GHOLSON ROAD
Revolutionaries and Texas Rangers

By

Donna Gholson Cook

ISBN: 1-4140-0476-1 (e-book)
ISBN: 1-4140-0475-3 (Paperback)
ISBN: 1-4140-0474-5 (Dust Jacket)

Library of Congress Control Number: 2003097328

This book is printed on acid free paper.

Printed in the United States of America
Bloomington, IN

1stBooks – rev. 12/15/03

In memory of my father and mother

Who always believed in me and encouraged me

And whose spirits still guide me

It's all for nothing, if you don't have freedom.

Braveheart

Contents

PART ONE: VIRGINIA AND KENTUCKY

PART TWO: TEXAS

List of Illustrations

List of Maps

Preface

On June 26, 1960, my parents and I were visiting my father's Aunt Kate and Uncle Will Pitts in Lampasas, Texas. I remember being very excited when Aunt Kate presented us with our copy of Margaret Baker Mitchell's book, GHOLSON AND ALLIED FAMILIES. That was the beginning of my fascination with family history, and the Gholson family contains some truly interesting characters. By 1995, my daughters were grown, I had finally finished college (only thirty years after I started), and I found that I had a little more time on my hands. I began to search for information about my father's family, and discovered new information about my Gholson ancestors in almost every library I visited.

This is not a genealogy or a family history in the traditional sense. There are several of those in existence about the Gholson family, including an excellent updated version of the Mitchell book, compiled by Ronald Lee Gholson, the pages of which contain thousands of names of the descendants of Anthony$_1$. GHOLSON ROAD tells the story of selected important events in the history of America, and the parts played by Anthony$_1$ Gholson and some of his descendants from the seventeenth through the nineteenth centuries. If I had known that my great-grandfathers participated in the American and Texas revolutions, I would have paid more attention in my classes in American and Texas history. Even though I got a late start, I have thoroughly enjoyed researching and writing this book, and I sincerely hope that the reader, Gholson or not, will gain a better understanding of the events that shaped our nation and the daily lives of the first colonists and their descendants.

DONNA GHOLSON COOK

ACKNOWLEDGMENTS

My sincere thanks to my supportive husband and daughters, who have encouraged me every step of the way, and all of the friends and relatives who have offered help and encouragement. One of the best Christmas gifts I have ever received from my husband Lewis was my own Limited Edition set of *The New Handbook of Texas*. He also spent hours using an astronomy imaging program to achieve the best quality possible in converting my color photographs to black and white.

I would also like to express my appreciation to the following:

To David and Binnie Hoffman, historical architects, for purchasing the deteriorating rock house built by B. F. Gholson, and for undertaking the most authentic restoration possible. They have graciously shared their plans for the house and their historical information and photographs, and I wish them well in their enormous task.

To my aunt, Marjory Gholson Morris, granddaughter of B. F. Gholson, for family photographs and her willingness to be interviewed often and at great length in frequent telephone conversations. Through her I was able to learn more about this great man from someone who spent many of her childhood days with him.

To Sammy Gholson and Martha Gholson Holland for sharing the autobiography of Samuel Sullivan Gholson.

To Bonnie Gholson Gentry, who trusted me with her irreplaceable Gholson family albums.

To Dee Dee Gholson, for sharing her information and photographs.

To Robert Gholson, son of Theodore Roosevelt Gholson, for sending me his father's notes used in a speech at the dedication of the historical marker at the grave of B. F. Gholson.

To Faye Wilson Dillard, genealogist, for her excellent and thorough search of hundreds of county records from the Robertson's Colony area.

To Robert Santiesteban and Carol M. Finney at Texas General Land Office for their expertise and assistance in helping me to obtain copies of early Texas land grants and related maps.

To John Anderson and Eddie Williams at the Texas State Archives for their help with photographs and documents. Ms. Williams has now retired, and I wish her a long and happy retirement.

To Ronald Gholson, for the hundreds of hours spent in updating the 1950 book by Virginia Baker Mitchell, *Gholson and Allied Families*.

To Gary Spurr at The University of Texas at Arlington for answering questions, sending information, and helping me to assemble my own set of *Papers Concerning Robertson's Colony in Texas*.

To Margaret Brown Altendahl for her book, *Relatives of the Browns of Mill Springs, Kentucky*, which contains a wealth of information about the Gholson family.

To Dr. Todd Auker, who restored my lost vision. Without his surgical skill, this book would have never been completed.

To the following who responded to my requests by mail: Arkansas History Commission; Central Texas Genealogical Society; Coryell County Genealogical Society; Daughters of the Republic of Texas; Falls County Historical Commission; The Filson Club; Hamilton County Genealogical Society; Harrison County Genealogical Society; Lampasas County Historical Commission; Library of Congress; Library of Virginia; Mills County Historical Commission; National Archives (military service records); Orange County Historical Society; Robertson County Historical Foundation; Steubenville (Kentucky) Baptist Church; Texas State Historical Association; Virginia Genealogy Society; Wayne County (Kentucky) Historical Society; West Texas Historical Association; Western Publications, formerly of Stillwater, Oklahoma; and U. S. Geological Survey for a wonderful website and excellent maps.

My travels took me to a number of different cities where I used the following libraries and manuscript collections, and my research was made easier by helpful staff members: Center for American History in Austin, Texas; Clayton Genealogy Library Branch of the Houston Public Library; Contra Costa County Library, Pleasant Hill, California; Fort Worth Public Library; Institute of Texan Cultures; Kentucky Historical Society; New England Historic Genealogical Society; San Antonio Public Library; State Library of North Carolina; Sutro Library, San Francisco; Texas Ranger Museum and Library; Texas State Library and Archives; Toronto Public Library; and Waco Public Library.

Much information was taken from the courthouse records of the following Texas counties, several of which I visited personally: Bell, Coryell, Falls, Hamilton, Harrison, Lampasas, McLennan, and Mills.

I am especially grateful to historians of the past who had the foresight to realize that they were living an important part of history, and who made the effort to record events as they happened, giving us an understanding of what life was like at the time. A huge contribution was made by J. Marvin Hunter, editor and publisher of *Frontier Times* magazine in Bandera, Texas. His diligence and high standards gave us a very important source for the history of Texas and the Southwest, and specifically, the activities of the early Texas Rangers, including B. F. Gholson. Mr. Gholson's grandson, Theodore Roosevelt Gholson, also spent many hours interviewing his grandfather and typing the interviews, which somehow found their way to the Center for American History. Samuel Sullivan Gholson wrote a lengthy autobiography, relating his trail drive experiences and some of the events he shared with his brother, B. F. Gholson, such as their narrow escape from the hangman's noose as a result of mob rule during the Civil War. Two books that I found very informative and entertaining contained the stories of Noah Smithwick and E. C. "Teddy Blue" Abbott, but probably the single book of the most value to my research in the area of early Texas was a small, out-of-print book by William Ransom Hogan, *The Texas Republic*. The book that touched me the most was *Surviving on the Texas Frontier, The Journal of an Orphan Girl in San Saba County*, by Sarah Harkey Hall.

I am very grateful for The History Channel, which has done more to renew interest in history than any other source, in an objective, unbiased manner. A special thanks to Bob Boze Bell for his publications and his work with The History Channel to keep the memory of the Old West alive.

After writing letters to hundreds of agents and publishers, I found 1st Books Library, and I would like to express my sincere thanks to Amber Olmstead, Darci McWilliams, and all of the others whose names I do not know. Both Amber and Darci were friendly, helpful, and competent, and they answered each of my many questions with the utmost patience and courtesy. Publishing with 1st Books Library allowed me the ability to retain complete control over my manuscript, while giving excellent service in the printing and marketing processes. I would also like to thank the hundreds of agents and publishers for their rejection slips, many of which were courteous, thoughtful, and contained helpful information.

My deepest appreciation to Dr. Malcolm S. McLean for his magnificent work in compiling *Papers Concerning Robertson's Colony in Texas* and for editing my chapter regarding the colony. His help and encouragement is greatly appreciated, and meeting him and Mrs. McLean was truly an honor.

The author and Dr. Malcolm D. McLean, at his home in Georgetown, Texas, September 19, 2000. Photo by Rebecca Brassfield.

Introduction

The best times I had as a child were at my Uncle Preston's ranch, or Uncle Prep as we called him. My parents and I often spent weekends at their ranch, usually sleeping in one of the cabins, often with several other aunts and uncles and cousins. His ranch was not far from my great-grandfather Benjamin Franklin Gholson's place, near Evant, Texas. I didn't have a chance to know my great-grandfather, but I feel very lucky that so many of his recollections have been preserved for me to discover and compile into a book.

Uncle Prep was everyone's favorite uncle. He would often slip me a dollar bill with a warning not to tell Aunt Ruth. She ruled the roost. When it was time for him to get a haircut, she would give him a quarter to go into town and get a haircut and buy a sack of Bull Durham to roll his own cigarettes.

Aunt Ruth may have been tight fisted with the considerable money that they made raising turkeys, but she sure could cook. Uncle Prep and my father and I would go to the field and gather a basket of roasting ears (corn on the cob) and she would have the water boiling when we got back with them. We husked the corn, and she would either throw the ears into the boiling water or cut the kernels off the ears to make cream style corn. That was the best corn I have ever eaten. I was skinny as a rail, but I could easily eat three or four ears, along with everything else. I would watch her wring the neck of a chicken to fry for dinner (the noon meal) and she would serve it with biscuits, gravy, sliced tomatoes from the garden and warm peach cobbler topped with cream from their own milk cow. She churned her own butter until she discovered that she could use the hand mixer to beat the cream into butter, but it was not long before the little motor burned out.

The heat of the day was often spent playing cards or dominoes and talking about the "olden days." Then Uncle Prep would load his old pickup with bales of hay to feed the cattle and I would ride around with him while he scattered the bales around the pasture.

Uncle Prep always had a couple of huge black and tan 'coon hounds. I was grown before I realized that the word was an abbreviation for "raccoon." My Dad would never allow me go hunting with them at night because it was past my bedtime, but I loved playing with the dogs during the day. I didn't realize until I was working on this book that this tradition had originated hundreds of years before, in early Virginia and Kentucky.

There was a river running through Uncle Prep's place and my Dad taught me to fish. He had me practice casting a lure in the direction of a bucket until I could hit it with a fair degree of accuracy before he turned me loose on the fish and the trees on the riverbank. There were always guns in the house, but he told me to leave them alone until I was big enough to learn to shoot, and I did. I was probably around ten or twelve years old when I was allowed to ride in the back of the truck with an ancient .22 rifle while Uncle Prep drove around the country roads looking for armadillos. When he saw one, he would stop the truck and say to me, "There's one, Donna, get it!" I would shoot the armadillo and Uncle Prep would cackle.

Maybe it was because I was an only child that I enjoyed the company of the older members of the family and the stories they told, but it seems that the older I get, the more important it becomes to pass the stories along to current and future generations. I loved the stories about the Indians and at times, I wished that I could be kidnapped by the Indians and grow up like Cynthia Ann Parker. Now I realize that I was very fortunate to have grown up at the time and place that I did. I hope that you obtain a small portion of the enjoyment out of reading this book that I experienced in writing it.

DONNA GHOLSON COOK

EXPLANATORY NOTES

SURNAME ORIGIN
Records of the Gholson family have been traced at least as far back as 1283, when Ralph de Gulston was mentioned in connection with the building of Conway Castle in Wales. This and other references to Gholsons in England can be found in James M. Black's book, *The Families and Descendants in America of Golsan, Golson, Gholson, Gholston,* Virginia Baker Mitchell's *Gholson and Allied Families,* and the Revised *Gholson and Allied Families,* published in 2002 by Ronald Gholson. According to *A Dictionary of British Surnames,* variations of the name *Gholson* appeared as early as the *Doomsday Book* in 1066. The variations listed are *Goldston, Goldstone, Gouldstone, Goulston, Goulstone, Golston, Goldson, Golson, Gulston, and Gulson.* There are also references to the variations in the years 1180, 1185, 1202, 1214, 1312, 1523, 1524, 1795, and 1798. There are many different spellings of the name in references used, but in this book, the spelling *Gholson* was used for ease in reading.

THE CALENDAR
Until 1752, the new year began March 25th. January, February, and the first twenty four days of March were the last three rather than the first three months of the year—coming after December of that year. In the year of change (1752), events taking place during those three months were often written "1751/52." "8 ber" was sometimes written as an abbreviation for October under the old style calendar—being the eighth month following the new year's day of March 25. Thus, December was the 10th month, not the 12th.

MONEY
Monetary units in the American colonies were commonly pounds, shillings, and pence until 1792, although cured tobacco was also a common medium of exchange at the rate of a pound for a pence. Congress adopted the dollar in 1786, and in 1792, Virginia began to use dollars and cents for accounting purposes and the collection of taxes.

TITLES

In order to understand the social order of early Virginia, a few terms need explanation. The title "Gentleman" or "Gent" was a designation for those men of considerable wealth and large land holdings. The title "Planter" was usually given to those with greater land holdings than the subsistence farmer and engaged in the growing of a number of crops, including the lucrative ones, tobacco and hemp. Indentured servants were bound by contract to work for a limited period of time, usually around five years, for the planters who paid for their passage. After the work period expired, there was no social stigma attached to the former indentured servants, who were free to pursue the life of their choice, which often included marrying a member of the master's family. Upon the release of indentured servants, the master was obligated to give them sufficient grain to sustain them for one year, two suits of clothing, and a supply of tools, including a gun. Another title which was used frequently was "tithable." This refers to a person who was subject to the capitation tax, which was the only American tax for many years. This tax usually applied to males over sixteen and servants of both sexes over that age. Eventually, wheeled vehicles also became "tithables."

EDITING

My first inclination was to rewrite the long quotes in a more readable style. I rewrote some short quotes in what I thought was better form and sent it to Doctor Malcolm McLean, editor and compiler of *Papers Concerning Robertson's Colony in Texas*, for his opinion. His reply illustrated that my attempt to improve it had actually blurred or changed the meaning, and he advised that I quote the material exactly as I found it. I followed his advice, because the best possible historical accuracy was more important to me than easy reading. In quoted material, most spellings and punctuations have been left exactly as they appear in the original manuscript. Only a few very obvious typographical errors were corrected, and only if there was absolutely no doubt as to what the author intended. One of the greatest variations was in the different spellings of the same name. If the Gholson name was spelled differently, I used the spelling of *Gholson* for consistency. In the case of other proper names, I usually retained the spelling as found in the original source. In the days when few people knew how to read or write, a number of creative spellings were used. If it seemed likely that the meaning of a word would not be obvious to the reader, the modern spelling or an explanatory word or two were added in brackets. If there was a disparity between sources, I made a decision as to which source I considered to be the most reliable, using legal documents and military records as primary sources. In most instances, the primary sources matched the eyewitness accounts amazingly well, the most notable exception being the stories told by Samuel Gholson, one of the first Texans. I have not changed, added, or omitted anything in an attempt to be politically correct. For example, to be consistent, the original Americans are referred to as Indians, because that is what they are called in the sources I used. There was no intent to offend anyone, but simply to relate the historical accounts as they were told by those who lived them, in the language of the day.

TIMELINE

1500-1599:
1500 Voyages of discovery by Columbus, Cabot, Vasco da Gama,
   Magellan
1517 The Reformation
1572 Dr. Theodore Gulston born
1578 Humphrey Gilbert obtained a charter from Queen Elizabeth to
   colonize
1585 Walter Raleigh established Virginia
1588 England defeated the Spanish Armada
1596 Will proved in England mentioned Anthony Goulson

1600-1699:
1604 King James I of England made peace treaty with Spain
1606 Virginia Company of London created
1607 Settlement of Jamestown began
1610 Dr. Gulston received doctor's degree at Oxford
1616 Dr. Gulston entertained Sir Thomas Dale and Powhatan's counsellor
1618 Powhatan died
1619 Dr. Gulston bought ten shares in the Virginia Company
1620 Dr. Gulston was made one of the King's Council for the Company
1620 The *Mayflower* sailed from Holland
1621 Dr. Gulston recommended Dr. Pott for physician-general of Virginia
1622 347 Virginians massacred by Indians
1624 Population of Virginia was 1292
1624 Virginia was converted into a Royal Colony
1629 King Charles I dissolved Parliament in England
1632 Dr. Theodore Gulston died in his home in St. Martin's on Ludgate
   Hill
1632 Seventeen laws passed in Virginia - Church of England
1634 Dr. Gulston's brother John was a Justice of the Peace in England
1634 Henry Gouldson and family left England for America
1641 Anthony Gunston transported to America by John Bayly (Bayles)
1642 Sir William Berkeley arrived in Virginia
1644 Indian attack

1660 Virginia and Maryland began passing laws banning interracial marriages and forbidding blacks to own property; also forbade blacks to bear arms or travel without written permission

1670 Increase in the number of slaves

1670 Plows came into use

1671 Governor Berkeley opposes educating the common people

1675 William Goulston listed in shippers by the *Joanna* from London for Virginia

1685 Anthony$_1$ Gholson born in Spotsylvania County about this time

<u>1700-1799</u>:

1705 Anthony$_1$'s son William born

1716 Virginia's Royal Governor Spotswood led his party out of Williamsburg to claim the Appalachian mountains for England and to stop the advance of the French in the interior

1724 Church of England had very little competition remaining

1725 Anthony$_1$'s first recorded transaction of a purchase of 200 acres in Spotsylvania County, St. George Parish, in 1725

1727-1733 Anthony$_1$ Gholson was caretaker and overseer of the road in Spotsylvania County

1728 Anthony$_1$ obtained a grant from King George II for 1000 acres on Terry's Run in Spotsylvania County; sons Anthony and William received grants at the same time

1729 Anthony$_1$ summoned by the Grand Jury for not revealing a bastard child

1733 Anthony$_2$ (William's son) born around this time

1738 Anthony$_1$ had sold all of the 1000 acres

1739 Anthony$_1$ and his wife Jane sold the 200 acres to Zachary Lewis

1740 Anthony$_1$ bought 400 acres from John Chew and wife

1744 Anthony$_1$ named as guardian to Hannah Durram

1744 Anthony$_1$ sold 120 acres

1747-1774 William bought and sold many tracts of land

1750 Joseph Collins took the oath as Captain of a Troop of Horse

1750 Voyage described by Gottfried Mittelberger

1754-63 French and Indian War

1756 Collins' troop joined the Culpeper County Militia to fight the Indians above Winchester

1757 Joseph Collins died

1761 Anthony$_1$ sold the remaining 280 acres

1763 Anthony$_1$ executed deeds of gift

1764 Anthony$_1$ died; wife Jane executed deed of gift

1764-1786 Eleven children born to Anthony$_2$ and wife Elizabeth

1765 Stamp Act

1767 Tax on tea

1768-1786 Anthony$_2$ rented land from George Washington in Frederick County

1769 Daniel Boone left Virginia to go hunting in Kentucky - May 1

1770 Boston Massacre

1770-71 Daniel and his brother spent the winter hunting, trapping and exploring in southern Kentucky

1771 Daniel and brother left Kentucky for home in March

1771 Letter written by George Washington to his brother Samuel Washington discussing the best way to collect Anthony$_2$ Gholson's rent

1772 Samuel Gholson born in Botetourt County, Virginia

1773 Daniel and other families left Clinch River area to move to Kentucky - turned back by Indian attack

1774 Request to English Parliament to repeal acts passed in previous decade

1775 Daniel led a party to blaze a trail through the wilderness - March 10

1775 Patrick Henry's speech - March 23

1775 Colonel Henderson left for Kentucky, following Boone's trail - March 28

1775 Paul Revere's ride - April 18

1775 Battle of Lexington, beginning of Revolutionary War - April 19

1775 Henderson's party arrived at Fort Boone - April 20

1775 Patrick Henry confronts Lord Dunmore - April 28

1775 Lord Dunmore reconvened the House of Burgesses - May

1775 Washington appointed general and commander in chief of Continental troops - June 15

1775 Anthony$_2$ signed petition in Berkeley County, West Virginia, protesting an election

1775-1786 William's first wife, Susannah (Collins) died during this time

1776 Henderson's request rejected to have Kentucky admitted as the 14th colony

1776 Jefferson was asked to draft the Declaration of Independence

1776 Declaration of Independence approved by Congress - July 4

1778 Anthony$_2$ lived in Beverley Manor, Augusta County, Virginia, where he bought 374 acres

1779 Anthony$_2$ had sold the 374 acres and moved to Botetourt County - court martial summons issued for Anthony$_2$, for missing musters in Augusta County

1780 Anthony$_2$ Gholson received a grant of 992 acres in Kentucky

1780 Virginia invaded by British forces led by Benedict Arnold

1780-1801 Numerous land transactions for Anthony$_2$ in Botetourt

1781 Richmond captured and burned by second British invasion - January

1781 Battle of Guilford Court House

1783 Anthony$_2$ served on a jury

1783 Anthony$_2$ purchased 200 acres in Fayette County

1784 Anthony$_2$ purchased 680 acres

1784 House built for reception of deer skins and hemp, which were accepted as payment of taxes in Botetourt County, with Anthony$_2$ appointed as inspector

1785 Anthony$_2$ bought 1000 acres

1785 Micah Taul born

1785-1788 Anthony$_2$ was surveyor of the road

1790 Anthony$_2$ sold 1000 acres

1790-1800 Anthony$_2$ assembled 1180 acre plantation

1792 Kentucky became the 15th state of the Union

1792 Postal service extended to Kentucky

1792 Anthony$_2$ was overseer of the road

1793 Anthony$_2$ built a new gristmill

1794 Anthony$_2$ obtained permit for another gristmill

1796 New Wilderness Road completed

Late 1700s Increase of Presbyterians, Methodists and Baptists

1800-1899:

1800 William died about this time

1800-1801 Wayne County, Kentucky, established

1801 Anthony$_2$ sold 1180 acres in Virginia

1801 Anthony$_2$, with family and slaves, crossed the mountains to Kentucky from Virginia - one of the founders of the town of Monticello

1801 Anthony$_2$ donated land for the construction of a Baptist church

1801 Micah Taul elected first county clerk of Wayne County - March 16

1801 Micah married Dorothy Gholson, daughter of Anthony$_2$ - May 20

1801 Samuel Gholson married Mary Ann "Polly" Slaton - June 24
1802 Anthony$_2$ purchased 105-acre tract in Wayne County
1803 Louisiana purchase ratified
1804 Anthony$_2$ helped organize Big Sinking Baptist Church
1807 Anthony$_2$ purchased 220-acre tract
1812 War declared against Britain June 18
1812 Kentucky volunteers reported for duty - August
1812 Hull surrendered Fort Detroit - August 16
1812 Chauncey was placed in command of the American naval forces on Erie and Ontario - September
1812 Chauncey turned Lake Erie over to young Commodore Perry
1813 Deeds of gift signed by Anthony$_2$
1813 Taul's troops returned home - March
1813 Kentucky troops called up again in June, to rendezvous in August
1813 Perry defeated British fleet in Battle of Lake Erie - September 10
1813 Taul's company, including Samuel Gholson, arrived at Lake Erie
1813 Battle of the Thames - October 5
1813 Tribes signed armistice agreement with General Harrison - Oct. 16
1814 Micah Taul elected to Congress
1814 Defeat of Napoleon in the spring allowed Britain to focus on America
1814 British burned the White House - August 24
1814 British attacked Fort McHenry - September 14
1814 Samuel Gholson enlisted in Captain Vickery's company - Nov. 10
1814 Treaty of Ghent ended War of 1812 - December 24
1815 Anthony$_2$ donated land for Baptist church and cemetery at Steubenville
1815 Battle of New Orleans - January 8
1815-16 Anthony$_2$ died around this time
1818 Samuel's son Albert born in Kentucky - May 24
1819 Samuel and two others tried and acquitted on rape charge in Wayne County, Kentucky; defended by Micah Taul
1820 Samuel and Mary Ann and children lived in Livingston County, Kentucky
1821 Samuel lived in Arkansas Territory - Dec
1823-4 Military districts were formed in Texas and militia units were composed of all males between eighteen and fifty-five
1824 Samuel lived at Cadron in Arkansas Territory around this time

1826 Isaac West, Jr., purchased Samuel's interest in the firm of Gholson and Bradberry in Arkansas

1826 Micah moved his family to Alabama

1827 Micah's wife Dorothy died

1829 Micah's son Thomas was murdered

1829 Samuel's son Alvades died in Illinois when thrown by a horse

1830 Mexican government issued a decree to ban further immigration to Texas from America and to control slavery

1831 Charles Cocke, codefendant in rape trial, murdered Zebulon Edmiston in Clark County, Arkansas

1832 Samuel and son Albert left Jackson, Tennessee, for Texas - April 3

1832 Samuel and Albert reached San Felipe - July 29

1832 Charles Cocke apprehended in Texas and extradicted to Arkansas

1832 Pack train robbery at what is now Gholson Gap

1833 Charles Cocke hanged in Arkansas - April 29

1834 Samuel's son Alhanon convicted of counterfeiting in Arkansas

1834 Santa Anna assumed authority in Mexico and began dismantling the federal government

1835 William Travis gathered a small band of men and a small cannon and forced the garrison at Anahuac to surrender and return to Mexico - June 29

1835 Battle of Gonzales, Albert Gholson participated - October 2

1835 Texans left Gonzales for San Antonio with cannon to confont General Cos

1835 Samuel Gholson signed a deed in Nashville, Tennessee - Oct 2

1835 Battle of Concepción, Albert participated - Oct 28

1835 Battle of San Antonio - Dec 5-9; Milam was killed Dec 7, Albert was nearby

1836 Samuel and Albert voted for delegates to the convention at Washington-on-the-Brazos - Feb 1

1836 Texas declared its independence from Mexico - March 2

1836 Fall of the Alamo - March 6

1836 Battle of San Jacinto, Albert commanded Barron's company - April 21

1836 First major Indian raid on Fort Parker - May 19

1836 Albert was in Capt. Pierson's company providing security along La Bahía road - June 30-July 30

1836 Albert was in Capt. Robbins' company on the Red River - July 30-Sept 30

1836 Election held for the new Republic of Texas; Albert and Samuel voted; Sam Houston defeated Henry Smith and Stephen F. Austin in a presidential election - Sept 5

1837 Samuel's son Alhanon killed in duel in Arkansas?

1837 Robertson County established - Dec 14

1837-8 Albert was in Capt. Barron's company, one year enlistment

1838 Samuel and other citizens of Robertson's Colony signed a petition to the government for protection from the Indians, April 23

1838 Sam Houston signed treaty with the Comanches - May 29

1838 Albert received Bounty Warrant for service from June 30-Sept 30, 1836

1838 Albert helped bury the Navarro County surveyors killed by Indians - Oct 8

1838 Albert married Elydia Anderson, born 1822 in Missouri - December

1838-9 Samuel lived in Robertson County

1839 Indians attacked the homes of George Morgan and John Marlin; Bryant's defeat - Jan

1839 A. G. Golston, 2nd Lt under Capt. Nimrod Doyle in the Robertson County Volunteer Rangers; also Samuel, same dates - Mar 8-Jun 10

1839 Mary Ann Gholson (Samuel's wife?) married William Carson in Madison County, Tennessee - Dec 10

1840 Deed from Samuel Gholson to son Albert and John Chisum

1840 Albert's first son born, Samuel Sullivan - Nov 13

1840 Samuel lived in Harrison County until at least 1848

1841 Samuel married Sarah Bullock in Harrison County - August 9

1841 Sam Houston elected to a second term, after a term by M. B. Lamar

1842 Samuel married Brittanna Cannon in Harrison County - August 21

1842 Albert's second son born, Benjamin Franklin - Nov 17

1843 Malaria epidemic along the Brazos - summer and fall

1843 Albert moved his family to Harrison County because of family illness

1843 Albert moved his family to Limestone County

1843 Elydia died near Old Springfield at age twenty-one - Sept

1844 Albert moved to Blue Ridge, now Falls County

1845 Samuel tried for card playing in the Republic of Texas

1845 Annexation, under Anson Jones, President of the Republic - Dec 29

1846 Albert married Mary Mathis (Matthews) in Harrison County

1846-7 Mexican War

1847 Samuel voted in an election in Nashville, Milam County - Sept 4

1847 Daughter born to Albert and 2nd wife in Falls County

1848 Treaty of Guadlupe Hidalgo established Rio Grande River as boundary - Feb 2

1849 Son born to Albert and 2nd wife in Falls County

1850 Mary Ann (Albert's mother) was living with Albert's family

1850 Micah Taul died - May 27

1850 Samuel still living with Brittanna in Harrison County

1850 Albert signed petition protesting selection of Viesca as county seat of Falls County - August

1851 Adams (now Marlin) became the county seat of Falls County - Jan

1851 Albert served as a juror in Falls County - Feb

1851 Albert elected as a justice of the peace, precinct three, Falls Co. - March

1851 Albert appointed as a reviewer for road to be built to Springfield - May

1851 Albert sold his land on Blue Ridge and moved to the west side of the Brazos

1852 Albert charged in Falls County on two counts of assault with intent to kill - April 22

1852 Samuel died in Wood County - July 4

1852 Albert moved to an area north of Waco (now the town of Gholson) between the Brazos and Aquilla rivers - Nov

1854 First school built in the town of Gholson

1854 Assault case against Albert dismissed - May 10

1855 Albert moved to Mills County, establishing the first ranch on North Sims Creek - June 12

1855 Frank's first visit to Langford's Cove (now Gholson Gap) - June 19

1856 Albert lost 2214 acres he owned on the east side of the Little Brazos because of his failure to pay his 1853 taxes - Sept 28

1856 Indians investigated the location of settlers along the streams

1856 Tribal council near the forks of the Brazos - Nov

1857 Comanche and Kiowa tribes began depredations on the settlers - March

1857 War council of nine tribes - only two joined the coalition to conduct war upon the settlers

1857-73 Indian wars

1858 Post office established in the town of Gholson

1858 Albert moved from Mills County back to Coryell - August

1858 Frank and Sam joined Capt. Williams' new company of rangers at San Saba - Oct 2

1858 Frank and Sam helped bury the Jackson family - Oct 28

1858 Frank with ranger party struck the trail of the Indians with the kidnapped Jackson children - Nov 6

1858 Jackson children recaptured in Nolan County, near Sweetwater - Nov 9

1858 Reached Camp Colorado with the Jackson children - Nov 16

1858 Langford Cemetery established

1859 Son born to Albert and 2nd wife in Coryell County

1859 Albert found his sons in Capt. Williams' company and made them come home - Mar 2

1859 Murder of Mr. and Mrs. Riggs and Mr. Pierce - Apr

1859 Sam left home and started freighting - Nov

1859 Indians moved across the Red River from Texas reservations

1860 Frank left home for Fort Belknap and joined the ranger company of Capt. Smith, later led by Sul Ross - Mar 4

1860 Albert shot and killed at 42 by neighbor in Coryell County - June 10

1860 Frank was with the company on an expedition against the Northern Comanches in the Wichita Mountains when he received word that his father had died, and he rode through dangerous Indian territory with Lt. Gault, with advice from Placido and Caddo Tom - Aug 11

1860 Battle of Pease River, recapture of Cynthia Ann Parker - Dec

1861 Lt. Bob Carter killed by Indians - Oct 19

1862 Sam joined Sheridan's company of Confederate soldiers - summer

1862 Frank married Adeline, the sister of his brother's wife - Jul 18; reared nine children

1862 Sam joined the company of Capt Gallasby [Gillespie?] to muster Oct 5 in Lampasas

1862 Sam and Frank narrowly escaped death at the hands of a mob - Oct

1862 Hanging of Doctor Steward by the mob - Oct 11

1862 Sam and Frank enlisted in Colonel Pyron's Second Texas Cavalry, Company F - Oct

1862 Company F ordered to Buffalo Bayou - Dec; dismounted and sent to Galveston

1863 Frank participated in the Battle of Galveston - Jan 1

1863 Sam was sent to Big Sandy to establish a horse camp; while hunting for horses, he found the leader of the mob that tried to hang him and took care of him - Feb 10; Gen. Magruder ordered him and the other two horse hunters brought in; Sam evaded capture and deserted until Aug 1864

1863 2nd Texas Cavalry under Gen. Tom Green defeated Banks - Jun 15

1864 Frank deserted - Feb 2

1864 Sam rejoined the Confederate Army in Arkansas - Aug

1865 Lee surrendered to Grant - Apr 9; Sam was in Lampasas on furlough

1865 Frank given an honorable discharge - May 4; apparently he returned to the army after he deserted

1865-6 Sam was sheriff of Hamilton County

1866 First Texas herds crossed the Red River

1866 Bill Willis attacked by Indians - Dec 25; died Feb 3, 1867

1867 Abilene, Kansas founded

1868 Sam arrived at Fort Sumner, New Mexico with herd - Feb 15; delivered to Charles Goodnight

1869 Sam moved to Coleman County - May 15; partners with G. K. Elkins from 1869-1871

1870 Frank moved to Gholson Gap and bought 244 acres from Sam Sneed for $400 cash - Oct 12

1870 Sam, John M. Elkins, and others in Indian fight in Taylor County

1871 Frank and Asa Langford, Sr., posted bond for Thomas Holly

1871 Sam joins John M. Elkins to hunt Indians on Jim Ned Creek

1872 Frank's cowhands in confrontation with Indians at Beef Pen Spring

1872-5 Frank and a stone mason built rock house

1873 Sam Gholson met young James Gillette - spring

1873 Gholson's outfit fights Indians on the banks of the Concho - summer

1873 Indians try to steal Frank's horses - Apr

1873 Sam's cowhands kill Indian who stole their horses

1873 Frank scaled down his cattle operation

1873 Asa Langford, Jr. and Richard Dublin worked for Joe Franks' outfit

1874 Capias for arrest of Asa Langford, Jr. for murder - June 20

1874 Langford killed by a posse - Oct

1880 Sam bought into the Llano Cattle Company

1883 Indians stole Sam Gholson's horses--possibly the last depredation in the area

1900-

1932 Frank died - Apr 3

1940 Adeline died

1967 Dedication of historical marker (or 1968?)

1977 Frank's rock house purchased by restoration architects

Gholson Line
Anthony Gholson to Benjamin Franklin Gholson

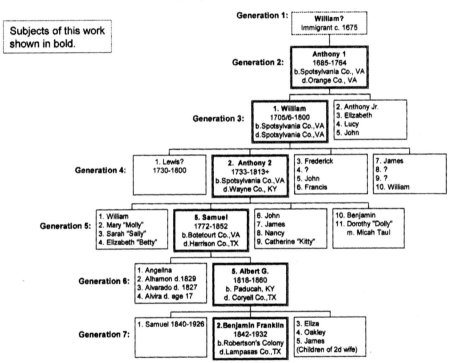

Subjects of this work shown in bold.

Generation 1:
William?
Immigrant c. 1675

Generation 2:
Anthony 1
1685-1764
b.Spotsylvania Co., VA
d.Orange Co., VA

Generation 3:
1. **William**
1705/6-1800
b.Spotsylvania Co., VA
d.Spotsylvania Co., VA

2. Anthony Jr.
3. Elizabeth
4. Lucy
5. John

Generation 4:
1. Lewis?
1730-1800

2. **Anthony 2**
1733-1813+
b.Spotsylvania Co., VA
d.Wayne Co., KY

3. Frederick
4. ?
5. John
6. Francis

7. James
8. ?
9. ?
10. William

Generation 5:
1. William
2. Mary "Molly"
3. Sarah "Sally"
4. Elizabeth "Betty"

5. **Samuel**
1772-1852
b.Botetourt Co., VA
d.Harrison Co., TX

6. John
7. James
8. Nancy
9. Catherine "Kitty"

10. Benjamin
11. Dorothy "Dolly"
m. Micah Taul

Generation 6:
1. Angelina
2. Alhamon d.1829
3. Alvarado d. 1827
4. Alvira d. age 17

5. **Albert G.**
1818-1860
b. Paducah, KY
d. Coryell Co.,TX

Generation 7:
1. Samuel 1840-1926

2.**Benjamin Franklin**
1842-1932
b.Robertson's Colony
d.Lampasas Co.,TX

3. Eliza
4. Oakley
5. James
(Children of 2d wife)

XXXV

PART ONE

VIRGINIA AND KENTUCKY

Donna Gholson Cook

Chapter 1: The Immigrants

Anthony₁ of Virginia c. 1685 - c. 1764
William of Virginia c. 1705 - c. 1795-1800

Changes were already brewing in the world before Europeans began coming to the American continent. The Italian Renaissance had been going on for a couple of centuries. The printing press allowed the dissemination of newly-accumulated knowledge, resulting in a more educated population. The voyages of discovery around 1500 by Columbus, Cabot, Vasco da Gama, and Magellan provided hope for new places to live and a new way of life. The Reformation began in 1517 when a German priest named Martin Luther challenged corrupt practices of the Church authorities at a time when the Church was the temporal and religious authority. The work of scholars such as Copernicus and Galileo revolutionized commonly held scientific beliefs. All of these factors, along with increased difficulty in trading with the East, added momentum to the desire to go to the newly-discovered American continent, the source of unlimited wealth. At the same time, the flow of products and silver into Europe from America caused extreme inflation and made life in the Old World more and more difficult.[1]

Theodore Gulston was a child in England in 1578 when an Englishman named Humphrey Gilbert recognized the possibility of colonizing the new lands and obtained a charter from Queen Elizabeth to begin. Unfortunately, Gilbert died when his ship sank, but his half-brother Walter Raleigh carried on alone, establishing in 1585 a colony that he called Virginia, in honor of the queen. That attempt did not succeed, nor did one two years later, and then England became too preoccupied with the Spanish War to try again for another twenty years.[2] In 1588, England defeated the Spanish Armada in a naval battle that launched England as a world power, but the struggle between England and Spain continued, as did the competition for the New World.[3] In 1604, England's King James I made a peace treaty with Spain, giving England the opportunity to again turn its attention to the colonization of America.[4]

There were many reasons for the English to migrate to America. With the worsening situation caused by inflation, excessive regulation of industry by the government, the difficulty in joining the craftsmen's guilds, and the peasants being driven off the land, more and more people were becoming unable to support themselves and their families.[5] Most emigrants came from the middle and lower-middle classes, although class distinction was less pronounced in America than it had been in England. Most were not farmers before they moved to America.[6] They may have to come to America for religious freedom, economic or other reasons, but there was one thing that they did not want to change—they wanted to remain Englishmen and to recreate the culture they left behind. Some of them did not like the changes taking place in England and saw America as a place where they could retain old customs.[7] They brought with them farming tools, livestock, seeds, chests full of personal belongings, and a determination to recreate England in the wilderness of America.[8] To their surprise, instead of a wilderness, they found large fields which had been cleared and planted in corn by the Indians, although not many Indians had survived the smallpox epidemic spread by European fishermen.[9] The Indians were generally helpful, but in Virginia they were more numerous and posed a greater threat than in New England.[10]

English merchants began to realize that there were opportunities to make money in the new land and they began to pool their resources to form joint stock companies. In 1606, the Virginia Company of London was created. In May 1607, the settlement of Jamestown was begun. In a year, half of the several hundred settlers were dead, but those remaining were eventually able to support themselves. Captain John Smith became the leader of the colony and the "marriage of his lieutenant John Rolfe with Pocahontas, the daughter of the Indian chief Powhatan, caused a sensation in the English capital."[11] Powhatan managed to maintain peace between his people and the colonists, but after his death in 1618, his warlike brother conducted raids upon the settlements, which began a cycle of war resulting in the end of the Powhatan Confederacy.[12]

Fig. 1.1 - *Portrait of Pocahontas*, photograph of a painting in the
United States Capitol, copied from original by William Sheppard,
dated 1616, at Barton rectory, Norfolk, England. Detroit
Publishing Co. No. M 18753. Gift; State Historical Society of
Colorado; 1949. Library of Congress No. LC-D416-18753.

Dr. Theodore Gulston, believed to be related to the first members of
the Gholson family in America,[13]

> was a celebrated London physician and a prominent
> member of the Virginia Company. He was born in 1572,
> studied at Merton College, Oxford, where he took his
> doctor's degree, April 30, 1610, was fellow (Dec. 29,
> 1611,) and Censor of the College of Physicians, and
> practised with great success in London. In 1616 he
> frequently entertained Sir Thomas Dale and Uttomakin,
> Powhatan's counsellor, who had been sent to England. On
> June 14, 1619, Dr. Gulston was appointed on the committee
> of the Virginia Company in regard to the college. On Dec.
> 15, 1619, he bought ten shares of land in Virginia from
> various persons. He was made one of the King's Council
> for the Company in England, on July 8, 1620, and in July
> 1621, he recommended Dr. Pott for appointment as
> physician-general of Virginia. Dr. Gulston was

distinguished as a Greek and Latin scholar, and translated several works from Greek into Latin.[14]

Dr. Gulston was also the founder of the Gulstonian lecture series at the College of Physicians, Cambridge.[15] His name is listed frequently in the *Records of the Virginia Company of London* as an attendee at court sessions, beginning in May of 1619.[16]

Dr. Gulston's brother John was a justice of the peace in England in 1634.[17] At that time, justices of the peace were the law enforcers of the countryside in England and were the only people outside the armed forces who had the right to bear arms.[18] They were members of the gentry, appointed by the Crown. "The office could be an exasperating burden, but one few gentlemen dared to refuse; it was an honor to receive, a duty to accept, and a training ground for those eager to serve in Parliament."[19]

A justice of the peace carried heavy administrative duties. He fixed wages, licensed alehouses and checked that they observed hours, apprenticed boys to trades, found homes for orphans, saw to the care of the poor and infirm, disciplined the obstreperous, inspected roads and bridges, punished all legal infractions, large and small. He kept, or was supposed to keep, the king's ministers informed on all aspects of local life that might be relevant to the welfare of the nation. The increasing number of impositions upon him from London under the early Stuarts convinced some of the justices they had little to lose in moving to America.[20]

It is worth noting that succeeding generations of Gholsons were road inspectors and were also involved in various phases of law enforcement. John Gulston married Jane, the daughter of Richard Ketridge, and they had eleven children, the youngest of whom was named William.[21] This William may have been the first member of the family to move to America.

Dr. Theodore Gulston died in his home in St. Martin's on Ludgate Hill on May 4, 1632.[22] In his will, he left a portion of his estate to his brother John's children.[23] Theodore's brother Nathaniel also had a son named William, but Nathaniel's son William lived a distinguished life in England and died there in 1684.[24] John Gulston's son William may have been the same William Goulston who was listed in shippers by the *Joanna* from

London for Virginia in March 1675.[25] Since Anthony₁ was born about ten years later, the timing would be about right for William to have been his father. In early Virginia, first-born children were named for their grandparents, and second-born for parents.[26] Since the second son of Anthony₁ Gholson was named Anthony, after himself, and the first son's name is William, it is reasonable to assume that Anthony₁'s father was also named William.

The directors of the London Company had many ideas as to the source for profit from the new colonies, but none of them guessed that it would be tobacco. The smoking habit had been brought to England by the Spaniards and the demand for tobacco was just beginning when it was discovered that Virginia had an excellent soil and climate for growing it. The planters soon grew rich and as their wealth grew, their sense of independence increased.[27]

Also assisted by the Virginia company was a group of thirty-five Puritans who sailed from Holland in September 1620 with sixty-six adventurers on the *Mayflower*. Their patent was invalidated when they landed at Cape Cod two and a half months later because they were outside the jurisdiction of the Virginia company.[28] There was a disagreement about who would lead the two groups on board the *Mayflower*, considering their differences in goals and moral values, and the *Mayflower Compact* was drawn up "for the general good of the colony."[29] There was no lucrative crop in Massachusetts, as there had been in Virginia, resulting in no profits for the financial backers, but the colony survived.[30]

The colony of Massachusetts was established following the 1629 dissolution of Parliament in England by King Charles I and his Personal Rule. In the following ten years, the number of colonists grew to fourteen thousand, some of whom began moving out to start other colonies.[31]

Many of the early colonists were lured to America by an intense advertising campaign conducted through poems, pamphlets, sermons and any other media available. After the Indian massacre in Virginia in 1622 had dampened the enthusiasm of many prospective emigrants, the Reverend John Donne was paid in stock by the Virginia Company for preaching a sermon in which he "declared that continued support of the colony would advance both the interests of England and the Kingdom of God."[32] The advertising was apparently favorable enough to outweigh the many tales of horror on the other extreme, such as the rumor that New England had flying rattlesnakes that could kill a man by breathing on him.[33]

Most of the first immigrants to Virginia had origins in the southern and western parts of England.[34] Between 1606 and 1625, more than 5600 people left England to start a new life in Virginia. By 1625, only about 1100 remained alive.[35] The first big challenge was to survive the voyage. Gottfried Mittelberger described the conditions on one of the immigrant ships which landed in Philadelphia on October 10, 1750, in his *Journey to Pennsylvania*. "During the journey the ship is full of pitiful signs of distress—smells, fumes, horrors, vomiting, various kinds of sea sickness, fever, dysentery, headaches, heat, constipation, boils, scurvy, cancer, mouth-rot . . ."[36] There is a shortage of food and water. The water is "very black, thick with dirt, and full of worms."[37] The little bit of spoiled bread that is available is "full of red worms and spiders' nests."[38] There are "so many lice, especially on the sick people, that they have to be scraped off the bodies."[39] Small children seldom had the strength to survive the voyage, often dying from measles or smallpox.[40] To compound the misery, a storm would arise and for several days everyone on board was in fear that the ship would sink.[41] Even when land was finally reached, those who could not pay for the voyage were forced to remain on board until they were purchased, and those who were ill had little chance of that.[42]

In the years just before the Revolutionary War, there were many like Anthony₁ Gholson's family who had come to America at least a hundred years before but new settlers were arriving by the thousands.[43] Many of the English who came to Virginia in the early years were members of distinguished families but left because of the rule of primogeniture (inheritance of the family estate by the oldest son), hoping to improve their situation in America.[44]

The parents or grandparents of Anthony₁ Gholson of Virginia were on board one of those leaky little ships from England that arrived on the coast of America before Anthony₁ was born in Spotsylvania County around 1685. His father may have been Dr. Theodore Gulston's nephew William. Anthony₁ was probably a son or grandson of a pioneer because he signed his name with a capital "A" rather than a signature. If he had come directly from England, he would have probably been able to read and write, but the pioneers' constant battle for survival left little time for education.[45]

Others who may have been related to Anthony₁'s English ancestors include the following:

- On November 6, 1596, a will was proved in England, mentioning one Anthony Goulson among the friends of the deceased, John Davenaunte.[46]
- Henry Gouldson, age 43; Ann, his wife, age 45; Ann Gouldslon (*sic*), age 18; and Mary Gouldson, age 15 (probably the daughters of Henry and Ann), "took shipping in the *Elizabeth*, of Ipswich, Mr. William Andrews, bound for New England, the last of April 1634."[47]
- Antho. Gunston was one of fourteen persons transported by John Bayly (Bayles), who entered a claim for 700 acres (50 acres per head) on the north side of the Charles River on October 18, 1641.[48]

~

The new American colonists came from every nation in Europe, taking as much as two months to cross the ocean. At the end of a miserable and dangerous voyage, they found a land which contained abundance and opportunity, but they also faced hostile natives and fatal diseases not known in Europe. The first Europeans to come to America were mostly single men. If a wife was left behind in England, the man would send for her when settled and confident of being able to support a family. Since there were so few women in the colonies, those who were there had little trouble marrying well.[49]

More than forty percent of the Chesapeake area immigrants to America were indentured servants who were required to work for several years for whomever paid their passage. At the end of the indenture, they were free to live as they chose.[50] The master could buy or sell the indentured servant, or bequeath him as private property.[51] Most were young single working-class males,[52] but every occupation and profession was represented in this group—laborers, schoolteachers, craftsmen, doctors. While they endured hardships, they could look forward to a freedom from their bondage in a few years. On the dark side of the indenture system, many parents traded their children's freedom for their own. The children were bonded servants until the age of twenty-one and often did not see their parents for years, if ever.[53] The indentured servants supported the society in the North. The Southern equivalent of the indentured servant was the multitude of slaves brought by shiploads from Africa[54] who had to endure much more horrible conditions than the colonists who came voluntarily.[55] There were also prisoners sent to America because of the overcrowded prisons in England.[56]

As to terminology, the settlers who came to America from the British countries were called "imports" and were automatically citizens. Those who came from countries considered "foreign," such as Germany, were "immigrants" and had to become naturalized.[57] The first wave of colonists through the first half of the seventeenth century was predominantly English, but they were followed by Scotch-Irish, German and French settlers. There was enough land for everyone and the westward movement was beginning.[58] They were developing an independent streak in which the seed was germinating that would later result in the American Revolution.

Chapter 2: Life in Early Virginia

1600-1800

Anthony₁ of Virginia c. 1685 - c. 1764
William of Virginia c. 1705 - c. 1795-1800
Anthony₂ b. 1733 Virginia, moved to Kentucky 1801, died c. 1816

To the colonists who survived the voyage, America must have seemed like heaven on earth after the horror stories they had been told about what they would encounter in the new land. There was an abundance of wild fruits and berries, huge flocks of wild turkeys, thousands of ducks, and rivers and streams filled with fish. Unfortunately, the colonists were too ill and exhausted from the voyage and too poorly equipped to take advantage of the abundance. Most of them had no guns for hunting. Vacant land, streams, and wood were plentiful, and these three things "worked together slowly to transform the Englishman into something he did not plan on—a new breed of man."[1]

> America might be a land of promise, but "the promise was to the diligent rather than to the adventuresome." There was wood for fires, but he must first "cut and fetch it home" before he could burn it. There was wood for housing, but he "must build his house before he would have it." In short, men had in America "all things to do, as in the beginning of the world," and one of the first things to do was clear the land.[2]

The farmers were also limited by their simple and inefficient tools. It was more than a hundred years before any real improvements were made and tools such as scythes and axes approached the quality seen today. Plows did not become common until the 1670s.[3] The most useful crop was corn, which the settlers learned how to grow from the Indians, and no part of the plant was wasted, even the husks, which were used to stuff mattresses.[4] In addition to the dishes made from corn (called *maize* by the

11

Indians), the settlers had kitchen gardens and fruit trees, usually apple and peach. While there were some chickens and goats brought from England, the hog was the staple meat. The hogs ran loose in the woods and when they were butchered, no part of them was wasted.[5] Cattle were highly valued and became the first industry for American farmers,[6] but protecting them from rustlers and wolves was difficult.[7]

Farmhouses in seventeenth-century America usually consisted of a hall at the ground level with a loft above for sleeping and storage space. There was no kitchen, bathroom, or closets. Cooking and eating were done in the downstairs hall and all family members used an outhouse.[8] "In the Chesapeake more than half the households contained personal belongings worth less than sixty pounds."[9] The family ate from a long board, hence the expression "room and board."[10] If the family was prosperous, they might own a bedstead or two, which was kept in the hall. As many as a dozen family members might live in this small area, from infants to elderly, and the style of living changed very little for two hundred years.[11]

The necessity to move frequently to a new area usually meant that the seventeenth century tobacco planters lived in a hovel, because all of their energy went into making a large cash crop of tobacco. Gardens and orchards were neglected, and the planters often did not plant enough corn to feed the family through the winter. "Those who charged him with laziness failed to note that he grew the most demanding crop produced in colonial America."[12] From February to October, the seeds were planted, transplanted, kept free of weeds and pests, cut, hung in sheds to dry, taken down, the leaves stripped and pressed into hogsheads, weighing between 1000 and 1300 pounds. All of the year's chores were done in the next three months—building fences, clearing fields, and cutting firewood.[13]

Robert Beverley, an early Virginia historian, kept an excellent and thorough record of the world around him. He wrote about the song of the mockingbirds and the beautifully colored hummingbirds flocking around the honeysuckle. He described the summer thunderstorms and the wonderful smell of the woods.[14] He mentioned finding a bullfrog that was so large that "six French-Men might have made a comfortable Meal of its Carcase."[15] He found very little wrong with Virginia and downplayed the three things that he found annoying—thunder, heat and vermin. He had a remedy for every minor nuisance, such as mosquitoes or "musketaes" and ticks.[16] Beverley attributed most of the illnesses of people to their own poor judgment. Either they ate too much fruit, they dressed too warmly, or they became too damp and chilled. He credited the good health of the population to the use of herbal remedies and, interestingly enough, to the shortage of doctors. ". . . there is not Mystery enough, to make a Trade of Physick there, as the Learned do in other Countries, to the great oppression of Mankind."[17]

In reality there were medical professionals sent to the colonies by the London Company and their fees were considered exhorbitant even in 1655, but a large part of the fee was for the time spent in travelling to the patients, unlike those in England.[18]

> Another innovation broke more sharply with English medical traditions. There medical practice was divided into three branches—the physician, addressed as "doctor," who was a university graduate with a sound grounding in medical theory; the surgeon, addressed as "mister," who was considered little more than a craftsman; and the apothecary, who compounded and sold drugs. All three came to America in the early ships and tried to practice as they had at home. The cumbersome arrangement collapsed quickly, and for a simple reason—there was not enough business in the thinly populated land to keep all three fully employed. By the end of the century the American doctor served as physician to his patients, did his own surgery, and concocted his own drugs.[19]

The mortality rate in Virginia was high—twice that of rural Massachusetts, with about half of all children dying before they became adults.[20] Many diseases as they were described at the time are difficult to identify today, but malaria and smallpox are identifiable by the symptoms. There was an outbreak of smallpox every ten or fifteen years, as new generations of susceptible children were born. The resulting deaths were slow and horrible, with the whole body breaking out in sores which stuck to the bed when the patient turned over, leaving large patches of skin behind. Smallpox killed hundreds of Indians and settlers alike.[21] Fever was cured by bleeding the patient, then purging the intestines.[22] Rattlesnakes were used in many cures, such as cooking the flesh in a broth and feeding it to the patient, mixing its gall with chalk for stomach aches, and using its oil for gout.[23] Starvation caused some of the early colonists to become cannibals.[24]

Due to the frequent epidemics of deadly diseases, orphaned children were common, and there was hardly a household that did not include one or more of these children.

> In tidewater Virginia during the seventeenth century, most children—more than three-quarters, in fact—lost at least one parent before reaching the age of eighteen. One consequence was to enlarge the importance of other kin; for when a nuclear family was broken in Virginia the extended family picked up the pieces. Another consequence was to change the structure of the household in a fundamental way. Historians Darrett and Anita Rutman observe that in "just about any" household one might find "orphans, half-brother, stepbrothers and stepsisters, and wards running a gamut of ages. The father figure in the house might well be an uncle or a brother, the mother figure an aunt, elder sister, or simply the father's 'now-wife,' to use the word frequently found in conveyances and wills."[25]

Anthony[1] Gholson was named in a guardian's bond in 1744 as guardian to Hannah Durram, orphan of Robert Durram.[26] He had previously been summoned in 1729

> to answer the presentment of the Grand Jury for keeping a bastard child unknown within this two months Last past, the Court having heard his Excuses and the said Anthony[1] having assumed to keep the said child of the Parish are of the opinion that the said Anthony[1] be Excused and accordingly order that y[e] sd presentment be dismissed.[27]

Anthony[2] reared two of his grandchildren after the death of their mother, Anthony[2]'s daughter Kitty, wife of Bartholomew Hayden,[28] and he was also guardian for the two sons of Peter Evans for conducting a suit after their father died.[29] In spite of the high death rate, Virginians seemed to be relatively unconcerned about dying, in contrast with the Puritans in Massachusetts who seemed obsessed with the topic.[30] They did, however, make a great show of funeral ceremonies, often involving huge quantities of food and alcohol. Virginians were usually buried in a family plot, rather than a public burying ground as in the New England tradition.[31]

The opportunity for villagers to form bonds as they had in England was lost in America because the growing of tobacco quickly depleted the soil and colonists moved every few years.[32] However, the sense of community that was lost was transferred to the family and to neighbors within fifty miles or so.[33] In 1624, the population of Virginia consisted of 1048 men and 244 women and children. Most of the men were single— called "adventurers" by the London Company.[34] When young Sir William Berkeley arrived in Virginia in 1642, the colony was a chaotic collection of roughly 8000 hard-drinking, uncivilized occupants. In Berkeley's thirty-five years as governor, the population grew to around 40,000 with a refined socio-economic system and "a governing elite which Berkeley described as 'men of as good families as any subjects in England.'"[35] It was before or during Berkeley's tenure that the parents or grandparents of Anthony₁ Gholson arrived in Virginia. Anthony₁ was not among Virginia's elite, but he did acquire enough land to become a prosperous planter.[36]

Fig. 2.1 - Portrait of Sir William Berkeley. Courtesy of The Library of Virginia. POR-Berkley, Sir William, 1606-1677. Lab# 02-0389-01, CA9-430.

The uniform religion for the colony was the Church of England as promoted by seventeen laws passed in 1632 by the Virginia Assembly. Puritan and Quaker groups attempted to gain a foothold but were quickly squelched. By 1724 the Anglican church had very little competition and shaped the culture of the colony. In the late 1700's there was an increase of Presbyterians, Methodists and Baptists.[37] Shortly after moving to

15

Kentucky in 1801, the grandson of Anthony₁ Gholson, whose name was also Anthony (hereafter referred to as Anthony₂), donated land for the construction of a Baptist church.[38]

Virginians developed an unusual way of speaking that did not resemble the speech of their New England contemporaries. Many common words were from old English expressions that were considered outdated in Britain, such as *bide* or *tarry* for stay, *botch* instead of blunder, *porely* or *pekid* for unwell and *favor* rather than resemble.[39] Many of these expressions are still commonly used by Virginians and their descendants in the southern states. The peculiarities of Virginia speech originated in seventeenth-century regional dialects spoken in the south and west of England. "The dialect of rural Sussex in the nineteenth century startled American travelers by its resemblence to Virginia speech."[40] In addition to retaining the old expressions for three centuries after they were considered archaic in England, Virginians added new words based on Indian and African expressions. The Virginians' speech pattern was soft and melodious, contrasted with the nasal whine of New Englanders. Dating back to the seventeenth century is the expression *you all* or *y'awl* in place of the plural *you*.[41]

The name of the county Botetourt was pronounced *Boat'a'tote*, and for some unknown reason the name Crenshaw became *Granger*.[42] Also originating in England was the addition of the letter *y* between words, especially names, that ended and began with consonants, resulting in names like *Billy* and *Bobby*.[43] Many of the family names as they were pronounced bore little resemblance to the written version,[44] making it easy to understand why the name Gholson was spelled so many different ways, along with the fact that many people, including Anthony₁ Gholson, could not read or write even their own names.[45]

Literacy in 17th century Virginia among the elite was near one hundred percent but dropped to about fifty percent for the less wealthy male property owners, was lower among the laboring class, and almost nonexistent for women.[46] In the 18th century, the differences in the literacy rates increased between rich and poor, rather than decreasing, and the rich actively suppressed the education of the lower classes to keep it that way.[47] The ruling class deliberately restricted printing to keep reading material from the masses, while collecting impressive libraries of their own.[48] Governor Berkeley spoke for the Virginia elite in 1671 when he was asked about the state of education in Virginia:

"I thank God," he declared, "there are no free schools nor printing, and I hope we shall not have these [for a] hundred years; for learning has brought disobedience, and heresy, and sects into the world, and printing has divulged them, and libels against the best government. God keep us from both!"[49]

Although there was not an effort to educate the poor and help them to become rich, they were given help as needed. According to Thomas Jefferson in his *Notes on Virginia*,

The poor who have neither property, friends, nor strength to labor, are boarded in the houses of good farmers, to whom a stipulated sum is annually paid. To those who are able to help themselves a little, or have friends from whom they derive some succors, inadequate however to their full maintenance, supplementary aids are given which enable them to live comfortably in their own houses, or in the houses of their friends. Vagabonds without visible property or vocation, are placed in work houses, where they are well clothed, fed, lodged and made to labor. Nearly the same method of providing for the poor prevails through all our States; and from Savannah to Portsmouth you will seldom meet a beggar.[50]

Virginia had a definite patriarchal society, and marriage "was a social condition which everyone was expected to achieve. Bachelors and spinsters were condemned as unnatural and even dangerous to society."[51] In 17th century Virginia, so few immigrants were female that almost all women were able to marry, but there were only enough wives for about three-fourths of the men, and a man's ability to find a wife depended greatly upon his social status.[52]

There was a vast difference between Virginia and New England in sexual mores. In Virginia, pregnant brides and unwed mothers were common.[53] There were multiple rules applying to sexual behavior. While women were held to strict standards, men were encouraged and expected to engage in sex with any and all women, willing or not. In the diary of William Byrd II, he described his sexual adventures with "relatives, neighbors, casual acquaintances, strangers, prostitutes, the wives of his best friends, and servants both black and white, on whom he often forced himself, much against their wishes."[54] He always asked for God's forgiveness after the incident but continued to repeat the behavior again and again.[55] Rape, which was punishable by execution in Massachusetts, was punished lightly if at all in Virginia.[56]

Love was expected to follow marriage, not necessarily precede it. The recommended course was to take a wife that one could learn to love. Parents took an active role in deciding on a spouse for their children. Although children were seldom forced to marry against their will, they could be denied their inheritance if they did. "Amongst landed families, marriage was regarded as a union of properties as well as persons, and the destinies of entire families were at stake."[57] Among the common people, women were responsible for the same household chores they had performed in England. Of necessity, they also became a partner in the fields, although deference to the man still remained. Women were not usually encouraged to read, write, or discuss political matters, as they were not considered intelligent enough, although there were exceptions in the upper class.[58] Thomas Jefferson wrote the following letter to his daughter Maria, while he was in New York in 1790:

> Where are you, my dear Maria? how do you do? how are you occupied? Write me a letter by the first post, and answer me all these questions. Tell me whether you see the sun rise every day? how many pages a day you read in Don Quixote? how far you are advanced in him? whether you repeat a grammar lesson every day? what else you read? how many hours a day you sew? whether you have an opportunity of continuing your music? whether you know how to make a pudding yet, to cut out a beefsteak, to sow spinach? or to set a hen? Be good, my dear, as I have always found you . . . [59]

Daughters of the top families in Virginia were instructed in running a household and supervising servants, as well as the social graces they would need to fill their role. Because the social life was so important, music, dancing and etiquette were essential skills for a young woman to acquire.[60] Although the slaves relieved southern women of most of the manual labor, great skill was required to maintain order, feed and care for them.[61] There were wooden floors to be sanded and polished, and every well-to-do family had large amounts of pewter and silver which needed frequent polishing. Huge collections of linen had to be maintained, without washing machines and steam irons.[62] Almost all food and clothing used by a family was grown and processed at home. Livestock was raised, slaughtered and cured, and grains were grown, threshed and made into flour. With the exception of a few items such as sugar and spices, all food originated with the family or a neighbor.[63] Candles and soap were made at home, in long and tedious processes, and even medicines were made by "the gathering and drying of herbs, the making of ointments and salve, the distilling of bitters, and the boiling of syrups ..."[64] Some of the drudgery was relieved by turning work into social occasions, such as quilting bees, sewing bees, and many other "bees."[65]

The greatest burden placed upon the colonial woman was "the incessant bearing of offspring."[66] Anthony$_1$ Gholson and his wife, or wives, had at least five children;[67] his son William was the father of between seven and eleven;[68] and William's son, Anthony$_2$, was the father of eleven.[69] Children were an asset rather than a liability and more children meant more workers and the ability to generate more wealth for the family.[70]

Every member of an early Virginia family had a role to play, beginning at a very young age, and the welfare of the family depended upon every member. Planting, tending and harvesting crops consumed much of every member's time and energy. The day began and ended with prayers, and relatives who could not care for themselves were cared for and given whatever tasks they were able to carry out.[71]

Virginia gentlemen were generally honest, hospitable and courteous toward each other, but in addition to their weaknesses of gambling and womanizing, many of them drank excessively. It was quite common to drink all day, from breakfast until bedtime, remaining in a "state of stupefaction"[72] except for those special occasions when they became exceedingly drunk. A Kentucky land transaction mentioned the old still house belonging to Anthony$_2$ Gholson[73] and he was undoubtedly following the example of his father in Virginia, as archaeologists have excavated stills in earlier Virginia compounds. The colonists distrusted water and had no coffee or tea until well past the mid-seventeenth century, but an early Virginian stumbled upon a way to make whiskey from corn mash.[74] They soon learned to make hard cider and peach brandy from the fruit of their orchards. "Regardless of laws passed . . . and sermons preached, excessive drinking remained common."[75]

As to recreation of Virginians, Robert Beverley observed, "They have Hunting, Fishing, and Fowling, with which they entertain themselves an hundred ways."[76] The various methods of hunting game included hunting hares on foot with dogs, hunting turkeys, trapping wolves, and hunting varmints such as raccoons and opossums with dogs by moonlight. The dogs would chase the game up a tree by the time the hunters caught up with them, "and then they detach a nimble Fellow up after it, who must have a scuffle with the Beast, before he can throw it down to the Dogs; and then the Sport increases, to see the Vermine encounter those little Currs."[77] Because of the danger of encountering larger animals such as bears and panthers, they also took the larger dogs along at night. Beverley also described the many methods of fishing and bird hunting.[78] Anthony[2] Gholson's family members were no exception and were described as "elegant people and wouldn't work, but loved to hunt."[79]

Night time posed a special set of problems and fears for early Virginians and the rest of the world before the invention of electricity. Roger Ekirch, Virginia Tech historian, has studied the preindustrial night for many years and shared his knowledge with Joyce and Richard Wolkomir in a *Smithsonian* magazine interview in the January 2001 issue. In prior centuries, "people relied on torches, hearth fires, smoking candles, walnut oil"[80] although only the rich could afford candles, and "for our ancestors, night meant fear of demons, witches and nighthags."[81] The difference between day and night was profound and although night provided anonymity for criminals and carousing gentry, many people in a variety of jobs worked at night, including bakers and dyers as well as those who performed offensive jobs such as emptying cesspools and collecting garbage. Methods of combating the darkness included wearing light-colored clothing or riding a white horse, but accidents happened frequently, especially when alcohol was involved. "People fell into ditches, ponds and rivers and off bridges; they were thrown by horses unfamiliar with dark paths."[82]

> People began as children to memorize their local terrain—ditches, fences, cisterns, bogs. They also memorized the magical terrain, spots where ghosts and other nighttime frights lurked. "In some places, you never whistled at night, because that invited the devil," says Ekirch. "You might wear charms or amulets around your

neck, and nail horseshoes to your home to fend off witches."[83]

Sleeping patterns were also different. Instead of sleeping from dusk until dawn, people slept in segments, awaking after four hours or so, lying in bed and meditating or even visiting with neighbors for one to three hours, then going back to sleep for another four hours. "People, as a matter of course, routinely referred to their 'first sleep' and their 'second sleep.'"[84] Beds were often the most valuable piece of furniture in the house, and it was common for an entire family to sleep in the same bed, often joined by visiting relatives or other travelers.[85] When Anthony₁ Gholson gave his property to his children before he died, two of his sons, William and Anthony, Jr., each received "one Feather Bed & its Furniture."[86]

Eighteenth-century Virginians were inordinately fond of horses and were said to be "foaled, not born."[87] It was fortunate that they loved horses, as riding was necessary to get from one place to another.[88] Those who could afford it had expensive horses and handsome carriages, but even the poorest Virginian had a saddlehorse to ride. Walking was avoided like the plague, except when incidental to hunting. According to J.F.D. Smyth's observations of Virginians, recorded in 1772 in *A Tour in the United States of America*, "a man will frequently go five miles to catch a horse, to ride only one mile upon afterwards."[89]

The number one sport in eighteenth-century Virginia was horse racing, on which large sums of money were wagered. Fine horses were imported and carefully bred to bring out the most excellent qualities. It was during this period that the quarter horse was developed for great speed over a distance of a quarter of a mile in southern Virginia and North Carolina.[90] Not only did the Virginians bet on horse racing, but on card games, crops, the weather, and the like, with bets being enforced as contracts by the courts.[91]

In managing a plantation, the planter would oversee every detail, but if he owned slaves, it was the slaves who did all of the work, planting tobacco on the good soil and corn on the inferior soil. The best land was found under hardwood forests, so the trees were girdled to kill them and tobacco was planted between the stumps. Tobacco was grown for about three years, then the land was planted in wheat for a year or two before allowing it to revert to the forest, so planters had to continually move their plantations.[92] Jefferson predicted that when tobacco production declined, it would be replaced by cotton in the eastern parts of the state, and hemp and flax in the western parts.[93]

In 1784, a house was built for reception of deer skins and hemp, which were accepted as payment of taxes in Botetourt County, with Anthony$_2$ Gholson appointed as inspector. The post was an important one, because "much depended in those days on the quality of fiber secured, there being so many uses for it (rope etc.)."[94] The house was built on Thomas Madison's Stone House tract of land, and was described as follows:

> 18 x 24 feet, of round logs, 16 feet high, the lower story 10 feet, plank floors above and below, with a good door with sufficient lock and key, covered with lapped shingles 18 inches to the weather clear of sap, the whole to be finished by the first of March in a workman like manner, for the reception of deer skins and hemp, agreeable to Act of Assembly. Anthony Gohlson was appointed inspector for the skins and hemp received, which were accepted as payment of taxes in the county.[95]

In a letter to John Adams, written at Monticello in 1812, Thomas Jefferson states, "We consider a sheep for every person in the family as sufficient to clothe it, in addition to the cotton, hemp and flax which we raise ourselves. For fine stuff we shall depend on your northern manufactories."[96]

The Virginia planters and their families were great socializers, often dressing in their finest clothing and going to join neighbors for elegant dinners and dancing, singing, card playing, drinking and holding philosophical discussions. The dances included minuets, reels and country dances, with music provided by French horns and violins.[97] The ability to dance was taken very seriously, and children were forced to learn to dance as a form of discipline, in contrast with the Quaker and Puritan colonies, where it was discouraged or forbidden.[98]

When it came to food, prosperous Virginians retained their English tastes, eating roast beef and fresh fruits and vegetables at every opportunity. The less prosperous often ate a "mess" of greens and salt meat or a bowl of hominy. Characteristics of Virginia cooking were roasting, simmering or frying, and highly seasoned dishes. For all social classes, feasting was an important ritual, taking place any time significant events occurred—weddings, christenings, holidays, or deaths.[99]

Although Virginians seemed indulgent in rearing their children, compared with the New England colonists, they instructed them very well in "formal rules of right conduct."[100] All children of all social categories were forced to learn them, but more rules applied to children from the higher ranks.

> Among the earliest writings by George Washington was a list of 110 "rules of civility and decent behaviour in Company and conversation," which the young scholar had been compelled to inscribe in his best copybook hand:
> 1st Every action done in Company ought to be with some sign of respect to those that are present . . .
> 19th Let your countenance be pleasant but in serious matters somewhat grave . . .
> 26th In pulling off your Hat to Persons of Distinction, as Noblemen, Justices, Churchmen &c make a reverence, bowing more or less to the custom of the better bred . . . [101]

In the families of the American colonists, "Youngsters were taught . . . that what they did reflected first on the family, then rippled out to affect the entire community."[102] Children were given chores and responsibilities as early as three years of age and often had very little supervision during the day. "John Adams was given a gun when only eight, just old enough to lift it, and alone, under no watchful adult eye, he spent hours, day after day, in the marshes bringing down birds, or trying to."[103] There was no generation gap, as fathers and mothers worked with sons and daughters on a daily basis to teach them the things necessary to know to sustain life. Some children did not fare as well, as they were apprenticed out at an early age because the parents were unable to take care of them for one reason or another.[104]

There was a great difference in the attitude of Virginians toward Indians and Negroes. They saw Indians as noble savages with the capability of being transformed into civilized citizens, even though the Indians had no desire to become civilized.[105] The beginning of the end of friendly relations between the settlers and the Indians came in 1622 when Indians in Virginia suddenly and without warning killed 347 settlers across a hundred-mile area, followed by another attack in 1644, which gave the settlers an excuse to exterminate them.[106]

Much has been written which holds that after the first third of the century white settlers carried out a conscious criminal conspiracy to exterminate the Indian and that America ever since has been forced to bear a burden of guilt for what the past did to an innocent people. There is another view. "The American aborigine was the victim of a process," Bernard W. Sheehan has written in a perceptive essay on Indian-white relations in early America. "The crime, if there was one, was the inexorable breakdown of the native's cultural integrity, in part the result of conscious policy and in part the inevitable consequence of competition between two disparate ways of life."

Sheehan's judgment echoes that of Robert Beverley, who in 1705 published the first sympathetic study of Indian culture. Beverley ended his lengthy account about the way of life among Chesapeake Indians—"their dress . . . management of children . . . cookery and food . . . war and peace . . . concerning religion . . . diseases and cures . . . handicrafts"—with words that are hard to improve on nearly three centuries later:

> They have on several accounts reason to lament the arrival of the Europeans, by whose means they seem to have lost their felicity as well as their innocence. The English have taken away great part of their country and consequently made everything less plenty amongst them. They have introduced drunkenness and luxury amongst them, which have multiplied their wants and put them up to desiring a thousand things they never dreamt of before.[107]

The "noble savage" idea did not extend to Negroes, as shown by the following quote from *Undaunted Courage* by Stephen E. Ambrose:

When they looked at a Negro, they saw something less than a human, something more than an animal. Never in their lives did they imagine the possibility of a black man's becoming a full citizen. William Clark tried to adopt a part-

Indian boy as his own son. He would not have dreamed of adopting a black boy as his own son.[108]

In the early days of settlement, there were many more blacks in the North than in the South, but they were treated much like any other indentured servant. Slavery grew slowly in the South during most of the seventeenth century, partly because most slavers did not stop there, bypassing Virginia for more lucrative markets in the West Indies and Brazil. It was also less of a financial risk for a planter to buy an indentured servant for a few years than to buy a slave, due to the high death rate.[109]

Not all blacks in early seventeenth-century Virginia were slaves. Some were indentured servants, and some could even purchase white servants and testify against whites in court. There was even some tolerance for interracial marriage. Then beginning around 1660, Virginia and Maryland began passing laws banning interracial marriages and forbidding blacks to own property. They also forbade blacks to bear arms or travel without written permission.[110] Around 1670, several factors caused an increase in the number of slaves, including the following:

- There was a greater chance that they would live a longer life, making the investment less risky;
- The slavers began to tap into a market that had been ignored; and
- The role of the black man in society had deteriorated over the previous fifty years, making it more difficult for a black man to live free.[111]

Although in the beginning there were many similarities between the early colonies of New England and Virginia, it did not take long for them to develop their own distinct cultures. New England continued to maintain a rigorous religious focus with attention turning to commerce and trade.[112] The second and third generation Virginians, on the other hand, lived the aristocratic life on the plantations they had inherited and the social skills and knowledge obtained by being educated in England.[113] They became somewhat lazy due to the warm climate and ease of growing crops, preferring to hunt and socialize, rather than work, and the Gholsons were no exception. However, even though they admired and emulated English society, the Virginia aristocrats would prove themselves to be quite capable of rebelling against British authority when the time came.[114]

Chapter 3: Virginia – The Planters and the Land

Anthony$_1$ received a 1000-acre grant
from King George II in 1728.
His son William received a 500-acre grant at the same time
and married Susanna Collins in 1725.
Their son Anthony$_2$ was born in 1733.
William's father, Anthony$_1$, died between Aug 1763-Dec 1764.

The right of property to an Englishman, native or colonial, was the primary and essential right on which all others rested. Attacks on property in the form of illegal levies or taxes had been the characteristic aggression of autocratic rulers.[1]

The fact is that . . . "power always follows property. Men in general, in every society, who are wholly destitute of property, are also too little acquainted with public affairs to form a right judgment, and too dependent upon other men to have a will of their own. . . . Such is the frailty of the human heart, that very few men who have no property have any judgment of their own. They talk and vote as they are directed by some man of property, who has attached their minds to his interest." They were not, therefore, "independent men"—that magic status on which true republics must rest, men who owned property and thus could call their souls their own.[2]

Property . . . was the basic liberty, because until a man was secure in his property, until it was protected from arbitrary seizure, life and liberty could mean little.[3] *John Adams, Vol. I*, by Page Smith

The possibility of acquiring land was a dream that attracted thousands of Europeans to the colonies. In Europe it had become almost impossible to acquire land that was not already in the family, but in America an abundance of land awaited anyone who wanted it.[4]

> Private land ownership was dear to the Englishmen but was foreign to the Indians. The Indian considered all creation common property equally accessible to all and for the benefit of all. To the Indian, whose very existance [*sic*] depended upon his ability to hunt, fish and plant a small number of crops, the free use of the land was essential. The right to the land upon which the English chose to settle was claimed by the Powhatan Confederation. The English, on the other hand, did not recognize any sovereign right to the land or the use thereof in the Indian but rather claimed title and exclusive right to possession and use of the land under the generally accepted (in Europe) doctrine of title by discovery and later under the prevailing doctrine of effective occupation.
>
> Though some land was purchased from the Indians and some was given to the English by the Indians, it is generally conceded that most of the land acquired by the English in Tidewater Virginia was taken from the Indians without benefit of either purchase or gift. It was seized by conquest, eviction and appropriation and the Indian was denied further access to it.
>
> The Virginia Company of London or the London Company, and later the English Crown, recognized the problem and many attempts were made to protect the rights of the Indians, all to no avail. As the flow of settlers increased and the demand for tobacco land grew, there was very little desire or willingness on the part of the new residents of Virginia to recognize that the previous inhabitants had any rights at all to the land.[5]

Virginia was converted into a Royal Colony in 1624.[6] For each person transported to Virginia, the London Company assigned the rights to fifty acres of land, called "headrights," to the person who paid for their transportation.[7] Any freeman who paid his own passage received fifty acres for himself and for each member of his household.[8]

Virginia's Royal Governor Spotswood envisioned creating an English nation in North America as he led his party out of Williamsburg in 1716 to claim the Appalachian mountains for England and to stop the advance of the French in the interior. He and his party, whom he called the Knights of the Golden Horseshoe, climbed to the top of the Blue Ridge range on September 5, 1716, and looked down into the great valley and across to the Allegheny Mountains. Then they descended to the Shenandoah River (named by the Indians and meaning *Daughter of the Stars*) where they buried a bottle containing Virginia's claim to the land for King George I.[9] For the next century, the American frontier was pushed back by Anthony Gholson and his descendants and thousands of others like them.

~ The first Anthony Gholson in America ~
c. 1685-1764

It is not certain how many generations of Gholsons had been in America before Anthony₁ Gholson was born sometime around the year 1685. His first recorded transaction was a purchase of 200 acres of land for fifty pounds of tobacco in Spotsylvania County, St. George Parish, in 1725,[10] which he and his wife Jane sold in 1739 to Zachary Lewis.[11] In 1728, he obtained a grant from King George II for 1000 acres on Terry's Run in Spotsylvania County.[12] By 1738, he had sold all of the 1000 acres.[13] His sons William and Anthony, Jr. received grants of 500 acres each at the same time he received the 1000 acres.[14] Anthony₁ bought 400 acres in 1740 from John Chew and wife, and sold 120 acres in 1744 and the remaining 280 acres in 1761.[15]

Most of those who settled in Virginia during the first hundred years had not moved beyond the fall line of the main rivers so that they could easily transport their tobacco to ships bound for England.[16] As the soil in that area began to be depleted from tobacco growing, landowners began acquiring new lands in the Piedmont and Valley sections of Virginia.[17] Moving inland from the water courses necessitated the building of roads to move the tobacco to seaports. When road building began, it became a function of the county courts to build and maintain the roads.[18] The following description of the road system is taken from Thomas Jefferson's *Notes on Virginia*:

> The roads are under the government of the county
> courts, subject to be controlled by the general court. They

order new roads to be opened wherever they think them necessary. The inhabitants of the county are by them laid off into precincts, to each of which they allot a convenient portion of the public roads to be kept in repair. Such bridges as may be built without the assistance of artificers, they are to build. If the stream be such as to require a bridge of regular workmanship, the court employs workmen to build it, at the expense of the whole county. If it be too great for the county, application is made to the general assembly, who authorize individuals to build it, and to take a fixed toll from all passengers, or give sanction to such other proposition as to them appears reasonable.[19]

There are several references to Anthony₁ Gholson as caretaker and overseer of the road between 1727 and 1733 in Spotsylvania County. On August 1, 1727, Anthony₁ was appointed to serve as overseer of the highways,[20] then he petitioned for more hands to be added to his road gang but the petition was rejected.[21] On February 5, 1729/30 (see Explanatory Notes), he petitioned for discharge as overseer and his petition was granted.[22] On April 7, 1730, he was ordered to help Thomas Pulliam, who had been appointed overseer, as his replacement.[23] On November 6, 1733, Anthony₁ was ordered to help Joseph Thomas to keep the road clear.[24]

The wealthiest Virginians owned as many as several hundred thousand acres of land, often split into many tracts. Robert Carter of Lancaster County owned approximately 333,000 acres.[25] Anthony₁ Gholson was not one of the wealthiest, but he was a prominent member of the community in Spotsylvania County and engaged in a number of legal transactions between the time of the 1000-acre grant and his death in his late seventies sometime before December 1764.[26]

On July 23, 1763, not long before he died, Anthony₁ executed a deed of gift in Orange County, Virginia, to four of his five children, as follows:

- To son William, slaves named Tom and Little Tom, and one feather bed and its furniture;
- To son Anthony, slaves named Bob and Cupid, and one feather bed and its furniture;
- To daughter Elizabeth Rice, female slaves named Venus and Mary;
- To daughter Lucy Step [Stapp], female slaves named Phillis and Greece [or Creece], which he loaned to her during her natural life, with

the slaves and their future children going to Lucy's children after her death; and one feather bed and its furniture; and

- To his granddaughter, Jane Pollard, female slave named Sarah.[27]

The above deed of gift reserved the use of the slaves and furniture to Anthony[1]'s widow, Jane Gholson, for her lifetime. On August 8, 1763, Anthony[1] executed a deed of gift to his son John for one lot of land purchased from Nathaniel Geer, the slaves Judy and Ben, all of his stock of horses and cattle, and all of the remainder of his estate.[28] Jane then executed a Deed of Gift on December 3, 1764, giving all of the slaves named above to her son John, for her lifetime, then they would revert to her other children as stipulated by her deceased husband, Anthony[1].[29]

~ William Gholson, son of Anthony[1] and Jane ~
c. 1705-1800

Anthony[1] Gholson's eldest son William was born around 1705 in Spotsylvania County. His first recorded transaction was the 1000-acre grant received jointly with his brother, Anthony, Jr. in 1728. He owned many slaves and many tracts of land in Spotsylvania County and Orange County, in the foothills of the Blue Ridge mountains in Virginia's Piedmont section, with his name appearing frequently in record books between 1747-1774. Even though William bought and sold numerous tracts of land, no record has been found of the settlement of his estate. He was married twice. His first wife was Captain Joseph Collins' daughter Susannah, who died between 1775 and 1786. His second wife's name was Joan, but the names of her parents are unknown.[30]

William and Susannah had at least seven children, possibly as many as eleven.[31] Their first son may have been Lewis Gholson of South Carolina. The other children were Anthony[2], who moved to Kentucky in 1801, Frederick, John, Francis, James, and William, Jr., and possibly one or more additional children.[32] William may have lived with his son William, Jr. until he died. It does not seem likely that he crossed the mountains into Kentucky with his son Anthony[2] in 1801, as he would have been well into his nineties at the time.[33] William, like his father Anthony[1], signed his name with a distinctive mark, Anthony[1] using a large capital "A" and William using an "M" with a slash through it.[34]

~ The second Anthony Gholson ~
Son of William Gholson & Susannah Collins Gholson
c. 1733-1816

William's son Anthony$_2$, named after his grandfather, was born around 1733 in Spotsylvania County. Anthony$_2$ married Elizabeth (parents' names unknown) in Spotsylvania County and they had eleven children during the years 1764-1786, William, Mary (Molly), Sarah (Sally), Elizabeth (Betty), Samuel (who moved to Texas), John, James, Nancy, Catherine (Kitty), Benjamin, and Dorothy (Dolly) who married Micah Taul, whose life is described in Chapter 6.[35]

Anthony$_2$ rented a 113-acre parcel of land from George Washington in Frederick County above Worthington's Marsh from 1768 until 1786 or later and became delinquent in his rental payments. The following excerpt is from a letter written by George Washington to his brother Samuel Washington on December 6, 1771, discussing the best way to collect Gholson's rent:

> You wrote me word sometime ago that a Tenant of mine, was desirous of raising money in your hands for the discharge of his Rent; if you think there is a probability of his doing of it, I should much rather take it in that way, than by distress, & should be glad if you would order it so accordingly, & ask the other's [*sic*], as you may accidentally see them, in what manner they purpose to pay; as I am resolvd, so soon as Gholson's Rent for the present year becomes due, to destrain for the whole; as I also will for all the Arrearages of Kennedy's after March when I think by his Lease I have a right so to do.[5] . . .
>
> . . . 5. Anthony[2] Gholson rented a 113-acre parcel of GW's Frederick County land above Worthington's Marsh from 1768 until at least as late as 1786. Rental was set at £4 a year. Gholson did not make his first payment until 19 Oct. 1772, at which time he paid £18.15.0 to cover his arrears through 1771 (Ledger A, 305; Ledger B, 31; Frederick County Deed Book, 22 Mar. 1769, pp. 10-12).[36]

In 1775, Anthony$_2$ lived in Berkeley County, now West Virginia, which adjoins Frederick County, Virginia. He signed a Petition of

Freeholders of Berkeley County to the "Honourable the Moderator and the Delegates of the Colony of Virginia in Convention assembled"[37] protesting an election in Berkeley County. The nature of the protest can be found in the following excerpt from the petition:

> That Colo. Adam Stephen without consulting any person in the County as far as your Petitioners have been able to learn arrogated to himself the sole power of appointing the time of Election and notifying it to the public. That the time fixed upon by him for the election succeeded so quickly to the Notification and the Notification was given in so partial and private a manner that a great number of Freeholders did not hear of the election until it was over and many of those who did attend were not acquainted with it till the very day of the election.[38]

On July 27, 1775, the Convention declared the election irregular and ordered a new one.[39]

Some of Anthony$_2$'s moves in Virginia can be traced by records from Augusta and Botetourt counties. In 1778, Anthony$_2$ lived in Beverley Manor, Augusta County, where he bought 374 acres, which he sold in 1779.[40] He was a member of Captain Tate's Augusta County militia during the Revolutionary War.[41] Then in 1779, the names of delinquent taxpayers returned by the deputy sheriff for Augusta County listed "Anthony$_{[2]}$ Golston, gone to Botetourt"[42] where he and his family lived in the Buffalo Creek Community on the Roanoke River, north of the present city of Roanoke.[43] The fact that Anthony$_2$ had moved may account for the missed musters resulting in numerous court martial summons issued for him in the last half of 1779 and may explain why he was acquitted.[44]

There were many legal transactions involving Anthony$_2$ Gholson in Botetourt County, Virginia, between 1780 and 1801. In 1783 he served on a jury.[45] The largest tract purchased in Botetourt County was 680 acres from Reverend Caleb and Rosanna (Christian) Wallace in 1784. Rosanna's brother was Colonel William Christian of Botetourt County, who was married to Anne Henry, a sister of Patrick Henry. The population of the region was sparse, such that there were frequent interactions between seemingly ordinary people and others who have become legendary figures in history. In addition, "Thomas Madison, owner of some of the land adjoining that purchased by Anthony$_2$ Gholson, was a son of John Madison, a cousin of President James Madison. Thomas Madison was married to Susannah Henry, another of Patrick Henry's sisters."[46]

The Botetourt County Court minutes show that Anthony$_2$ was appointed Surveyor of the Road on May 10, 1785.[47] The minutes for November 8, 1785, show that James Robertson was "appointed to allot the hands to work on the road under David May and Anthony[2] Gholson."[48] Anthony$_2$ was the Surveyor of the Road until the appointment of David Goods on September 9, 1788.[49] Then on February 16, 1792, Anthony$_2$ Gholson was appointed Overseer of the Road.[50]

In 1785, Anthony$_2$ assembled about 1000 acres which he sold in 1790. Then between 1790 and 1800, he again assembled several tracts[51] into a plantation of 1,180 acres in Botetourt County's Buffalo Creek Community, which was called the "Big Spring Estate." He sold all of the tracts to Daniel Stoner in September 1801. The transactions prompted a comment from Rev. Caleb Wallace that the "rich men were buying up all the land getting it into their own hands."[52]

An important development in early America was the sawmill, which utilized the numerous fast-running streams for power to turn the abundant wood into lumber for export and for use at home.[53] Another type of mill, the grist mill, required a larger investment, because of the necessity to import the stones from Europe which were used to grind grain. When the stones reached a seaport, they had to be hauled to the site of the grist mill and assembled and dressed by an expert.[54] Anthony$_2$ Gholson built a new grist mill in 1793[55] and on January 14, 1794, he was given a permit to build another one on his land on Robinson's Creek.[56]

> Grist milling . . . was a highly specialized craft. The ideal miller combined the skills of carpenter, cooper, joiner, blacksmith, and mason. He needed to be able to judge with eye and hand the quality of the grain, its age, its moisture content, its temperature, and then determine the proper speed to rotate his stones for the particular batch in hand. ...
>
> Others in the community might have more prestige, but no one exceeded the miller in practical importance. His presence could mean the difference between a subsistence existence and prosperity. Without him all grain had to be ground by hand and few farmers could produce enough

surplus flour by that process to send to market. Flour the miller shipped to port towns returned in the form of pots and pans, axes and hoes, bolts of calico. Some millers opened small stores to serve the neighborhood. Often a hamlet cropped up around the mill site as it slowly became the economic and social center of the area. . . . the gristmill and to a lesser extent the sawmill, both powered by water, worked for the backcountry of early America as an "entering wedge of a slowly emerging market economy." Both served the isolated settler as a window on the world beyond the farm.[57]

After the Revolution, there was a decline in the price of tobacco due to overproduction, and the profit margin dropped drastically,[58] prompting many Virginia families to move to western Virginia, Kentucky and south into the Carolinas and Tennessee.[59] "At the time of the great migration into the Shenandoah Valley, Botetourt County encompassed the area which is now several counties in Virginia, part of West Virginia, and the entire states of Kentucky, Ohio, and Illinois."[60]

In 1801, the hardy sixty-eight-year-old Anthony$_2$ Gholson crossed the mountains into Kentucky with his family, including married sons and daughters, and his slaves.[61] The thought of moving west had probably been on his mind since 1780 when he received a grant of land in Jefferson County, Kentucky (in Virginia until 1792) for 992 acres on Bayles Trace. "These entries were the location of lands issued for service, sometimes as early as the French & Indian Wars (1753 on) but usually for Rev. War."[62] In 1783, there is a 200-acre tract entered in his name in Fayette County, then in 1802 there is a 105-acre tract entered in Wayne County, and in 1807 an additional 220-acre tract.[63] On May 2, 1803, two years after Anthony$_2$ moved his family to Kentucky, President Thomas Jefferson signed a treaty to purchase the Louisiana Territory from Napoleon for $15,000,000, doubling America's territory and opening the land from the Mississippi River to the Rocky Mountains for expansion.[64]

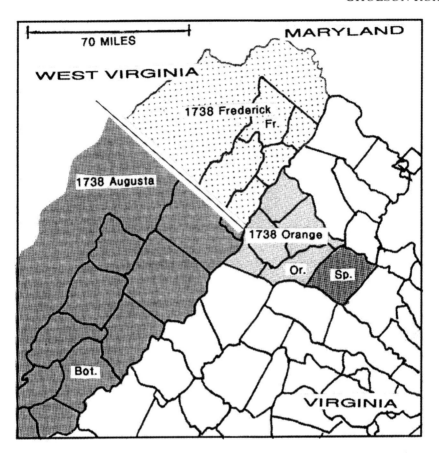

Map 1

Current north central Virginia Counties showing
area covered by the following counties in 1738:

Augusta
Frederick
Orange
Spotsylvania

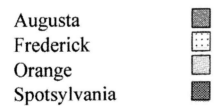

Map drawn by D. Cook. Copyright 2003.

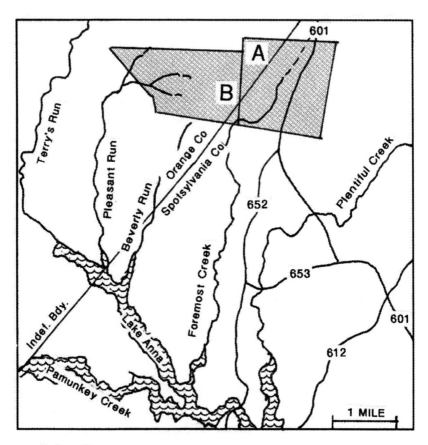

Map 2

Virginia Land Grants, 8 September 1728, then
Spotsylvania County, now Orange/Spotsylvania.
Courtesy of the Library of Virginia.

A. Anthony$_1$ Gholson, 1000 acres,
   Patent No. 13, 1725-1730, pp. 441-442

B. William Gholson and Anthony Gholson, Jr.
   1000 acres, Patent No. 13, 1725-30, pp 382-3.

Land grant outlines obtained from *Orange
County Land Patents*, 2nd Edition, by Joyner.
Topography from USGS 7.5 minute quads Lahore
and Belmont, photorevised 1973 and 1983, resp.
Map compiled by author. Copyright 2003.

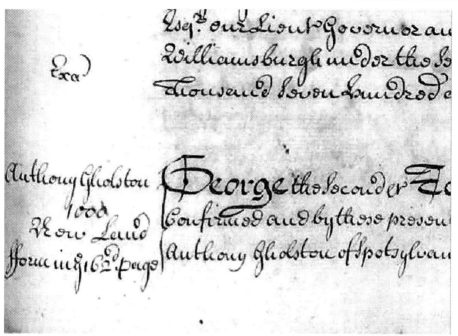

Fig. 3.1 - Sample corner of land grant to Anthony Gholston for 1000 acres by King George II. State Records, Land Office (RG4) Register of the Land Office, Original Patents and Grants 1728-1933, Patent Book 13: 1725-1730 [Microfilm Reel 12] 1000 acre grant to Anthony Gholson, 28 September 1728, pp 441-2. Archives Research Services, The Library of Virginia, Richmond, VA.

Chapter 4: Virginians in the American Revolution

William's son Anthony₂ was born in 1733
and was 43 years of age in 1776.

". . . the War for Independence was largely fought and won in the South."[1]

Virginia's role in the American Revolution was a complex one; often it was a dominant one. Her statesmen and soldiers were involved in nearly every phase of the political, social, and military upheaval which transformed a group of thirteen isolated English colonies into a unified and independent republic. A Virginian was the second commander in chief of the Continental armies . . . and later the first president of the new nation.

Other Virginians conquered the Old Northwest, fought and won at Stony Point, fought Indians on the Ohio and in Georgia, and stormed the citadel of Quebec. Virginians tasted defeat at Charleston and Camden, suffered hunger and disease at Morristown and Valley Forge, rotted in prison hulks, and died as captives in New York City. Cannon, muskets, and powder for the Continental forces were fabricated in Virginia. Enemy armies twice invaded her, and a major British force surrendered within her borders. The names of Washington, Jefferson, Madison, Monroe, Marshall, and Mason are still venerated; those of Woodford, Lawson, Scott, Weedon, and thousands of others are lost in obscurity. Nevertheless, the future president and the nameless private each shared a common experience, and each played his own unique and vital part.[2]
A Guide to Virginia Military Organizations in the American Revolution

By the end of the Seven Years War, England owned territory stretching from Canada to the Gulf of Mexico, and the decisions that were being made regarding these lands began to irritate the colonists, particularly those in the middle and southern colonies. Some of the colonists, including George Washington, were making plans to buy land from the Indians when England issued a proclamation forbidding them to buy and settle the lands. Washington and others ignored the ban.[3]

King George III decided that the colonies would pay for the protection they were receiving from the military along with a portion of the expenses of the British government. The first step was to strengthen the Molasses Act which imposed a duty on foreign imports, eliminating the colonists' means of making money with which to repay their creditors in England. This did not prove to be effective, so it was decided that a fee would be charged to stamp all legal documents in the colonies, and the Stamp Act was passed in 1765. This would not have presented a major problem, except that it riled the journalists by including a tax on newspapers. The journalists made an appeal to those who were willing and able to organize and lead the resistance—men such as Patrick Henry in Virginia and Samuel Adams in Massachusetts. There was no general objection to the Stamp Act in America, but it was greatly opposed by the English creditors, as it hindered the ability of the colonial merchants to pay back the money they had borrowed, "because the duty had to be paid in bullion already needed for meeting the adverse trade balance with England."[4]

The Stamp Act was repealed, but in 1767 a tax was levied on American imports of several items, including tea. Although this angered the colonists, it was still not a good enough reason to revolt. After the colonists boycotted English goods, the duty was dropped for all of the items except tea.[5] Just when the trouble appeared to be over, British troops in Boston fired on a group of civilians who were throwing snowballs at them on March 5, 1770, killing five, and the Boston Massacre added fuel to the revolutionary zeal of Samuel Adams and others. A communication network of seventy-five towns was established. "The Virginian agitators, led by the young Patrick Henry, created a standing committee of their Assembly to keep in touch with the other colonies, and a chain of such bodies was quickly formed. Thus the machinery of revolt was quietly and efficiently created."[6]

Fig. 4.1 - *Patrick Henry*, photograph of a painting by George B. Matthews, 1857-1935, in the United States Capitol. Detroit Publishing Co. No. M 9855. Gift; State Historical Society of Colorado; 1949. Library of Congress No. LC-D416-9855.

Colonial anti-British sentiment was finally galvanized by the English government's effort to rescue the East India Company from bankruptcy. The company was given the authority to ship tea to the colonies duty free, thus destroying the American importers and their distributors. The Patriots, as they had begun calling themselves, disguised themselves as Indians, boarded ships that carried the first duty-free tea into Boston Harbor and destroyed the tea by dumping it into the water.[7] As a result, the British Parliament assumed authority, suspending the Massachusetts assembly and closing the port, and ordered that troops be quartered in the other colonies to maintain order. Instead of isolating the resisters as Britain hoped, these actions brought them together. A congress held in Philadelphia in September 1774 drafted a document which requested that the English Parliament repeal thirteen acts which had been passed during the preceding decade, but the petition was rejected.[8] Americans switched from tea to coffee, thereafter considering it unpatriotic to drink tea.[9]

None of the colonial governors sent by the Crown were very well liked, but Lord Dunmore, Governor of Virginia, was disliked more than most. Dunmore and Patrick Henry had been engaged in a power struggle for some time, with the most recent confrontation arising from Henry's speech at the Second Virginia Convention. All of the leading Virginians were present at that convention on March 23, 1775, in Saint John's Church in Richmond, including Thomas Jefferson and George Washington. Since Anthony$_2$ had rented land from Washington and purchased land from Patrick Henry's sister-in-law, he must have been personally acquainted with them and may have even been in attendance. The meeting was not expected to do anything other than ratify the acts of the First Continental Congress and approve delegates to the Second. Then Patrick Henry rose to speak.[10]

Most of the planters had no intention of opposing the king and were shocked when Henry demanded that a militia be raised in Virginia. They were really hoping to settle their differences and restore their former relationship with the king. Fighting the powerful Crown was the last thing on their minds.[11] Henry could not be persuaded to sit down and shut up, and he went to the podium again. His words became known as one of the greatest speeches ever given:

> Reconciliation? What reconciliation? We are infested with armies and fleets sent from England. A military presence with only one purpose—to force our submission.
>
> And what is our reply? More argument and petitions? Sir, we have been trying that for the last ten years. We have nothing but the same old arguments to present. We have already done enough petitions, remonstrations, protestations.
>
> There is no longer any room for hope. If we wish to be free—if we mean to preserve inviolate those inestimable privileges for which we have been so long contending . . . we must fight! I repeat it, sir, we must fight! An appeal to arms and to the God of Hosts, is all that is left us!
>
> They say we are weak. But when shall we be stronger? Next week, or next year? Shall we wait until there's an army stationed here, a guard at every door? No.

We are not weak. We are invincible in the holy cause of liberty. Three million people invincible by any force which our enemy can send against us.

There is no retreat, but in submission and slavery! Our chains are forged. Their clanking may be heard on the plains of Boston! The war is inevitable—and let it come! I repeat, sir, let it come!

Gentlemen may cry, peace, peace—but there is no peace. The war is actually begun! The next gale that sweeps from the north, will bring to our ears the clash of resounding arms! Our brethren are already in the field! Why stand we here idle? What is it that gentlemen wish? What would they have? Is life so dear, or peace so sweet, as to be purchased at the price of chains, and slavery? Forbid it, Almighty God! I know not what course others may take; but as for me, give me liberty, or give me death![12]

His words were enough to light a fire in any soul, but his actions during the speech gave his words an even greater impact:

He delivered those words with a kind of wild theatricality. According to one account, "an unearthly fire burned in his eye" and "the tendons of his neck stood out white and rigid like whipcords. His voice rose louder and louder, until the walls of the building, and all within them, seemed to shake and rock in its tremendous vibrations." When he spoke of chains and slavery, he "stood in the attitude of a condemned galley slave, loaded with fetters, awaiting his doom. His form was bowed, his wrists were crossed; his manacles were almost visible." But when he exclaimed, "Give me liberty, or give me death!" he flung his arms wide as though shattering his bonds and struck the left side of his chest with a clenched fist as though driving a dagger into his heart.[13]

After a moment of stunned silence, Patrick Henry received a standing ovation. The convention continued—the acts of the First Continental Congress were approved and delegates were chosen for the Second. The delegates included Peyton Randolph, George Washington, and Patrick

Henry. Thomas Jefferson was chosen as an alternate for Randolph.[14] Before the convention ended, each county was asked to raise "at least one company of infantry and one troop of cavalry."[15]

Lord Dunmore had forbidden the gathering at the Second Virginia Convention and the sending of delegates to Philadelphia. Both orders were ignored, and even more worrisome to Dunmore was the forming and training of militias. The news about Lexington had not reached Virginia when Dunmore sent a group of British seamen to confiscate the twenty-one and a half barrels of gunpowder which belonged to Williamsburg and take them to a ship. His excuse was that he might need the gunpowder in case of a slave uprising, but the planters demanded it back for the same reason. Since there were 140,000 slaves in Virginia, outnumbering the whites two to one, this was not an unreasonable fear.[16] The conflict escalated, with a threat from the colonists to march on Williamsburg, followed by a threat from Dunmore that if they did, he would arm the slaves and burn the city. The troops dispersed, fearing that he would carry out his threat. Patrick Henry was not so easily intimidated and postponed his trip to the Second Continental Congress to gather a group of frontiersmen to march on Williamsburg.

> Although he often liked to pretend to be an unlettered country rustic, Henry was hardly a frontiersman himself. His father was a judge of the Hanover County court, as well as a county surveyor and a colonel in the Virginia militia. And Henry himself had an excellent education—from his father, at home, and also from his uncle Patrick, who taught him Latin, Greek, and the Bible.
>
> In later years, Henry was to be widely known for rarely reading anything, but in youth he consumed books by the dozen, especially history, from which he could snatch apt examples and quotations. People soon discovered that this adolescent with his red hair that early subsided into a fringe and his excitable blue eyes was also an eager talker and a debater. From earliest youth, Patrick Henry liked a good fight.[17]

With French, Spanish and Dutch assistance, the Patriot militia began collecting powder and supplies at Concord, where the Massachusetts assembly had reconvened contrary to the orders of Parliament. General

Thomas Gage, who was the British military governor of Massachusetts, planned to confiscate the ammunition and arrest Adams and Hancock. The colonists monitored the activities of the English soldiers, and when Gage assembled his troops, the colonists' military supplies were dispersed to other towns. Samuel Adams and John Hancock went to Lexington. Paul Revere was at his post in the North Church steeple on April 18, 1775, when he saw eight hundred of Gage's men marching down the Concord road in darkness. After signaling with lanterns, Paul mounted his horse and raced to Lexington to warn Adams and Hancock. By sunrise when the British troops arrived at Lexington, the local militia was in place on the village green. The British officer at the head of the column ordered the colonists to disperse, then the militia commander ordered his own troops to disperse, but a shot was fired, starting a battle in which a number of the militia members were killed. It was April 19, 1775, and the Revolutionary War had begun.[18]

On April 26, seven days after the battle at Lexington, the news reached George Washington who was at home on his plantation, Mount Vernon. He immediately left for the Second Continental Congress in Philadelphia, taking with him his impressive Virginia militia uniform. The uniform would leave no doubt in the minds of the delegates that Washington was ready for a fight.[19] On June 15, he was appointed general and commander in chief of the Continental troops, to the dismay of John Hancock, who was expecting to be asked to accept the position.[20] Washington had the military experience and leadership skills, and being a southerner, he brought the union together, but he was modest and did not feel that he was the most qualified.[21]

Fig. 4.2 - *George Washington in the Uniform of a British Colonial Colonel*, 1772, by Charles Willson Peale, Washington - Custis - Lee Collection, Washington and Lee University, Lexington, Virginia. This is the first of seven portraits painted during Washington's lifetime by Peale, and the only one of him before the Revolution.

Peyton Randolph, the speaker of Virginia's House of Burgesses, was traveling by coach on April 27 when an express rider gave him the news of the battle of Lexington. Randolph was a wealthy and well-educated planter and was the cousin of Thomas Jefferson. He had been the president of the First and Second Continental Congresses and was chairman of the Virginia group which was a part of the colonial network organized to oppose British rule.[22]

Randolph and the other tidewater planters were fighting to stay in power in the House of Burgesses as Patrick Henry and the small farmers like Anthony$_2$ Gholson from western Virginia tried to gain control.[23] Henry had been elected to the House of Burgesses at twenty-nine, about the same time as the Stamp Act was enacted.[24] He introduced his seven resolves, stating that Parliament had no authority to impose taxes on Virginia and that Virginians did not have to obey orders of Parliament.

The bill passed in a modified form, marking the shift of power from the tidewater planters to the counties in Western Virginia.[25]

On Friday, April 28, 1775, the news of Lexington reached Williamsburg, Virginia's capital.[26] This would have normally been an active time of the year, but Governor Dunmore had closed the House of Burgesses the previous year and still refused to allow it to open. When his servants brought him the news of Lexington, he was already preparing to leave to escape from Patrick Henry and his troops who were marching toward Williamsburg. Dunmore had confiscated Williamsburg's gunpowder supply and the colonists were incensed.[27] On the night the news of Lexington reached Williamsburg, Patrick Henry's troops were camped about sixteen miles from Williamsburg. Henry demanded that Dunmore return the gunpowder or pay for it. Dunmore gave Henry a draft for the cost of the gunpowder, and Henry prepared to travel to Philadelphia to attend the Second Continental Congress. Dunmore returned to his palace and declared Henry an outlaw.[28]

Life returned to a somewhat normal state, but in addition to the spring planting activities, the militia continued to grow and drill and march.[29] The Virginia militia was composed of all white males between sixteen and fifty who attended monthly and quarterly musters, often electing their own officers, and "those who reported to the rendezvous were usually untrained, unarmed, and uninterested."[30] However, young men formed a social bond and gained experience with muskets, enabling them to defend their communities if needed.[31]

In order to convince citizens to move to the American colonies, the English government had promised to guarantee all of the personal freedom and property rights to the colonists that they enjoyed in England, including the right of Protestants to keep and use weapons. These rights were restated in the charters of Virginia and other colonies. The English common law was adopted in its entirety, unless the situation made it impractical, and the colonists added their own laws as they became necessary.[32] A major emphasis of the colonial governments was to "ensure that the populace was well armed,"[33] however Catholics were considered as potential subversives and Indians and black slaves were generally excluded from owning firearms.[34]

> Colonial law went another step beyond English law and required colonists to carry weapons. A Newport law of 1639 provided that "noe man shall go two miles from the

Towne unarmed, eyther with Gunn or Sword; and that none shall come to any public Meeting without his weapon." Early Virginia laws required "that no man go or send abroad without a sufficient partie well armed," and "that men go not to worke in the ground without their arms (and a centinell upon them)." They even specified that "all men that are fittinge to beare armes, shall bring their pieces to the church uppon payne of every offence, if the mayster allow not thereof to pay 2 lb of tobacco."[35]

Thomas Jefferson wrote the following description of the militia in his *Notes on Virginia*:

Every able-bodied freeman, between the ages of sixteen and fifty, is enrolled in the militia. Those of every county are formed into companies, and these again into one or more battalions, according to the numbers in the county. They are commanded by colonels, and other subordinate officers, as in the regular service. In every county is a county-lieutenant, who commands the whole militia of his county, but ranks only as a colonel in the field. We have no general officers always existing. These are appointed occasionally, when an invasion or insurrection happens, and their commission determines with the occasion. The Governor is head of the military, as well as civil power. The law requires every militia-man to provide himself with the arms usual in the regular service. But this injunction was always indifferently complied with, and the arms they had, have been so frequently called for to arm the regulars, that in the lower parts of the country they are entirely disarmed. In the middle country a fourth or fifth part of them may have such firelocks as they had provided to destroy the noxious animals which infest their farms; and on the western side of the Blue Ridge they are generally armed with rifles.[36]

The colonists strongly believed in maintaining a militia for self defense but they had a fear of standing armies which had grown out of generations of prior experience. Soon after the beginning of the reign of

George III, it began to appear that these fears were justified.[37] The militia acts gave the British Crown more power over the militia and the ability to place it under the regular army. Then the proceeds from import taxes were used for the upkeep of the army in the colonies.[38] By 1775, the militia had come to be considered unreliable by the Crown, and the colonists were not confident in the ability of the militia to protect them. By the early part of 1775, patriots had begun to organize a selected group of individuals they trusted into a smaller militia of "minute men."[39]

In May 1775, Lord Dunmore reconvened the House of Burgesses while Patrick Henry and the other radicals were occupied in Philadelphia. Peyton Randolph turned over his position as chairman of the Continental Congress to John Hancock and returned to Williamsburg to preside over the House of Burgesses. Lord North, representing the Crown, had offered conciliatory proposals, but the proposals were rejected and Thomas Jefferson wrote the official reply.[40] Dunmore responded by offering emancipation to the slaves, which eliminated any hope of reconciliation between England and Virginia.[41] Thomas Jefferson personally carried the document rejecting Lord North's proposal to Philadelphia.[42] In 1776, Jefferson was given the opportunity of a lifetime when he was asked to draft a document declaring America's independence from Great Britain. After heated debate, the Declaration of Independence was approved by Congress on July 4, 1776.[43]

Thomas Jefferson was governor of Virginia when it was invaded by British forces led by Benedict Arnold in the fall of 1780. In January 1781, the capital of Richmond was captured and burned by a second British invasion. The state government was moved to Charlottesville, but the state archives were lost, destroyed, or captured, and Jefferson's home at Monticello was also raided.

> Interestingly, Jefferson was so eager to secure Virginia's claims to the Ohio country that he had tried to send part of the Virginia militia to the region a few months earlier. The militia units, however, had mutinied and refused to leave Virginia.[44]

~

Anthony[2] Gholson may have also served in the French and Indian Wars, as he received a grant of 992 acres in 1780, in Jefferson County, Kentucky, on Bayles Trace.[45] These grants were given for service in both the French and Indian and the Revolutionary Wars. He served as a private under Captain James Tate in the Augusta County militia during the Revolutionary War.[46] Augusta County had been formed in 1745 from Orange County, which was originally part of Spotsylvania County.[47] Captain Tate's company fought the British on March 15, 1781, at the battle of Guilford Court House in North Carolina, but Anthony$_2$ had moved to Botetourt County in 1779 and probably was not a participant. Numerous court martial summons were issued for Anthony$_2$ in the last half of 1779 for missing musters, but he was acquitted, possibly because he had moved from the county.[48] British General Cornwallis held the field and technically won the battle of Guilford Court House but "had lost 800 men, including many of his best officers—twice the casualties suffered on the American side."[49] Captain Tate was one of the Americans who lost his life in the battle.

~

From the DAR Patriot Index:
> Anthony$_{[2]}$: b c 1733 VA d a 1-20-1817 KY m Elizabeth — Pvt VA[50]

Chapter 5: Over the Mountains to Kentucky

Anthony₂ moved his family to Kentucky in 1801 at age 68.

... to the frontier the American intellect owes its striking characteristics. That coarseness and strength combined with acuteness and inquisitiveness; that practical, inventive turn of mind, quick to find expedients; that masterful grasp of material things, lacking in the artistic but powerful to effect great ends; that restless, nervous energy; that dominant individualism, working for good and for evil, and withal that buoyancy and exuberance which comes with freedom—these are traits of the frontier, or traits called out elsewhere because of the existence of the frontier.[1]
~ *Frederick Jackson Turner*

Many hunters had already passed through Cumberland Gap on the way to the good hunting grounds in Kentucky when Daniel Boone and his friend John Finley and four others left Boone's cabin on May 1, 1769. Daniel knew that his wife Rebecca would get along, with the vegetables from the garden and the game shot and trapped by his eleven-year-old son James, and he hoped to bring back a profitable collection of skins and furs.[2] "Dressed in coonskin cap, buckskin jumper, and leggings, Boone disappeared for weeks at a time into the dense Kentucky wilderness, always to return."[3]

Fig. 5.1 - *Daniel Boone*. Courtesy of the Library of Virginia. POR-Boone, Daniel, 1734-1820. LAB# 03-1574-01, A9-17407.

As Daniel and his party approached the Gap, they were surprised to find a settlement under construction, led by Joseph Martin of Virginia. This settlement would be the last stopping point on the way to Kentucky for many settlers for years to come. Boone and the others crossed the divide and continued through the gap with its fifteen-hundred-foot cliff on the right side and a lower and rounder hill on the left. They followed an old Indian trail down to a ford on the Cumberland River and continued until they eventually reached Red Lick Fork, where they made their camp.[4]

Fig. 5.2 - *Cumberland Gap,* steel engraving by S. V. Hunt after painting by Harry Fenn. Copyright by D. Appleton & Co. Illustration in *Picturesque America.* Library of Congress No. LC-USZ62-52628 DLC (b&w film copy neg.).

There was such an abundance of game that the hunters had no trouble gathering a collection of furs and skins, but then Boone and his brother-in-law John Stuart had a run-in with a group of Indians. The Indians took their furs, captured them, and held them for a week before they were able to escape. By the time they made it back to camp, the camp had been plundered and their hunting companions had started home, so they did the sensible thing and resumed hunting. They had been hunting for a few weeks when Daniel's brother named Squire and a friend came to look for them because of their long absence. As soon as the rescuers found out that they were safe, they joined in the hunt themselves. The four of them continued trapping for several months, but then Stuart was killed by Indians, the other two left, and Daniel was left on his own to explore the wilderness. Squire took a load of furs home, then came back and the two brothers spent the winter of 1770-1771 hunting, trapping and exploring in southern Kentucky.[5]

By the time Daniel and Squire started home in March 1771, they had a good collection of furs and Daniel had decided to bring his family to Kentucky as soon as possible. Before Daniel and Squire reached home, however, another group of Indians took their guns, horses, supplies and their furs. For two years of work, the only thing they had to show was the batch of furs previously brought home by Squire.[6]

Still undaunted by his desire to move, by September 1773, Daniel had convinced a few other families to move to Kentucky, so forty people left the Clinch River area and started west. Boone's family and some neighbors were in the leading group and Captain William Russell was leading the second group. Boone sent back his son James, who was then seventeen, to give Russell directions on combining the two parties for the dangerous part of the trip. With James were Russell's son Henry and six others, including two of Russell's slaves, Adam and Charles. The group was attacked by Indians and were killed, with the exception of the slave Adam and one of the others, both of whom managed to escape.[7]

After the settlers buried the dead, they discussed whether to continue on or go back. Only Boone wanted to go on, but he eventually gave in and returned with the others.[8] The months that followed would bring more Indian conflicts before Boone could return to Kentucky.[9]

Daniel's next opportunity came when Colonel Richard Henderson of North Carolina asked him to be his agent and adviser in negotiating the purchase of roughly 20,000,000 acres of land from the Cherokee. The land encompassed the area between the Cumberland River and the Kentucky River, south of the Ohio River, as well as lands drained by tributaries of the Cumberland River.[10] In addition, Henderson secured a wide strip of land to provide access to the purchased land. He then gave Daniel Boone the job of cutting a road to Kentucky.[11]

Daniel gathered an assortment of axmen, friends, neighbors and others, and they left Long Island (Kingsport, Tennessee) on March 10, 1775, to blaze a trail of two hundred miles. As they approached Cumberland Gap, they again encountered Captain Joseph Martin, rebuilding the settlement he had left shortly after Boone's first visit.[12]

The axmen continued on, cutting the path through the mountains. As they came through a gap in the last mountain range, they saw the plains of Kentucky, covered with blooming clover and huge flocks of turkeys and other game. They knew they had found paradise.[13] After two more days, they were camped fifteen miles from the place where they planned to build a settlement, when a band of Shawnee Indians attacked them just before dawn. Two members of the group died and Boone built a barricaded shelter on the spot to care for the remaining wounded member, who soon recovered enough to be moved to the intended settlement location on the Kentucky River.[14]

Colonel Henderson had not bothered to consult any government authorities before he undertook to make the treaty with the Cherokee. The treaty and his plans for relocating 500 settlers did not meet the approval of Virginia and North Carolina authorities, including Colonel George Washington.[15] Henderson was not about to be deterred and left Long Island on March 28, 1775, with a group of around thirty horsemen. He followed the newly blazed trail, arriving at Martin's Station two days later. By the time he left there, his group had increased to around forty to fifty.[16]

Henderson's party was near Cumberland Gap when he received the letter from Boone describing the Indian problems.[17] He continued on, even though they met many persons returning from Kentucky because of their fear of the Indians. On April 20, 1775, they arrived at Fort Boone. Henderson took command and began revising Boone's plans, but gave him some recognition by naming the new capital Boonesborough.[18] Then he asked to have the area, which he called Transylvania, admitted as the fourteenth colony. In 1776, Virginia and North Carolina persuaded the first Continental Congress to refuse and Henderson's dream died. Instead, Kentucky became the westernmost county of Virginia.[19]

Among the many who used the road cleared by Daniel Boone's party was Thomas Lincoln, Abraham's father.[20] The road remained the same until Isaac Shelby took office as governor of Kentucky, which became the fifteenth state of the union in 1792.[21] Shelby decided that the road needed to be improved.[22] With the limited funds that could be raised, Colonel John Logan and Colonel James Knox supervised crews in widening and shortening the road.[23]

Shelby's next step was to improve the mail service. The federal government had established the postal service in 1789, and Kentuckians demanded that it be extended to them, which was done in August 1792.[24] Attempts to establish a route either overland through Cumberland Gap or down the Ohio River both had unsatisfactory results. Finally, both routes were used, although the Ohio River was not navigable in the winter.[25]

By the end of his administration, Governor Shelby approved an act which called for major improvements. A good wagon road to Virginia was badly needed.[26] Daniel Boone, who was then sixty-two years old, poor and without land, wrote to the Governor to ask for the job.[27] Daniel had never been paid for the original job and hoped to earn the money for the rebuilding work. The governor, however, appointed Colonels James Knox and Joseph Crockett to make the improvements. The route cut by their surveyors seldom touched Boone's route, which was abandoned, and the new road became the Wilderness Road.[28]

To advertise the completion of the improved route, the following announcement was made in the *Kentucky Gazette* on October 15, 1796, and printers in other states were requested to publish the notice:

> THE WILDERNESS ROAD from Cumberland Gap to the settlements in Kentucky is now compleated. Waggons loaded with a ton weight, may pass with ease, with four good horses,—Travellers will find no difficulty in procuring such necessaries as they stand in need of on the road; and the abundant crop now growing in Kentucky, will afford the emigrants a certainty of being supplied with every necessary of life on the most convenient terms.
> JOSEPH CROCKETT
> JAMES KNOX
> Commissioners[29]

~

In the fall of 1801, the year that President Thomas Jefferson was inaugurated, Anthony$_2$ Gholson at age sixty-eight crossed the mountains from Virginia to Kentucky with his family and as many as eighteen slaves.[30] In all likelihood, they travelled along the new and improved Wilderness Road. There were more than a hundred thousand people in Kentucky, with more coming every day.[31] A man named Moses Austin had come across the road in December 1796 who, like the Gholsons, would also wind up in Texas where he would establish the Austin colony with his son Stephen.[32]

When Anthony$_2$ Gholson and his family arrived in Kentucky in the fall of 1801, Wayne County had just been created, the first meeting of the county court having been held in March of that year. A log building was constructed for a courthouse and fifteen-year-old Micah Taul was appointed clerk of both courts, the county court and the court of quarter sessions.[33] Much of the court business in the early years was concerned with building and maintaining roads, which were vital to reach the mills that were located on the rivers.[34] The judicial system in Kentucky was changed in 1804-1805, abolishing the District and Quarter Sessions Courts, and replacing them with Circuit Courts.[35]

A tract of public land had been set aside for the town site.[36] Four families lived in the town at the time, the families of William and Joseph

Beard, Roger Oatts, and Henry Garner. Joseph Beard was a merchant and his clerk was Ben Gholson, the young son of Anthony[2]. The first trustees of the town were Anthony[2] Gholson, George Singleton, Roger Oatts, John Hammond, and Isaac Crabtree. The first constable was Joseph Wheeler. When a jail was eventually needed, Roger Oatts, tavern keeper, was designated as the first jailer and he used a log house adjacent to his tavern for the jail.[37]

Augusta Phillips Johnson described the birth of the town in *A Century of Wayne County, Kentucky*:

> It is county court day: then as now, the good citizens have assembled—a clerk is to be elected—the town is to be named. Some are gathered at the town spring, others are drinking, fighting, and pillaging "for fun." A squad of militia, commanded by Lieutenant Bill Jones, is drifting near the spot where the old jail stood. We can see in the crowd, Joseph Chrisman, William Cullom, Anthony[2] Gholson, Isaac West, Bartholomew Hayden, John Buster, Louis Coffey, Squire Baker, Thomas Eades, Solomon Dunagan, Leonard Dodson. These first settlers came mainly from West Virginia, North Carolina, and Tennessee.[38]

Joseph Chrisman, his brother Isaac, Bartholomew Hayden, and Micah Taul each married daughters of Anthony[2] Gholson. Bartholomew's sister married Anthony[2]'s son Benjamin.[39]

When the town was named, there was some controversy over which name to choose. Micah Taul suggested calling the town Monticello, after Thomas Jefferson's home, but the Jones family, who lived in the area, wanted the town named after them. When Taul's suggestion was adopted by the court, the Jones family developed a grudge against him. Later Micah was elected to a post of military captain instead of William Jones, who had his eye on the position.[40] Jones became so enraged that he attempted to whip Micah, but as Micah described it, "His rage unmanned him and as luck would have it I whipped him, according to the fighting phrase of the day. After a hard fight, fist and skull, biting, gouging &c, I came off victorious."[41] It took years for Jones to get over the humiliation of being beaten by the much smaller Taul, but eventually, Jones and Micah became close friends.[42]

Anthony₂ Gholson built a large house for his family near Steubenville which was owned by the Bohon family for over one hundred years. The house, below and to the east of the Steubenville cemetery, was owned by the Al Landreth family from 1972 until 1977, when it was destroyed by fire. "A call was made to the Monticello Fire Department but due to the lack of a $100 guarantee as required, they failed to respond and the home was completely leveled."[43] The following description was written by Margaret Gray who was born in the house, a fourth generation descendant of the Bohon family, who would have had to have moved into the house in 1820, prior to the birth of John L. Bohon:

> It was a log house put together with mortar. It had six rooms and three porches. The road used to go in back of the house for quite awhile, then was closed off. There was a huge stone fireplace in the east end of the kitchen, which was closed up and the chimney torn down in the thirties. The rocks were used to make a fence at the old Correll front yard by the Stubenville [*sic*] cemetery. There was a huge room for a cellar under the house. You entered from a door in the floor of our dining room and went downstairs.[44]

During the Civil War Battle of Mill Springs, wounded soldiers were brought to the house, a part of which was used as a hospital.[45]

Fig. 5.3 - Photo of Anthony Gholson home near Steubenville, Kentucky. Courtesy of the Monticello *Outlook* and the Wayne County Historical Society.

There are many references to Anthony[2] Gholson in the Wayne County, Kentucky deed books from 1801 until his death and through the administration of his estate. In deeds of gift executed August 18, 1813, Anthony[2] gave away slaves and household furniture, which would seem to indicate that Elizabeth had died, although she was still alive in 1810.[46] In 1815, Anthony[2] donated land for a Baptist church and cemetery at Steubenville, about ten miles northeast of Monticello.[47] The log church was built with wooden pegs and "was razed in the eighties [1880s] and a frame house built."[48] The wooden pegs were actually superior to metal nails, because while nails can rust away or split the wood, the wooden pegs breathed with weather changes and eventually welded into the wood.[49] Anthony[2] died intestate at some time between September 26, 1815, and March 1816, and documents in Wayne County, Kentucky deed books show the disposition of estate, including legally transferring the property to the church, as the deed had not been recorded during his lifetime.[50] He was also one of the organizers of the Big Sinking Baptist Church in January 1804.[51] A tribute to him was written in the Bible of one of his descendants, stating that he "was a Baptist, an ardent supporter of the faith, and gave the ground for both the church and the burying-plot (wherein he lies in an unmarked grave) at Steubenville, where he spent his latter years."[52]

The Boone and Gholson families, along with countless others, are examples of the backwoodsman's advance across America. Daniel Boone's son explored the Rocky Mountains and he and his party "are said to have been the first to camp on the present site of Denver. His grandson, Col. A. J. Boone, of Colorado, was a power among the Indians of the Rocky Mountains . . ."[53]

As Americans moved westward, the first group were the pioneers, who depended upon native crops and hunting to survive. When they felt the urge to move on, the next class of emigrants moved in to introduce a bit more civilization in the form of roads, bridges and additional cultivated fields. Following them were the "men of capital and enterprise"[54] who created substantial buildings and towns. There were a few in the first two classes who remained behind to advance in society, but there were far more who often sold out and moved, perhaps only a few hundred miles.[55] The Gholson family was a good example of the movers. Anthony[1] Gholson and his son William moved gradually across Virginia, then William's son Anthony[2] moved to Kentucky, and Anthony[2]'s son Samuel moved to Tennessee, Arkansas Territory and Texas.

Chapter 6: The Family of Anthony₂ Gholson of Virginia and Kentucky

CAPTAIN JOSEPH COLLINS & SUSANNAH LEWIS

Anthony$_2$ Gholson's mother was Susannah Collins, daughter of Captain Joseph Collins, who fought in the French and Indian War (also known as the Seven Years' War), and Susannah Lewis, probably the daughter of Zachary Lewis. On November 6, 1750, Joseph Collins took the oath as Captain of a Troop of Horse. The troop was to join the Culpeper County Militia to fight the Indians above Winchester in 1756. He is also listed as a Captain of Company of Foot.[1] The French and Indian War (1754-1763) marked the turning point where Americans began to feel less dependent on the British and began to think of themselves as Americans and not British.[2]

Joseph Collins died in 1757, a reasonably wealthy man, and an inventory of his estate gives some insight as to how few possessions were owned, even by the wealthy, at that time. The list of items is also informative as to the way of life. His property, excluding land, was worth about £470, and £300 of the total was represented by the value of eight slaves:

> 1 negroe man Named Osea
> 1 negroe Woman Named Sooe
> 1 negroe Girl Named Indey
> 1 D° Named Phillis
> 1 D° Named Hannah
> 1 D° Named Winney
> 1 negro Boy Named Peter
> 1 D° Named Munk[3]

The following items comprise the remainder of the estate (value of individual items omitted):

> 5 Head of horses
> 1 Cart & wheels

5 Feather Bedds & Furniture
1 Desk
2 Black Walnut Tables
1 Black Walnut Coubbard
1 large looking glass
1 Gunn
1 Hone 3/6 one Razor 1/3 one Strop 1/3
1 Mans Saddle
1 P^r of Pistols & holsters
1 Large brass kettle
4 Iron Pots & three P^r pothooks
2 Iron Pot Racks
16 head of Sheep
3 Wooling Wheels & one flax D^o
1 Large Pine Table & one Small D^o & one p^r of
money scales
20 Head of Cattle
3 Chests
A parcel of Old Pewter with some Lumber
1 Silver hilted Sword
1 Old frying pan 1/3 one small Trunk 2/16
3 Iron wedges & old lumber Iron with it
1 Cross Cut Saw & old Jointer
1 P^r of Hillards
1 Brass warming pan
a parcel of Chairs
a parcel of Corn about fifty Barrells
a Parcel of fine earthen ware
a Parcell of Coarse Ditto
1 Case of Bottles
1 Candle Stick & one nut meg greatter
a Parcel of old Books & 1 Brush
a Parcel of Butter pots and Bottles
3 Bells & one Curry Comb
2 Small Casks
1 Washing Tub & two pails
1 Pocket Ivory Case & some brass forks
1 Loom & Gears
To Some spun wool & Cotton

2 Slain Cowhides
1 Womans Saddle & Bridle
A Parcel of Tan[d] Leather
A Parcel of Reap Hooks & one Smoothing Iron
40 head of Hoggs
One Hundred Gallon Cask & one Rundlett
1 Cask & Laundering Tub & one Chest[4]

~

MICAH TAUL

Fig. 6.1 - Portrait of Micah Taul. Courtesy of the Wayne County Historical Society.

Micah Taul was one of the most fascinating characters associated with the family of Anthony$_2$ Gholson in Wayne County, Kentucky. Micah became the County Clerk of Wayne County just before he turned sixteen and married Dorothy Gholson, Anthony$_2$'s youngest daughter, when he was seventeen. At twenty-eight he was the youngest commissioned colonel in the State of Kentucky, commanding the 7th Regiment,[5] which included Dorothy's brother Samuel Gholson.[6]

Micah wrote his memoirs in 1848-1850, the last two years of his life, leaving an excellent record of his experiences in the early colonization of Kentucky, some of the major battles in the War of 1812, and an eyewitness account of the governing of America in the nation's formative years. In addition, his memoirs contain much information about the family of Anthony$_2$ Gholson, his father-in-law, whose life was undoubtedly as interesting as Micah's, if he had only written it down. A fairly accurate birthdate for Anthony$_2$ can be assumed as 1733 because of Micah's description of Anthony$_2$ as around eighty in 1813 when he rode ten or twelve miles from his home to meet and welcome Micah home from the war of 1812.[7]

Micah was born in Maryland, just north of the city of Washington, on May 14, 1785, the youngest of six sons. His parents moved to Fayette County, Kentucky when Micah was two years old and Kentucky was a wilderness. Most of the education Micah received was from his brother Benjamin who was a school teacher.[8] He described Benjamin as "the very best man I ever knew"[9] and it was through Benjamin that he was given a job in a clerk's office at the age of thirteen.[10]

When Micah was about seven years old, he had his first experience with death when his brother Pentecost drowned in the Kentucky River.[11] His brother Jonathan was a farmer who died "by falling from a tree on the end of an axe handle."[12] Micah's brother Levi married Nancy Copher, whose mother was the daughter of George Boone, brother of Daniel Boone. Levi suffered for many years from what is described as a "hemorage of the lungs."[13] Micah's brother Samuel also had poor health, but was a good farmer and raised a large family with his wife, Polly. Micah described his brothers as being "remarkable for their morality and steady habits."[14] He wrote in his memoirs that "neither of them was ever intoxicated with spiritous liquor,"[15] which was quite unusual for that time and place with its population of "plain, honest, rough"[16] backwoodsmen.

Micah loved school and realized at an early age that he did not want to be a farmer. His handwriting was so good that at the age of thirteen, upon his brother Benjamin's recommendation, he went to work in the office of a Revolutionary War captain named David Bullock who was Clerk of the County Court of Clark County.[17] While working for Bullock, Micah was very impressed with the court speeches of a young lawyer named Henry Clay, so impressed that he decided to pursue a career as a lawyer.[18] The young Micah worked diligently and advanced quickly in the office of Captain Bullock.[19]

Wayne County was established in the 1800-1801 legislative session from portions of the counties of Cumberland and Pulaski. Micah was the candidate for clerk of both the Quarter Session and County Court. He had the recommendations of Captain Bullock, the Quarter Session judges and many other prominent citizens.[20] There were many qualified candidates for the position, including the county surveyors for Pulaski and Cumberland counties. The first court day was March 16, 1801, drawing many residents of the new county to watch the proceedings. Six judges undertook the job of electing a clerk. Micah, having started with one vote in the voting process, eventually won five votes out of six. He was elected clerk of both courts two months before his sixteenth birthday.[21] He had passed an examination the previous October which established his qualification for the job, having answered every question correctly.[22] One of the Quarter Session Judges was Colonel Isaac Chrisman, whose wife Sarah was a daughter of Anthony[2] Gholson and the sister of Micah's future wife, Dorothy.[23]

The description of Micah's first encounter with Dorothy is taken directly from his memoirs, as follows:

> In the fall of the year [1801], Anthony[2] Gholson removed from Botetourt County, Virginia to Wayne County, Kentucky. He had previously purchased a valuable tract of land and plantation five miles N.E. of Monticello on the road to Pulaski. His son John and his youngest daughter, Dorothy, were one day ahead of the family, when they passed Isaac West's where I boarded. It was a cool, damp evening, the young lady was wrapped up in a large blue cloth cloak, her face veiled and an umbrella over her. I guessed that they were members of that family, and as they passed I remarked to my brother Jonathan, who was then with me, that "that young lady was to be my wife." I saw her a few weeks afterward at a wedding (Abel Shrewsberry to Miss Tabitha Van Hoagan) and soon became enamoured of her. On the 20th of May six days afterward I was 17 years old, we married with the approbation of both of our families.[24]

Micah acknowledged that at seventeen he was very young, and his wife was even younger, but he was doing a man's job. He began to study law, buy property, and build cabins. His father gave him a young male slave named Frank who remained with the family until he died in Alabama, and Dorothy's father Anthony$_2$ gave her a young female slave named Agnes who was still with the family at the time the memoirs were written.[25] Micah and Dorothy's first son, Thomas Paine Taul, was born two months before Micah's eighteenth birthday.[26]

Thomas Jefferson's Louisiana Purchase was ratified in 1803 and Kentucky was called upon to furnish 5000 troops to take possession of the land if it was not surrendered. Micah raised a company in Wayne County with no difficulty, but the need to fight did not arise at that time.[27]

Micah and Dorothy's second son was born in October 1804 and they named him Algernon Sidney. A third son died a few days after he was born.[28] A daughter named Louisiana was born in March 1808.[29]

By that time, Micah was a lawyer. Between his farm, his clerk positions and his law practice, he had a good income. He said in his memoirs, "It was then fashionable among the profession to play cards, for money. . . . I seldom sat down to a card table without losing a great deal."[30] Later, gambling on cards became unfashionable and he quit.[31]

Micah's role in the War of 1812 led to his election to Congress in 1814, with the enthusiastic support of the men who had been in his regiment in the war. He was Clerk of the Circuit Court of Wayne County at the time and resigned the position, to which his nephew John Chrisman, who had been working in his office, was elected. In November 1815, Micah left Monticello for Washington on horseback, which was still the chief mode of travel at the time.[32] "The Capitol was at that time in ruins, and Congress sat in a house prepared for the purpose about 150 or 200 yards east of the Capitol."[33] Fellow Kentuckian Henry Clay was elected Speaker of the House and Micah was appointed to the Committee of Enrolled Bills. Micah described himself as a silent member but one who actively participated. The popularity of Micah and most of the rest of the Kentucky delegation sagged when they voted for an unpopular bill,[34] and he chose not to run again. He redeemed himself during the next session, however, by making a speech in favor of the repeal of the bill, even though he was no longer a member of congress.[35]

Fig. 6.2 - Portrait of Henry Clay, statesman, 1777-1852. Lithograph by Charles Fenderich, 1805-1887. Library of Congress No. LC-USZ62-1095.

In 1817, Micah was in the audience on the day James Monroe was sworn in as president "on a temporary platform erected in front of the house in which Congress had held its sessions."[36] He rode home the next day in the company of the senator from Tennessee, Colonel John Williams, and a representative from that state named Bennett Henderson who became the minister to Guatemala under John Adams. Micah returned home to practice law and placed his sons under the tutelage of Samuel Wilson, leaving one child at home, daughter Louisiana who later married General Bradford.[37]

During the summer Micah became dissatisfied with Wayne County and decided to move. After visiting several places in Alabama and Tennessee, he decided to move to Winchester in Clark County, Kentucky, which turned out to be the second greatest mistake he ever made, by his own description, the worst being voting for the unpopular bill in congress. He chose the Winchester area because he was partly raised there and he was able to be near his brothers again. He quickly built up his law practice.[38] For several years he was "the most popular lawyer at the bar of Paris in Bourbon County, one of the most populous and wealthy counties in the state."[39] However, he made the mistake of becoming associated with a noted criminal attorney, whom he described as "a man of decided talent and commanding eloquence, but I always thought he had as much character as he deserved."[40] Together they won the acquittal of a defendant in a murder trial and a few years later they won acquittals in a trial of two men accused of beating an old man to death. The men were acquitted due to contradictions in the dying man's declaration, but the people were not pleased with the verdict and they hanged the judge, jurors and lawyers in effigy on the town square. When an influential resident of the county attempted to cut them down, he had to leave town to keep from being mobbed. One of the defendants left the state and the other was shot and killed a few weeks later.[41] No attempt was made to find and prosecute the killer.[42]

Micah won another controversial criminal case in the spring of 1819 or 1820 in which he said, "three men were charged with having committed an outrage on the person of a female in Wayne County, where I still continued to practice."[43] This was another case in which public sentiment ran high against the defendants. Several prominent citizens asked Micah not to defend them and told him that the three men were guilty without any doubt. "Two of the men were married men of respectable families and were on bail; the third was a widower of not more than ordinary standing in society, and had been committed to jail for want of bail."[44] In talking with the defendants, Micah became convinced that they were only guilty of poor judgment, and not the offense as charged, and he decided to defend them.[45]

The man in jail was the first to be tried. The judge made a great show of protecting the woman with armed guards as she went from the house where she was staying to the courthouse and back, where the judge and attorney general were also staying with the excuse of guarding her, but in reality were attempting to manipulate the public sentiment against the defendants.[46] Micah decided to do a little manipulating of his own. The judge was already disliked, and it was easy to create antagonism toward him as Micah mingled with the crowd. Through Micah's subtle efforts the people began to change their attitude toward the defendants. When the trial of the man in jail began and the woman was brought to the courthouse under guard, Micah "took the liberty of 'looking daggers' at the Judge and interchangeing indignant glances with others."[47] The woman was a believeable witness and Micah was beginning to have doubts as to whether he would be able to disprove her testimony. After the testimony was finished, a respectable man came to Micah and told him something that contradicted the witness on a material point. Until that moment the man had given the information to no one, because the public was so inflamed against the defendants that he feared for his safety.[48] One can only imagine what his information may have been, as Micah did not reveal the nature of it. After the new evidence was heard, the jury returned a verdict of "not guilty" and the local citizens realized that they had made a mistake in condemning the men. Micah's argument took two hours, during which the judge left the courtroom. The judge had become an enemy for life when Micah had beaten him in the congressional election in 1814.[49] In fact, the judge did not like anyone in Wayne County because when he ran for congress in 1812 and 1814 he had received only eighteen votes there.[50]

The other two defendants were tried and easily acquitted. Micah purposely avoids mentioning their names, but he said "One of them is a respectable man with a large family, residing at present in Texas—one was hung a few years ago, in Arkansas, for murder."[51] That defendant was Charles Cox, also known as Cocke.[52] There is little doubt that the one who moved to Texas was Micah's wife's brother Samuel, which would explain why Micah was willing to take the case in the first place and his reluctance to give the names of the defendants. According to Micah's memoirs,

> They got themselves involved in this great difficulty by dissapation; they had been the preceding day at a deer hunt, fish fry, etc., where they had indulged freely in drinking, as well as eating, they were 15 or 20 miles from home and started to go home after night but stopped at a "doggery" [a low class drinking establishment] by the way side where they became involved as above.[53]

The possibility of Samuel being one of the defendants would also explain an excerpt from an 1898 letter published in *A Century of Wayne County, Kentucky*, which states, "Sam Gholson was very wild and did a great many naughty things and Ma says every time she asks the early settlers here about them, they tell her about Sam. They seem to remember him better than the rest."[54]

Not long after the case was finished, Micah made a trip to Missouri with the idea of possibly moving there. Some of his old friends were members of the legislature, including Bennett Clark, brother of George Clark of Kentucky, and Colonel Jesse Boone, the son of Colonel Daniel Boone. Daniel died that winter and the legislature adjourned to honor his memory.[55]

Micah decided not to move to Missouri, although he felt that he would have done well there. He visited Tuscaloosa, Alabama in 1821 but was not impressed.[56] He lost money on his land holdings but was able to get his sons into college. Thomas graduated in 1821 and Algernon in 1822, both from Transylvania University in Lexington.[57] Thomas became a popular lawyer in Nicholas County and the head of the bar.[58]

The health of both of Micah's sons began to decline, and in 1825 he decided to move his family to Huntsville, Alabama. "Thomas was sent with the blacks to Huntsville where he hired them out,"[59] followed by Micah, Dorothy and their daughter Louisiana in February 1826. Algernon was so ill that he could not travel and was left to board with a man named Hay Taliaferro in Winchester, Kentucky. By the end of the journey, Dorothy was ill and depressed. The weather had been so wet that by the time they reached Huntsville, "the town and country was almost covered with water."[60] They finally headed back north and settled in Winchester, Tennessee, "handsomely situated on the west side of the boiling fork of Elk river a few miles from the western base of the Cumberland mountains, in the County of Franklin."[61]

The day after they arrived in Winchester, Thomas returned to Kentucky to check on Algernon, who was so ill that Thomas could hardly move him to his Uncle Benjamin's house, ten miles away. Thomas wrote to his family to tell them of Algernon's condition and Dorothy and Louisiana left for Kentucky as soon as they received the letter. Algernon died not long afterward, before his father could see him again. He had just obtained a law license but had not yet begun to practice. Micah and his wife were devastated and Dorothy's health was so affected by the trip that she never recovered.[62]

Micah began to practice law in Winchester, as did his son. Thomas met his future wife, Caroline, who was the daughter of Colonel William P. Anderson of Franklin County. They were married on Thomas' birthday, March 7, 1827, when he was twenty-four years of age. Dorothy's health continued to decline and she died in December 1827 after months of terrible pain.[63] Micah wrote the following tribute to his wife in his memoirs:

> I feel myself wholly incapable of doing justice to the
> memory of this admirable woman, the wife of my youth—
> in person she was small and very delicate—her weight at
> no time of her life exceeded 100 pounds, generally she

weighed about 95; she was, however, generally very healthy—in mind she was a giantess. Her early education like my own, was limited, but she was fond of reading, and I made it a rule when at home, to read everything I did read in her hearing. As a daughter, wife, mother, mistress, friend, sister, neighbor, she was blameless. As a housekeeper she had no equal. Order and neatness everywhere prevailed. To cap the climax of her character she was a devout Christian—a member of the Baptist church. She was baptised in Cumberland river by the Rev. Thos. Chilton about the year 1810 or 1811—Her sister, Nancy Gholson attended her for several months in her last illness . . ."[64]

Thomas was a candidate for attorney general in the fall but lost by one vote.[65] His health was growing worse and he and his wife spent the winter in New Orleans, returning to Winchester in 1828, his health not improved. In 1827 the editor of the *Huntsville Democrat* newspaper had been killed by a prominent local attorney.[66] None of the local attorneys wanted to prosecute the case, so they approached Thomas, offering him a large fee for the job of prosecution.[67] The trial was held and the man was acquitted. The effort was too much for Thomas' health. He moved to Huntsville, where he soon ran into the man whom he had prosecuted. Only the intervention of mutual friends prevented a fight between the two. Thomas was never paid the large fee that had been promised to him.[68] Later in the year 1828, Thomas' wife Caroline gave birth to a stillborn daughter and she also died shortly after the birth.[69]

Before Caroline died, she had made arrangements for Thomas to spend the winter in Cuba for his health. He was preparing to go when he was involved in a fight in Winchester with a "furious drunken old Irishman . . . which resulted in Thomas shooting him with a pistol, somewhere near the hip, which fortunately did not prove mortal."[70] Thomas at the time weighed less than 100 pounds and did not have the strength to fight the man who was threatening him, so he shot him in self defense. Micah was near enough to hear the shot and when he found out that his son had shot the Irishman, he gave Thomas a good horse and sent him away. "Several very sprightly young gentlemen began to fly about and curse and swear and call for horses, and very soon were rushing in every direction but the right one in pursuit of him."[71] Martial law was imposed upon Winchester and Micah was closely watched, but in spite of that he was able to send Thomas off to Cuba in a few days, opposing Thomas' desire to stay and stand trial.[72]

Thomas spent the winter in Cuba and his father and sister met him in Tallahassee when he returned in May of 1829. He had gained weight, his health had greatly improved, and he was determined to return to stand trial.[73] Before a trial could take place, however, Thomas was murdered on the town square in Winchester in August of 1829 by his deceased wife's brother Rufus Anderson, who did not even know Thomas well enough to recognize him.[74] Micah's wife Dorothy had been buried in the Anderson family cemetery, but her body was disinterred and buried alongside Thomas in Winchester's public cemetery. Also buried in that cemetery were the bodies of two infant children by his second wife.[75] Micah believed that his son's murderer was acquitted by a jury of men who went into the trial with no intention of finding him guilty, mainly due to the political influence of the defendant's father.[76] A few years later the acquitted murderer was killed in a fight with the attorney general who had prosecuted him,[77] but Micah's obsession with the injustice of the trial apparently never left him until his own death on May 27, 1850, in Mardisville, Talladega County, Alabama, about two months after he finished his memoirs.[78]

~

JOSEPH AND ISAAC CHRISMAN

Anthony$_2$ Gholson's daughter Mary "Molly" was married to Joseph Chrisman who "served with George Rogers Clark in his Northwest Campaign and was with him at the capture of Vincennes."[79] George Rogers Clark was the brother of William Clark, of the Lewis and Clark expedition.

Anthony$_2$ Gholson's daughter Sarah "Sally" was married to Joseph Chrisman's brother, Lieutenant Colonel Isaac Chrisman.[80] Isaac Chrisman was one of the Quarter Session Judges when Micah Taul passed the examination which qualified him to become County Clerk of Wayne County, Kentucky, at age fifteen.[81]

~

BARTHOLOMEW HADEN

Anthony$_2$ Gholson's daughter Catherine "Kitty" was married to Bartholomew Haden, who "served as a Second Lieutenant under his brother-in-law, Micah Taul, during the War of 1812."[82]

Chapter 7: Kentuckians in the War of 1812

Samuel Gholson, Son of Anthony[2]
Micah Taul, Son-in-Law of Anthony[2]

About thirty years after the end of the Revolutionary War, America again went to war against Britain. The reasons for the War of 1812 were obscure, and the war did not have the patriotic fervor behind it that the Revolutionary War had inspired. Maritime issues were a primary cause, but there was also the issue of the conquest of Canada. The idea appealed to many Americans, if for no other reason than to put a stop to the British influence over the Indians in the area.[1] Two-thirds of the occupants of the lower part of Canada were French, and the inhabitants of upper Canada were about a third American, leaving very few loyal British to carry on a war in Canada. Thomas Jefferson and other Republicans believed that Canada could be easily taken and Kentucky statesman Henry Clay bragged that the Kentucky militia alone would be able to conquer Montreal and Upper Canada.[2] Clay, who was a personal friend of Micah Taul[3], was young, articulate, and was elected Speaker of the House on his first day in Congress. "Staunchly nationalist and rabidly anti-British, the young Republicans regarded the Napoleonic Wars in Europe as an unparalleled opportunity to defend national honor, assert American interests, and conquer Canada and Spanish territory in Florida and the Southwest."[4] Under Clay's leadership, the War Hawks controlled the Twelfth Congress.[5] A series of events led to a war bill which was narrowly passed by Congress and signed into law by President Madison on June 18, 1812. None of the Federalists supported the bill.[6]

Two months later, Kentucky was asked to furnish volunteers. Lieutenant Colonel Isaac Chrisman, who was married to Anthony[2] Gholson's daughter Sarah,[7] was in charge of the regiment from Wayne County and Micah Taul was a major. Micah had volunteered as a private, but the men elected him to command them, and he reluctantly agreed.[8] In August of 1812, the Kentucky volunteers reported for duty, with Micah's company being attached to the regiment of Colonel Barbie, at whose residence the regiment gathered. The regiment had been ordered to go to Indiana but the orders were "changed for the northwest, in consequence of the surrender of Detroit, and the army at that place under Gen. Hull."[9] General Hull had been appointed to lead the western campaign, being the only candidate who was remotely qualified at the time. He had served with distinction in the Revolutionary War, but at age fifty-nine his body had been weakened by a stroke and his spirit by personal tragedies.[10] British General Brock managed to trick Hull into believing that all of the soldiers and civilian inhabitants of Fort Detroit would be massacred by a large group of Indians. Hull became so fearful and despondent that he surrendered the fort on August 16, 1812, without consulting any of his officers, to the disgust of everyone inside, "even the women."[11]

Micah Taul wrote in his Memoirs,

> The sensation in the country everywhere, at the news of "Hull's surrender" was great. I was in Lexington and saw Mr. Clay, at his house, while there he received a letter from Gen. Meigs of Ohio, containing certain intelligence of facts Allen's and Lewis's Regiment had been ordered out sometime before to re-enforce Gen. Hull, but they had not reached his headquarters before he surrendered. They were somewhere in the State of Ohio ... We were encamped near New-port, opposite Cincinnati, a few days—our encampment was on the ground, where the town of Covington now stands, it was then a farm owned and occupied by a man of the name of Kennedy. From this place we marched to Piqua on the Miami, where we remained a week or ten days, and then moved to St. Mary's 30 miles, where we were stationed all winter.[12]

Unfortunately, the soldiers had not come prepared to stay all winter and had left home in "linen or cotton hunting shirts and pantaloons, and they were nearly worn out."[13] When winter came, the ground was covered with two feet of snow and the streams were frozen.[14]

After Hull's surrender, the popular and respected William Henry Harrison was made a major general in the militia by Kentucky leaders, even though he was not a citizen of Kentucky.[15] This obstacle, and the fact that only one major general was authorized and the position was already filled, were overcome by making him a brevet major general.[16] The Kentuckians and other westerners pressured the administration until General Harrison was given command of the army in the Northwest.[17]

General Harrison appealed to Governor Shelby of Kentucky for clothing for the freezing volunteers, and around Christmas, the soldiers received an abundant supply of clothes and blankets from wives, mothers, and sisters in Kentucky. They were later able to buy supplies from the local citizens, hunt game, and build log cabin barracks.[18]

General Harrison was on the post at St. Mary's when he received a warning that he was about to be attacked by an army of British and Indians near Fort Defiance.[19] The Kentucky troops, including Taul's regiment, marched twenty-six miles in the rain and mud to Fort Jennings on the Au Glaise the next day. The following day, General Harrison ordered Taul's regiment to return to St. Mary's, and the "forced march was the cause of much sickness and several deaths."[20]

The soldiers were able to return home after that expedition. Taul wrote,

> Our term of service, six months, expired, I think the first of March [1813] and we were marched to Cincinnati distant about 100 miles, paid off in part and discharged. Our friends in Wayne County met us at Cincinnati with horses. I arrived at home the third Sunday in March. The day was unusually fine for the season. We had stayed the night before at Somerset in Pulaski County from whence it was 9 miles to the Cumberland river, then the line between Wayne and Pulaski County. A large number of persons had collected on the Wayne side of the river to receive and welcome us home, and amongst them was my venerable father-in-law Anthony[2] Gholson, then near 80 years of age, who had rode from his residence that morning 10 or 12 miles to greet me on my return. The reception was a most cordial one. The people of the country generally were apprized of our being on the road home, and they had assembled in large numbers at the different homes on the road to see us.[21]

Micah remembered it as one of the happiest days of his life. He had returned to a healthy family and he had brought home all of the Wayne County men in his command in good health. The following day was court day and he was able to personally greet the families of the men under his command.[22]

Only two months later, in June 1813, General William Henry Harrison called for 5000 mounted volunteers which again brought the Kentuckians into action.[23] The United States forces were stronger in the campaign of 1813, having more experienced officers and troops available than in 1812. General Harrison had replaced General Hull in the Northwest and Andrew Jackson was coming forth as the leader in the Southwest. Troops were paid more and legislation had been passed to make the army operate more efficiently.[24] Micah Taul easily raised a company in Wayne County, which included Second Lieutenant Bartholomew Haden,[25] his brother-in-law,[26] and another brother-in-law, Samuel Gholson, who was a private.[27] Micah was very proud of his company, as reflected in his memoirs:

> Some time in August we were called upon to rendezvous at Cincinnati by the 30th of the month. I immediately issued an order for my company to assemble on the day appointed at Monticello, well-mounted and prepared in all respects to take up the line of march. Accordingly on the day every man attended, well clad, and as well as I can remember well-mounted. I don't think there was an indifferent horse in the company. I am very sure there was not an indifferent man. I well remember when we marched into the city of Lexington, several of my acquaintances said to me, "Yours is the best looking and the best mounted Company that ever marched into this place." They were in a truth a noble looking set of fellows—stout, able-bodied, well-dressed Mountaineers, in fine health.[28]

Upper Canada was again targeted by the American campaign of 1813. It was very important for the Americans to gain control of the Great Lakes, especially Erie and Ontario, because the lakes provided the best way to transport troops along the northern frontier. British control of the lakes had previously gone undisputed.[29] In September 1812, Captain Isaac Chauncey was placed in command of the American naval forces on Erie and Ontario and ordered to gain control of them.[30] By the end of 1812, Chauncey had decided to focus his attention on Lake Ontario and had turned Lake Erie over to the twenty-seven-year-old Commodore Oliver H. Perry.[31] The naval commanders were short of manpower and were forced to use soldiers, including one hundred Kentucky sharpshooters furnished

Donna Gholson Cook

by General Harrison. Perry and his fleet of nine vessels sailed for Put-in-Bay in the Bass Islands at the west end of Lake Erie.[32]

On September 10, 1813, Commodore Perry, with the wind at his back, sailed his ship, the *Lawrence*, into the middle of the British fleet. He had ordered the other ships to follow him, but Lieutenant Elliott held back the *Niagara*, leaving Perry to fight the British ships unassisted. At the end of a two-hour battle with two of the largest British ships, all three of the ships were damaged and eighty percent of Perry's sailors were injured. Refusing to surrender, Perry took a rowboat over to the *Niagara*, somehow escaping injury, and assumed command. He sailed back into the British fleet of six vessels and after three hours he had killed or wounded the first and second in command on all of them.[33] This battle was the most important one fought on the Great Lakes and it allowed the United States to regain the position that was lost in 1812.[34] "Perry's message to Harrison, 'We have met the enemy and they are ours,' signaled the end of the British threat to the old Northwest."[35]

Fig 7.1 - *Battle of Lake Erie, 1813*, U. S. Capitol painting by W. Powell, Theodor Horydczak, photographer, c.a. 1890-1971. Library of Congress No. LC-H814-T01-C01-504 DLC (b&w film dup. neg.)

Fig. 7.1 - Detail.

Taul's company, in which Samuel Gholson was a sergeant,[36] "arrived at Gen. Harrison headquarters, on the margin of Lake Erie, near the mouth of Portage River on the 11th or 12th of September just as they were landing the prisoners taken on board the British fleet on the 10th."[37] Taul described the prisoners as a "motley set of fellows, a large number of them were negroes, who had run away from their masters in the U.S."[38]

Micah said in his memoirs, "The army encamped here in a very unhealthy location several days, and I was unfortunately taken sick."[39] The science of medicine was in its very early stages, cleanliness was hard to enforce in the camps, and epidemics were common. He did not specify the nature of his illness, but diseases such as "dysentery, typhoid fever, pneumonia, malaria, measles, typhus, and even smallpox were common and often fatal."[40] Doctors "bled and blistered their patients and subjected them to assorted emetics, cathartics, and diuretics designed to purge the body of disease. . . most of the drugs were worthless or even poisonous."[41]

The detachments of soldiers were taken on small boats to Put-in-Bay, and from there to one of the smaller islands nearby. According to Micah, five thousand men were camped on a nine or ten acre island for two or three days, and in that length of time it became "the filthiest spot I ever saw."[42]

> When we landed on it, it was literally covered with snails.
> Here I became so much worse I could not be moved when
> the army was about to embark for the Canada shore, distant
> about nine or ten miles. I gage [gave] orders to have me put
> into a boat, but Gov. Shelby hearing of my situation, came
> to see me in company with Dr. Mitchell, his surgeon
> general, who gave it as his opinion, that if I was removed at
> that time, and put into one of the boats, that I would not

reach the Canada shore alive. The Gov. peremptorily forbade my being removed. A large number besides myself and friends, who were left with me, were also left on the filthy, desolate Island, mostly without provisions, among others was Major Robert P. Henry, son of Gen. C. Henry, who like myself was too sick to be removed. A few nights afterward at a late hour, an officer of the Navy, having the command of a small vessel, called for the purpose of taking us to Detroit. He came first to my Quarters, and superintended my removal to his vessel, and afterward sent for Major Henry, who had with him a few friends. I had with me some four or five. He immediately gave orders for the vessel to sail leaving at least 100 poor fellows on the island. Maj. Henry and myself remonstrated against his sailing without taking all on board, which he could have done in perfect safety. But he was about "half seas o'er," and was deaf to our entreaties. He landed us the next day at Detroit. The poor fellows left on the Island subsisted for two or three weeks on damaged meat that had been thrown from the vessels while lying at anchor of the islands. Finding starvation staring them in the face, they ultimately got off by patching up an old boat that had been left or had drifted up on the island.[43]

By late September of 1813, General Harrison had about 5500 men, including 3000 Kentuckians with their horses, ready for battle at the western end of Lake Erie. By the time they arrived at Detroit and Malden, the British had fled. British General Henry Procter decided to take a stand at Moraviantown, fifty miles east of Detroit, with 800 regulars and 500 Indians.[44] Procter needed to placate Tecumseh to keep him from deserting, so he promised the Indians that the army would make a stand at the fork of the Thames River. After learning that the site would not be a good location to mount a defense, Procter broke his promise and continued his eastward retreat. An angry Tecumseh, with the help of a few of his followers and a few British soldiers, attempted to ambush the Americans at the forks. Harrison had been warned of the attack and dispersed the enemy before they could resist, and Tecumseh also retreated.[45]

Colonel Richard M. Johnson was in command of about 950 Kentucky mounted volunteers, divided into two battalions. He placed one of the battalions under his elder brother, Lieutenant Colonel James Johnson, to go against the British regulars. "Having no family, unlike his brother James, Richard Johnson reserved the more hazardous task for himself: assaulting the unpredictably dangerous Indians."[46]

> Finding the British lines thin, [Richard] Johnson asked for permission to make a frontal assault with his mounted troops. Although a cavalry charge like this was extremely unorthodox, Harrison agreed to the plan. "The American backwoodsmen ride better in the woods than any other people," he said. "I was persuaded too that the enemy would be quite unprepared for the shock and that they could not resist it."
>
> Shouting "Remember the Raisin!"—the rallying cry commemorating the massacre in January, 1813—Johnson's troops galloped toward the enemy. The right wing easily burst through the British line and then dismounted and caught the British in a crossfire, forcing them to surrender. "It is really a novel thing," said an American officer, "that raw militia stuck upon horses, with muskets in their hands instead of sabres, should be able to pierce British lines with such complete effect."[47]

Fig. 7.2 - *"Remember the River Raisin!" Moraviantown, Upper Canada, October 5, 1813.* Ken Riley; National Guard Heritage. Courtesy National Guard Bureau, Department of the Army.

The Indians were more capable of defending their position against the Kentuckians than were the British regulars, which was not a good omen for Richard Johnson's troops. Because of the swampy condition of the battleground, the Kentuckians' horses became more of a hindrance than a help and Colonel Johnson ordered them to dismount. A fresh regiment of Kentucky militia arrived to reinforce the tired troops, making it difficult for the Indians to sustain their offensive. Colonel Johnson, as well as his horse, had been badly wounded when he was suddenly confronted by a lone Indian. The Indian fired his musket, striking Johnson on the hand, then raised his tomahawk to kill Johnson, but Johnson managed to draw his pistol and shoot the Indian in the chest. Many of those who participated in the battle stated that the Indian was Tecumseh,[48] and while some honored him, "several jubilant Kentuckians cut long strips of skin from his thighs for souvenir razor strops."[49] It is not certain whether the Indian killed by Johnson was Tecumseh, but he was killed about that time and Colonel Johnson was given the credit for killing him, breaking the Indian confederacy and giving him the vice presidency in 1836.[50]

From Micah Taul's Memoirs,

> The battle of the Thames was fought on the 5th of October, 1813, and the army consisting almost exclusively of Kentucky volunteers under Harrison and Shelby, including Col. Johnson's Regiment of mounted men (the horses of the other Kentucky Volunteers had been left at Portage, returned to Sandwich in upper Canada, opposite Detroit, on the 10th of October). Many were sick and unable to march on foot and were transported across the lake in vessels furnished by Commodore Perry—But before a passage could be procured for me, the vessels were so much crowded, that I could not get in, and I had to recross the lake in an open boat—It was then freezing cold—The weather was stormy and lake very rough, making our passage not only laborious and disagreeable but absolutely dangerous—We had two boats and about 150 men with which we coasted the lake and arrived at Portage in 6 or 7 days. Here we found the most of our horses—but in bad condition. We left for home on the 20 or 21st of October. Our encampment was in a wet prairie, near the lake—when we left the ground was frozen hard enough to bear our

horses. I was something better than I had been—was able to ride a horse. The first morning after taking up the line of march for home, I was taken with the mumps, from which I did not recover until after I got home.[51]

The Battle of the Thames was an important victory for the Americans, undermining the British authority in the Northwest. Harrison and Perry had "turned the tide in the West and had secured the whole region to the United States."[52] Several tribes signed an armistice agreement with General Harrison on October 16.[53] Taul's soldiers were dismissed in Marysville and he went home to recover his health.[54]

After the defeat of Napoleon in the spring of 1814, Europe was at peace for the first time in over ten years, and Britain was able to focus its attention on punishing the Americans. The size and quality of the American army had greatly improved by the spring of 1814. Many soldiers were discharged in the winter of 1813-14, but an appealing bounty attracted many new soldiers and veterans. By early 1815, American soldiers numbered around 45,000. The Americans decided to take advantage of its control of the west and focus on Upper Canada again.[55]

A number of battles occurred during the spring of 1814 and the British were eventually able to maneuver into position to attack Washington. American officials had been slow in realizing the possibility of an attack on the nation's capital but on July 1st the president created a special military district around the area.[56] The defenders fled after they were unable to repel the attack of the British troops. Through the efforts of Dolley Madison, the cabinet records and some White House treasures were saved. On August 24, 1814, the British entered the White House, ate the dinner which had been prepared, drank the wine, collected some souvenirs and set fire to the building. They also burned the Capitol building.[57] On September 14, 1814, the British attacked Fort McHenry. Francis Scott Key had boarded a British ship to secure the release of a prisoner, and the British refused to allow him to leave until after the attack. As he paced the deck all night, watching the mortar shells exploding over the fort, he was inspired to write "The Star-Spangled Banner." The song became popular immediately, but it took more than one hundred years for Congress to make it the national anthem in 1931.[58]

The next British campaign was against the Gulf Coast. New Orleans was targeted with the intention of cutting off the back country of America from a seaport.[59] Andrew Jackson had assumed command of the Gulf

Coast region in May of 1814. In November, he attacked the Spanish-owned seaport of Pensacola with 4100 troops and destroyed the forts, then marched to Mobile, then to New Orleans, arriving there on December 1.[60]

New Orleans in 1814 was a small but growing French-Spanish town that had only come under American domination eleven years earlier, with French and Spanish being the primary languages spoken. Houses were built close together, with the larger ones being on raised foundations to permit air circulation and prevent the wood from decaying. The streets were muddy and uncobbled, with open gutters.[61] The three most impressive buildings were the St. Louis Cathedral, the Presbytere, and the Cabildo, the latter containing the Sala Capitular, a long narrow room in which the documents were signed on December 20, 1803, transferring the Louisiana Territory from France to the United States. The Cabildo now houses the Louisiana State Museum.[62] The largest and finest house in town was built by a man named Moore and later became the Orleans Hotel.[63]

When General Jackson arrived in New Orleans on December 1, 1814, the mood of the people "radiated disloyalty and defeatism"[64] but Jackson's energy and determination soon changed their attitudes and militia began to pour in. Jackson even accepted an offer of help from the Baratarian pirates in the area, and he got along so well with Jean Laffite that Jackson made the pirate his aide-de-camp. Not only did they boost the numbers of the Americans, but they proved themselves to be skilled in artillery and familiar with the local terrain. The pirates' aid was so valuable that President Madison pardoned them after the war.[65]

When Jackson heard of the approach of the British, he took some troops to meet them well outside New Orleans. The close fighting resulted in a number of wounds. Pakenham arrived the next day with more British troops but failed to take advantage of the fact that his army was much larger than Jackson's.[66]

> This enabled Jackson to pull back unmolested and establish a new line behind a canal about two miles from the British. In the days that followed, the Americans constructed earthworks along the edge of the canal between a cypress swamp on the east and the Mississippi River on the west.[67]

Fig. 7.3 - Replica cannons on the line of defense at Chalmette National Monument, site of the Battle of New Orleans. Photo by Donna Gholson Cook, February 2002.

Fig. 7.4 - Lewis Cook with replica of cannon used in the Battle of New Orleans. Photo by Donna Gholson Cook, February 2002.

Pakenham decided to continue to New Orleans, advancing toward the well-defended American line. The British placed batteries of guns behind casks of sugar, believing that they would offer as much protection as sand, but Jackson's cannon fire penetrated the casks and killed the gunners.[68]

The British attack was begun by Colonel Thornton's routing of 700 Louisiana and Kentucky militia, followed by the main British force advancing in the fog. The fog suddenly lifted, leaving the British troops exposed, in what was described by Sir Winston Churchill as "one of the most unintelligent manœuvres in the history of British warfare."[69]

> When the British got within 500 yards, the Americans began firing their cannons. When they were within 300 yards, American riflemen opened up; and when they got within 100 yards, those with muskets opened fire. "The atmosphere," said one American, "was filled with sheets of fire, and volumes of smoke." The effect of this fire—particularly the grape and canister from the American artillery—was utterly devastating. According to a British veteran of the Napoleonic Wars, it was "the most murderous [fire] I ever beheld before or since."
>
> All along the battle line the British were mowed down before they could get near the American earthworks. Only a small column advancing along the river got to the American line, but these troops suffered such a withering fire that they had to fall back. The fire was so intense that many hardened British veterans turned and fled. Others hit the ground and remained there until the battle was over. Pakenham did his best to rally his men, but as he rode across the battlefield he made a conspicuous target. One horse was shot out from under him, and shortly after commandeering another, he was "cut asunder by a cannon ball."
>
> General John Lambert, who took command after Pakenham fell, broke off the engagement. It had lasted only a half hour on the eastern side of the river, and yet the toll was terrific. One eyewitness said the field was a terrible sight to behold, "with dead and wounded laying in heaps"—all dressed in scarlet British uniforms. Those who had thrown themselves to the ground in the heat of battle got up when the fighting ended. A few fled but most surrendered. One officer who was far from American lines reportedly surrendered because *"these d—d Yankee riflemen can pick a squirrel's eye out as far as they can see it."*[70]

One of these riflemen was Samuel Gholson of Kentucky, who was serving a six-month enlistment that began November 10, 1814, in Captain Adam Vickery's Company of the Kentucky Detached Militia, commanded by Lieutenant Colonel Gabriel Slaughter.[71]

> Smith's *History of the Battle of New Orleans* says:
> "No troops engaged on the American side did more fatal execution upon the enemy's rank and file than did these Kentucky troops. Every man of the regiment was in rifle range and all did deadly work."[72]

Another source tells a different story about the value of the Kentucky militia to the battle. According to C. Edward Skeen, the Kentuckians showed up late, ill clothed and poorly armed. Jackson was reportedly furious with their lack of order and their insubordination, and their failure to defend the right flank near the woods.[73] However,

> A court of inquiry mostly exonerated the Kentucky militia on the right bank because of a lack of arms and poor troop placement. Gen. John Adair, who commanded the Kentuckians on the right bank, sought to get Jackson to withdraw his harsh judgment of the Kentuckians. Jackson, however, refused to concede Adair's point, and this triggered an angry response in the press in Kentucky that lasted many years and was dredged up again during Jackson's presidential campaigns in 1824, 1828, and 1832.[74]

Ironically, the Battle of New Orleans was fought on January 8, 1815, two weeks after the Treaty of Ghent had been signed on December 24, 1814,[75] to end the war. "The British lost over 2,000 men (including close to 500 captured). The United States, by contrast, lost only about 70 men, and only 13 on Jackson's side of the river."[76] The battle preserved America's claim to the Louisiana Purchase, but the war accomplished very little. It did, however, enhance the reputations of a number of participants, "helping catapult four men into the presidency—James Monroe, John Quincy Adams, Andrew Jackson, and William Henry Harrison—and three men into the vice-presidency—Daniel D. Tompkins, John C. Calhoun, and Richard M. Johnson."[77] It boosted the career of others including Henry

Clay, and it sent Micah Taul to Congress in 1814.[78] Despite few concrete achievements, the War of 1812 was significant because "it promoted national self-confidence and encouraged the heady expansionism that lay at the heart of American foreign policy for the rest of the century."[79]

Map 3
Kentucky Militia Involvement in the War of 1812.
The United States in 1810. Map drawn by D. Cook.
Copyright 2003.

Map 4
War of 1812, Northern Front activities involving
the militia of Wayne County, Kentucky.
Map drawn by D. Cook. Copyright 2003.

Chapter 8: Gone To Texas

Samuel Gholson & family in Western Kentucky,
Tennessee, & Arkansas Territory, 1820-1832

Sam Gholson was very wild and did a great many naughty
things and Ma says every time she asks the early settlers
here about them, they tell her about Sam. They seem to
remember him better than the rest. — *A Century of Wayne
County, Kentucky*[1]

Just about every big family has at least one troublemaker, and in the
family of Anthony[2] Gholson, Samuel was it. Samuel Gholson was born in
Botetourt County, Virginia in 1772[2] and was a child when his father
fought in the Revolutionary War.[3] He was one of the middle children of
the large family and was twenty-nine and unmarried when his father
moved the entire household, including numerous slaves, from Virginia to
Kentucky.[4]

On June 24, 1801, soon after arriving in Kentucky from Virginia,
Samuel married Mary Ann "Polly" Slaton.[5] It may have been an indication
of Samuel's rebellious nature that their five children were given names
which, for the first time in generations, were not traditional family names.
In 1820, Samuel and Mary Ann and all of their children, ranging in age
from two to fifteen, lived in Livingston County, Kentucky.[6] From there,
they moved to Arkansas, then Tennessee. It is uncertain how far Mary
Ann and the children moved with him, but they probably were together at
least as far as Arkansas, since the oldest daughter married a man in
Arkansas and stayed there.

- The first child was a girl named Angeline, who married Jenkin
Williams in Arkansas, and lived there until she died.[7]
- The oldest boy, Alvades (aka "Alvadus") died in his twenties in
February 1829 at Exelet, Illinois, when he was thrown from a horse
and killed.[8]
- According to the information told to Samuel's grandson, his son
Alhanon was robbed and killed in Santa Fe in the fall of 1827.[9]
However, Samuel may have attributed an early date of death to his son

to cover up the crimes committed in the last years of Alhanon's life. It is very likely that Alhanon was the young man known as "Alhanson" Gholson who was in trouble with the law in Arkansas in 1834. He was possibly also the Gholson who was killed in a duel in 1837 in Arkansas across the Mississippi River from Memphis, Tennessee. These events will be described in newspaper articles quoted later in this chapter.

- The fourth child was Alvira (aka Elvira), a daughter who died unmarried at seventeen years of age.[10]
- The fifth child, Albert, was born on May 25, 1818, Kentucky.[11] Samuel and Albert moved to Texas in 1832, but Mary Ann apparently did not accompany them, because in 1836, Samuel was described as having "no family except a grown son . . ."[12]

In 1834, after Samuel and Albert moved to Texas, Alhanon may have had the dubious distinction of being the first person convicted in Arkansas Territory for passing counterfeit money.[13] The following article appeared in the ARKANSAS GAZETTE on September 16, 1834:

> *A Counterfeiter detected.* —A few days since, a young man by the name of GHOLSON, was apprehended in this town, for passing a counterfeit $50 note, purporting to be on the *City Bank of New-Orleans*, on one of our merchants. He was immediately detected and apprehended, and twenty-five notes of that denomination, (making $1250), and on the same bank, found on him, and, in his saddle-bags, was found a sheet of paper containing numerous indubitable evidences of his expertness in counterfeiting not only the signatures of the President and Cashier of the above bank, but of the officers of the U. S. Bank and several of its branches. He underwent a thorough examination before Mr. Justice More, and was by him committed to Jail, to await his trial at the Circuit Court next month. The prisoner recently resided in the Western District, Tennessee, and his father, some 8 or 10 years ago, resided at Cadron in this Territory.[14]

The article went on to describe the appearance of the notes, to make it easy for the public to recognize similar counterfeit notes. Six weeks later, an article from the same newspaper dated October 28, 1834, tells of the trial of *Alhanson* Gholson, which "occupied two entire days"[15] and involved "a great number of witnesses,"[16] resulting in conviction and the sentence of twenty-five lashes and a fine of $100. The lashing was carried out, but as he had no money, with the exception of his counterfeit notes, he was released without paying the fine. The notes taken from the prisoner were cancelled by defacing them.[17] The article is followed by a postscript:

> Since the above was put in type, we understand Gholson has stolen a valuable race horse at the house of Mrs. Black, in the Big Prairie, belonging to Gen. Wm. Montgomery, and has made off with him.[18]

One would think that it would not take a very smart criminal to realize the folly of stealing a race horse from a general.

Now, back to the duel. Although only the surnames were given, it may have been Alhanon who was killed in the duel described in the following article from the ARKANSAS TIMES AND ADVOCATE on May 29, 1837:

FATAL DUEL

> Two gentlemen, by the names of Jackson and Gholson, crossed the river on yesterday morning to the Arkansas side, accompanied by their seconds and several of our citizens to settle, agreeably, to what is called the laws of honor, a difficulty which is said to have originated a few days since. The preliminaries having been setled [*sic*], at a distance of 30 feet, the word being given both pistols were discharged co-instantly. Mr. Gholson received the ball of his antagonist directly through the heart, and expired immediately without speaking; and Mr. Jackson was severely wounded, though, we understand, not dangerously, in the back. Comment from us is unnecessary. —*Memphis Gazette*[19]

Again showing amazing ineptitude, this Gholson managed to lose the duel even after shooting his opponent in the back. No later mention of Alhanon or Alhanson Gholson has been found.

~

Samuel's participation in the War of 1812 was described in a preceding chapter, as was the rape trial in which he was acquitted after being defended by his brother-in-law, Micah Taul. Samuel and his family left Wayne County, Kentucky shortly after the trial, possibly having worn out his welcome. He was on the delinquent tax list for 1820 with a notation "gone away."[20] Samuel was recorded in Wayne County, Kentucky in December 1819,[21] but in the 1820 census for Livingston County, Kentucky, Samuel and family were listed as residents of that county.[22] By December 1821 he was living in Arkansas Territory.[23] In 1824, Samuel was fifty-two and living at Cadron in Arkansas Territory.[24] Cadron was located near the Arkansas River "at a point slightly south of the mouth of Cadron Creek, west of modern Conway, in Faulkner County."[25] In Thomas Nuttall's journal of his travels through Arkansas Territory in 1819, he describes the tiny settlement of four or five families in a cove of rocks, which "affords a safe and convenient harbour, and a good landing for merchandize."[26] There had been efforts toward townlot speculation and a few years earlier there were forty or fifty families living there but most of them had moved on and Nuttall correctly doubted that a town would ever succeed on that location.

> Some high and rich body of alluvial lands would be better suited for the situation of an inland town, than the hills and the rocks of the Cadron. Modern cities rarely thrive in such romantic situations. There is scarcely a hundred yards together of level ground and the cove in which Mr. M'Ilmery lives is almost impenetrably surrounded by tiresome and lofty hills, broken into ravines, with small rills of water. It is true, that here may be obtained a solid foundation on which to build, without danger of dislocation by the perpetual changes and ravages of the river, but in an agricultural settlement something more is wanting than foundations for houses.[27]

Nuttall noted a need for a "house of public entertainment"—a tavern—and thought that the area did have promise as a resort, being on one of the main routes through the territory.[28] Local industry was clearly needed. Goods were expensive and difficult to obtain. If grain had been grown, there was no grist-mill to grind it. Flour sold for $12 per barrel, sugar twenty-five cents a pound, and coffee fifty cents a pound, although there were maple trees to tap for sugar and sassafras and spice bush to use for tea.[29] The hilly lands were good for grazing cattle and the sandy loam areas would support a good cotton crop.[30] Children had little opportunity for education because the population was so scattered.[31] There was some surveying being done in the area[32] which may have been the reason for Samuel to move there, since he was a surveyor in Texas.

When Nuttall returned to the area almost a year later, there were more travellers and some emigrants, and the place is beginning to sound more like the sort of place that would have attracted Samuel.

> The only tavern, very ill provided, was consequently crowded with all sorts of company. It contained only two tenantable rooms, built of logs, with hundreds of crevices still left open, notwithstanding the severity of the season.
>
> Every reasonable and rational amusement appeared here to be swallowed up in dram-drinking, jockeying, and gambling; even our landlord, in defiance of the law, was often the ring-leader of what it was his duty to suppress. Although I have been through life perfectly steeled against games of hazard, neither wishing to rob nor be robbed, I felt somewhat mortified to be thus left alone, because of my unconquerable aversion to enter this vortex of swindling and idleness.[33]

~

As is the case all too often with Samuel, it is difficult to prove or disprove his claim that he was one of the Santa Fe traders.[34] He did own an interest in the firm of Gholson and Bradberry, which may have been his link to the Santa Fe trade. According to the July 15, 1826, *Jackson Gazette,* Isaac West, Jr. purchased Samuel's interest in the firm in 1826 and stated that he would "continue to offer an assortment of goods for sale."[35]

~

> A century ago [1846] the expression "Gone to Texas" (or simply "G.T.T.") chalked on the doors of houses in the

Southern states gave information that the former occupants had departed for the frontier Republic, sometimes with a suddenness explainable only by a desire of the dweller to avoid an appearance as a principal in a court action. Many of the immigrants traveled to Texas by Gulf steamer and schooner. Some journeyed overland by wagon or horseback, possibly with a portion of their trip by stagecoach or river boat. A few simply walked.[36]

The preceding excerpt was somewhat mild as compared to the following from Dewees "Letters from Texas" in 1831:

"It would amuse you very much, could you hear the manner in which people of this new country address each other. It is nothing uncommon of us to inquire of a man why he ran away from the States! but few persons feel insulted by such a question. They generally answer for some crime or other which they have committed; if they deny having committed any crime, or say they did not run away, they are generally looked upon rather suspiciously."[37]

Samuel's friend and codefendant in the Kentucky rape trial, Charles Scott Cocke, also moved to Arkansas. In 1831 he was living with his family in Clark County where he murdered a man named Zebulon Edmiston. Cocke escaped and fled to Texas where he was apprehended in 1832, and he was extradicted to Arkansas Territory and executed by hanging on April 29, 1833. He had come to Arkansas about 1827 using the name Charles Scott and had reportedly fled from a murder charge in Alabama. He was said to have committed other murders in Tennessee. Edmiston's widow offered a reward for her husband's killer, providing the necessary incentive for his capture.[38] Is it more than a coincidence that Cocke was apprehended in Texas the same year that his old friend Samuel moved there? Is it possible that Samuel was still Cocke's partner in crime?

Samuel was, after all, sixty years old in 1832 when he moved to Robertson's Colony with his fourteen-year-old son Albert. According to his story, he and Albert had joined a train of covered wagons leaving Jackson, Tennessee on April 3, 1832, and landed at San Felipe, Texas, around July 29 of the same year.[39] The cost of moving to Texas was only about ten dollars a head in 1833. In a wagon train, some of the wagons would carry "women and children and others the furniture, spinning wheels, looms, and provisions; white and Negro men on horseback, herding horses, mules, oxen, cows, sheep, and hogs . . ."[40] Alternative transportation was also employed. Some made part of the trip by steamboat, as soon as they became available in the mid-1800's. Prospective settlers were advised to visit Texas and select a location before moving and to bring "furniture, cooking utensils, wagons, farming implements, and tools, as well as supplies of provisions and plain clothing, in order that they could begin life on the frontier without undue handicaps."[41]

San Felipe was having a growth spurt when Samuel and Albert reached it in 1832. The settlement was founded by Stephen F. Austin in 1824 on the west bank of the Brazos River. In 1828 there were about 200 residents, "three general stores, two taverns, a hotel, a blacksmith shop, and some forty or fifty log cabins. Ten of the inhabitants were Hispanic, and the rest were of American or European origin; males outnumbered females ten to one."[42] By 1835, San Felipe had boomed to 2000-3000 inhabitants and was the center of American activity in Texas,[43] at that time a province of Coahuila-y-Texas.[44] When Samuel Gholson arrived in San Felipe in 1832 in the midst of this boom, he had lost three of his five children to death and his wife was apparently no longer with him. He and only his youngest son came to Texas with a train of immigrants. Despite this misfortune, or perhaps because of it, he seemed to become a better citizen as he began a new life in the land which was to become Texas.

Fig. 8.1 - Covered wagon, one of the main forms of transportation of early settlers moving to Texas. Photo by Donna Gholson Cook at Fort Parker, April 2002.

PART TWO

TEXAS

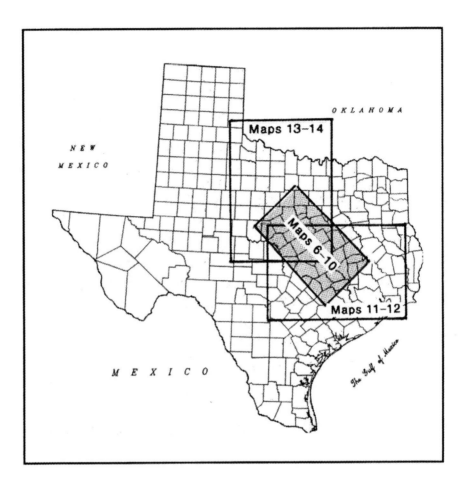

Map 5

Index map for Texas Maps 6-14.
Map courtesy of the Texas General Land Office.

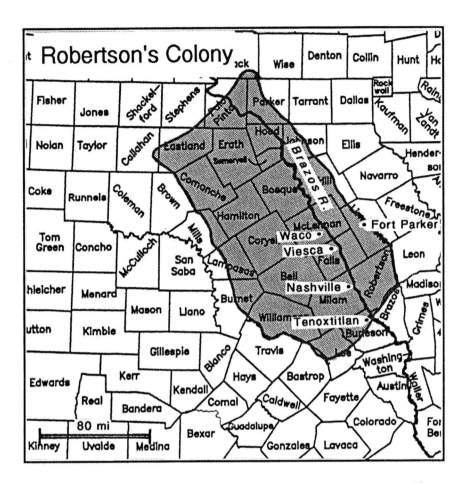

Map 6
Robertson's Colony 1834-1835 shown
with boundaries of current Texas counties.
Map drawn by D. Cook. Copyright 2003.

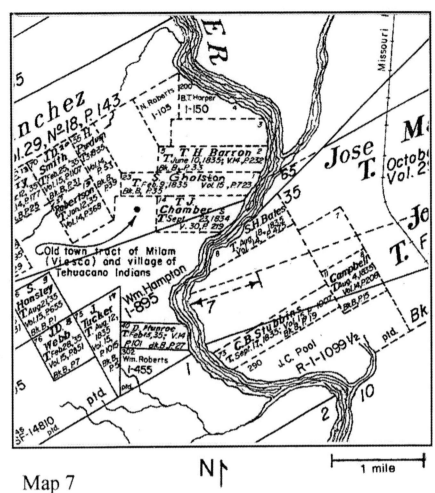

Map 7

Samuel Gholson's tract on the west bank of the
Brazos River, near the mouth of McCullough slough.
Dated Feb. 9, 1835, title to one labor of land (177.1 acres)
was obtained through Sterling C. Robertson's empresario
contract with the Mexican State of Coahuila and Texas.
Excerpt from the base map entitled: "Falls Co., General
Land Office of the State of Texas. Bob Armstrong,
Commissioner. February 6, 1976. Compiled by P. R.
Connally. Drawn by Joan Kilpatrick. Scale: 1 inch =
2000 varas."

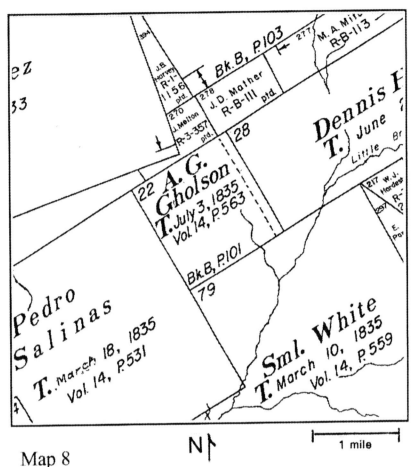

Map 8

Albert Gholson's tract on the west side of the Little
Brazos River, east of the Brazos River and Samuel's tract.
Dated July 3, 1835, title to a quarter-league of land
(1107.1 acres) was obtained through Sterling C. Robertson's
empresario contract with the Mexican State of Coahuila and
Texas. Excerpt from the base map entitled: "Falls Co.,
General Land Office of the State of Texas. Bob Armstrong,
Commissioner. February 6, 1976. Compiled by P. R.
Connally. Drawn by Joan Kilpatrick. Scale: 1 inch =
2000 varas."

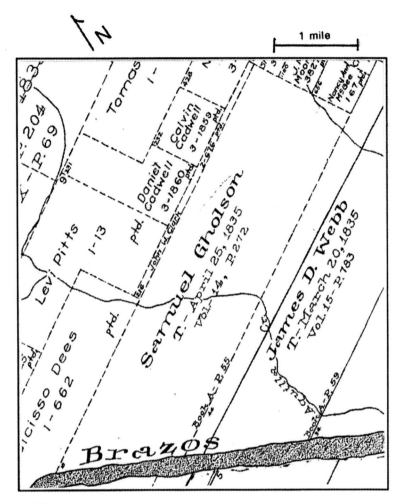

Map 9

Samuel Gholson's tract on the east bank of the Brazos River, near the mouth of Aquilla Creek, north of the town of Waco. Dated April 25, 1835, title to one league of land (4428.4 acres) was obtained through Sterling C. Robertson's empresario contract with the Mexican State of Coahuila and Texas. Excerpt from the base map entitled: "McLennan County, General Land Office, Austin, Texas. Bascom Giles, Commissioner. Sept. 30, 1946. Compiled by W. S. Brewington. Drawn by Tommye Buie. Scale: 1 inch = 2000 varas."

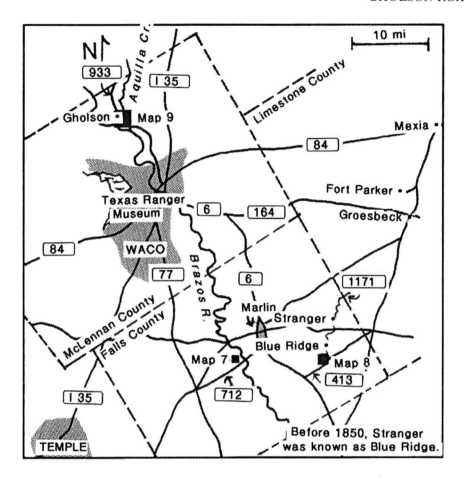

Map 10
Location map for 1835 land grants in Falls and McLennan
counties as shown on maps 7, 8, and 9. Map compiled
by author. Copyright 2003.

Chapter 9: Robertson's Colony

Samuel & Albert Gholson: 1832-1836

On March 2, 1822, a group of seventy men known as the Texas Association met in Nashville, Tennessee, to draft a memorial (petition) requesting permission from the Mexican government to settle in Texas. Robert Leftwich was designated to make the trip to Mexico City to deliver the document. Finally, on April 15, 1825, he obtained a colonization contract from the state government of Coahuila and Texas to bring in the first 800 families. In the course of several legal actions, the name evolved from the Texas Association (1822-1825), to Leftwich's Grant (1825-1827), the Nashville Colony (1827-1831), the Upper Colony (1831-1834), and Robertson's Colony (1834-1835). The boundaries were finally established to include all or part of thirty present-day Texas counties—Bastrop, Bell, Bosque, Brazos, Brown, Burleson, Burnet, Callahan, Comanche, Coryell, Eastland, Erath, Falls, Hamilton, Hill, Hood, Jack, Johnson, Lampasas, Lee, Limestone, McLennan, Milam, Mills, Palo Pinto, Parker, Robertson, Somervell, Stephens, and Williamson.[1]

Sterling Clack Robertson had been one of the original members of the Texas Association, and in 1830, he began to recruit families to come to Texas. After years of legal battles involving Robertson, Stephen F. Austin and others, a contract was awarded to Robertson as empresario on May 22, 1834. The area was approximately 100 miles wide and 200 miles long, beginning at the San Antonio-Nacogdoches Road, following the Brazos River to the northwest, and was centered around Waco.[2] In 1819, the *Texas Republican* described the Brassos [Brazos] River as 750 miles long and the "largest river in Texas—300 yards in width, and navigable for large keels. From the appearance on its banks, it must rise and fall 100 feet; its banks well timbered, and a rich prolific soil."[3]

While Samuel and Albert Gholson were in route from Tennessee to Texas between April 3 and July 29, 1832,[4] Robertson was serving a nine-month jail sentence in Tennessee on an 1829 manslaughter conviction,[5] and James Bowie's expedition was searching for hostile Indians in the areas of the headwaters of the Pedernales, Llano, San Saba, Colorado and Brazos rivers. They found no hostile Indians, but Bowie's report mentions minerals that he collected on the expedition and, according to a postscript in a letter from Nestor Clay to his father-in-law, they found an incredibly rich silver deposit:

> P. S. I had like to have forgot to tell you of the quantity of silver oar [ore] we found. I think from the experiment made & the silver smelted that we may calculate on a fortune some day from it.
>
> According to another version, Rezin P. Bowie, Jim's brother, had gone down into the Lost San Saba mine, hacked off some ore, "with his tomahawk," and had carried it to New Orleans and had it assayed. "It panned out rich."[6]

Whatever the source of his wealth, Bowie did seem to have plenty of money.[7]

Robertson was given until April 29, 1838, to bring the number of colonists up to the required 800 families. Families who farmed were to be given one labor of land (177.1 acres), and a league of pasture land for stock (4,428.4 acres). Single men would receive one-quarter league (1,107.1 acres).[8] Samuel Gholson received a Mexican title dated February 9, 1835, for one labor of land,[9] and another dated April 25, 1835, for one league of land.[10] Samuel's son Albert received a Mexican title for a quarter-league dated July 3, 1835.[11] He was seventeen at the time.

The boundaries of the land grants were determined by surveyors and distances were usually measured in varas (one vara is approximately 33-1/3 inches) but were sometimes given in more vague terms, such as a half-day walk.[12] J. G. W. Pierson was appointed principal surveyor.[13] Samuel and Albert Gholson were surveyors in Robertson's Colony, and Albert's compass and chain were still among his possessions when he died in 1860.[14] Some interesting actions were required to finalize a survey, as a way of marking a person's territory:

> Surveyors were required by Spanish and Mexican law to point out to grantees each and every corner of the grant and to tell him "in a loud voice" that he was invested with the property pointed out. The grantee indicated his acknowledgement of the grant by throwing rocks, shouting aloud, firing guns, and making other and sundry noises.[15]

Survey corners were established with bearing trees marked with the owner's initials or mounds of earth at least three feet high, and surveyors were required to make correct notes and plots. In return for their work, they were paid either in property or in cash.[16]

In addition to using Spanish surveying methods, Texas before the Revolution operated under Spanish law with a unitary judiciary, which suited the needs of the colonists better than the more complicated English system of two separate courts (law and equity). After the Texas Revolution, English law took the place of most Spanish law, with several major exceptions—trial procedures, land titles and water rights, and rules regarding family relationships.[17] For inheritance purposes, the designation of an independent executor streamlined the probate procedure. Also, a husband was allowed to protect his home by killing his wife's lover without punishment.[18] Until March 26, 1834, Texas settlers were required to subscribe to Catholicism,[19] although they did so with a general lack of enthusiasm. An ambiguous law passed in 1834 supposedly legalized Protestant preaching, but as one preacher observed, "the populace, with few exceptions, apparently were not very anxious for the establishment of 'the institutions of Christianity.'"[20]

The capital of Robertson's Colony was located near the Falls of the Brazos, long used as a fording point, not far from the present town of Marlin. It was named Sarahville de Viesca in honor of Robertson's mother, Sarah, and Agustín Viesca, the Mexican official who headed the legislature when the contract was awarded to Robertson. All land titles were issued in Viesca until the colonization process was interrupted by the Texas Revolution. Robertson was not able to fulfill the quota of 800 families, but was given credit for introducing 600 families by the Supreme Court of the State of Texas in December 1847.[21]

A description of Marlin in 1836 is found in Newton C. Duncan's recollections, published in the *Galveston News*, October 1, 1895:

> Marlin in '36 was nothing more than the family of John Marlin, who lived at the Marlin springs, on the edge of the Brazos bottom, about two miles from the site of the present town, with the families of Colonel Sam Golston [Gholson] and George Morgan, sr., for neighbors.
>
> John Marlin lived in a double log house made of hewn cedar logs. His family consisted of himself, wife and six

children, four sons and two daughters; his oldest son William P., his oldest daughter Louisa; next sons Rufus, Ashley and Oakley D., and his youngest daughter Emily, and staying with them was B. W. Holtzclaw, who had just returned from the San Gabriel, where he had been locating lands. He had been attacked by the Indians, and having his negro servant killed by them, he was forced to return.

Colonel Sam Golston's [Gholson's] family consisted of himself and son, A. G. Golston. Albert G. Golston was killed on Owl Creek, in Bell county. Colonel [Sam] Golston died in east Texas. Albert Golston left two sons by his first marriage, Sam and Frank.[22]

Samuel Gholson was one of the settlers living "at or near Viesca in 1834-6"[23] and indeed a plat map of Viesca shows a lot owned by S. Gholson in Viesca on the Brazos River bank across from the mouth of Gleason's Creek.[24] A document signed by Samuel Gholson on December 10, 1834, in the absence of the alcalde "is the earliest document we have found mentioning the Jurisdiction of Viesca, the Alcalde, and the First Regidor, indicating that a municipal government had been formally organized according to Mexican law."[25]

Samuel lived with only his son Albert, who was eighteen in 1836, but he was generous in opening his home to other settlers in need of a temporary place to stay. Newton C. Duncan wrote a biographical sketch of Levi (aka Levy or John) Taylor, stating that the Taylor family of five had lived with Sam Gholson and that Duncan himself had also stayed in the Gholson home. Not long after that, the Indians began their attacks. The first major Indian raid was the attack upon Fort Parker in May 1836, which will be described in Chapter 10. Soon after, the Taylor family and several others moved back to Grimes County, hoping to be in less danger from the Indians.[26] Unfortunately, the move did not save them. On March 8, 1837, Levi Taylor was killed by Indians while searching for a cow in a creek bottom. After Levi's death, his wife moved with her three young children to live with the family of Joshua Hadley. On the night of June 7, Indians attacked the Hadley house, and Mrs. Taylor decided to move her family again to another residence a half mile away. On the way, the Indians ambushed them and killed Mrs. Taylor and her daughter. The two boys ran back to the Hadley home. The Indians shot one boy in the hand, but the other escaped unharmed.[27]

Other settlers in the Viesca area were Reverend Z. N. Morrell, the well-known frontier preacher and author of *Flowers and Fruits from the Wilderness*, Sterling Clack Robertson, John Goodloe Warren Pierson, Joshua Hadley, Alexander Thomson, Albert G. Perry, Jeremiah W. Simpson, and Thomas Chalmers.[28] On the east bank of the Brazos were the families of John and James Marlin, George and Jackson Morgan, and Mrs. Jones, most of whom were killed in an Indian raid in 1839, which will be described in detail in Chapter 10.[29] Among the settlers in the western part of Falls County were the McLennans, who settled on Pond Creek in 1835.[30] At that site, in June 1836, "Indians killed Laughlin McLennan and burned his mother to death . . . and three McLennan children were carried into captivity where two died. The third child was not released until 1846."[31]

~

Fig. 9.1 - Brazos River as seen from the east bank, just below the falls, near the site of Sarahville de Viesca. Photo by Donna Gholson Cook, January 2000.

Fig. 9.2 - Replica of a log cabin at Fort Parker, similar to those used by early Texas settlers. Photo by Donna Gholson Cook, April 2002.

When new settlers arrived, their first stop was at the Falls of the Brazos to make an application for land and locate their homesites. With the help of neighbors, a cabin was quickly completed. As soon as the foundation and walls were completed, the neighbor ladies prepared a feast of the best food and drink available.[32] Texas "cabins were located with more attention to elevated ground and proximity to water than to land lines and roads."[33] Most common were one- or two-room log cabins, with a lean-to for added storage space.

The two-room or double log cabin, like the house of John Marlin described above, often had a long porch and "open central hall, designed to catch the breezes that tempered the scorching Texas sun."[34] The double log cabin was also known as a dog-trot or dog-run house. The logs, often unhewn, were notched at the corners for joining, with the open spaces filled with rocks, moss, mud, or wood chinks. There was usually a fireplace at a gabled end, and a few cabins even had an attic. The same type of construction was also used for churches, schools, jails, and other types of buildings.[35] There were few windows, and glass windows were rare. Roofs were overlapping oak clapboards and the chimney was a

107

mixture of sticks and clay. Floors were either "dirt, sawed boards, or split logs with the flat side up."[36]

> Among the prized possessions of the first to settle in Robertson County were flint-lock rifles, pistols, powder horns, a hunting knife, and necessary powder and lead. The axe, hammer, saw, and auger were as essential as were arms for defense. The pioneers prized their slate and pencil, sealing wax, ink powder, and their candle wicks and moulds.[37]

Some of the best descriptions of Texas in the early nineteenth century are found in the journal of Noah Smithwick, who was nineteen when he became obsessed with the idea of going to Texas. He left Hopkinsville, Kentucky, with a little money, a change of clothes, and a gun, and traveled by stagecoach to the [Cumberland] river, then a flatboat loaded with ice to New Orleans to meet the future.[38] He described the Texas frontier in his *Recollections* as having

> an abundance of game, wild horses, cattle, turkeys, buffalo, deer and antelope by the drove. The woods abounded in bee trees, wild grapes, plums, cherries, persimmons, haws and dewberries, while walnuts, hickorynuts and pecans were abundant along the water courses. The climate was so mild that houses were not essential; neither was a superabundance of clothing or bedding, buffalo robes and bear skins supplying all that was needed for the latter and buckskin the former.[39]

At the time he wrote this, he must not have experienced a real blue norther of the kind that come through Texas several times each winter!

Corn had been a major food source for inhabitants of Texas since prehistoric times[40] and it was the most essential food of the Robertson's colonists and their livestock. "Not only was it comparatively easy to grow, harvest, and prepare for eating, but it provided the basic food resource for the maintenance of the frontier. Once matured, corn could be prepared for consumption in many ways."[41] The pith of the stalk was made into molasses. The fresh grain could be toasted, boiled, or fried. When hardened, it could be grated and made into bread, but most corn was ground into meal. The meal could be boiled in water to make corn meal mush, or cooked in a variety of ways, with or without other ingredients. Most families owned a steel hand-operated mill to turn corn into meal.[42] Other staples were venison, wild turkey, and bear meat.[43] Hogs were easily raised and a dependable source of food. There was fish, rabbit, buffalo and beef.[44] Yams, melons, pumpkins and other fruits and vegetables were gradually introduced. Native pecans were highly nutritious and grew wild along the rivers[45] and pecan pie made with corn syrup is still a favorite dessert of Texans today. Table implements were primitive, consisting of such items as bowie knives and pocket knives, cane forks, and drinking gourds.[46] Flour, sugar and coffee were usually available to anyone affluent enough to afford them,[47] and coffee was the most indispensable nonalcoholic drink. When the coffee ran out, substitutes were made from "parched corn, wheat or okra seeds."[48]

Tobacco and liquor were used excessively. Men of all social classes chewed tobacco, older women smoked pipes and younger women dipped snuff.[49] Many types of liquor were available and overindulgence resulted in many social problems, ranging from idleness to killings.[50] Women often made homemade wines and cordials but drank with more discretion than the men.[51] Home brew was made from a variety of fruits and vegetables.

Buckskin was often the only material available for clothing for the earliest Texas settlers, but it had its drawbacks. Francis R. Lubbock, comptroller of the Republic of Texas, told of an Indian-hunting trip he undertook wearing buckskin and taking no extra clothing.

> When rain drenched his suit, he dried it—and himself—near the campfire only to discover when he was thoroughly warm and dry that his breeches had shrunk to above his knees and were stuck so tightly to his skin that they had to be cut off. But the "old stagers" knew better than to dry buckskin near a fire, and Texas pioneers continued to wear it on hunting and fighting expeditions throughout the period of the Republic. Headgear often was fashioned from coonskin, and one individual who lived near Washington on the Brazos won local notoriety by donning a snakeskin vest, "a very odiferous affair."[52]

As the settlers began to raise cotton, homespun replaced the buckskin, except for hunting expeditions. Pioneer women "carded, spun, and wove cotton and wool, sometimes even concocting their own homemade dyes"[53] from bark and berry juices. Women wore sunbonnets and a man might wear a hat made of straw or palmetto.[54] Many men wore long hair. "Whiskers were worn to suit the fancy of the individual man, but many Texans were clean shaven at least part of the time and nearly everyone owned a razor."[55]

In 1835, three years after Samuel Gholson moved to Texas, slaves accounted for about twelve percent of the immigrant population.[56] In 1850, only about one farmer in three owned any slaves at all, and half of those farmers owned fewer than five. Most of the slaves were located on the larger plantations along the coast. William Bollaert, who lived in Texas for four years and kept a record of his observations,

> testified that Negroes were well treated on the whole, and added that he could "bear witness that they are not over-worked, or ill-used"; most of them were "family Negroes," who were permitted to stay on the plantations in their old age and not sold to masters indifferent to their welfare. On well-regulated plantations, each slave family had its own log cabin, with a half or full acre of land behind it for a garden, as well as pigs and poultry which the family consumed or sold.[57]

Although most Texas farmers did not own any slaves, they generally approved of the institution and hoped to own a few eventually, to increase the profitability of their farming operations. However, Colonel James Morgan, who owned at least fifteen slaves, expressed his frustration with the system in the following words:

> I am a slave holder, was bred in a slave holding Country— am tired of slaves and slavery. I am the slave for my negroes—while they are happy and content I am unhappy and the loser by them—I wish to be free and hope to see Texas free'd of slavery—because it will be to *my interest* as a land holder.[58]

No record was found to indicate that Samuel owned slaves, but his son Albert owned four at the time of his death in 1860.[59]

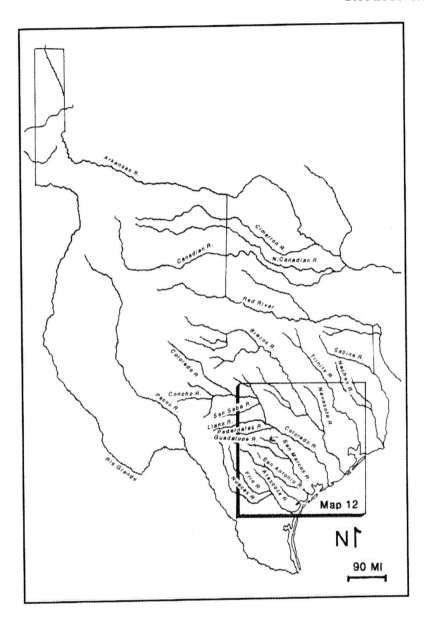

Map 11
The Republic of Texas in 1836, with major rivers.
Map compiled by author. Copyright 2003.

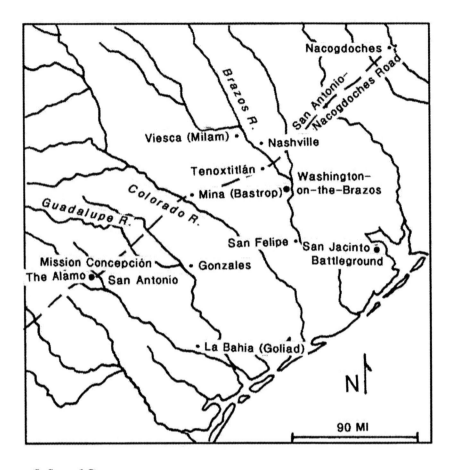

Map 12
Location map for selected events in the Texas Revolution.
Map compiled by author. Copyright 2003.

Chapter 10: The Republic of Texas—Early Texas Rangers

Samuel & Albert Gholson: 1835-1845

~ The Birth of the Republic of Texas ~

Most of the early colonists in *Coahuila y Texas* intended to become good citizens of Mexico, but the Mexican colonial policy tried to restrict the rights of the colonists in several areas and did not provide the credit, banks and roads necessary to establish a market economy. By decree issued on April 6, 1830, the Mexican government attempted to ban further immigration from America and to control slavery. Stephen F. Austin correctly predicted that the decree would only stop the immigration of prosperous Americans. In spite of the turmoil, Texas exported $500,000 worth of cotton and hides in 1834.[1]

In 1833 and 1834, the Coahuila y Texas legislature was diligently trying to respond to the complaints of the Texas colonists. The English language was recognized for official purposes. Religious toleration was approved. The court system was revised, providing Texas with an appellate court and trial by jury.

In Mexico City, however, a different scenario was developing. Santa Anna assumed supreme authority in April 1834 and began dismantling the federalist government. Among the most offensive changes dictated by Santa Anna was the reduction of the state militias to one man per each 500 population. The intent was to eliminate possible armed opposition to the emerging centralist government.

But liberals in the state of Zacatecas in central Mexico rebelled. Santa Anna's response was particularly brutal, as he tried to make an example of the rebels. Troops were allowed to sack the state capital after the victory over the insurgents.

Trouble also was brewing closer to the Texans.[2]

As the power of the Mexican states began to erode, some Texans advocated a complete break from Mexico and others wanted to calmly ride out the storm.[3] However, there were many young, single men like Albert Gholson who were just eager to participate in a good fight, no matter what the cause.

> The establishment by Mexican authorities of custom houses with armed guards was resented by the settlers, but did not lead to any widespread feeling for rebellion even after June 29, 1835, when William Travis gathered a small band of men and a small cannon and forced the garrison at Anahuac to surrender and return to Mexico.[4]

The Mexican generals became increasingly determined to squelch any rebellion and decided to try to disarm the Texans, beginning with a six-pound cannon that the DeWitt colonists in Gonzales had been given to fight Indians. Having very little actual value, the cannon

> was practically useless, having been spiked and the spike driven out, leaving a touch-hole the size of a man's thumb. Its principal merit as a weapon of defense, therefore, lay in its presence and the noise it could make, the Indians being very much afraid of cannon. But it was the match that fired the mine, already primed and loaded.[5]

When a few Mexican soldiers went to Gonzales to retrieve the cannon, the locals refused to give it up. When additional Mexican reinforcements arrived, the Gonzales officials called for volunteers, and dozens of Texans responded,[6] including seventeen-year-old Albert Gholson, who "rendered his first service at Gonzales under Captain Carey White, taking part against the Mexicans in an engagement there."[7] Stephen F. Austin, the most respected member of the community, commanded the militia of about 300 volunteers who brought their own weapons. None of them, including Austin, were professional soldiers.[8] Travis was also there "simply as a recruit."[9] "On Oct. 2, 1835, the Texans challenged the Mexicans with a 'come-and-take-it' flag over the cannon. After a brief skirmish, the Mexicans withdrew, but the first rounds in the Texas

Revolution had been fired."[10] The distraction created an opportunity for Mexican General Cos, brother-in-law of Santa Anna, to move a large Mexican army force into San Antonio undetected.[11] On October 12, the Texans left Gonzales with the cannon and started for San Antonio to confront Cos where he had fortified the Alamo and the town plazas west of the river with his force of 650 men.[12] Because of problems in transporting the cannon, they were forced to abandon it at Sandy Creek, halfway to San Antonio, leaving it to be appropriated by anyone who happened along, Mexican or not. It had served its purpose.[13]

Noah Smithwick was a gunsmith by trade and arrived at Gonzales just after the initial battle, in time to help with the arms and ammunition. Among the preparations they made, ". . . we cut slugs of bar iron and hammered them into balls; . . . formed a company of lancers and converted all the old files about the place into lances, which we mounted on poles cut in the river bottom."[14] After making preparations and learning a few military tactics, the volunteers began their march to San Antonio and Smithwick described the appearance of the new Texas army.

Buckskin breeches were the nearest approach to uniform, and there was wide diversity even there, some being new and soft and yellow, while others, from long familiarity with rain and grease and dirt, had become hard and black and shiny. Some, from having passed through the process of wetting and drying on the wearer while he sat on the ground or a chunk before the camp fire, with his knees elevated at an angle of eighty-five degrees, had assumed an advanced position at the knee, followed by a corresponding shortening of the lower front length, exposing shins as guiltless of socks as a–Kansas Senator's. Boots being an unknown quantity; some wore shoes and some moccasins. Here a broad-brimmed sombrero overshadowed the military cap at its side; there a tall "beegum" rode familiarly beside a coonskin cap, with the tail hanging down behind, as all well regulated tails should do. Here a big American horse loomed up above the nimble Spanish pony ranged beside him; there a half-broke mustang pranced beside a sober, methodical mule. Here a bulky roll of bed quilts jostled a pair of "store" blankets; there the shaggy brown buffalo robe contrasted with a gaily checkered counterpane on which the manufacturer had lavished all the skill of dye and weave known to the art–mayhap it was part of the dowery a wife brought her husband on her wedding day, and surely the day-dreams she wove into its ample folds held in them no shadow of a presentiment that it might be his winding sheet. In lieu of a canteen, each man carried a Spanish gourd, a curious specimen of the gourd family, having two round bowls, each holding near a quart, connected by a short neck, apparently designed for adjusting a strap about. A fantastic military array to a casual observer, but the one great purpose animating every heart clothed us in a uniform more perfect in our eyes than was ever donned by regulars on dress parade. So, with the Old Cannon flag flying at the head, and the "artillery" flying at the heels of two yokes of long-horned Texas steers occupying the post of honor in the center, we filed out of Gonzales and took up the line of march for San Antonio.[15]

Albert Gholson was a member of the motley band of rebels. On the way to San Antonio, Sam Houston visited them briefly. Smithwick described his first encounter with Houston, which may have been Albert's first look at the man also.

At the Cibolo, Sam Houston came up with us. It was my first sight of the man who more than all the others was destined to win enduring fame from the struggle we were inaugurating. I have a vivid picture of him before my mind's eye as he rode into our camp alone, mounted on a little yellow Spanish stallion so diminutive that old Sam's long legs, incased in the conventional buckskin, almost touched the ground. He made a speech to us, urging the necessity of concerted action among the colonists: arguing that it should be for independence, otherwise we could expect no assistance from other powers. He also advocated the enlistment of the Cherokees as allies, and owing to his great influence with them, he could no doubt have used them to advantage. They were Uncle Sam's wards, however, and he said "no." Houston immediately returned to San Felipe to take part in the convention.[16]

Upon arriving in the San Antonio vicinity, Gholson[17] and Smithwick were part of a small force that fought in the battle of Concepción. That force also included Smithwick's friend Jim Bowie who had joined them at Cibolo, and Fannin, leader of the "Brazos Guards" at the Battle of Gonzales.[18]

By the time the Texans camped along Salado Creek east of San Antonio in mid-October their numbers had grown to over 400 men, including James Bowie and Juan N. Seguín, who brought with him a company of Mexican Texans. Bowie and James W. Fannin, Jr., led an advance to the missions below San Antonio in late October, while Cos brought in 100 reinforcement men. On October 25 the democratic Texans conducted a debate over strategy. Sam Houston, who had come from the Consultation government, urged delay for training and for cannons to bombard the fortifications. Austin and others won support to continue efforts at capturing San Antonio.

From San Francisco de la Espada Mission on October 27, Austin sent Bowie and Fannin forward to Nuestra Señora de la Purísima Concepción de Acuña Mission with ninety men to locate a position nearer the town for the army. There on the foggy morning of the twenty-eighth Cos sent Col. Domingo de Ugartechea with 275 men to attack the advance force. The Texans drove off the assault from a position along the bank of the San Antonio River, inflicting over fifty casualties and capturing one cannon. Austin arrived after the battle of Concepción to urge an attack on San Antonio but found little support among his officers.

Cos then resumed defensive positions in San Antonio and the Alamo, while the Texans established camps on the river above and below the town and grew to an army of 600 with reinforcements from East Texas led by Thomas J. Rusk. After discussion among the Texan officers produced little support for an attack, some volunteers went home for winter clothes and equipment. Yet the arrival of more East Texans in early November offset the departures.[19]

Fig. 10.1 - "Fall of Bexar" colored lithograph by Lewis & Brown, NY, 1845. Texas State Library & Archives Commission No. 1979/121-1.

The following account of the Battle of San Antonio was written by one of the participants:

STORMING OF SAN ANTONIO DE BEXAR IN 1835.
(From the State Gazette, 1849.)

In December 1835, the Texan forces under General Burleson invested San Antonio, then held by General Cos, with twelve or fifteen hundred regular troops. It had been determined by the officers, after consultation, not to attempt carrying the place by storm against the great odds, but to go into winter quarters. At this juncture a deserter from the town gave information that the place was not as strong as had been represented, and he advised an immediate attack. Colonel Ben Milam at once made a call for volunteers, in these words: "Who will go with old Ben Milam into San Antonio?" Officers and men, to the number of about four hundred, responded with a shout. General

Burleson was requested to hold his position with the rest of the army until the result of the attack should be known, which he promised to do. The attacking force was divided into two companies, the first under command of Colonel Milam, assisted by Colonel Frank and Major Morris; the second under the command of Colonel F. W. Johnson, assisted by Dr. Grant and Colonel Austin. Arnold, Cook, and Maverick, and Deaf and John W. Smith acted as guides. Colonel Neil was sent to make a feint on the Alamo, which he did in good style, and then joined Milam in town. The attack was made early on the morning of the 5th of December, the signal being the discharge of a cannon near the Alamo. The enemy were unprepared. Their bugle sounded a wild alarm, and their drums beat hastily to arms. Silently cutting down the sentinels at their posts, the Texans entered the town amid the roar of artillery. Grape-shot and musket fell thick around them doing but little execution, as they had got near enough to be sheltered by the walls of the houses. Having effected an entrance, the desperate fight was waged from house to house, by making holes through the soft adobe walls, and dislodging the enemy, driving him before them step by step, and street after street. We proceed in the language of the narrator.

"The order was given for fifteen or twenty men to take possession of the roofs of some houses; ten succeeded in gaining the roof, but it was a hot berth, for the enemy poured a deadly fire upon us, killing and wounding several. In the main plaza, or public square, was a large church, in the cupola of which was a party of the enemy's sharp-shooters, who were picking us off. The weather being very cold, and a stiff norther blowing, we had great difficulty in loading our rifles, as the wind blew the powder away. At this moment, Deaf Smith, the spy of the army, the Harvey Birch of Texas, appeared upon the roof of the house where we were, but as he raised himself up and shouted to us the order to come on, he received a ball in the shoulder which disabled him.

119

Fig. 10.2 - "Erastus 'Deaf' Smith" courtesy of the Texas State Library
& Archives Commission, No. 1999/1-18.

There were now but five men remaining of the ten who
had mounted the roof, and finding that it was certain death
to remain in that position, we attempted to return to the
ground. We soon cut a hole through the roof large enough
to admit of a man's body, and placing myself in my
blanket, I requested my comrades to lower me through the
opening into the house. Down I went, holding on tight, as I
did not know how far it was to the bottom. It was an
uncomfortable position to be in, but my friends did not
leave me long to my apprehensions, for the blanket slipping
through their grasp, down I went ten or twelve feet into the
middle of a fire which was burning on a dirt floor,
scattering embers and ashes in all directions. Jumping up,
the first thing that met my gaze was a Mexican officer

about to make an attack upon me, but jerking my pistol from my belt, I fired at him before my somewhat disordered faculties assured me that my foe was not an officer, but an officer's uniform hanging in such a position as to resemble one. My friends hearing the report, supposed it to be a gone case with me, but their fears being relieved, they joined me in the room below, from which the late occupant had evidently beat a hasty and undressed retreat." Then the fight continued from house to house, and from street to street, for five days, the loss of the assaulting party being comparatively small. On the 7th, the brave Milam, while leading* a charge, was instantly killed by a rifle ball in the head, from a sharp-shooter. The impetuous Captain Thomas Wm. Ward, also, lost a leg in the fight. On the night of the 9th, a combined attack was made upon the priest's house and other buildings upon the public square, and after a determined resistance, the enemy retreated and fled precipitately across the river to the Alamo where they afterward capitulated.

By this affair General Cos and twelve hundred Mexican troops, together with a large quantity of army stores and munitions of war, fell into our hands.[20]

*An almost identical version of this article from the *Texas State Gazette* was printed in *Frontier Times*, and instead of "leading a charge," that version states that Milam was "loading a charge."[21] Another account lends credibility to the "loading a charge" version, as it states that Ben Milam was killed while crouching beside a rock wall and peering over the top after the shooting had ended, assessing the situation. Only the top of his head and his eyes were exposed when he was shot in the middle of the forehead.[22] Albert Gholson was within about forty feet of Ben Milam when Milam was killed.[23]

Fig. 10.3 - "Benjamin Rush Milam" painting by Charles B. Normann.
Texas State Library & Archives Commission No. 1979/39-8.

Most of the Texas volunteers went home after the Battle of San Antonio[24] and the Texans were overconfident after the easy victories in 1835. While the Mexicans were organizing their army, the Texans were negligent in developing a coordinated plan for defense. Sam Houston held the title of commander-in-chief but had little authority. In January 1836 he sent James Bowie to San Antonio to evaluate whether the Alamo was defensible, and if not, to destroy it.[25] Houston needed the approval of Governor Henry Smith to demolish the Alamo, but Smith unfortunately did not agree with the plan. Bowie arrived at the Alamo on January 19 and was impressed with the work that had been done on the fort under the leadership of Col. James C. Neill. He was convinced that the strategic location must be maintained to protect the settlers from the enemy. Governor Smith ordered William B. Travis to report to Colonel Neill, and under duress Travis took his thirty troopers to the Alamo, arriving on February 3.[26] On February 8, David Crockett arrived at the Alamo with a group of volunteers.[27] On February 14, Neill had to leave due to family illness, leaving Travis in command.[28]

> Neill had not intended to slight the older and more experienced Bowie, but Travis, like Neill, held a regular army commission. For all of his notoriety, Bowie was still just a volunteer colonel. The Alamo's volunteers, accustomed to electing their officers, resented having this regular officer foisted upon them. Neill had been in command since January; his maturity, judgment, and proven ability had won the respect of both regulars and volunteers. Travis, however, was unknown. The volunteers insisted on an election, and their acting commander complied with their wishes. The garrison cast its votes along party lines: the regulars voted for Travis, the volunteers for Bowie. In a letter to Smith, Travis claimed that the election and Bowie's subsequent conduct had placed him in an "awkward situation." The night following the balloting, Bowie dismayed Bexar residents with his besotted carousal. He tore through the town, confiscating private property and releasing convicted felons from jail. Appalled by this disorderly exhibition, Travis assured the governor that he refused to assume responsibility "for the drunken irregularities of any man"–not even the redoubtable Jim Bowie. Fortunately, this affront to Travis's sense of propriety did not produce a lasting breach between the two commanders. They struck a compromise: Bowie would command the volunteers, Travis the regulars.[29]

On February 23, Santa Anna's army arrived and "hoisted a blood-red flag, the traditional Mexican symbol of no quarter, no surrender, no mercy. Travis and Bowie defiantly answered the display with a cannon shot."[30] Travis sent a plea for help to Gonzales. The Mexicans continually bombarded the Alamo for the following days and nights. Because he was ill, Bowie turned over his share of the command to Travis on February 24. The defenders were able to slip out to gather firewood and burn buildings used by the Mexicans for cover without suffering any casualties. Messengers came and went, and thirty-two reinforcements from Gonzales were able to get into the Alamo on March 1 without losing a man.[31]

Fig. 10.4 - Earliest known photograph of the Alamo. "Alamo, Texas 1849" [San Antonio]. Alamo Daguerreotype, 1849. Prints and Photographs Collection, Center for American History, The University of Texas at Austin, DI Number 00775.

By March 5, Santa Anna had 4,000 men in camp, a force he felt sufficient to subdue the Alamo.

Historians disagree on the date, but the story goes that on March 3 or 5, Travis called his command together and explained the bleak outlook. He then asked those willing to die for freedom to stand and fight; those not willing could try to get through enemy lines to safety. Even the sick Jim Bowie vowed to stay. Only Louis (Moses) Rose, a veteran of Napoleon's retreat from Moscow slipped out of the Alamo that night.

At dawn March 6, Santa Anna's forces attacked. When the fighting stopped between 8:30 and 9 a.m., all the defenders were dead. Only a few women, children and black slaves survived the assault. Davy Crockett's fate is still debated. Mexican officer Enrique de la Peña held that Crockett was captured with a few other defenders and was executed by Santa Anna.

Santa Anna's victory came at the cost of almost one-third his forces killed or wounded. Their deaths in such number set back Santa Anna's timetable. The fall of the Alamo also brutally shook Texans out of their lethargy.[32]

Fig. 10.5 - "General Santa Anna" from print first published in U.S. 1837. Texas State Library & Archives Commission No. 1/102-500.

At the same time the Alamo was under seige, the Convention of 1836 was underway at Washington-on-the-Brazos. On February 1, 1836, in the town of Milam (formerly Sarahville de Viesca, renamed to honor the fallen leader Ben Milam), Samuel Gholson and his son Albert cast votes for delegates to the convention. The delegates elected to represent Milam were Sterling C. Robertson and George C. Childress.[33] Texas declared its independence from Mexico on March 2, 1836, but this fact was probably not known by the defenders of the Alamo.[34] As a result of the convention, Sam Houston was finally in full command of the Texas army. When he heard of the fate of the Alamo defenders, Houston ordered James Fannin to abandon La Bahía presidio at Goliad and retreat to Victoria, but his delay in obeying the order resulted in the capture and execution of Fannin and about 350 of his troops by the Mexican army.[35]

Fig. 10.6 - Restored Independence Hall at Washington-on-the-Brazos.
Photo by Donna Gholson Cook, March 2000.

The situation in Marlin after receiving the news of the fall of the Alamo was described by a resident, Newton C. Duncan, who was a child at the time:

> When the Alamo fell into Mexican hands the report came to us that General Cos was to overrun our section with his troops, his object being to capture Sterling C. Robertson, who was impresario [empresario] of the colony of which Marlin was a settlement. Robertson's headquarters were at Viesca, across the Brazos. All the male members of the Marlin settlement were absent from home, having gone in pursuit of Indians, who were threatening the settlement. One still morning, at a time of the day when no human noise interfered with the transmission of sound, the report of two large guns reached our ears. The ladies of the

settlement immediately held a consultation of war. It was decided that the guns we had just heard were those of the advancing Mexicans. The ladies decided that to retreat to the Brazos bottom, there to conceal themselves and families until the men of the colony returned or the Mexicans be gone, was the wisest thing to do, each family seeking concealment by itself. Acting upon this policy Mrs. Cavitt started with her little children and her negro women and their children to find a hiding place, endeavoring to secrete herself and those in her charge in a briar thicket. She soon found that her object was defeated, for the negroes and the briars mixed, and the yells of those dusky sons and daughters of the south, which could not be stopped, would betray her hiding place. She returned to her home. Mrs. Marlin started for the bottom with her two small children, and on reaching there her little daughter Emily, finding out the cause of their hiding, became so much frightened that she screamed at the top of her voice and would not be pacified. So Mrs. Marlin was forced to return to her home and if the worst came to the worst to face the advancing foe. Mrs. [Mahala] Duncan started to find concealment for herself and two little boys, one of whom [Newton C. Duncan] is the author of this bit of reminiscence, amid the friendly thickets of the Brazos. We had as an appendage to our household at this time a hound puppy, and when we sought concealment the pup sought it also. Evidently he feared the Mexicans as much as we did. On our way to the bottom the pup fell in with some red ants, and being severely stung, he began to howl, and howl as I know now only a hound pup can howl. He howled loud enough for Cos and every Mexican in Texas to hear him, and the more we tried to persuade him to desist the more determined he was to howl, until in our frantic despair my mother decided it was better to face Mexicans than to longer endure the yells of that hound. So we bent our steps homeward, and I must say that from that day to this, that hound pups and red ants have never occupied a warm place in my affections. All having returned to our homes, we determined to await developments. The next twenty-four hours were anxious hours to those in the little Marlin settlement, but God never gave to a country more noble and self sacrificing women than were the mothers of Texas in her pioneer days, and well may we say peace to their ashes and incense to their memory. It turned, out, however, that the guns that we had heard were those of the returning settlers, who were encamped on the opposite side of the Brazos, two families, Graham and McKey, from three forks of Little river, that settlement having been previously abandoned by its settlers through fear of the Mexicans and Indians. The guns fired by McKey and Graham were known as British muskets. They made a report equal to a modern cannon, and besides in those days of Mexican and Indian atrocities, you could hear a shot further than nowadays, for the sense of hearing was developed to a very high degree.[36]

Returning to the activities of the Texas army, we find Houston camped on the Colorado River gathering his army and within about a week he had 1200-1400 men in his camp. On March 27 he moved his army to San Felipe on the Brazos, then back toward the San Jacinto River. Through the intelligence gathering of Houston's scouts, led by Erastus "Deaf" Smith, Houston was able to track the movement of the Mexican army.[37]

THE BATTLE OF SAN JACINTO.
(From A Brief History of Texas.)
On the morning of the 19th of April, the Texan army crossed over and marched down the right bank of the Buffalo Bayou to within half a mile of its junction with the San Jacinto River. Here they formed in line of battle on the edge of a grove of trees, their rear protected by the timber, while before them was the open prairie.

A few days before this, the army of the young Republic had received two pieces of artillery as a gift from some of the citizens of Cincinnati, Ohio. These were named the "Twin Sisters," and were placed in position. On the morning of the 20th of April, and soon after General Houston had dispersed his forces, Santa Anna came marching up in battle array. A volley from the "Twin

Sisters" brought him to a sudden halt, and falling back to a clump of trees a quarter of a mile distant, he formed in line of battle. In return for the *feint* of the evening, Colonel Sherman, at the head of his mounted men, made a gallant charge upon the Mexican army, which, although it did not accomplish any decisive result, seemed to inspire our men with fresh enthusiasm.

The 21st of April dawned bright and beautiful. It was felt by those who were to participate in its stirring scenes, to be the day upon which the conflict for Texas was to be decided.

On this side was arrayed the whole available army of Texas, embracing 750* men. On that, were the best troops of Mexico, to the number of 1,800, and commanded by an able and wily general. The men of Texas were aware that every thing for them depended upon the issue of the fight, and every heart was beating quick and every nerve well strung.

The men of Mexico were flushed with pride at recent successes, and felt secure of the result.

Early in the morning General Houston sent Deaf Smith, the celebrated Texas spy, with two or three men, to destroy Vince's bridge across the bayou over which the Mexican army had passed, thus cutting off their only available avenue of escape. The daring exploit was executed almost in the presence of the foe. It was now decided to be the moment to attack Santa Anna in his intrenchments. With the stillness of death the patriot army moved, in three divisions, to the charge. No music heralded the advance. No sound but the quiet tread of determined men broke the stillness of that spring morning. When within two hundred yards they received the volley of the enemy's advanced column without quailing, and then increased their pace to a "double quick."

When within seventy yards the word "FIRE" was given, and six hundred Texas rifles belched forth their deadly contents. Then the shout, "ALAMO" and "GOLIAD," rang along the entire line, and they rushed forward to a hand to hand encounter. But Mexican valor had already given way before the impetuosity of that charge, and in a few minutes more the boastful legions of the "Napoleon of the West" were in full retreat. The rout soon became general. Finding the bridge destroyed, the Mexicans plunged into the bayou, where many were drowned or slain by their pursuers. Seven hundred dead Mexicans upon that day atoned for the butchery at the Alamo and Goliad; and seven hundred and thirty prisoners were in the hands of the victorious army.

Santa Anna in vain tried to escape. He was discovered, on the morning of the 22d, hiding in the long grass with a blanket thrown over his head, and was taken to the quarters of General Houston.

At the time Santa Anna was brought before him, Houston, who had been severely wounded in the battle, was lying on a mattrass under a tree which constituted his headquarters. The President of Mexico, bowing low before him, said, "I am General Antonio Lopez de Santa Anna, a prisoner of war at your disposal." General Houston requested him to sit down, which he did, at the same time asking for opium. A piece of this drug was brought him, which he eagerly swallowed. He then at once proposed to purchase his freedom, but was answered, "that was a matter to be negotiated with the government of Texas." He however persisted saying to Houston, "You can afford to be generous, you have conquered the Napoleon of the West."

General Houston asked him "how he could expect mercy after showing none at the Alamo?"

He replied, that "by the rules of war, when a fort refused to surrender, and was taken by assault, the prisoners were doomed to death." General Houston answered him that "such a rule was a disgrace to the civilization of the nineteenth century." He was then asked "by what rule he justified the massacre of Goliad?" He replied that "he had orders from his government to execute all that were taken with arms in their hands."

General Houston told him that "*he* was the government–a Dictator had no superior, and that he must at once write an order for all his troops to abandon Texas and return home." This he did, and the dispatch was sent by a trusty messenger to his subordinates.

How to dispose of Santa Anna was a troublesome question. Among the soldiers the feeling existed that his life only could atone for the cruelties perpetrated by his order. But prudence as well as humanity dictated another course, and his life was spared. The following agreement was entered into between him and the President of Texas:

First. That he would never again take up arms against Texas.

Second. That he should order all Mexican troops in Texas to return home.

Third. That he should cause to be restored all captured property.

In consideration of the fulfillment of these conditions he was to be set free. When the time came for his release, the storm of popular indignation was so great, that President Burnet thought best to order his longer detention as a prisoner of war.

Santa Anna was liberated by President Houston, in January, 1837, and sent to Washington, D. C., whence he returned to Mexico.[38]

*See General Rusk's Report

Fig. 10.7 - "Sam Houston, New York, 1856" from a photograph by
Frederick. Texas State Library & Archives Commission No. 1/102-
271.

Lieutenant Albert G. Gholson commanded Captain Thomas H.
Barron's company in the Battle of San Jacinto. Captain Barron had
previously fought with Albert's father Samuel as a member of the
Kentucky militia in the Battle of New Orleans, and lived in Arkansas
Territory, as did Samuel.[39]

> From before until after the Texas Revolution he [Barron]
> served as captain of Texas Rangers at Viesca, Nashville,
> Washington-on-the-Brazos and Tenoxtitlán, where he was
> commandant. In January 1836 a ranging company was
> formed at Viesca with Sterling C. Robertson as captain and
> Barron as sergeant. Soon thereafter, Barron was promoted
> to captain. As the struggle for Texas independence
> heightened, Barron, now in middle age, was allowed to
> return home to assist in moving families and slaves ahead

of the advancing Mexican front in the Runaway Scrape. At the battle of San Jacinto on April 21, 1836, his company, in his absence, was commanded by Lt. Albert G. Gholson.[40]

From the recollections of B. F. Gholson, Albert's son:

After San Antonio was taken and the army was ordered to evacuate this city and fall back to Gonzales, my father, with a majority of the army, obeyed the command.

By the time the army reached Gonzales new companies were being organized in the different localities of the colonies. Captain Tom Barron was organizing a company near Washington, on the Brazos. Some of the men said to Captain Barron "We would like to have Albert Gholson for our first lieutenant, but he is not here. He is off in the army."

Barron said to them "If enough of you will vote for him that will bring him to the company." So he was elected by vote of the men, unknown to him and Captain Carey White was notified. He transferred Albert G. Gholson from his company to Captain Tom Barron's company. Thus he took his position at a youthful age under Captain Barron.

When Houston took command of the army at Gonzales, the army fell back from place to place, the Mexican army pursuing. This brought about what was known as "the runaway scrape." During this time Captain Tom Barron, being a middled aged man, and having some family and quite a lot of negro property, was allowed, with others, to go home and help move the families and slaves out of danger and to assist others to places of safety. My father, Albert G. Gholson, being unmarried, remained with the army in command of the Company. Before the return of Captain Barron the battle of San Jacinto took place, so my father commanded Barron's Company on that occasion. He was in the thick of the firing at Vince's Bridge. I have heard him tell the story of the battle many times. He says that there was a wholesale capture of Mexicans there, and that it will never be known just how many were killed in the Bayou. I remember a conversation between my father and another comrade of his about this very thing. The other man said "I was stationed below where the main fighting took place, and I'll declare to you, Albert, from the blood that was coming down that stream it seemed that two thousand men were shot in the stream."

"Yes," said my father, "but there were many horses shot too, and some of the blood you saw was horse blood." My father was also in the chase to the Bayou where the bridge was destroyed.

Concerning Deaf Smith, my father says that he knew him well, that there was a lot of Smiths in the army, and that he was called "Deaf" Smith to distinguish him from the other Smiths. He was hard of hearing, but was by no means deaf. He spoke of Smith's ability in high terms.[41]

When the farms and homes were abandoned in the Runaway Scrape, the settlers lost almost everything they had worked so hard to accumulate:

Since Gonzales had been burned when General Houston left, then the Mexicans came through gathering up plunder, and, finally, the Comanches came, took what they wanted, and left, it was a bizarre landscape indeed through which this party was traveling. Here is [Noah] Smithwick's description:

The desolation of the country through which we passed beggars description. Houses were standing open, the beds unmade, the breakfast things still on the tables, pans of milk moulding in the dairies. There were cribs full of corn, smoke houses full of bacon, yards full of chickens that ran after us for food, nests of eggs in every fence corner, young corn and garden truck rejoicing in the rain, cattle cropping the luxuriant grass, hogs, fat and lazy, wallowing in the mud, all abandoned. Forlorn dogs roamed around the deserted homes, their doleful howls adding to the general sense of desolation. Hungry cats ran

134

mewing to meet us, rubbing their sides against our legs in token of welcome. Wagons were so scarce that it was impossible to remove household goods, many of the women and children, even, had to walk. Some had no conveyance but trucks [barrows?], the screeching of which added to the horror of the situation. One young lady said she walked with a bucket [of water] in hand to keep the trucks on which her mother and their little camping outfit rode from taking fire.

And, as if the arch fiend had broken loose, there were men–or devils, rather–bent on plunder, galloping up behind the fugitives, telling them the Mexicans were just behind, thus causing the hapless victims to abandon what few valuables they had tried to save. There were broken-down wagons and household goods scattered all along the road. Stores with quite valuable stocks of goods stood open, the goods on the shelves, no attempt having been made to remove them.[42]

The flight was marked by lack of preparation and by panic caused by fear both of the Mexican Army and of the Indians. The people used any means of transportation or none at all. Added to the discomforts of travel were all kinds of diseases, intensified by cold, rain, and hunger. Many persons died and were buried where they fell. The flight continued until news came of the victory in the battle of San Jacinto. At first no credence was put in this news because so many false rumors had been circulated, but gradually the refugees began to reverse their steps and turn back toward home, many toward homes that no longer existed.[43]

~ Early Texas Rangers ~

Stephen F. Austin may have been the first to use the term "ranger" in Texas around 1823 when he attempted to form a ranging unit, although the term had been used much earlier in the English colonies to describe "a body of men who operated apart from the regular military establishment, irregulars, men who literally ranged the frontiers."[44] In the early days of Texas, civilian posses were formed as necessary to defend the settlers against Indian raids[45] but between 1823 and 1824, military districts were formed and militia units were composed of all males between eighteen and fifty-five.[46] On October 17, 1835, in the process of developing a system of government for Texas, several ranger districts were proposed by Daniel Parker, each with its own superintendent. Twenty-five rangers were to be stationed between the Brazos and Trinity rivers, ten on the east side of the Trinity, and thirty-five between the Brazos and the Colorado.[47] In November additional rangers were employed and the area was extended, and when a resolution organized a regular army to fight the Mexican army, the resolution included an article authorizing a corps of 150 rangers.[48]

> The formation and status of this ranger force was clarified on November 24, 1835, by the passage of an Ordinance and Decree to "establish and organize a Corps of Rangers" to be commanded by a major, with three companies of fifty-six men led by a captain, a lieutenant and a second lieutenant.
>
> The men were to be enlisted for one year, rather than the two years of the Regular Army, and would receive a dollar and twenty-five cents a day for themselves and their horses. Officers were to be paid the same as Dragoons in the United States Army, plus the pay of ranger privates.
>
> Privates had to furnish a good horse, saddle, bridle and blanket, in addition to weapons and a hundred rounds of powder and shot. If these were not available, the company commander could purchase any item necessary and deduct the cost from the ranger's pay.[49]

After Texas gained its independence from Mexico, the Mexican army was not as threatening, but Indian raids became more frequent and the focus of the rangers turned to protecting the settlers from the Indians. One of the great policy differences between Sam Houston, the first president of the Republic of Texas, and Mirabeau B. Lamar, the second president, was in the manner in which they dealt with the Indians.[50]

> President Sam Houston repeatedly vetoed legislation that would have led to the strengthening of the armed forces to protect the settlers from the Indians. Instead, he tried to make treaties with the various tribes. Meanwhile those tribes continued to receive arms and ammunition from the officials of both Mexico and the United States, which they used to murder more Anglo-American settlers in Texas.
> . . . whereas it might be said that, for Houston, the best Indian was a lithesome lass very much in love, the only good Indian for Lamar was a dead Indian.[51]

Texas historian Walter Prescott Webb stated it even more bluntly. "Where Houston pursued peace, Lamar . . . favored war. Houston loved Indians, if he loved anything; Lamar hated them, but his hatred for Indians was probably secondary to his hatred for Houston."[52]

The first major Indian raid in the area was an attack on Fort Parker on the extreme eastern edge of Robertson's Colony on May 19, 1836, and many other raids followed. The Indians attacking Fort Parker were mostly Comanches, but members of several other tribes also participated. They killed almost everyone in the fort, taking a few captives, including Cynthia Ann Parker and her brother John, Rachel Parker Plummer, and her young son.[53]

> EXCERPT FROM *RACHAEL PLUMMER'S NARRATIVE*
> [Entered under May 19, 1836]
> On the 19th day of May 1836, I was living at Parker's Fort on the head waters of the River Navisott [Navasota]. My father (James W. Parker) and my husband (L. T. M. Plummer) was cultivating my father's farm, which was about a mile from the Fort.–In the morning, say 9 o'clock, my father and my little brother, (Wilson,) and my husband went to my father's farm to work; I don't think they had left the Fort more than an hour, when some one cried out Indians! Indians!! All appeared at once in a complete state

of confusion. At this time the Indians were something the
rise of a quarter of a mile from the Fort; my oldest sister
started to my father's farm to alarm my father and
husband;–I saw her no more! I was in the act of starting to
my father, but I knew I was not able to take my little son
(Jas. Pratt Plummer.) All the women had by this time left
the Fort, whither I knew not, but I supposed they had all
started towards my father's farm. My old grand-father, and
grand-mother, and several others, started through uncle
Silas Parker's farm, which was immediately adjoining the
Fort; Mr. G. E. Dwight started with his wife and child and
his mother-in-law (Mrs. Frost) and his children; as he
started uncle Silas Parker says, Good Lord, Dwight, you are
not going to run; he said no, I am going to take the women
and children to the woods. Uncle [Silas] said, stand and
fight like a man, and if we have to die we will sell our lives
as dear as we can. Mr. Dwight promised to return, which I
have do doubt he intended to do. Uncle Benjamin Parker
said he would go out to the Indians, who had now almost
come to a halt, and had sent on two Indians to the Fort to
inform the people of the Fort that they were friendly, and
had come for the purpose of making a treaty of peace with
the Americans. Uncle Benjamin Parker started out to the
Indians, who had now come within two-hundred yards of
the Fort, their white flag still waving in the air. In a few
moments Uncle Benjamin came back to the Fort, and told
those who were in the Fort, that he was convinced that the
Indians intended to fight, and told the people in the Fort to
put every thing in the best possible order, tho' there was
only my two uncles and Samuel Frost and his son Robert B.
Frost, now left at the Fort. Benjamin said that he would go
back to the Indians and try to compromise, or see if the
fight could not be avoided. Uncle Silas told him not to go
back, but to try to defend the place as well as they could but
Benjamin started off again to go with the Indians. Uncle
Silas observed to me, I know that they will kill Benjamin,
and said to me, do you stand here and watch the Indians'
motions till I can run into my house (I think he said) for my
shot pouch. I suppose that he had got a wrong shot pouch,

as he had four or five rifles. I stood and watched the Indians till I saw them gathering round uncle Benjamin. I was now convinced that this was the time they intended to kill him. I started across the Fort and met Silas returning to the same place where he left me. He asked me if they had commenced killing Benjamin. I told him they were gathering around him. He said, I know they will kill him, but I will be good for one anyway. Those were the last words I heard him utter. I ran out of the Fort through a small back gate that led immediately into the farm; as soon as I passed the corner of the Fort, I was again in sight of the Indians, and I saw them stabbing their spears into uncle Benjamin, and shooting him with arrows. I do not now so completely recollect every particular circumstance, for I was much alarmed and was trying to make my escape. I soon discovered that a party of Indians had got ahead of me, and though I was vain enough to try to run to save myself, they soon headed me, and one large sulky looking Indian picked up a hoe and knocked me down. I well recollect their tearing my little James Pratt out of my arms, but whether they hit me any more I know not, for I had swooned away, how long I know not. The first thing I recollect was the Indians dragging me along by the hair of the head. I made several unsuccessful attempts to raise on my feet before I could possibly do so. As soon as I was able to stand, I heard a desperate screaming near the place where they had first taken me. I heard one or two shots, and am confident that I heard uncle Silas shout a most triumphant huzza, as tho' he had thousands to back him, but I dont know how many Indians was fighting him. I was soon dragged to the main body of Indians, my face and clothes was covered with blood from the wound of the hoe. I looked round for my little James Pratt, but could not see him–I expected they had killed him. There were two Commanchee women, one of them came to me and struck me several times with a leather whip that she had. I suppose it was to make me quit crying. I now looked at the place where uncle Benjamin was, and found he was fully dead.

All this was done, I think, in about one half hour. I now expected that my father and husband, and all the rest of the men, were killed. I soon saw a party of the Indians coming, bringing my aunt Elizabeth Kellogg a prisoner, and some bloody scalps–among them I could distinguish that of my old grandfather, Elder John Parker, I knew it by the grey hairs. I had not yet seen my little James Pratt, and had almost entirely given him up, when at a great distance I discovered him. An Indian had him on his horse–he was crying, and calling for mother, oh mother! He was just able to lisp the name of mother, being only about eighteen months old. It appears that the Indians were nearly all engaged in plundering the houses; they cut open our bed ticks and threw out the feathers, so that the air was literally thick with them. I saw them bring out a great many of my father's books and medicines–many of the books was torn up, and many of the bottles of medicine were broken, but they carried on several bottles of the medicine for a few days. I had but few moments to reflect on matters and things, for they soon started back the same way they came up, and killed a great number of our cattle as they went along. They soon convinced me that I had no time to reflect on what was past, for they commenced whipping me in such a manner that the wounds and bruises were not well for some weeks, in fact my flesh was never clear of wounds from the lash, and bruises from clubs, etc. for thirteen months, and to undertake to narrate the sufferings I endured for the next ensuing twenty-one months, would be utterly impossible. I am confident it can be of no possible benefit to any person to read a full statement of their barbarous treatment, and I assure my sanguine reader that it is with feelings of deep regret that I think of it, much less to speak or write of it.

About midnight they halted, but there was not near so many Indians as there was at the Fort, for they had been dropping off all the evening. In fact I never knew how many there were, for there was many of the different tribes; Tywaconies [Tawakonis], Cadoes [Caddos], Keacheys [Kichais], Wakos [Wacos], Towash, some Beadies

140

[Bidais], and I have but little knowledge how many others. There was the Commanchees [Comanches] somewhere from six to seven hundred, they composed the strongest party.

They now tied a platted thong round my arms, and drew my hands behind me; they tied the thongs so tightly round my arms that the marks of them are to this day plainly seen. They then tied a similar thong round my ankles, and drew my feet and hands together, beating me over the head with their bows; they now turned me on my face, and I was unable to turn over, and it was with great difficulty that I could keep from smothering in my blood, for the wound they gave me with the hoe; and many others, was bleeding freely. I could hear my little James Pratt crying for mother, and I could easily hear the blows they gave him, and sometimes his feeble voice was weakened by the blows. I leave my reader to reflect what were my feelings.–Such horrid, indiscribable yelling–enough to terrify the hearts of sages—while dancing round the scalps; kicking and sometimes stomping the prisoners, who now amounted to five in number, viz: Elizabeth Kellog, widow, uncle Silas Parker's oldest daughter Synthia [Cynthia] Ann, aged about eleven; his oldest son John, aged about nine years; my little son James Pratt, and myself–In my heart, I tried to pray that the Great Being would so arrange things that I might once more hear the sweet music of the English language, instead of the horrid savage yells. They never allowed the prisoners to speak to one another.

Next morning we started on about a north course. They tied me every night, as before described, for five successive nights–and during the term of five days I never eat one mouth full of food, and was allowed but a very scanty allowance of water.–Still, notwithstanding my sufferings, I could not but admire the country. It is a beautiful faced country–prairie and timber.–I saw a great many fine springs. I think it was about sixty miles from the Fort to the cross timbers. This is a range of timbered land from the waters of the Arkansas, bearing a southwest direction, crossing False Washita, Red River, the heads of the Sabine,

Neches, Trinity, Brazos, Colorado, etc. Going on southwestward, this range of timber is of an irregular width, say from five to thirty-five miles wide, and is also diversified country, abounding with small prairies skirted with woodlands of various kinds of timber, Oaks of all kind, Ash, Hickory, Elm, Mulberry, Walnut, etc.: tho' there is more Post Oak on the high lands than any other kind of timber. It will be a densly populated country through the cross timber, and all south of it almost entirely to the Gulf of Mexico, still there is some exceptions, for in some places the prairies are too large, and in others they are too poor. The country, south of the large or grand prairie and north of the San Antonio road, (which is from one hundred to a hundred and fifty miles in breadth) is with few exceptions the best watered country perhaps known, and presents the greatest prospect of health, with an abundant quantity of good land to afford dense settlements;–in fact there are but very few prairies that are more than five or six miles across. The prairie land is generally either of a deep black sandy or a dark mulatto sandy soil. The woodland is not generally as rich as the prairie, except the bottom land which is generally very rich–mostly clay. The Colorado country, as well as some parts of the Brazos, abounds with Live Oak, and also the country along the coast.

The country south of the San Antonio road is not as well watered as that to the north, although there are some parts of the country where there is an abundance of water, for instance that part lying between the Brazos and Trinity, and between the Brazos and Colorado. There is an immense region of Pine timber east of the Brazos, and south of the San Antonio road, which is generally rather on the thin order, but it is thought to be a very healthy part of the country. Progressing still farther south, that is getting within fifty or sixty miles of the Gulf, the prairies become almost entirely level and very poor, except on the water courses, where the land is very rich, being the best sugar and cotton land known, still the upper country is more desirable and promises better health. Concluding all in a few words, Texas is calculated to suit the feelings or taste of all people, for they can find a section of country as cold as they desire, (even perpetual snows) or as warm as they may wish for, so that garden vegetables may be gathered in the dead of winter.

After we reached the grand prairie we turned more east, that is the party which I belonged to. My aunt Elizabeth [Kellogg] fell to the Keachies, and my nephew and niece [John Parker and his sister, Cynthia Ann Parker] to another portion of the Commanchees.[54]

The narrative continues as the Indians travel out of Texas, but this portion has given some idea of the first few hours of the captivity of Cynthia Ann Parker and others from Fort Parker. The story will resume in a later chapter with the recovery of Cynthia Ann by a party of rangers including Albert's son, Benjamin Franklin Gholson.

Fig. 10.8 - Inside the walls of the restored Fort Parker, 10 miles northwest of Groesbeck. Photo by Donna Gholson Cook, April 2002.

Fig. 10.9 - Fort Parker Cemetery. Photo by Donna Gholson Cook, April 2002.

While Samuel Gholson had a tendency to stretch the truth, history reveals that Albert did not inherit the trait. In fact, historical records reveal Albert's involvement in significant events that his sons apparently did not know about, or did not consider important enough to pass along. A certificate signed by Captain J. G. W. Pierson, formerly chief surveyor of Robertson's Colony, states that Albert G. Gholson was a member of his company from June 30, 1836 to July 30, 1836, when he was honorably discharged.[55] *The New Handbook of Texas* describes the activities of Captain Pierson's company during that time period.

Based on reports that the Mexican Congress had repudiated the agreements that Santa Anna had made with the ad interim government of Texas and that Gen. José de Urrea was organizing a large Mexican army to invade Texas, on June 20, 1836, ad interim president David G. Burnet issued a proclamation calling for volunteers to meet the enemy. On June 30 in Washington County Pierson organized a militia company of seventy-four men. He reported his company to Brig. Gen. Thomas Jefferson Green, whose brigade was at Coles Settlement on a campaign against the Indians. On the same day Pierson was commissioned a captain of cavalry, Green's Brigade, Army of the Republic of Texas, by Green and ordered to proceed to the main army near Victoria by way of the La Bahía Road and to provide security to the settlers and chastise any Indians that had committed depredations against them.[56]

A certificate signed by Captain Jno. N. Dyer states that A. G. Gholson was a private in his company, which was previously commanded by Capt. Thos. Robins, [*sic*] from July 30, 1836, until September 30, 1836, when he was honorably discharged at the headquarters of Cavalry Placedoris Ranch.[57] Albert was in the company when it was involved in the following engagement and was probably wounded, although it is not known to what extent he may have been wounded:

> CAPTAINS ROBINSON AND ROBBINS
> August, 1836, these two officers, belonging to the Texas army, under the command of General Thomas J. Rusk were ordered out in charge of a small force of men to reconnoiter the position of some Indians who were encamped on a little stream called Sandy. While engaged in carrying out this order, they were boldly attacked by a large body of Indians at night, who had surrounded them under cover of the darkness. The Texans stood their ground and defended themselves bravely until eight were killed and nearly all the rest wounded. There was but one out of the sixteen men that escaped unhurt. The Indians captured all their horses and camp equipage. The loss of these brave men at this juncture was severely felt, as it was during the time that the thirty thousand inhabitants of Texas were battling for life and liberty against eight millions of Mexicans, aided by their Indian allies, and the services of every man were needed.[58]

On January 26, 1838, Albert received Bounty Warrant 2115 for 320 acres in Walker County from the Secretary of War for service from June 30 to September 30, 1836.[59]

On September 5, while Albert was in Captain Robbins' company, an election was held to choose the president, vice president, and congress for the new Republic.[60] A list of voters containing the name of Albert G. Gholston [Gholson] and several other Robertson colonists at "Head Quarters Rosados Ranch," places the company on the Red River on September 5.[61] Sam Houston won his first term as president of the Republic in that election. Samuel Goldson [Gholson] is also listed as a voter in the same election, on another list with no location given, but it was possibly Nashville, Tenoxtitlán, or in the field with a Ranger

145

company. On the list with Samuel's name were George Morgan, George W. Morgan and James Coryell.[62] By the end of 1836, the new Texas legislature had passed several acts to authorize the formation of a battalion of mounted riflemen, a Regular Army, and militia units.[63]

> Any volunteer unit that furnished its own weapons, clothing, equipment and horses, or paid for these items out of the members' pay, was considered a ranger company. it was partially a matter of furnishing all equipment and partially a matter of the type of service: ranging the frontier, scouting, spying.[64]

Since the Gholsons and many other early Texans came from Kentucky and Tennessee, many of the early rangers used the Kentucky rifles they had brought to Texas.[65] Most rangers had at least one pistol[66] and the newly-invented Colt revolvers found their first market in Texas.[67] Each ranger also owned a large knife, which doubled as a weapon and camp tool.[68] Riding with the rangers was undoubtedly an exciting life for Albert Gholson and many other young men in early Texas.

> As the population increased and more and more single men came to Texas, there was a larger group of non-family young men to fill the ranger units, men for whom an Indian chase or turning back a Mexican raid was more exciting than farming. These were the natural fighters, but they were a relatively small part of the population. . . . Although there are countless examples of families fighting to the death to protect their homes, many driving off larger numbers of Indians, defending a house was not the same as being able to ride for days, track signs across endless prairies, then fight and survive.[69]

From the recollections of B. F. Gholson:

> When the Texas army disbanded my father returned home to what is now Falls county and engaged in farming and later in stock raising. He did not remain long in peace, however, for the Mexican Government encouraged the different tribes of Indians to depredate on the colonies. This

brought about the organization of Ranger companies in self
defense. Captain Tom Barron and my father, Albert G.
Gholson, organized a ranging Company under the authority
of the Republic of Texas, each of them holding the same
position as Captain and First Lieutenant that they had held
formerly in the army. This began in 1837 and they served
twelve months enlistment in the company, ending in
1838.[70]

There were good times and bad times in settler-Indian relations. There
were periods of relative peace and occasionally there were even friendly
interactions between them. A French physician visited Texas in 1838 and
wrote the following description after his encounter with a band of
Comanches:

While I was at San-Felipe-de-Austin, the arrival of some
hundred Comanche Indians was announced, they too
heading towards Houston to make a peace treaty. They rode
wild little horses called mustangs, and with their women
and children they formed a sizable caravan. A Texas officer
was serving as their guide. The Comanche tribe has
remained powerful; it is still feared in Texas, where
Spanish legends have given it a reputation for bravery and
ferocity which is all too accurate. These Indians halted on
the right and a short distance downstream from the town
right on the bank of the river. They all let their horses go,
and drove them out onto the prairie: their sole precaution
was to tie onto the more spirited of these animals long
leather nooses which hung down from their necks. The men
got out their pipes and began to smoke gravely, hardly
bothering to glance toward the town, and observing that
unbroken silence which is the salient trait of the Indians.
The women, as soon as they dismounted, ran to the river's
edge to cut some tree branches, which, when driven into the
ground, laced together, and covered by buffalo skins
(bison), served as tents. That of the old chieftain was the
first to be set up, somewhat removed from the location of
the others: it was the roomiest and the best constructed; this

task was in the hands of two women who apparently belonged to the old chief.

The Comanches are for the most part tall in stature; their skin is a deep red, and their hair is invariably jet black. Several, who appeared to me to be the leaders, let it grow very long, hanging halfway down their backs in tresses. Beautiful silver plaques two or three inches wide, placed at some distance one above the other, were attached to these tresses. The old chief had five of them.

Almost all these Indians had, just below the elbow, a large bracelet made of copper from which hung a great number of scalps, on some of which could still be seen traces of dark, dry blood. This copper band was replaced on some men by a roughly carved gold bracelet. One Indian of about twenty years of age wore above his elbow two such bands on which were suspended more than a dozen scalps, among which it was easy to distinguish the hair from heads other than Indians.

The braves were generally wrapped in large blankets dyed red or the color of wine dregs. Some wore buffalo skins with the hairy side turned inwards. All the squaws were without exception dressed in a sort of tight trousers made of tanned doe-skin and in a round jacket, often sleeveless, also doe-skin; some wore very roughly carved gold rings on their fingers. Almost all wore beaded necklaces, and it was obvious that spun-glass beads, either red or white, were especially popular with the Comanche maiden.

The children, the youngest of whom were at least six or seven years old, were usually nude. But of all these Indians, the one whose costume was the most bizarre was unquestionably the old chieftain. He wore a narrow red belt around the waist, a blue uniform with a red collar, the remains of epaulettes and metal buttons, the sort of uniform worn by our [French] National Guard or our infantry soldier, and a hat covered with oil-cloth like our postillions. This hat was a Mexican's whom he had killed a short time previously during a skirmish in the Rio-Grande Valley. Comanche life is little known to us. It is known that they are not farmers, and that, like certain South American tribes, they have learned how to train horses.

At first we had a great deal of trouble making these Indians understand us; only the young Texas officer spoke a few words of their tongue. Fortunately, there was among them a poor Mexican boy of about twelve years of age who could serve as interpreter. This child had been reared by the Comanches after the massacre of his family, and was their slave; he spoke their language very well and had not yet forgotten his own. I thought I noticed a certain musical quality in the Comanche language; its words are singularly complex and full of guttural sounds.

The old chief was aware of the potency of fire water, for one day when he was offered some, I saw him make a gesture to indicate that after having partaken of this dangerous potion one's head became heavy and one would fall into a deep slumber.[71]

While they were visiting Sam Houston, a treaty was signed on May 29, 1838, in one of Houston's futile attempts to protect the rights of the Comanches and the safety of the settlers.[72]

It is hard to believe that the band of Indians described above is the same group whose visit to Houston was described in the following newspaper article. The reporter who wrote the following article for the *Telegraph and Texas Register* did not share the French doctor's admiration of the Comanches. The truth must lie somewhere between the two descriptions.

A party of Comanches arrived in this city [Houston] on the afternoon of Saturday last [May 26, 1838]. As soon as their arrival was made known, our citizens were seen hastening in crowds to gaze upon the representatives of this formidable tribe which has for centuries been the scourge and terror of Mexico. All expected to meet a band of fierce, savage warriors, with sinewy limbs and gigantic frame, but what was their astonishment on arriving at the President's house, to behold probably about twenty-five diminutive, squalid, half-naked, poverty-stricken savages armed with bows and arrows and mounted on several horses and

149

mules! Every feeling of admiration was dispelled at once, and our citizens viewed them with mingled feelings of pity and contempt. They were received with great kindness by the President, and soon acquired a remarkable degree of confidence. The day after their arrival their squaws and children were scattered in all directions through the city, picking up old tin pans and the chippings of tin, glass bottles and similar rubbish, which they appeared to consider extremely valuable. They have evidently been less affected by the arts of civilized life than any other tribe within the limits of Texas. The Chief wore a Mexican hat, which he seemed to prize very highly. Judge Baker informed us that the hat was worn as a trophy; it had been captured from a Mexican officer, who had been killed by the chief a few months since. We imagine a formal treaty of peace has been ratified with them and [they] have merely visited our city from motives of curiosity. A number of presents were distributed to them on Wednesday, and on Thursday morning they set out on their return.[73]

On April 23, 1838, just before the Comanches visited Houston, Samuel Gholson and more than 150 other citizens of Robertson County signed a memorial to the Senate and House of Representatives of the Republic of Texas asking for protection from the Indians in the form of "a fiew pieces of Artillery one at least to each dens[e] settlement togather with some of the munitions of war . . ."[74] The signers of the memorial stated that they were "daily and hourly exposed to the mercy of the merciless Savages our Surveyors have been murdered togather with their hands and within the last 2 days one of our Neighbors was inhumanly butchered and his scalp born off in triumph by the Indians . . ."[75] An article in the *Texas Sentinel* reminded settlers not to leave their house without being armed:

A small party of about fifteen Indians recently attacked four or five men, who were at work on the plantation of Mr. CHILDERS, on Little river, and killed a young man named JAMES CHILDERS. That section has been the haunt of a small party of Indians for the last four years, as is well known; and yet it appears that these men were out at work *without arms.* We are surprised that our frontier settlers should be so foolishly rash as thus to expose themselves, unarmed, to the attacks of hostile savages. Had only two of these men been armed, the Indians probably would not have dared to make the attack. Settlers who thus reside directly in the hunting grounds of hostile Indians, should not venture even twenty rods from their houses, without arms. We know a settler who has resided nearly ten years on the very verge of the frontier, and yet has never suffered injury from his savage neighbors, for he has always been accustomed to carry a well loaded gun upon his shoulder whenever he went beyond the threshold of his cabin.[76]

In a letter from B. F. Gholson to his brother Sam, he wrote that in the fall of 1838 Albert was a member of the burial party for the seventeen surveyors killed by Indians in Navarro County.[77]

In the fall of 1838, twenty-four surveyors went out from Old Franklin to measure land in present Navarro County. They were led by Captain William F. Henderson and, after traveling by night to avoid Indians, they finally reached the area now called Spring Hill. Their purpose was to survey and locate land for settlers.

On the morning they were to start work, William Love discovered one of the compasses was out of order and agreed to return to Franklin with a Mr. Jackson to secure another. Before leaving, Love urged his companions to await his return before surveying and, in the meantime, to drive buffalo away from the area so Indians would follow them. The surveyors disregarded Love's suggestion, and started work while a band of Indians watched from a distant woodland.

Finally, the Kickapoos attacked and the surveyors took shelter in a ravine from which they fought until sundown, killing over twenty savages. In that time, too, the Americans lost twelve of their men. The battle continued on into darkness, and when the surveyors made their break from the ravine all but three were either killed or severely wounded.

The scene of the massacre was one of horror. Years later, survivors related the story of how seventeen of their number died, and their accounts were slightly different. William Henderson, who lived to become a famous lawyer; and Walter Lane a hero of the Battle of San Jacinto in 1836 and of Mexican wars, saw the holocaust differently; however both reports were of the bravery of the men of Old Franklin who fought so valiantly against impossible odds.

The battle occurred near the present town of Dawson and most of the Indians, numbering three hundred, were Kickapoos. They knew the surveyors would be followed by settlers who would drive their buffalo farther westward. They had assembled from distant places for winter meat and were determined to make their removal from their hunting ground costly.

The Indian attack started on a prairie and the surveyors took refuge in a ravine where they fought through the day and most of them died. In the thick of battle Euclid Cox, who had fought with Ben Milam in storming San Antonio in 1835, died a hero's death. Cox left the safety of the gully where his companions were pinned down and killed eight Indians with his pistol before a rifle ball struck him in the back. Mortally wounded, he asked James Barton, who survived the massacre, to take one of his dueling pistols to his wife and kept its twin to make his last defense. Cox continued to fight from an oak tree until he was clubbed to death.

John Violet, with his leg shattered, crawled eighteen miles through the woods to Tehuacana Springs and was not found for a week. Walter Lane was seriously wounded; and William Smith carried him from the ravine on his back as Indians fired at the survivors.

In the dark of night, the survivors made a break for a creek to the south and escaped by it to Tehuacana Springs, and back to Old Franklin. While William Love and Jackson were returning from Old Franklin, they came upon a band of Indians laying an ambush for the survivors and drove them away. Love then found Henderson and Smith carrying Lane in their arms and learned from them of the tragedy.

He carried the wounded Lane to Franklin and gathered a burial party to return to the scene of battle.

Arriving at Battle Creek, the men gathered the bodies which had been mutilated by vultures and wolves and buried them under an oak tree "so they would have morning sun and evening shade," according to one of the men in the burial party. Descendants of Euclid Cox erected a grave stone and fence to mark the place where the surveyors died. The monument is engraved as follows: "Sacred to the memory of our beloved dead, killed by Indians, October 8, A.D. 1838."

Among the dead at Battle Creek were Joseph Jones, Euclid Cox, Thomas Barton, Samuel Allen, Jim Heard, Asa Mitchell, William Tremier, Jim Bullock, Nathan Baker, Andy Houston, Dana Clark, James Neal, John Hand, John Ingraham, John David, Joseph Spikes, and William Smith. The survivors were Love, Jackson, Henderson, P. M. Jones, Lane, John Burton, and Violet.

The survivors returned to Old Franklin to mourn with the families of the dead. In later years, some of the men rose to high positions in the State and others suffered in their dangerous work. Walter Lane was a hero of Texas, Henderson a political power, and Jones was a respected citizen. William Love, one of the truly great men of early Texas, was killed in Navarro County in an argument growing out of conflicting land locations.

Soon after the tragedy at Battle Creek, George Washington Hill built a trading post at the spring where Franklin men were buried. William Love became Captain of the Robertson County Rangers stationed at Franklin. Albert Gholson, John Sherrod, Lee Davis, Charles Curtis, and W. L. Murry headed patrols to protect settlers. Hostilities did not end and Jose Maria, chief of the Anadarko Indians, came to central Texas to lead savages against white settlers. The tragedy of Bryant's defeat, in January, 1840, [correct date is 1839] where men from all parts of Robertson County died, added to the misery of families who prayed for peace.

But peace did not come, and the people at Old Franklin continued to fight for existence. Their ripened fields were burned in the fall and Indians raided their homes. Horses were stolen and no help came from the government.[78]

Albert Gholson married Elydia Anderson in December 1838, in a village named "Welch" which is now extinct.[79] Albert was twenty and Elydia was sixteen. After their marriage, they lived near the falls of the Brazos, not far from the Marlins and the Morgans. In January 1839, Indians attacked the homes of George Morgan and John Marlin. Forty-eight of the settlers, including Albert, decided to pursue and fight the Indians, rather than abandon their homes.

The Morgan Massacre and Bryant's Defeat

The year 1839 will long be remembered by all old Texans as one in which they were called upon to pass through many dangers, privations and hardships. The glorious victory gained by Texas heroes over the Mexican army upon the banks of San Jacinto, on April 21, 1836, failed to bring rest and security to the Texans. Marauding bands of Indians constantly raided the white settlements, and on every such occasion they stole and drove away the best horses of the settlers. In many instances the bow and arrow and tomahawk did their deadly work, and on other occasions women and children were carried away into a captivity worse than death. During this year many important battles were fought, among which may be mentioned that of Colonel John H. Moore with several hundred Comanches, which occurred above Austin, on the San Saba river, the battle of Brushy creek, in Travis county; the Flores and Cordova fights, and Bird's victory in Milam county. But the year opened with the Morgan massacre, the history of which we are about to narrate.

Many years ago, that veteran old Texan frontiersman and statesman, John Henry Brown, of Dallas, contributed to the current history of Texas a number of articles on the Indian wars and fights in Texas. The "Morgan Massacre" appeared among the number. The history of this sad tragedy, and that of the battle known as "Bryant's Defeat," will be given substantially in the language of Colonel Brown. We would here further remark that we are indebted to the same source for the accounts previously given in this book of the battles between the Cherokees and Wacos in 1829, and between the Cherokees and Tehuacanas in 1830, credit for which should have appeared in the proper place but for an oversight. But to the history of the Morgan massacre.

On the east side of the Brazos river, near the Falls, the families of the Morgans and Marlins lived, and with them the families of some of their married children. Some resided above and others below the present town of Marlin. There were a number of settlements on the river below Marlin for a distance of twenty miles, but above that place, with the exception of the families mentioned, the country at that time was an uninhabited wilderness–the time to which we refer was the winter of 1838-9. It was on Sunday night, the first day of January, 1839, that a portion of the families of James Marlin, Mrs. Jones and Jackson Morgan were passing the night together at the house of George Morgan, who lived at what is now called Morgan's Point, six miles above the town of Marlin. The remainder of the divided families were at the house of John Marlin, seven miles below the fort. John and James Marlin were brothers, the others of the same name were their children. A little after dark the house of George Morgan was suddenly attacked by Indians, who instantly rushed into the dwelling, thereby giving the inmates no time to prepare for defense. George Morgan and wife, their grandson, Jackson Jones, Mrs. Jackson Morgan, Miss Adeline Marlin, fifteen or sixteen years old, were all tomahawked and scalped in the house in a very few moments. Miss Stacy Ann Marlin, afterwards the wife of William Morgan, was severely wounded and left for dead. Three children were in the yard when the attack was made. One of them, Isaac Marlin, a child ten years of age, secreted himself behind the fence, and remained there undiscovered until the Indians had left. The other child, Wesley Jones, first ran to the house, but seeing

155

the red devils entering and tomahawking the inmates, he ran out unobserved by them, and was followed by Mary Marlin, another little child. They both escaped together. The young lady, before mentioned as having been severely wounded, retained her consciousness and feigned death. She was not scalped, but all the rest were. The Indians, after they had finished their bloody work, robbed the house of its contents, and then left. When the Indians departed, the little fellow, Isaac Marlin, who had secreted himself behind the fence, entered the house and felt the pulses of each one of the victims to ascertain if they were dead. His wounded sister, supposing him to be an Indian, remained motionless until he had left, when she crawled out. The little boy Isaac then took the path leading to John Marlin's, and ran the distance, seven miles, in a very short time–a swift messenger of death to his kindred there assembled.

Wesley Jones and Mary Marlin, the two little children before mentioned as having made their escape, did not reach Mr. Marlin's house until daylight the next morning, and the wounded Miss Marlin not until noon the next day. John Marlin, his brother James, William and Wilson Marlin, Jackson and George W. Morgan and Albert G. Gholson, after they were told of the terrible massacre by the little boy Isaac, hastened to the scene and found the facts to be as he had stated. The next day a great many came from the lower settlements to their assistance, and the dead were consigned to their graves amid the wailing of their grief-stricken relatives and friends. Ten days later, being the tenth day of January, the Indians, seventy in number, attacked the house of John Marlin and his son Benjamin (the surviving family of the latter are now residents of Milam county). Garrett Menifee and his son Thomas were present also when the Indians made their attack. They killed seven of the Indians and wounded others, without receiving any injury themselves. The Indians, not particularly relishing such a "friendly" reception, withdrew.

When the attack was made Menifee's negro man, Hinchey, was at work a short distance from the house and "put out" for the settlements below at "double quick." He ran twenty-five miles, and reached his destination in less time than a good horse could have traveled the same distance–in fact, as he admitted himself, Hinchey was badly scared. He reported the attack that was being made upon Mr. Marlin's house, and a company was soon raised and started to the assistance of the besieged party, but before they reached the place the Indians had left.

After some discussion upon the subject, those who were present came to the conclusion that they must either pursue and fight the Indians or abandon their homes and fall back to the lower settlements for safety. They chose the former alternative, and made their preparations accordingly. Their effective force available for pursuit was forty-eight men.

Benjamin Bryant, of Bryant's Station, whose surviving family now reside in Milam county, was called to the command. The next morning he and his company took the trail of the Indians and followed it until it struck the Brazos river near Morgan's Point. They crossed the river at that place, and on the west side they found a deserted camp which the red devils had but recently left. About a mile from this camp they came upon a fresh trail bearing in towards the river and followed it. They counted sixty-four fresh horse tracks upon the trail besides the moccasin tracks of a great number of foot Indians. They crossed the river where the trail entered it, and just as they did so they observed a smoke rising up from the prairie which was on fire, and supposing the Indians had fired Mr. John Marlin's house, they hastened down there with all the speed they could make. As the day was far advanced when they discovered their mistake, they halted and encamped for the night. The next morning, January 16, they started again and found that the Indians had been at the deserted houses two miles above and had plundered them. They then traveled on six miles further to Morgan's Point, where they discovered the Indians in the open post oak woods near a dry ravine.

The noted chief, Jose Maria, who was riding in front in perfect nonchalance, when he saw Bryant and his men coming, slowly rode back to the rear where he halted, pulled off his gauntlets, and taking deliberate aim, fired at Joseph Boren, cutting his coat sleeve. Jose Maria gave the signal for battle, and the action commenced. Captain Bryant ordered a charge, which was gallantly made, and in which he was wounded, and the command was transferred to Mr. Ethan Stroud. The Indians fired one volley at the Texans when they charged, and then fell back into a ravine. Before they did so, however, David W. Campbell fired at Chief Jose Maria, the ball striking him in the breast, but not wounding him seriously. At the same time Albert Gholson fired at the chief and killed the horse he was riding. The Texans followed the Indians to the ravine and fired upon them from the bank. The Indians then commenced retreating down the ravine in order to reach some timber known as the "River Bottom," and as soon as the Texans perceived the movement, a number flanked around and got into the ravine below them to hold them in check, which caused the Indians to fall back again to their original position. By this time the Texans had come to the conclusion that they had won the day, and in consequence they became careless and scattered about in all directions, every man acting as his own captain and fighting on his own hook.

The shrewd old Indian chief, observing this state of affairs, suddenly sprang from the ravine at the head of his men and opened a terrible and unexpected fire upon them. This threw the Texans into some confusion, and their commander seeing how matters stood, ordered his men to retreat to a point some two hundred yards distant where he intended to re-form them, and then charge the enemy again. He also desired by this move to draw the Indians some distance from the ravine, so that when he charged them again they could not easily avail themselves of its shelter.

This order, owing to prevailing confusion, was understood by many to mean an unqualified retreat, and a sudden panic seized upon the men. Taking advantage of their disorder, the wily old chief at the head of his men charged furiously upon the Texans, at the same time making the welkin ring with their demoniac yells. Several of the Texans were killed at the first onset, the rest were demoralized and the rout soon became general, and they were hotly pursued by the Indians for four miles. In this retreat ten men were killed and five wounded. All who were killed fell within one and one-half miles of the battle ground–the most of them being dismounted within half a mile. Plummer, Ward and Barton were killed at the ravine before the retreat began. Some individual acts of heroism and bravery deserve especial mention. David W. Campbell, not hearing the order to retreat, was about being surrounded by the Indians when the brave Captain Eli Chandler, who was mounted, rushed to his rescue and took him up behind him. Young Jackson Powers, having lost his horse, mounted on a pony behind William McGrew, and at the same moment his arm was broken by a bullet. Shortly afterwards his brother, mounted on a large horse, came up with him, who told him to leave the pony and get up behind him. He sprang from the pony with the intention of complying with his brother's request, but owing to the plunging of the horse and his own inability to mount quickly, because of his broken arm, the Indians came up with them before he succeeded in doing so. His brother defended him to the last, but when he saw him fall dead, he put spurs to his horse and escaped. William N. P. Marlin was severely wounded in the hip before the retreat began and was unable to mount his horse. David Cobb ran to him and lifted him on his horse at the imminent risk of his own life.

Wilson Reed, a daring young fellow, was knocked from his horse during the retreat by coming in contact with a tree. The Indians were close upon him, coming at full speed, yelling and brandishing their tomahawks, when he cried out: "Oh Lord, boys, Mary Ann is a widow;" but just then some one came riding by, took him up and bore him off unhurt.

The Indians lost about as many in this affair as the Texans although the latter were driven from the field. They were greatly elated by their double victory in that neighborhood, and became more daring than ever until checked by a signal defeat near Little river, known as "Bird's Victory."

The names of those who participated in the battle just described were as follows: A. J. Powers, Washington McGrew, _____ Ward, Armstrong Barton, _____ Plummer, Alfred Eaton, Hugh A. Henry, William Fullerton, A. J. Webb, _____ Doss, Charles Solls (or Salls), William N. P. Marlin, _____ Bryant, G. W. Morgan, Enoch M. Jones, John R. Henry, Lewis B. And William C. Powers, Henry Haigwood, Eli Chandler, Ethan Stroud, Joseph Boren, William McGrew, Andrew McMillan, Clay and David Cobb, Richard Teel, Albert G. Gholson, Michael Castleman, Wilson Reed (brother of William and Jeff Reed of Bell county and uncle of Volney Reed of Milam county), Wiley Carter, John Welsh, Britton Dawson, R. H. Mathews, David W. Campbell, Nathan Campbell, _____Smith, Jeremiah McDaniel, Walter Campbell, William Henry, Hugh Henry, John Marlin, Wilson Marlin, Joseph McCandless, John Tucker, Thomas Duncan (then a mere boy and afterwards a citizen of Bell county. He was mysteriously murdered about the close of the war), and one other whose name is not remembered. In the charge and retreat, the ten first names of the company in the preceding list were killed, and the next five were wounded. All who were killed fell within one and a half miles of the battle ground, the most of them within half a mile, being overtaken on foot. Plummer, Ward and Barton were killed at the ravine.

Jose Maria, so long the dread of the frontier, but afterwards the most pacific and civilized chief on the government reserve, has always acknowledged that he was whipped and retreating, until he observed the panic and confusion among the Texans. There is scarcely any doubt at all that if the Texans had observed the order of their commander to fall back to the designated point and there rallied that they would have gained a complete victory over the Indians, and probably the old chief himself would not have lived to tell the story of that disastrous fight.

Jose Maria visited Bryant's station years afterwards and offered Bryant his pipe to smoke. Bryant insisted that Jose Maria should smoke first as he had won the fight, and the old chief proudly followed the suggestion.[80]

Fig. 10.10 - The author and her father, Conner W. Gholson, great-grandson of Albert G. Gholson, at Indian Battlefield monument, State Highway 6, 4.5 miles south of Marlin. Inscription on monument reads, "At this site, near the pioneer home of George Morgan, a battle took place, January 16, 1839, between settlers in this region and Indians under Chief Jose Maria in which the colonists were defeated. A treaty with these Indians made soon after brought comparative peace to this region." Photo by Kristin Legaspi, January 2000.

The Army Papers in the Texas State Archives lists A. G. Golston, 2nd Lt under Capt. Nimrod Doyle in the Robertson County Volunteer Rangers from March 8, 1839 to June 10, 1839.[81] The Ranger Muster Roll in the Texas State Archives also lists Albert's father Samuel (Golston) as a private in the same company for the same period.[82] Samuel was sixty-seven years old at the time.

When Mirabeau Buonaparte Lamar became President of the Texas Republic in 1838, he announced as his goal "the extinction or total expulsion of all Indians." Under a new law, 800 men were enlisted to protect the frontier and eight ranger companies were organized. In January, 1839, William Love was elected captain of the Robertson County Rangers. The company served until 1840 and was then disbanded for lack of funds. Albert Gholson, John Sherrod, Lee Davis, Charles Curtis, and W. L. Murry served under Love.[83]

Chapter 11: Texas Becomes a State—Restless Years

Samuel Gholson d. 1852
Albert Gholson d. 1860

~ Statehood - 1845 ~

Sam Houston became a popular favorite after the victory at San Jacinto, and in September 1836 he defeated Henry Smith and Stephen F. Austin in a presidential election. In the same election, a proposal was approved to request annexation to the United States, but Andrew Jackson, who was the United States president at the time, was not interested. Although Houston did not achieve his goal of annexation in his first term, he did acquire a trade treaty with Great Britain and recognition as a nation by several other European countries. Under the new constitution, Houston was only able to serve one term of two years, but he was returned to office in 1841 after one term served by Mirabeau B. Lamar, who was opposed to annexation. Finally, near the end of Houston's second term, the United States became interested in annexing Texas, mainly to eliminate a rival on the same continent with strong foreign ties. The annexation was finalized on December 29, 1845, under Anson Jones, president of the republic, and soon after the entry of Texas into the United States, the Mexican War began. The fighting was mostly south of the Rio Grande and involved about 5,000 Texans. The war ended in March 1847 when General Winfield Scott captured Mexico City and the Rio Grande became the international boundary as a result of the Treaty of Guadalupe Hidalgo, signed on February 2, 1848.[1]

~ Samuel ~

Samuel Gholson made at least one trip back to Tennessee after moving to Texas, as evidenced by a deed he signed to Sterling C. Robertson in Nashville, Tennessee on October 2, 1835,[2] the same day that his seventeen-year-old son Albert was fighting with other Texans in the first engagement of the war for independence, the Battle of Gonzales. Samuel may have accompanied Robertson on a trip to the United States to recruit more colonists and to enlist aid in the fight for Texas independence.[3] On September 4, 1837, Samuel was in Nashville, Milam County, Texas, where he voted for a representative in the General Congress of the Republic.[4] [Robertson County was established on December 14, 1837, from portions of Milam, Bexar, and Nacogdoches counties.] He was in Robertson County in 1838-9[5] and by 1840 he had moved to Harrison County, Texas.[6] According to an instrument signed by his heirs after his death, Samuel lived in Wood County at the time of his death on July 4, 1852. He had a first cousin who was a doctor living in Wood County in 1852, Dr. Jacob Johnston Gholson,[7] so it is possible that he went to seek medical treatment from his cousin.

Although Samuel may have been somewhat more law abiding after his move to Texas at age sixty, he was tried and convicted in Harrison County by the Republic of Texas for card playing in 1845 at age seventy-three, along with seven others.[8] The laws against gambling had been passed a few years earlier, but apparently the Texans paid very little attention to them.

> Anti-gambling laws passed in 1837 and 1840 did little to discourage chance-taking at the card table. A few months after passage of the second law, a Houston newspaper (whose editors were not among the town's righteous elements) gleefully commented on the ineffectuality of the new law:
>> Since the law for the suppression of gambling has passed, we have seen more card playing than ever.—New games have been instituted and old ones revived. The Texians play at *rounders;* the Frenchmen at *vingt-et-un*; the Mexican at *monte*; the Kentuckian, Mississippian and Tennesseean at *poker*; the Dutch at *euchre*; the sons of Erin at *forty-fives*; and the negroes at *old sledge*. They all *cut* and *shuffle* to get rid of paying the liquor bill, for now that we have to pay 50cts per glass it takes but a few to spoil a V or an X. We hope congress will take this matter into consideration and repeal

a part or the whole of it. Houston *Weekly Times*, April 30, 1840.[9]

It is not clear at what point Samuel and his wife Mary Ann parted company, but a few years after coming to Texas, Samuel was described as having "no family except a grown son,"[10] so Mary Ann apparently did not accompany her husband and son Albert to Texas in 1832. She may have considered this abandonment and remarried in Tennessee, as the marriage records for Madison County, Tennessee reflect a marriage between Mary Ann Gholson and William Carson on December 10, 1839.[11] Nevertheless, she eventually wound up in Texas and was living with Albert's family in 1850, according to the census records of Limestone County.[12] Many wives did not accompany their husbands to Texas but followed them several years later, after they had some time to establish a homestead. Often, to their dismay, they found that the husband had remarried. Did Mary Ann fall into that category?

No record was found to indicate that Samuel and Mary Ann were ever divorced, but he was married a second time, to Sarah Bullock on August 9, 1841, in Harrison County.[13] Sarah died within a year, and Samuel married a third time on August 21, 1842, at age seventy, to Brittanna Cannon, born in Delaware.[14] There are many similarities between Brittanna and the daughter of a famous pirate in the Chesapeake Bay area, and several researchers are attempting to establish that she was that daughter. Like many others, Brittanna may have moved to Texas to escape her past, change her identity, and build a new life. The Republic of Texas Poll Lists for 1846 have a Brittanna Gholson listed in Harrison County, but Samuel is not listed.[15] The 1850 census for Harrison County shows the following:

> #698 Farmer ($500)
> S. Gholston,   71 m Va [should be 78]
> "B"   50 f Del
> #699
> C. T. Fields   26 f Del
> J.   12 m Ark
> W. C. Fields   6 m Tex
> J. W. Cannon (Farmer) 19 m Fla[16]

Also in the Harrison County census for 1850 is H. E. Cannon, age 53, possibly Brittanna's brother, with his family.[17] Samuel and Brittanna were together at the time of the 1850 census, but it is uncertain whether she was still with him when he died on July 4, 1852, at age eighty, in Wood County. A document that was signed by Mary Gholson as Samuel's widow would at the very least cast doubt upon the legality of Samuel's second and third marriages.[18]

~ Albert ~

Albert Gholson's first wife, Elydia, was born September 22, 1822, in Blue Ash, Missouri, the daughter of William Anderson, who brought his family to Texas in 1832.[19] Albert and Elydia were married in December 1838, and their first child was Samuel Sullivan, born November 13, 1840. The second was Benjamin Franklin, born November 17, 1842.[20] Both were born in Robertson's Colony, near the lower line of what is now Falls County.

In 1843, because of Indian troubles and family sickness, probably Elydia's, Albert moved to Harrison County. They may have lived with Samuel for the short time they were there. Elydia's health apparently did not improve, and it was not long until Albert moved the family to Limestone County,[21] where his young wife died near old Springfield in September 1843 and was buried in Stroud Cemetery.[22]

Elydia was only twenty-one when she died, leaving Albert a very young widower with two very young sons, ages three and one. The exact cause of her death is not known, but the fact that Albert had moved several times due to family illness[23] may have indicated that she suffered from malaria, with its miserable chills and fever. Families often moved to a different climate in an attempt to improve the health of the afflicted members.

Although malarial fevers were expected every summer, certain years brought more sickness than others. The summer and fall of 1843 were particularly difficult for the settlers along the Brazos, Guadalupe, Colorado, and Trinity rivers, and even the Indians were reported to be seriously afflicted. In August, 1843, Samuel A. Maverick wrote from La Grange that his "eldest son & eldest daughter have been at the point of death from the billious fever which has this year in consequence of heavy & constant rains prevailed here (on the Colorado) to an extent which has never been known before since the first settlement." [Maverick to R. N. Wier, August 15, 1843] "Bilious" fevers were thought to cause excessive secretions of bile and were extremely dangerous.[24]

The most common treatment for malaria involved the traditional "puke, purge, and bleeding"—heroic treatments which were supposed to reduce "irregular or convulsive wrong action" by "depletion" but actually sometimes killed the patient or often left him so debilitated that he fell victim to other diseases.[25]

After the death of Elydia, details of some of Albert's activities were related by his son Benjamin Franklin:

> After the death of Elydia (Anderson) Gholson, Albert G. Gholson moved to what was then known as "Blue Ridge," and located his headright which he had obtained from his service to Texas in the army. This was in what was later Falls County, Texas, in present-day Stranger. When Falls County was organized, [1850] Wilburn Jones had opened a store where Stranger now is, and it was known as "Jones' Store." Three places were voted for as possible county seats: site of Jones' Store as one; Adams Spring, as another (later renamed Marlin); and old Bucksnort as the third possible site. Adams Spring received the majority vote, was selected as the county seat, and renamed Marlin.[26]

In 1846[27] Albert married Mary Matthews [Mathis] in Harrison County and three children were born of that marriage, Eliza Jane, born 1847 in Falls County; Oakley, born 1849 in Falls County; and James P., born 1859 in Coryell County.[28] Albert and his wife Mary and their children are shown in the 1850 census for Limestone County, apparently living with or near his mother Mary.[29]

> GOLSTON, A. G., 33, m, farmer, b. Ky. 4,000. 371
> ", Mary A., 26, f, b. Mo.
> 1. " , Samuell G., 10, m, student w/in year, b. Tex.
> 2. " , Benjamin J. (or T.?), 8, m, b. Tex.

     3. " , Eliza J., 3, f, b. Tex
     4. " , Oakley, 1, m, b. Tex.
     GOLSTON, Mary, 66, f, b. Va.   500.   371[30]

In August 1850, Albert signed the petition protesting the selection of Viesca as the county seat of Falls County.[31]

> The falls of the Brazos gave the county its name. Since Falls County was established its boundaries have not changed. The legislature stipulated that Viesca would be the county seat, but the citizens petitioned for another location because most of the residents lived east of the Brazos River. The citizens voted 20-0 in favor of Adams, which officially became the county seat on January 30, 1851. Soon after, the town was renamed Marlin in honor of the Marlin family.[32]

For the next several years, Albert's life continued on an erratic path filled with ups and downs:

- Albert served as a juror in Falls County in February 1851 and in March he was one of two justices of the peace elected for precinct three.[33] "Under the Constitution of the Republic of Texas and the constitutions of 1845 and 1861, two justices of the peace were elected biennially from each militia captain's precinct."[34]
- In May 1851, the Commissioner's Court

> provided that 640 acres be set aside for the county cite, the Court House square to be 120 yards square with the streets 60 ft. wide running N & S, E & W. A. G. GHOLSON, H. B. COLMAN, Grandvill ROSE, G. W. MORGAN & Allensworth ADAMS were appointed as reviewers for road leading from this place by the nearest and best route to Springfield.[35]

- In 1851, he sold his land on Blue Ridge and moved to the west side of the Brazos, buying out Squire Meeks.[36]
- On April 22, 1852, in Falls County, The State of Texas charged Albert with two counts of assault with intent to kill two men named Jackson

Williams and Jefferson Matthews. The case was continued for several terms and finally dismissed on May 10, 1854, because of the failure of the witnesses to appear to testify. It is possible that they were in Falls County for only a brief period, as no other references to these two men were found in the county.[37]

- In November 1852, Albert sold the Meeks land and moved to an area north of Waco between the Brazos and Aquilla rivers, where he established a ranch and the town of Gholson still bears his name.[38]

Fig. 11.1 - Photo by Kristin Legaspi, January 2000.

GHOLSON, TEXAS (McLennan County). Gholson is at the intersection of Farm roads 933 and 1858, twelve miles northwest of Waco in northern McLennan County. The area was settled in the late 1840s, and the community that developed there was called Sardis. Its first school was built in 1854 [the student body probably included Albert's sons, Samuel and Benjamin Franklin]. A post office was established in January 1858, with John S. Bell as postmaster, but it was discontinued shortly after the Civil War. Among the early settlers had been the Gholson

169

brothers, Benjamin and Samuel, and the community gradually came to be called Gholson. . . .[39]

On June 12, 1855, Albert moved to what is now Mills County, establishing the first ranch with a good stock of cattle and horses on North Simms Creek at Blue Water Hole.[40] Around 1856-1858, Albert was a neighbor of David Morris, Sr. and family on Simms Creek. Andrew (Andy) Morris, the brother of David, Jr. was a participant in several events with B.F. Gholson which will be described in a later chapter.[41] David Morris, Jr. described Mills County in 1858:

> At this time, Mills County was a beautiful country, with an abundance of grass as high as a horse's back, flocks and flocks of wild turkeys, herds of buffalo, lots of deer, antelopes and bears, and other wild game too numerous to mention. There were also lots of bees and an abundance of honey to be found in the trees. The Indians became so hostile the settlers were in danger of losing their lives at any time and without warning. By the "light of the moon" the Indians would steal the horses and kill the cattle until it was a hard struggle for the settlers to make any more than a living. They could get a tract of 160 acres of land by filing on it and living there for three years and it became theirs, but were only allowed one homestead in this manner.
>
> The nearest mill was Straws Mill, which was about ten miles below where the town of Gatesville is now located.
>
> Lampasas was the nearest post office which was 30 miles away. If the settlers got their mail once a month they thought they were lucky.
>
> The settlements were mostly on rivers, creeks, or near springs. There was no water at other places as there were no wells drilled at that time.
>
> There were no cotton gins, no schools or churches. The wheat was cut with cradles and threshed by tramping it on the ground with horses and winding it out by hand and hauling it to the mill. The settlers had a hard time, but they blazed the trail to what was once one of the garden spots of the U.S.[42]

Fig. 11.2 - Low water crossing near the location of Albert Gholson's Blue Water Hole Ranch, the first ranch on North Simms Creek in Mills County, Texas. Photo by Donna Gholson Cook, March 2001.

On September 28, 1856, while Albert lived in Mills County, the Falls County Tax Collector sold 2214 acres he owned on the east side of the Little Brazos because of his failure to pay his 1853 taxes in the ridiculously small sum of $3.64.[43] The stay in Mills County was not a long one, because Indian raids made it necessary for Albert to move his family again, this time to Coryell County.

In March 1857, the Kiowas and Comanche Indians began their depredations on the frontier of Texas, and war was waged by them on a systematic plan for several hundred "moons." [Albert] Gholson knew, from his past experiences of Indian troubles in his early life, that it was necessary to move his herd of horses and the family and slaves to a safer place. He bought a farm in the lower part of Coryell County, on Owl Creek. Moved his family, stock, and slaves to that place and remained there the remainder of his life.[44]

Albert moved back east to Coryell County in August 1858 and lived only two more years. He died at age forty-two on June 10, 1860, after being shot by a neighbor, William Oakes[45] "down on Henson Creek, at the old John Farmer Spring."[46] He was buried on his farm on Owl Creek in Coryell County.[47] He left a widow and three young children in addition to his older sons, twenty-year-old Samuel Sullivan and Benjamin Franklin, just under eighteen, who had been on their own for a while. His youngest son, James, was born after the family moved to Coryell County and was only seventeen months old when his father died.

A search of records did not reveal the exact circumstances of the shooting, but did reveal some information about William Oakes. The following was taken from the Coryell County, Texas, 1860 Census and Mortality Schedule:

> Schedule 1 - Free Inhabitants in Owl Creek Beat in the County of Coryell, State of Texas, enumerated by me on the 16th day of July 1860, post office: Henson Creek, R. P. KNOWLES, Assistant Marshal, written page 38, stamped page 282R
> 252-252   OAKES, William, 30, male, herdsman,
> $1000/$1000, Kentucky
> Ellen, 19, female, Kentucky
> Mary, 4/12, female, Texas
> [Born 4-12?]
> Schedule 1 - Free Inhabitants in Owl Creek Beat in the County of Coryell, State of Texas, enumerated by me on the 18th day of July 1860,* post office: Henson Creek, R. P. KNOWLES, Assistant Marshal, written page 39, stamped page 283
> [*The actual counting must have been done prior to June 10, 1860, the day William Oakes killed Albert Gholson. Albert's financial status far exceeded that of any of his neighbors.]
>
> 255-255 GHOLSTON, A. G., 40, male, herdsman,
> $10000/$7200, Tennessee

172

Mary A., 34, female, Missouri
S.G., 19, male, waggoner, Texas
Ben F., 17, male, herdsman, Texas
Eliza, 13, female, Texas
Oakley, 11, male, Texas
James, 1, male, Texas[48]

A biography of William E. Oakes resembles the family of Albert's neighbor so closely that it would be difficult to argue that this is not the same William Oakes.

> William E. Oakes, b 1829 in Tennessee, d 1868 in Texas—was a son of Charles and Susan (Neal) Oakes of Tennessee who moved to Texas in 1845. William E. Oakes married Eleanor Turney—a daughter of Moses Turney—and they had a daughter, Mary Susan, b ca 1860 in Texas, who married James Clark, b 1849 in Mississippi—who was a younger brother to the man who in 1869 became her stepfather.
> William E. Oakes enlisted in the Union Army during the Civil War, in 1863, and raised a company known as Company B, 2nd Cavalry Regiment. He killed the enrollment officer, and escaped into Mexico where he raised another Union Company of Texas, and served as its Captain until the end of that war. He was subsequently appointed, in post-Civil War Texas, as a Delegate to the State Convention. After his death in 1868, his widow, Eleanor (Turney) Oakes, married July 28, 1869 to John Clark, b 1841 in Mississippi—becoming a stepfather to Mary Susan ("Sue") Oakes, who was to be his sister-in-law a few years later.
> The Clarks moved to Brown County, Texas.[49]

It is interesting to note Oakes' later appointment as a Delegate to the State Convention.

After Albert's death on June 10, 1860, there were many entries in the Probate Minutes of Coryell County, including the appointment of William F. Lemmon as administrator and the issuance of letters of guardianship for his children. The older sons, Sam and Frank, asked the court to appoint

John E. Everett as their guardian. His wife, Mary A. Gholson, was appointed as guardian for her children, Eliza J., Oakley, and James.[50]

Albert's estate included 3,524 acres of land, 108 head of cattle, eighteen horses, forty-five hogs, three yoke oxen, two wagons, a surveyor's compass and chain, and four slaves. A claim against the estate was presented by William Oakes for $30, dated February 1860. Did William shoot Albert because of the $30 Albert owed him? Another claim against the estate was presented by Drs. Embry and Bradford for $16.00, dated June 26th, 1860, most likely the doctors who treated Albert after he was shot.[51]

Appraisers were appointed in McLennan, Erath, and Hamilton Counties, the latter being Albert's former neighbor David Morris.[52] Another appraiser, John Farmer, owned the property on which Albert was shot.[53] On September 29, 1860, the appraisers of Albert's estate reported the following property in Coryell County:

Stock Cattle 108 head at 6$	$648.00
Horses 18 head at 65$	1170.00
1 Jack	50.00
3 Yoke oxen 50$	150.00
2 Waggons 60$	120.00
3 log chains 1.50	4.50
320 acres of land on Owl Creek	1500.00
1 negro woman & child	1500.00
45 head hogs 1.50	67.50
	$5210.00

In addition to the above, Albert owned 620 acres in Hamilton County, 2094 acres in Erath County, and 490 acres in McLennan County.[54]

A sale of personal property of Albert's estate on October 18, 1860, listed the following:

70 head of stock cattle,	J. E. Everett, $5.00	$350.00
63 head of " "	J. E. Everett, 7.00	441.00
1 yoak oxen	W. S. Dotson	40.00
1 " "	W. D. Coats	60.00
1 old steer	J. E. Everett	25.00
1 " "	Mary A. Gholson	17.00
1 Bay Horse	J. E. Everett	77.00

1 2 year old colt	Nathan Miligan	84.00
1 Black mare	J. E. Everett	50.00
1 Black mare and colt	J. E. Everett	81.00
1 year old filly	J. E. Everett	35.00
1 3 year old filly Bay	Nathan Miligan	150.00
1 3 year old sorral colt	J. E. Everett	70.00
1 2 year old black colt	J. E. Everett	41.00
1 3 year old black colt	J. E. Everett	75.50
1 bay mare & colt	J. E. Everett	107.50
1 bay mare & colt	J. E. Everett	176.00
1 Jack	John Castle	40.00
1 bay mare & 2 colts	J. E. Everett	150.00
1 Road Waggon	J. E. Everett	51.50
1 " Waggon	J. E. Everett	46.00
3 log chains	J. E. Everett	3.00
1 P____ Plough	J. A. Haynes	13.50
1 Surveyor's Compass & chain	Mary A. Gholson	21.00[55]

On January 28, 1861, the inventory by John E. Everett, Guardian of the estate of Sam and Frank Gholson, was received and recorded in the minutes of the probate court of Coryell County, consisting of 134 head of stock cattle at $6 for a total of $804.00. In 1862 Samuel became of legal age, and the guardian was directed to turn his property over to him. Samuel replaced Everett as guardian of his brother Frank.[56]

In a property sale of the Estate of A. G. Gholston [Gholson] Deceased on the 5th day of August, 1861, the following were sold:

D. W. Louyers[?] 3 cows & calves	$ 32.50
S. S. Gholston 31 head cattle at 6$ =	186.00
M. P. Knowles 1 beef steer	20.00
M. P. Knowles 1 do do	19.00
F. W. Fauntleroy 1 " "	7.75
S. S. Gholston 1 yok Oxen	51.00
F. W. Fauntleroy 1 stag	5.00
F. W. Fauntleroy 1 horse	75.00
B. F. Gholston 1 horse	70.50[57]

Chapter 12: Texas Rangers and Indians

Benjamin Franklin Gholson, 1858-1862

Frank was not quite a year old when his mother died, and his father married again when he was four. By the time he was eight, he had learned to ride a horse, and the following spring he was allowed to go on cow hunts with his father and older brother Sam and neighboring ranchers. The term "roundups" did not come into use until much later—at that time, they were cow hunts. During Frank's early years, the family ranch was at Blue Ridge near the present location of Stranger, later known as the Moffett Place. He was allowed to accompany his father on some of his freight-hauling trips to Houston, and he fondly recalled those trips as the beginning of his "camp life."[1]

> Supplies were hauled from Houston to that country [Falls County] in ox wagons. My father having three big teams, Tom Welch owning two big teams. Tom Welch made a business of hauling and kept my father's and his teams together on these trips. I was allowed to go on these trips occasionally.[2]

William Ransom Hogan described this slow but dependable method of moving freight in the early days:

> A large portion of the commerce of the Republic was carried by freight wagons, usually drawn by three to eight yoke of oxen or less often by horses or mules. The use of oxen had several advantages: their hoofs did not sink into the mud as readily as those of horses and mules; the purchase price of a yoke of oxen was about forty to fifty dollars [in 1846] compared with a figure at least three or four times as high for a pair of draft horses; and the oxen could subsist almost entirely on the prairie grass. Therefore, oxen-drawn wagons carried produce from the interior to markets and seaports and returned with goods and

176

provisions, a trip that required many weeks, or even months. A load for several yoke was three thousand to five thousand pounds, which could be transported at a rate of ten to fifteen miles per day in dry weather. If the streams were swollen by rains, progress was halted for days. Under such conditions, several "freighters" generally traveled together for mutual protection and assistance; by co-operating, teams could be doubled or goods lightened in crossing miry places and watercourses—all of which was accompanied by lurid swearing to which the oxen seemed to respond better than to whipping.[3]

Houston became the most important center of the freighting business because of the location of the capital there and the town's accessibility to water communication with Galveston Harbor. Trade with the Brazos River cotton-growing areas quickly sprang up, and the city became a "commercial mart" with a population variously estimated at two to three thousand souls. By 1840-41 the streets of Houston frequently were crowded with wagons being loaded to carry merchandise inland. In November, 1841, Josiah Gregg found that the town "has a brisk trade supporting from a dozen to 20 dry goods stores. It has indeed several tolerably extensive foreign importing houses." During the two following years the volume of trade lessened because of partial crop failures, river-boat competition, and bad roads. But early in April, 1844, the local press noticed "that the commerce of this city, which has been languishing to an unprecedented extent for the last two years is slowly and steadily reviving," and on May 22 that approximately a thousand bales of cotton had been brought into Houston in the preceding three weeks. A part of the explanation of the revival of trade, according to the editor, was that many wrecks and accidents had occurred in transporting cotton by river boat; two Brazos River steamboats had sunk in the preceding winter.[4]

As he tagged along with his father, Frank met many men who played important roles in early Texas.

I knew Sam Houston when I was a small boy. I have met Thos. Rusk a few times. I have known Gen. Ed Burleson. A few old pioneer preachers I have known were Z. N. Morel, [Morrell] I have heard him preach when I was a small boy also Sam Blaine, Hugh M. Childress. Hugh M. Childress was the officiating minister when I married. I knew old man Jim Marlin, the man for whom the town of Marlin was named for, also his brother, John. I knew his son, W. N. P. Marlin, who was a captain in Johnson's Regiment when I served in Ross' Co. of Rangers. Other sons, Rufus, Ash, and Oak Marlin. Knew Old Man Franklin for whom the town of Franklin was named, first county seat of Robertson County. He was also known as "Peg Leg Franklin" as he had a wooden leg. The first doctor in Falls County was Al Adams. He settled where the town of Marlin now stands, was then known as Adams' Mineral Springs.[5]

In the afternoon of June 19, 1855, a week after moving to Mills County, Albert rode with his sons Sam and Frank through the gap in the hills now known as Gholson Gap. Frank was thirteen when he rode into the cove that would become his home and camped within 150 yards of the spot upon which his rock house was built.[6] The area had been the location of a pack train robbery twenty-three years earlier in 1832, the same year Albert came to Texas with his father.

Early in 1925 a story was published in the Houston Chronicle and subsequently in many other newspapers of the robbery in 1832 of a train of pack mules loaded with silver. According to the story, the train was going to Loyola mission, on Red river, from San Antonio, and was in charge of Priests. They were set upon by a band of outlaws known as the Langford gang and were murdered. But when the would-be robbers undid the packs they discovered that they had been tricked, for the mules were loaded only with sand, the treasure having been hidden. The scene of the robbery was supposed to be at Gholson's Gap, which is almost on the county line of Lampasas and Coryell counties and is about a mile south of Evant, Texas.

Recently the writer [not identified] visited that portion of the country and, hearing of the story, went to see Uncle Frank Gholson, who lived near the cove bearing his name. He has lived in Texas since 1842, has seen pioneer life in all its phases, and still remembers vividly the early days. His memory is wonderful.

When asked about the above mentioned story he told what he says is a true version of it. He was anxious that a true account be given to the public in order that the reflection on the Langfords might be corrected. His wife was a Langford, so he knows the Langford history.

The old Mexican, Sanchos, who told the story of the robbery to Wicker and Caddell, was an old man living at Eagle Pass when Gholson was there during the Civil War with the Confederate army. Gholson knew him at the time, but did not know that Sanchos had ever been in the Lampasas county region. Sanchos later moved to Nacogdoches and it was while he was there that he told Wicker and Caddell the story and drew for them a map of the place where the treasure was buried. Wicker and Caddell came to Gholson's house and made a long search for the treasure. It was in this manner that Mr. Gholson heard the story and saw the map of the treasure.

Mr. Gholson says that the story printed in the papers in which reference was made to the Langford gang's operating about the time of the Texas Revolution is all wrong, for no settlements of any kind were made in the Gholson's Gap region till just before the Civil War. Old man Asa Langford, who was the first Langford to come to Texas, was born in September 1820, in Arkansas. In 1855 he came from Louisiana to Texas. It was thus impossible for any of the Langfords to have been even remotely connected with the robbery.

Sanchos' story to Caddell follows:

Just before the Texas Revolution there was a band of Americans in Texas, mostly outlaws, who operated on a systematic scale. They made friends and treaties with the Indians and came and went at pleasure among them. Their business was to rob money trains. They did not bother white men, so they were on friendly terms with them and came and went as they pleased. They were often among the colonists, but were not of them. Nor were they particular enemies of the Mexicans. They traded with the latter and were friendly with all except pack trains, which they made it their special business to rob. They operated on the different pack trails that ran between old missions or settlements or mines in Texas. These operations were all before 1836, and ceased after the battle of San Jacinto. On account of the coming into power of the new Texas Government the outlaws thought it best to go elsewhere. Most of them went to Utah; others went into the colonies or back to the states from which they came. They had leaders or Captains and were subject to some military discipline, but did not always stay together.

In making the trips over the various trails in Texas the pack companies would employ guards and drivers combined. Sanchos was one of these when the events in the story here told happened.

A pack train started from San Antonio to a mission on Red river. They had six mules loaded with money, both gold and silver, and others with supplies for the outfit. Two Mexican officers were in charge and there were twenty one people in all.

They crossed the Lampasas river near the mouth of Sims creek some sixteen or eighteen miles from what was later called Gholson's Gap. At this crossing they nooned one day and took off the packs. Three Americans rode up to them and ate dinner with them. They said that they were with a band of men going out about the San Saba mission, but had got lost off from their bunch. They inquired of the Mexicans if anything had been seen of these men. The Mexicans had not seen them, of course, for it is doubtful if they existed.

When the time came to start from the nooning place the Mexicans loaded their packs in the presence of three men, and when the caravan started the three men went off up the river rather in a west direction. The members of the caravan were suspicious of the three men, so after traveling up the trail some distance they decided to bury the money and go on to where there was an encampment of Mexicans at the crossing of the Leon river, where a gold mine was being worked. They could stay there until the danger blew over, then come back and get the money.

Two men were sent to a hill on which grew some cedars to get a cedar stob. This tree furnishes a wood that will not rot in the ground. Before these men came back the caravan stopped and all the money was put on three mules. These mules left the main trail, the men who led them walking in the grass to make as little sign as possible. They turned to the east of the trail, buried the money in one hole, both gold and silver, took seven steps east and drove the stob into the ground till only the top showed. They burned a figure seven on the west side of the stob, facing the treasure.

They then went back to the main trail and pack train and followed this trail a little farther. It was now late in the afternoon. They went into a canyon that ran north and south and there camped for the night. The next morning, instead of coming back to the trail, they went out to the head of the canyon on top of a mountain and stayed on top of this mountain till they came off at what was later called Gholson's Gap. They had taken care to have the pack mules that were formerly loaded with the treasure to be in the front of the pack and to be naked, thinking that if they met the robbers the latter would see the naked mules, would know that the money had been hidden, and would thus not attack the caravan.

In traveling on the mountain the mules were strung out for some distance, all ahead of the pack drivers. When they turned down the hill to go off the mountain at the gap the advance Mexicans were within some five hundred yards of the rear pack, Sanchos and one more Mexican being behind all. The other pack driver was up on the west side of the line of pack mules. The rear pack mules were barely off the mountain when a band of men in front of them and on the west side of the trail fired on the front Mexicans, killing and wounding a few at the first fire. The Mexicans retreated and went down a branch to a live oak grove. The three pack drivers ran in an easterly direction. The one farthest in advance and on the west side was overtaken and killed, but the other two made their escape, Sanchos being one of these.

The Mexicans who had escaped went east till they found more Mexicans on the Brazos river, near a natural falls, now in Falls county. All the others were killed, the last being killed in the grove on the branch.

The real commander of the outlaws was Captain John D. Lee. He was later put to death in Utah on account of the Mountain Meadow massacre.

This was the Mexican's story. Wicker and Caddell found the scene of the attack, but could only guess at where the pack quit the trail. They only knew that it was between the cedar hill and the gap. They could not locate the canyon where the party camped. Since then six Mexican pack saddles were found in a cliff by Jim Cormeans, who still lives near Evant.

Mr. Gholson is of the opinion that the original band of robbers got the money. He says that the trail was fresh and they were experts at the business, and if they did not find it no one else would stand much of a chance. There are many who think differently, however, and the story, with many variations, is widely told in Texas.[7]

Frank never gave up hope of finding buried treasure, making him the victim of practical jokers. He once said, "I have prospected for gold, silver and tin but never made a success of either one. While prospecting some devilish fellows wrote on a rock 'Turn me over and you will find gold.' When we turned it over the other side said 'Turn me back.'"[8]

Frank was not one to spend his time in school, but his knowledge of nature and Indian ways continued to grow as he roamed the Central Texas hills.

B. F. Gholson was educated to running steers instead of spending his youthful days studying the three R's in a log-cabin schoolhouse. In 1855 he passed through Langford's Cove, then a wilderness, inhabited only by Asa Langford and "Uncle Jimmy" Carter, two gentlemen now [1893] living and highly respected. The ever recurring prairie fire kept the underbrush all down and the lower limbs singed, making the surface of the country even prettier than it is now. In 1856 the Indians began investigating the location of the various white settlers along the streams, preparatory for an attack the next year upon the settlers, at a time to be agreed on in council of all the tribes in the far West. Indians could be seen reconnoitering the country. A complete mental plan of this whole country was made and the point of attack carefully located. Nine tribes were supposed to have been represented at the council of war. All, however, except two tribes, refused to join the coalition. These two tribes, made their own plans and conducted the war from 1857 to 1873, committing murders, kidnapping children, stealing stock, etc., the first persons killed in this community being old man Renfroe and his son. By a count kept by "Uncle Jimmie" Carter, forty-eight men of his acquaintance met their death at the hands of the red men.[9]

Texas settlers lived in constant fear of Indian attacks, as shown by the following excerpt from the journal of a young girl born in 1857 in San Saba County:

I was born in this perilous time and, by nature, I inherited all caution and care. My first recollection is of fear of Indians; sitting up at night listening to the whistle of the Comanches all around and shivering with fear and trembling. We were taught never to get but a short distance from our little hut, for it was no uncommon thing to get news of some family being massacred in the most horrible and cruel manner, with the capture of the women, and perhaps some little innocent girl being carried off with them. At the same time they would have the scalp of father and brothers to present to the captives and if they showed any grief, their torture was only increased until relieved by death. We would often venture out to the old vacated wigwams to gather trinkets left by the Indians; beads and such like. We always had strand after strand of them, which our childish hearts enjoyed. Although, once we were missed by our parents, we would hear the call, "Come here children, you will be picked up by the Indians," then we would take to our heels.[10]

At the time the Indians began their depredations upon the settlers, Albert had remarried and started a family with his second wife, and he decided to move the family from Mills County to a safer place. He moved to Owl Creek in Coryell County and started a horse ranch, leaving Sam and Frank to tend the cattle ranch in Mills County. The teenaged boys quickly grew bored and started making plans to head for California, while nearby the Jackson family made plans for an outing on Pecan Bayou to picnic and gather pecans. The day that started out as a picnic turned to tragedy when the family was ambushed by Indians. Frank and Sam were discouraged from continuing to California by a group of soldiers and returned with them to Camp Colorado, where they joined a new company of Texas Rangers. Frank was only fifteen and Sam was seventeen when they helped bury the Jackson family, then trailed the Indians for many miles to retrieve two kidnapped Jackson children.[11]

Frank told this story many times and several interviews are on record. The following version is reproduced in its entirety, as it is the most complete and descriptive. The other versions are very similar, but some contain a few additional details, which are shown in brackets at the appropriate places in the story. This is the story of Frank's first enlistment with the rangers.

When my father moved from Mills county he left me and my brother on this ranch with the cattle. We soon grew tired of this life and decided that we would like to go to California. We two, with A. N. Morris, an employee of the ranch, started out. Being well armed and well mounted we started out, made it across the Plains, going from the head tributaries of the Concho across to Castle Canyon, striking the Pecos river at what was known as Horsehead crossing. I understand that the Indians piled a great pile of horse heads there at an early date to show where to cross, hence the name.

There we were met by a band of United States soldiers, who told us that several tribes had gone on the war path to prevent emigration to California, that they themselves had been in a fight with the Apaches on Thursday before and had lost either fourteen or sixteen men. This was Sunday. On hearing this news we gave up our plan to go to California and returned with the soldiers to Camp Colorado, to which place they were coming. Camp Colorado was a Federal fort, garrisoned by United States troops and was located about nine miles east of Coleman city, on a high point between Jim Ned and Hoard creeks. There Louis Mulkey, a guide for the soldiers, told us that Captain John Williams was organizing a ranging company near San Saba, then a little new village.

This organization took place October 2, 1858, I and my brother being two of the recruits. After organizing, we marched up the Colorado river to what is now known as Bowser's Bend, and the company was divided into four detachments, each detachment being stationed about an equal distance apart so as to cover as much territory as possible by our scouting from the different detachments.

On the twenty-sixth night of October two of our men coming to headquarters camp reported having found an Indian trail coming toward the settlements. These two men were Frank Tankersley and George McReynolds. Early the next morning Captain Williams called for thirty men to follow this trail, and I was one of those who volunteered to go. Tankersley guided us to the place. We followed the trail down to what was known as Hanner valley, now known as Regency. A few settlers were here. So far the Indians had failed to get any horses. We went on down to Jones valley, so-called because old man Jones was an early settler there, still no horses had been secured by the Indians. We could tell this from the trail that they left.

At this place we learned that the Indians were two days ahead of us. We followed the trail till late that afternoon. I, being skilled in this sort of work, was made one of the trailers, it being my sole business to keep my eye on the

Donna Gholson Cook

trail. Directly I heard one of the men call out "Yonder goes a man a way down yonder, down the valley."

We continued the trail a short distance farther to where the Indians had crossed a small creek, now called Jackson branch. On coming up out of the bed of the creek, we discovered the body of a white man, with quite a number of arrow wounds in it. We also found a hack track, where the man had fallen out of the hack when he was killed. He was evidently driving along, unaware of danger when the shower of arrows struck him. We followed the hack track to where the hack and team had struck a grove of timber about five hundred yards from where the man's body was lying, where we found the hack standing. We also found the body of a boy about seven years old with both eyes shot out and his throat cut, lying on his back, with his head hanging off over the rear end gate of the hack. He had evidently been with the man in the hack and had never left the vehicle after the attack of the Indians and the running of the horses. The Indians had simply overtaken the running team and had not even taken the trouble to pull the boy out of the hack before murdering him.

A short distance to the east, in the bed of a dry gulley, lay a young ladies body. The throat had been cut and the head scalped, all the scalp being taken, not just a mere tuft of hair, and two large wounds were made with a knife in her left side, near her heart. Her body was horribly mutilated and she had been raped. Let me say right here, in passing, that Indians will never rape the bodies of young children nor older women, but they have been known to so mutilate the bodies of young ladies on more than one occasion under my observation, or within my knowledge. [A newspaper article, "Late Texas Ranger's Letters to Local Man Describe Indian Raids," gives the location of the mother's body: "The body of an old lady lay at the root of a tree some distance north of the hack. Her throat had been cut." The article was obtained from the Lampasas Historical Commission's B. F. Gholson file and was published in the *Nolan County News*, Sweetwater, September 17, 1942.]

This was late in the afternoon of October 28 and the people had been dead two days then. Captain Williams inquired who knew of any ranches in that region. Some knew of Mullein's ranch, some of James Fowler's ranch, Williams' ranch was mentioned and so was Kirkpatrick's. The Captain wanted men to go in pairs to the different ranches to get tools for digging purposes, or to get anything they could to wrap the bodies in for burial, as we would have to bury them without coffins. It was also desirable to learn who the murdered people were and to let the people at the different places know of the massacre, that they might be on their guard. I, for one, went to the Kirkpatrick ranch, which was down the Colorado river and on the opposite side from the scene of the murders.

When the men returned from all the ranches we learned that the murdered people were the Jackson family. Men from the ranches came that night and the next morning, bringing such tools and such materials for burial as they had. From these men we learned that there ought to be two more children. While the digging and burying went on a diligent search was made for the two missing children, but no sign of them could be found.

At the scene of the murder the Indians divided into two bunches. [Additional information from a sketch by T. R. Gholson in McCreary's "The Gholson House": "Going East about 18 miles and on top of a round mountain known as "Look Out" mountains, now in Mills County. These children were left with one warrior and two squaws, at this point."] A small bunch of Indians afoot and with only one horse in the party came directly east; the larger bunch went south, down the Colorado river, striking the settlements below. They had added the two horses from the Jackson hack to their collection. We followed them down as far as San Saba peak, which is now in Mills county, and decided that we were so far behind that the Indians would be able to make the rounds in the settlements and still be ahead of us, so we halted. Even though we were all well mounted and the Indians might not be, they had the advantage of us, for we could not follow the trail at night, while they could travel night and day. It is only in a region where the direction of a traveling party can be guessed at with some certainty, or where the trail is very fresh that any considerable progress can be made by a pursuing party at night.

Fig. 12.1 - Lookout Mountain, 1-1/4 mile south of Caradan in Mills County. Photo by Donna Gholson Cook, September 2000.

As neither of these factors were in our favor, we gave up the trail. We returned north and sent to the supply camp for more provisions, men and pack mules. We divided our men into small squads so as to cover the country from the Colorado to the Leon rivers and double track so as to see the ground twice a day and traverse the region thoroughly. We hoped in this way to intercept the Indians as they returned from their marauding expedition.

On the night of November 6 eight of us struck the trail where the Indians had passed out over our line earlier in the night. We followed it half a mile or more and discovered some revelings and fragments that we took to be portions of a white girl's clothing on the bushes or limbs that she might pass near if she were horseback. The two children were evidently kept on one horse, and this horse was turned loose in the herd, with them on it, and with no rope, bridle, or other means of guiding it. This we judged to be true from the crooked course made by the horse on which the children rode.

These signs gave us new courage, and we were sure that we were on a hot trail. Gideon P. Cowen, Second Lieutenant, was with this squad of eight men. He called for a volunteer to go east to meet the men from the Leon river. No one was willing to go alone. Then [He] then said: "Well, two of you go and tell them men or anybody else that you see that we are on the trail and that we are satisfied that it is the one that follows the children. Then come on and overtake us." Two men at once volunteered, leaving only six in our party. Romey Vaughn, a sergeant, then said: "I'll go back and meet the other boys alone."

This left only five of our party to follow the train [trail]. We found where the Indians had stopped long enough to water their horses, and at this place we discovered very plainly where the little girl had been allowed to dismount and walk along on the narrow sand bar of the branch. We saw where she knelt down and drank. Her tracks were very plain, and no other tracks of horses were near enough to erase them. We supposed that she had left a plain trail on purpose for us. The boy's tracks puzzled us. We could see only one shoe track. We felt sure it was the boy's track, but decided that he must be crippled, for he made only one track in a place. What he did with his other foot we could not imagine.[12]

A paragraph added to the end of an unrelated document in the Center for American History explains the mystery of the one shoe track:

I believe that I did not explain about the one track of the Jackson boy that puzzled us when we tracked him. The Indians took a knife belonging to Mr. Jackson when they killed him, but an Indian garb has no pockets so they took one of his shoes and made a scabbard.[13]

Returning to the narrative:

We continued the trail all day. About four o'clock in the afternoon Romey Vaughn, with two other men, caught up with us. Later in the afternoon, before crossing Pecan Bayou, we [saw] six men coming up the trail behind us. We halted to let them catch up with us and they halted too, thinking that we were the Indians that they had been following. We made friendly signs to them. Romey Vaughn rode out some distance from us, had a white hankerchief tied on his gun stick and wore a broad Mexican hat in an open place where the six men could see him plainly. Indians never [have] hats of this kind. He waved his white handkerchief on the end of his gun stick, then waved his broad hat indicating "Come on." When they came up we learned that they were citizens who had lost some horses down in Lampasas and Burnett counties, and were following the Indians hoping to recover them. They did not know that the Indians had killed anyone or were carrying away as captives and children.

Lieutenant Cowen told them: "We are Rangers. We are members of Captain John Williams' company. I am his second lieutenant, and we are now on the trail of a number of stolen horses and two captive children. We mean to spare no time, to use all the judgment possible, to travel by day or night as the circumstances require, and undergo any hardships or dangers that we may come in contact with, principally for the sake of those captive children. If you gentlemen want to go with us and will not in any way hinder us; if you will do as we do, fare as we fare and obey as my men do, we will be glad to have you. If you are not willing to abide by these regulations we would rather you wouldn't go."

They at once all agreed so to do and we moved on. After crossing the Pecan bayou we stopped and ate some supper and grazed our horses a while. One of the men who joined the company had a watch, so from then on we worked on time. The watch proved very valuable, as later events showed. After Lieutenant Cowen had showed us a star, he said to us: "That is precisely the way the Indians are going. Two of you take the head and follow in the direction of that star." We started toward this star, traveling till after midnight without stopping. We came to where the Indians had stopped to cook something to eat. We likewise stopped about two hours, grazed our horses and went on.

When daylight came Lieutenant Cowen started us off in a V shape. We traveled in pairs, in the general form of a figure V, several miles wide at the opening, that is, the two leading pairs of men were several miles apart. Each pair of men was several hundred yards away from his nearest neighbor, but in hollering distance of him. If any communication of a general nature was to be made, the man making it would shout it to the pair next behind him, this pair would pass on the word, and so on till it had passed clear around the V. We were hunting for the trail that we had abandoned due to our night travel. It was better to follow the trail in the day time, of course, but for the sake of speed we had guessed at the direction the Indians had taken and trusted to chance in order to travel at night. Pretty soon the two men in the lead on the right hand of the V found the trail and passed the news back. We followed the trail the balance of the day, stopping once in the morning, getting something to eat and resting our horses about one and one half hours, then again in the afternoon we came to a place where the Indians had stopped and cooked again. Here we again stopped a couple of hours. Our next stop was about eleven o'clock that night, when we again rested about one and one half hours.

When daylight came we found that we were riding right on top of the trail. Lieutenant Cowen told Tom Potts and me, who did most of the trailing, to take the trail. We were traveling a west course on the north side of a range of mountains, a lone mountain standing off alone north of the main range. The Indians had passed between this lone mountain and the main range. Tom and I while trailing traveled some eighty or more yards ahead of the rest of the company. We looked up from our work long enough to see a man sitting on a horse on top of that round mountain, with his horses head and his front looking back east toward us. He disappeared soon after we saw him, then reappeared, paused about long enough to give the rider time to count us, and disappeared again, this time for good.

We motioned to Lieutenant Cowen, who galloped up to us and asked us what we wanted. He questioned us rather closely when he heard our story, but made him understand that we positively saw a man on top of that round mountain. We knew that we were not mistaken, although the rider had disappeared in a gallop over the west side of the mountain. Orders were given to strike a gallop in close formation, the Lieutenant telling us that this rider was the rear guard and the rest of the Indians were not far off. His instructions to Tom and me were to keep our eyes continually on the trail. Some one from the rear called out: "Yonder they are. I see them now, away in front."

I looked up long enough to see a long string of horses in front of us, being driven in a run. The next I heard was: "They are fixing to fight. Don't you see them rounding up that herd?" But we soon discovered that they were roping fresh horses from the herd.

Some one yelled: "Look yonder. Two foot Indians are leaving the balance of them." By this time we were in a run. Cowen told Tom and me to give up the trail and we gladly did so, for we were rearing to go.

Cowen then ordered: "I will take part of the men and run in between the foot Indians and the horse herd. Rome, you take the other part and run in front of the foot Indians to keep them from going to the mountains, and lets kill them first."

We accordingly divided and I followed Cowen. But before we could get to them the two figures that we were pursuing hid. I[n] a few moments one of them rose from his hiding place and I heard him say: "They're white men; they're white men; they're white men. I saw their hats and I see their stirrups." We must have been about two hundred yards away at this time. Up he popped and he stayed up, and we soon saw that he was no Indian at all, but a white boy.

Some of the men jumped down off their horses and ran up to where the two had been hiding. Everyone became excited, for we realized that here were the two lost children for whom we were looking. One of the men, Romey Vaughn, ran up to the girl and began to comfort her as best he could. She was almost gone from starvation and excitement. Another one of the men, A. J. Brown by name, began to shout in regular camp meeting style, praising the Lord for all his goodness in permitting the children to be recovered. [Additional information from a sketch by T. R. Gholson in McCreary's "The Gholson House": "Gabe Choate calls out saying, 'What, Jack, are we going to have a revival right here in the wilderness?' and Jack answered, saying that God deserved praise in the wilderness under such circumstances as this, as much as in the churchhouse."] We let him shout without any interference, but when some one noticed that the Indians had disappeared we sat up and took notice. We then knew why it was that the Indians had so willingly given up the prisoners to save their own hides. This was the smartest trick that bunch or any other bunch of Indians with whom I ever had any dealings ever played, and it enabled them to get away without the loss of a man.

The boy told us that there were eight other Indians behind, so Cowen decided that we would not pursue the fleeing Indians, but would try to capture or kill the eight behind. The other Indians had roped fresh horses from the herd, so it would have been out of the question for us with our tired mounts to overtake them anyhow. [Additional information from a sketch by T. R. Gholson in McCreary's "The Gholson House": "So 8 of us ran on. The indians had left the herd and on their fresh horses had gone out of sight. When we ran on their trail about 1-1/2 miles to the top of a ridge we could see them, something like a half mile; running full speed, strung out one behind another. We counted them - 18 in number, and our horses being so completely broken down, we gave up the chase; stood there and watched them go out of sight, and then returned to the herd, finding them going back the trail to the nearest

193

water." A touching note from the autobiography of Samuel Sullivan Gholson provides insight as to the horrors inflicted upon the children: "Every man shed tears when they heard their story."]

Cowen and one of the men set to work to cook and try to feed the girl, who was so starved that she had lost her taste. They gave her some broiled bacon and finally got her appetite aroused. Then they had just as much trouble keeping her from eating as they had had getting her to eat. They took the lone watch that was in the company and fed her by it carefully, thus saving her life.

This was early in the morning. We remained at the place of rescue till about one o'clock. [An article by R. J. Gerald in the *Dallas News* on December 12, 1925, states: "This capture occurred near the head of Bitter Creek, in what is now Nolan County, about twelve miles southwest from Sweetwater." From a sketch by T. R. Gholson in McCreary's "The Gholson House": "The capture of these children and horses took place in Nolan county, 8 or 9 miles Southwest of Sweetwater, Texas, on the morning of November 9th, 1858."] How to proceed on the journey with the girl was a big problem. The only way we had of carrying her was horseback. We would double up a pair of blankets and put them behind one of the men, then we would set her up side wise behind him. We did not do this for the sake of fashion, but because the Indians had forced her to ride astride till she could do so no longer. When she would get tired we would change her to the front, or perhaps another man would take her. When she complained of any special misery, or appeared to be unable to go farther we would simply stop and let Lieutenant Cowen and Gabe Shaw administer to her needs. We traveled only about eight miles that first day. The journey to Camp Colorado, which was about one hundred fifty miles away, required eight days on account of the condition of the girl. The boy was in good condition physically, and needed no special care.

In the afternoon of November 16 we reached Camp Colorado. It was then garrisoned by Federal troops. A few families also lived near the fort. It was to the house of one of these settlers that the girl was carried. John Sinclair was the name of the man. One of our men, Steve Kemp was a brother-in-law to Sinclair and he insisted that she be carried there saying that his sister, Mrs. Sinclair and his two younger sisters who lived with her would be glad to keep the girl. She was so destitute of clothing that we had to keep her wrapped with blankets, her clothing having been torn from her body while she was riding through the brush on the uncontrolled horse in the herd of the Indians. When she was delivered into the hands of Mrs. Sinclair she was put to bed and Mrs. Sinclair at once went to the settlers store at the fort and bought quite a lot of cloth and other supplies. When she returned with the goods she sent her two sisters to notify the neighbor women who lived around the fort to come at once. They came and each one took away goods to make a certain garment. Lieutenant Cowen brought the Doctor from the fort, who examined the little girl, gave her some medicine and left some more for her to take. She was bathed thoroughly, her hair was combed and she was dressed in new clothing from head to foot, a change of clothing ready for her.

We remained at the fort till the second noon afterward, after which we resumed our travel toward headquarters camp. The little girl came out looking entirely different and feeling much better. Both the boy and girl went with us. When we reached our headquarters camp at Bowser's Bend the captain's wife, Mrs. Williams, had taken the opportunity offered of coming up from her home at Cherokee, San Saba county, with a supply train. She and the Captain were light housekeeping, so to speak, in a tent. When the boys at the supply camp saw us coming they yelled aloud "Gid Cowen and his men are coming with the horse herd and the captive Jackson children."

When we rode up among the tents I saw Mrs. Williams come out of her tent and walk directly to Lieutenant Cowen. She knelt down and kissed the little girl and howdied with the little boy. She then said: "Lieutenant, with your permission I will take charge of this little girl what time I am here." He at once granted the permission.

She then said "I and the Captain are staying in that tent. I am here only for a short time." She took the little girl by the hand and started toward the tent. Then she stopped and said "With your permission, Lieutenant, I can take the little boy also."

Before Lieutenant Cowen could reply, however, the boy spoke up. "Oh no, I don't [want] to go. I want to stay with these men that have brought me home." So he was allowed to remain with the men.

In a few days Mrs. Williams had to return home when she could get a guard for protection. There were a few ranches below our headquarters and on the opposite side of the Colorado river. On some of these ranches there were families, while on others there were only men. The nearest ranch to headquarters that had any family on it was that of Tom Priddy. His father-in-law and mother-in-law, Mr. and Mrs. George Tankersley lived there. Tom was a member of Williams' company. When Mrs. Williams started home she went by the Priddy ranch, carrying the little girl with her in a buggy and left her at this ranch. The children remained here till their borhter [*sic*] John Jackson, who was a grown man and who was living at the town of Lampasas at the time, got word of the recovery of the children and came to headquarters camp after them. A guard was sent with him to go by the Priddy ranch and get the children. He brought them back to Lampasas some time afterward, and put them in school there. From there he went to Austin, carrying the children with him, saying that if the Indians ever got them again they would have to come down into the settlements after them.

The boy was known as Tobe Jackson. Strangely enough, the exciting happenings that ended in our recovery of the children affected him more in the long run than they did the girl. He seemed unable to get the terrible events off his mind and finally lost his mind and died in an asylum. For some time before his death he would escape whenever he could and make his way back to the scene of the murder of his family, where searchers would find him. He died at Austin soon after reaching manhood. Rebecca, the girl, grew to womanhood, married Jack Stroud, lived to an old age, reared an intelligent creditable family of several children, two of her daughters being school teachers for several years in Hamilton county. She left Texas several years ago after the death of her husband and died in Melrose, New Mexico, in 1926.[14]

Sam and Frank served with Captain Williams until March 2, 1859, when their father found them and demanded that they be discharged. As they were minors, Captain Williams could not hold them and gave them honorable discharges. The ranch employee, Andy Morris, remained until the six-month term was out. They were paid $5 per month in state scrip and furnished their own pistols, guns, mounts and blankets. After their father brought the boys home, he attempted to keep them in school, but having had a taste of freedom, they did not stay for long. Sam left in November 1859 and started freighting for the public with a team of three broken oxen and five wild steers. Frank left again in the spring of 1860 to join the ranger company of Sul Ross.[15]

In the spring of 1859, between Frank's first and second enlistments with the rangers, he was living about six miles from the scene of the murders of several settlers by Indians in the northwest part of Bell County near Sugar Loaf Mountain. The following account was published in Hunter's *Frontier Times*:

Murder of Mr. and Mrs. Riggs and Mr. Pierce

VETERAN B. F. GHOLSON, who now resides at Evant, Texas, has kindly furnished the following account of the murder of Mr. and Mrs. Riggs, and a Mr. Pierce by Indians in Bell county in the Spring of 1859.

A new settlement was being formed in the northwest part of Bell county near Sugar Loaf Mountain by homesteaders and newcomers who were not familiar with Indian warfare. During the light moon of April, 1859, the Indians raided this settlement and killed a man by the name of Pierce and a Mr. Riggs and his wife and captured a boy and Riggs' two little girls, but these escaped. I lived about six miles from where these murders occurred. My brother, S. S. Gholson, had gone to mill at Sulpher Springs (now Lampasas) with an ox wagon and, on learning that Indians were in the country, I hastened to meet him. I encountered him on his return about thirty miles out and we reached home in safety, after which we hurried forward to join in the pursuit of the Indians.

Mr. Pierce, Mr. Riggs, Mr. Elms and a few others lived in that particular settlement, near Sugar Loaf Mountain. Mr. Pierce and Mr. Riggs were engaged in hauling cedar from a nearby cedar brake. Mr. Riggs lived nearest the cedar brake and it was his custom to wait the coming of Mr. Pierce each morning, then they would proceed together to the brake with their wagons. On this sad April morning, Mr. Pierce accompanied by a small boy by the name of Dave Elms, came along and Mr. Riggs not being quite ready to start, Mr. Pierce drove on towards the cedar brake which he had scarcely reached when the Indians sprang from their ambush, surrounded his wagon and killed him. While they were killing Pierce, the boy attempted to escape by running but the Indians pursued and captured him. When the Indians ran on to Pierce, Mr. Riggs had stayed with his wagon but on witnessing the attack he abandoned his team, ran back to his home and taking his wife and three children started to his brother's place which was in sight of his own home. All this was in full view of the Indians, and when they had murdered Pierce and had captured the boy, they turned their attention to the fleeing family. Leaving one of their bucks to guard the boy, Dave, they overtook the Riggs family, killed and scalped Mr. and Mrs. Riggs, and carried off the two little girls, leaving the baby boy unhurt. After having committed this atrocious deed, the Indians returned to Mr. Riggs' home and appropriated such articles as suited their fancy and that they could carry off.

When the savages caught the boy, Dave Elms, they stripped him bare and because he resisted, they whipped him unmercifully. The Indian left to guard him became deeply interested in the tragedy just then being enacted and when his whole attention was fixed on the slaughter of Mr. and Mrs. Riggs, the boy disappeared and got away. After his escape, the first man he met was Mr. Ambrose Lee, whose home was in the settlement. Mr. Lee seized his gun and went to where Dave told him Mr. and Mrs. Riggs had been killed and where he found their mutilated bodies and the little babe crawling around on the ground in the blood of its father and mother. Mr. Lee was the first to reach the scene of the tragedy. A. M. Woods was the second. After having plundered the Riggs home, the Indians went south about ten miles, taking all the stock that came in reach; then turning west, they came in sight of a man on horseback. Four of their number gave pursuit, overtook, killed and scalped him, taking his horse and all his effects. The Indians driving the herd of stolen horses along near the body of this unfortunate man while he was yet alive and the little captive girls, who had witnessed the chase and the killing, heard his groans as they passed the dying victim of savage ferocity. This man's name was Peevy, but I have forgotten his initials.

The Indians had out spies on each side of their course and after traveling some distance their spy on the north side reported a body of horsemen approaching. They immediately changed their course and took down a rough hollow or canyon in order to keep out of sight of the men discovered by their spy. Each one of the Riggs girls was mounted behind an Indian. The savages were going in a run and the smallest girl fell off the horse she was riding. The elder girl saw her fall and seeing that the Indian behind whom she had been riding made no halt or any effort to recover the child, jumped off. The Indian she was riding with made a grab for her and caught her by the clothing and held to her for some distance, her head and arms almost dragging the ground. Finally she seized a bush and held to it with such strength and persistency that her skirt was torn off and left in the hands of the savage, while she was left bruised and bleeding on the ground. The Indians had no time to look after their late captives.

This brave little girl made her way back to where her little sister had fallen. It was now late in the evening and the air was chilly. The little child had sustained severe bruises in her fall on the rocks but, with her sister's aid was able to travel. They began the painful and weary journey back in the direction they had come. After nightfall they came to an old vacant cabin long since abandoned by some pioneer. In this house they passed the night. The little sister complained of cold and hunger. There was no food to be had but the elder sister, herself but a child showed the qualities of the Texan heroine. She removed every remaining thread of her own clothing and with these remnants she wrapped the shivering form of her little sister, forgetting of her own comfort, thinking only of that of the little sister! Does history record a deed more sublime?

Next morning these two little girls followed a path which led them to another abandoned house where they found that the occupants had left only a short time before—frightened away probably by the Indians—leaving their household effects. With lacerated and swollen feet, weary exhausted, the little waifs could go no further. Sometime during the day a man came to the house. I do not remember his name but he was a stranger and had not heard of the Indians being in the country. He mounted the two girls on his horse, walked and led the animal and took them to Captain Dameron's, where they found quite a number "forted up." There were also a few men present for protection, the others had gone forward in pursuit of the Indians. Here at Captain Dameron's these two little girls were tenderly cared for until they were delivered to their relatives.

Dave Elms has been known, ever since that fatal April day, as "Indian Dave Elms." I think he now lives near Rock Springs in Edwards county.

(EDITOR'S NOTE—The two Riggs girls, in after years, resided in Bandera county. One of them married a man named Benton, and now lives in Arizona.)[16]

Fig. 12.2 - Fort Belknap, established 1851, the largest military post in northern Texas until the Civil War, located 2 miles south of Newcastle. Photo by Rebecca Brassfield, September 2000.

Frank was seventeen and working on his father's ranch in when he joined Captain J. M. Smith's company on March 4, 1860, at Fort Belknap. Sul Ross, age twenty-two, was Smith's First Lieutenant and became the company commander when Captain Smith was promoted. Sam Houston was governor at the time, and Ross was destined to become governor of Texas in 1886. In the summer of 1860, the company was on an expedition against the Northern Comanches in the Wichita Mountains when Frank and Lieutenant Gault both received word that their fathers had died and they were needed at home. Lieutenant Gault's family was in Virginia and he needed another man to go with him to Texas and he would leave for Virginia from there. Sul Ross gave them honorable discharges on August 11 and they set out for Texas. Two Indians, Placido and Caddo Tom, gave them instructions on how to survive the trip, but when their friends told them goodbye, they did not expect them to see them alive again. In an interview, Frank told the story of their dangerous journey:[17]

Fig. 12.3 - "Placido, Chief of the Tonkawa" from Thrall's *A Pictorial History of Texas*, 1879. Texas State Library & Archives Commission No. 1999/1-1.

The next service I did as a Texas Ranger was with a company organized by Capt. J. M. Smith early in March of 1860. L. S. Ross, better known as Sul Ross, was elected First Lieutenant under Smith. T. H. Calehaugh and A. F. Gault were elected Second Lieutenants. This company had one First Lieutenant and two Second Lieutenants instead of first, second and third. When we had fully organized at Waco the ladies of Waco made us a flag bearing the Texas star. On the morning of our departure Miss Ellen Earl presented us that flag with an address. The address was replied to by Lieut. Sul Ross. We marched directly to Fort Belknap. When we arrived there other companies of Texas Rangers were assembling. There were nine of these companies in all. Col. M. T. Johnson had authority to organize those companies into a regiment, which was done on the parade ground at Fort Belknap, near where Newcastle now stands. S. P. Ross, better known as Pete Ross, held a commission as Captain. He was instructed by Sam Houston, then Governor of Texas, to go to Fort Cobb, then headquarters for the Indian Territory, enlist Plasedo [Placido], chief of the Tonkawas, to pick forty-five warriors from that reservation and join the regiment with them when we reached the Indian Territory, which he did. Col. Johnson was at the same time in command of the regiment.

We marched directly to the Wichita Mountains, then in Indian Territory—now Oklahoma. We established headquarters and supply camp on Otter Creek and began scouting for the Northern Comanches from that point. The Comanches had received word through those reservation Indians that a strong force of Texas Rangers was coming in search of them. So in due time they started their women and children and all the stock property they had in the direction of Pike's Peak. The entire tribe went north except a sufficient number of warriors whom they left behind with instructions that when the tribe has gotten out of the way to divide into squads from the Red to the Arkansas Rivers. Special instructions were given them to fire the entire line on a certain day and then to pass over the ground and refire all the water courses passing through the territory so as to burn both sides of the Canadian, Washita and other streams across their line. (This we afterward learned through the reservation Indians just as the wild tribe had learned of our coming.) This being in June and it being very dry at the time, with the wind blowing from the south, they succeeded in so completely burning the country that the rangers, being mounted and depending on grass for their mounts and pack animals, made almost a complete failure of this expedition against the Northern Comanches. We never did find the north and west ends of that fire, though Col. Johnson took 400 men from the different companies and went in search of the west end of it. They were attacked high up on the Canadian some 200 miles from headquarters at night and lost a great many of their horses, leaving a good part of the men afoot. Those who had their horses divided time with those who did not, taking it turn about riding and walking and walking and riding until they got back to headquarters.

Lieut. Gault and I received word of the necessity of our return home, so we were honorably discharged on Otter Creek Aug. 11, 1860. Our discharges were headed as follows: "Texas Ranger Headquarters, Near Fort Radsminskie [Camp Radziminski], an Abandoned United States Fort."

It was a dangerous attempt for two men. We were given valuable instructions by the officers and men as to how to travel, also by Plasedo and his old warriors. Plasedo said to us in broken English, "All time ride at night. No much time ride in daytime. In daytime one sleep and one guard. All the time one eye open. Maybeso Conanch' no get you." So we bid all the boys and the Tonkawas good-bye and started. The boys said to us, "We never expect to see you again." We traveled all that day and a good part of the night. After that we traveled at night only, unless absence of water on the way forced us to go on until we came to water. The third night out, not more than twenty miles from Red River, the Texas line, at about midnight, we saw some lights kindled up to the west. They continued to kindle up until we could count thirty-two dim lights. The dimness of the lights was due to the fact that nothing except buffalo chips was available for fuel. We traveled on and discovered a large herd. Thinking it might be buffalo, we rode carefully up close enough to hear horses snort as they were grazing. We at once decided that this was the herd that belonged to the lights just west of us. We turned around to the east, leaving the herd to the west until we got past them. We did not see any Indians or herders. We traveled on some twelve or fourteen miles and went down off of a tableland into a broad prairie.

We halted at the foot of this tableland to sleep until morning. Our rule was not to unsaddle our horses until the last thing else was done. We had two horses apiece, riding one and leading one for a pack horse. When we had unpacked and had staked our horses (we carried stake pins), before we had unsaddled the ones we were riding they began looking back in the direction we were riding from and showing signs of fright. We had halters prepared to keep them from making any noise when in danger. We at once applied our smother halters and stopped them from making any noise. By this time a band of Indians was riding off of a bench or tableland about 400 yards to the northeast from us. We hugged close to the foot of the hill. We could hear the roar of the herds. Behind the Indians was a bunch of horses driven by more Indians and behind those Indians were more horses driven in a similar way. Several bunches of Indians and horses divided in that manner went off of the high ground, traveling to the southeast. The pack horses were mostly behind. We could hear the rattle of wigwam poles, owing to the manner in which they were carried. Occasionally we could hear the Indians talk among themselves, and could hear them hit the packs as they would strike at the pack horses with whips or ropes. At the rear we could hear the jabber of the squaws and children. When they were gone we remained where we were until daylight and then traveled on a few miles. Seeing a smoke nearly in front of us, we hesitated for a while as to what to do. We decided that the Indians had gone on or we would see that big herd of horses somewhere. We ventured down and found the fires burning and the water muddy, but all were gone. So we remained there all that day. We learned that a band of Indians had separated from the main band at that place. This small band had gone in our direction and the larger one had borne to the east. When night came, we took up our line of march again, trying to obey Plasedo's instructions. We did not make a long ride that day because when we struck the old road running from Fort Belknap to Fort Cobb on the Washita, we stopped and waited until daylight. When daylight came, we saw moccasin tracks thick but the Indians were gone. We looked around a little and found that a fire had been built on the south bank of the Little Wichita and had gone out immediately. This indicated that it had not been used. Nearby lay a dirty hickory shirt, commonly worn by frontiersmen and Mexicans. The shirt indicated that who ever wore it had been shot through the body with a big bullet, as it had a hole in each side of it around which were blood stains. We failed to find the man. There was a large hole of water in the creek near the fire and the shirt.

From this place on we had a road which we knew and so decided to ride in the daytime. Starting at about 11 o'clock in the forenoon, we rode until after sundown and came to Dave Peaveler's stock ranch. There we spoke to the first white people we had seen since leaving the ranger camp. Mr. Peaveler was an old man and has some grown sons who were working his ranch. This was the most northern ranch at that time. The Indians had been there the night before and carried off a lot of the ranch horses. Two of the young Peavelers, John and Lewis, were gone in pursuit of the Indians. The younger son, a lad, remained at the ranch with his father and mother and other occupants of the place. He still survives. He is known as Capt. France Peaveler. We remembered each other when we met at one of our ranger reunions. I met him at ex-ranger reunion last August.

Nothing else of interest occurred during the rest of this trip. When we got to my father's farm, Lieut. Gault stayed all night and then went on to Waco. He told me he would be in Waco several days. About the fourth day afterwards, I went to Waco, but he had gone to Virginia, his native State. I never met him again. I learned that he was made a Lieutenant Colonel on the staff of one of our Confederate Generals, but it has slipped my mind which one it was. He became a prominent lawyer in Washington, D. C., after the Civil War, and remained there until his death about ten years ago. He was an uncle of the Galt whose widow married President Wilson. This last information I obtained from a Mr. Nicholson of Dallas. He was a Government field agent and said he had heard Col. Gault tell of this trip of his and mine.

The company of rangers came in about three weeks later than we did and were disbanded at Waco.[18]

Fig. 12.4 - *Population of an Indian village moving*, photographic reproduction of an illustration from *Harper's Weekly*, May 21, 1870, p. 324. Library of Congress No. LC-USZ62-102450.

In his third ranger term, Frank Gholson was a member of the ranger party involved in the Battle of Pease River and the recapture of Cynthia Ann Parker. Cynthia Ann was captured as a child when the Indians attacked Fort Parker in 1836, as described in Chapter 10, and lived as a part of the Comanche tribe until her unwilling return to the Parker family in 1860. She was the wife of Chief Peta Nocona and the mother of several of his children, including the last chief of the Comanches, Quanah Parker. Frank Gholson's account reflects his empathy for the Indians and his admiration of their courage, first giving background information about the treatment of the tribes in Texas.[19]

~ The Battle of Pease River ~

There is a difference of opinion about whether those Indians that used to raid in this country were government charges. We once had all these Texas Indians that belonged in Texas on a Texas reservation. That was done after the annexation. They came under treaties and were put on reservation here in Texas. Fort Belknap was the headquarters, in Young County. There were remnants of several tribes. There was remnants of the Comanches that had accepted the treaty, and the main tribe didn't do it. That bunch was kept by Cooper because they was at variance with the other tribes. The Caddoes, Delewares, Phawnees, Wacoes and other tribes were kept there until 1858.

There was a division in the minds of the people on the frontier. Some said them Indians was complying with the treaty, and was being fed by the government and overlooked by the soldiers, and that it was Indians not under treaty that was doing this devilment, and others said these were the Indians that did it and were only taking part with those wild tribes. Althrough my ranger days I thought it was the wild tribes, but I found there was more Indians in the world than there was on those reservations.

But in 1859 there was much strife between people on that question. Texas asked the general Government to take charge of these Indians and put them over in the territory that was then set apart for Indians; and they had some five tribes on that reservation then, with Fort Gidson [Gibson] as headquarters.

In 1859 these Indians were moved off this reservation, all of them, and they wasn't willing to go. They was required to go with the assistance of the soldiers and two companies of rangers, who delivered them into the hands of the Indian agents, on the other side of the Red River.

I am of the opinion that right there things changed. I don't believe them Indians had been doing anything to cause this move, but the majority of the people got to think they were. They were forced to go over there, and they had made their treaty to stay in Texas. I wouldn't be surprised, then, if they didn't depredate from then on.

That was the reason that our company was organized, by order of Gov. Sam Houston. It is said that there were violations on the part of the white people, somebody would mistreat some Indians somewhere that was being friendly.

In some other part of the State somebody else would do something of the same kind.

In 1856, according to the statements of some prisoners who was in the hands of the Indians and had been recovered there was nine tribes of Indians come together in the fall. The nearest I can fix that time is November, 1856. And it was said they come together on and around and near the forks of the Brazos, which would be the Yellow prong and the Double Mountain prong of the Brazos, and that was where the council was held.

They described it that they held a meeting there near the forks of the river, near Double Mountains. I don't know just where the council ground was. It was there about the forks somewhere. They designated the time as in the light of the moon in November. He (the one telling this) called himself Juan Leon. He was a prisoner being used as a horse herder and hide dresser. They enslaved most of the Mexicans.

When I first enlisted in the rangers was in 1858. That was in another company. This Pease River fight was when I was in Sull Ross' second company, and served in each of them. We was organized on the first day of October on the bank of the San Saba, near the new village of San Saba, but that was the first company.

I went on then until this March enlistment under Smither [Smith] here in Waco in 1860. I came here (then Hamilton County, now Mills County) and worked on my father's ranch till March of 1860, when I went. Then was when we went into the regiment, ordered by Sam Houston, and formed at Fort Belknap.

Fig. 12.5 - "Sul Ross - 1875 Constitutional Convention" enlarged portrait detail from composite. Texas State Library and Archives Commission No. 1/170-1.

Sull Ross was born in 1838. That was 1860. I believe he was born in April. He was 22 years old and a little better. Six months was a ranger term. I was in three times, and this was the last. This company was organized in October, and this fight come off in December, while we was in the service of that organization. Smith's company came to be Ross' later on. When we was organized in a regiment Captain Smith went in as a field officer and Ross took his place in command of the company.

Sam Houston was governor at the time and wanted to send out a regiment of rangers against the Northern Comanches that spring, and in due time he commanded certain men to raise companies; as, Smith of Waco, Darnell of Dallas, Burleson of Austin and so forth. Then the companies would organize in different parts wherever enlisted.

Well, we went up the Brazos River yonder and got to Fort Belknap. One company got there today, one the next. Col. M. T. Johnson was there in command authorized to organize them into a regiment. We came from Waco, and the other fellows from wherever they was from. When we got there Johnson had authority to organize a regiment.

Johnson had his authority from the governor, and also these captains had, because he has commissioned them. The lieutenants and sergeants was elected by the men. Captain Darnell and Smith ran for lieutenant-colonel, for we needed some field officers, needed a lieutenant-colonel and a major and an adjutant. Smith got a majority of the votes. The whole regiment voted.

Sull, we elected him first lieutenant here in Waco. When they raised Smith, we just moved Sull up by all of the votes, and named Callahaw [Tom Kelliheir] to Sull's place, and Allen Galt to Callahaw's place. Captain Fitzhugh got to be major. Joe Johnson was to be adjutant.

Well, word was brought from Fort Cobb of some men who had been over there with some beef and supplies. Gooch and McKay were contractors to furnish corn and so forth to the fort, and when they returned to Fort Belknap they had learned from some friendly Indians that there were several bands of Indians camped over there in what was supposed to be their winter quarters. There was a man named Stewart who had been in that Country up there the year before, and he said he believed he knew where the place was and believed he could find it.

Well, we went to hunt that bunch of Indians. I don't know now whether this man Steward went voluntarily or whether he was promised pay, but he went along with us as a guide, not to keep us from getting lost, but to find those Indians.

We struck the river about 20 miles up, but still didn't find any Indian signs, fresh signs. That river was running from West to East. We went northwest till we struck that river, went across it, and hadn't found any fresh signs. We turned then up the north side of the river and camped one night of the north side. That night there came a rain and freeze, enough to wet the top of the ground, and it was a cold rain.

The next morning we started up the river. We first picked a buffalo trail, for the river was bad about quick sand, so looked for buffalo trails for a place to cross it. We crossed right over behind them, for if a bunch of buffaloes can cross the sand it is safe to cross until there comes another rise. We took up the south side, still we didn't see any fresh Indian signs. We had crossed the river again and camped on the North side about 10 miles up, and found another buffalo trail, and crossed back to the south side and camped.

All this time we had some men ahead of us, six or eight men, from four to 10 miles ahead, and we had some on that side, and some on this side, to look out for signs, or if they saw a body of Indians to come and report to the command. They beat on up the river till night, and we had four men ahead and we stopped there. When the men ahead wanted to find the command they knowed what direction it was, and at night they would see the fire light. In the day time that country you could see all over the country.

It was just at dusk that night that two of our men that was in the front of us, rode into camp. We was camped one company right above the other. Ross' was ours, and Cureton's Minute Men was the furtherest down. Anyhow, that was the way it was. They rode in, two men of our company, and told us – told Ross and the balance of us that was a mind to could listen in – that they had found some fresh signs and said it was about seven or eight miles from there. The understanding was that these two men would come and lead us up to that place, and that the other two would examine and see what they could learn.

When Ross talked to Cureton, he said "Ross, it is just impossible for me to move up tonight. Part of the men's horses wouldn't be able to go 10 miles, they are so fagged;" He says, "Why not wait till morning and then we will all start together? By that time our horses will be rested for travel."

Ross said, "No, them two men that was left there would wait until somebody came to them," and he says, "If they can't move you can follow us early in the morning, and I will take them soldiers and my company and go up there where those two men are, and we will be on the river so you can find us by just coming up the river."

Those men that couldn't move that night were Minute Men. Them fellows was considered rangers too, but they were Minute Rangers. Twenty soldiers went with us that night. And there was a Mexican with us, Anton, that was really Ross' cook. He was brought a locuse [brought along because?] he had been raised in that part of the country. 1860 was a dry year, and Captain Smith had told Sull, "That is the best man you can take. He will know all the lasting water is in that country." There were 41 rangers that went, just 61 men, except the Mexican, and he wasn't an enlisted man.

We stayed up all that night, kept moving up the river, and having a man ahead to see if he could see any lights of any kind in a low valley we would have to have been ahead or away up above them to see the lights. Either on the north or the south they would have been hid. We didn't see them, at any rate, and would just keep moving up. They boys that had been left had gone on up five or six miles, and they had found some more signs closer than that. They said the Indians were still going up the river. That was what caused us to keep on going up the river.

The Indians had killed a polecat; and they found close to the river where the squaws had cut down a hackberry tree, and there were Indian Children's tracks around it in the sand where they had been hunting hackberries, so then we knew they wasn't far off. From there on we kept about 12 men in front, instead of four.

Just about daylight, when it was beginning to get good light, the Indians were found in that place where the high hills were on all sides ecept [except] up and down the stream. They were packed up and some of them had done started when discovered. The balance were leaving as they got ready. There were 61 horses and mules packed with buffalo meat. As we later found, instead of staying there all winter, they were drying after killing their winter meat. At this time the game was poor, and they killed it there. They were killing and preparing the meat, and we later learned there was a bigger camp thirty five miles above that.

They would have anywhere from two to four hundred pounds on a horse, just owing to what the horse could work under. Unless they had plenty of pack animals they didn't have any mercy on the horses and mules. We got 375 horses and mules in all (after the fight). There was 19 of them mules had "US" branded on them. They had robbed some government train. The mules looked like they had had them for some time. Most of them was old.

I guess, women and children and all, there was between 500 and 600 Indians. Some histories say we killed them all, but the devil we did, there was more than 150 or 200 warriors.

Well, just as soon as we went up on top of this narrow hill that was cut in two by this creek we was discovered. The yell that was sent up from the Indians notified the rest and we just charged off the hill and across that little creek, which was boggy in places. There was some Indians going that way, and they fired into them and turned them this way. They just came up through the valley like they were running a race.

They had dogs with them and some of them barked and growled, and some run and some stopped with the Indians till they got killed. They didn't have a great many dogs, I guess, as many as fifteen.

Ross said "Twelve of you men with the best horses go to the front, and try to head them front Indians off." The Indians were strung out from the battle grounds as far as the eye could see. Twelve of us got off as quick as possible, as soon as we could hear what he wanted us to do. There was a string of Indians, and here is a Indian village right over there. There is a narrow ridge over there cut in two by a creek (indicating the position on the floor as he told it) he sent 20 men around the end of the ridge, around the point, where the creek narrowed. Them was the regulars that were at Ross' command. He told them to run around the end of that point.

When the Indians undertook to run they went right off to the West. The Comanche chief ran off up there, when he turned back with some warriors who came back with him. When he was with them the Indians in front bore a little to the North. When he turned back here, them Indians resumed their course, took the same course nearly exactly west.

When he comes back he forms a circle, a kind of oblong circle, right in front of our men. Them Indians that went in that circle dismounted and throwed their horses next to us, made a breastworks of the horses. That was to check us till the others could get away. That was his idea. Right while that talk was going on was when he come.

That was when Ross told ten or twelve men with the best horses to go after the Indians to delay them till something could be done. We got clear away from where those fellows were fighting around the circle. So all twelve of us kept together. Now they were going this way to the west, and running on the South side of the river. When we fired into them, it shoved them over a little to the north. Finally about 4 miles from there, they crossed the river and we crossed right behind them and run in and turned them almost to the North. Every time we fired a volley the Indians would turn a little to the north, until finally when we quit them they were going nearly exactly north. We turned them from west to north.

After crossing the river there, there were branches and gullies leading off from the river, one at one place and one at another. Before our run was ended we went on higher ground, going to the Red River. Every once in a while we would see a big bunch of Indians, but mostly women and children, going in those dry draws. We were on the opposite side, I remember three different good, big bunches, just quitting the run and running down in the draws, but not all in the same draw.

215

Fig. 12.6 - River at Copper Breaks State Park, site of the Battle of Pease River. Photo by Donna Gholson Cook, September 2000.

That was about the plan of it. There was a kind of half circle made. I don't know how much that run around was, but it was about 12 miles to go straight back to the battle grounds. We kept together, just counceled among ourselves as we went. If we had separated and gone up the draws, we would likely have all been killed.

Every once in a while as we were on this run there would be two or three guns and six-shooters shot. There must have been a few more six-shooters among the Indians than there was guns, because we could tell, was close enough when one was fired to know what it was. I will say that there wasn't more than one firearm to 20 Indians. They didn't have any guns.

Macoma [Nocona] the chief (identity known later) back on the battle field, took his position in the circle and his warriors, too. There was about 17 Indians killed in there, and five at one volley. No rangers were killed or wounded. After 17 was down Nacoma spoke out something. (I am done now, but that is what the boys said. They didn't know what it was, but soon saw what it was.)

Most of the Indians were then down behind dead or wounded horses for protection, or breastworks. When those words was spoke, they rose right up and mounted the nearest horses to them. Nacoma came up himself and when he mounted one squaw that was over there about the same place, and up she jumped behind him. At that time all was mounted that was going to be able to get up, just five warriors and the squaw. What he said was to let every man take care of himself and get out of there or die.

That was the only way the boys knew what the order meant. He went himself. Well, as he went out Lieutenant Mike Sommerville was the nearest man in the direction he wanted to go. Mike was a great big fat fellow. He fell almost to the ground as an arrow went over him. By this time Sommerville had recovered the Indian had passed.

Ross fell right in behind. That Indian then had that squaw still behind him. Ross ran in behind them and shot the last rider first. He shot one shot that went clear through her and wounded Nacoma. That didn't stop them until death struck her. They got five or six hundred yards from this circle place, and she just made a loud scream, a wild death scream and come to the ground, and she brought old Nacoma with her off of the horse. That put them on the ground afoot, and here was Ross coming right behind them.

When she got to the ground Nacoma got loose. About the first shot Nacoma made with his arrow he hit Ross' horse. Nacoma was letting the arrows come thick and fast. Sull shot random shots and one of these shots struck his right arm.

When he got that arm broke, Sull had shot him two or three times before he broke that arm, he turned to the only sapling close. It was a mesquite, I suppose 20 feet high, and he took hold of it with his hand this way, that is the way Sull and them boys told it.

Fig. 12.7 - Mesquite tree at the site of the Battle of Pease River. Photo by Donna Gholson Cook, September 2000.

The next man that come to him was that Mexican cook, and the cook had been in the hands of the Indians before, and he understood their language, when he (Nacoma) took hold of that sapling, he commenced looking right off, way toward the northwest, and commenced talking in his own language.

When the Mexican came up Sull was afoot and the Indian was afoot and a hold of the sapling and there stood the Indian's horse. Sull asked the Mexican, "Who is he?" He said, "Well, he is Nacoma." We all knew him by reputation, but not by sight, Sull said, "Well, what is he talking about?" The Indian was not noticing them, was looking way off yonder and talking. "Oh, he says, the blank-blank he talk to his god;" Sull says, "What is he saying?" Well he says he wants his gekovah [jehovah?] to give his token if he has done his duty as a chieftain, or ever failed his tribe, or failed or refused to do his duty any time in behalf of his tribe." Ross said, "But can you talk to him?" The Mexican said yes. Ross said, "Tell him then if he will surrender he will not be shot any more;" The Mexican broke loose talking to him in his own language.

That was the first time, I suppose, that Nacoma had noticed the Mexican. Quick as he spoke Nacoma turned and looked at the Mexican as much as to say, "Who is that talking my language?" I never knowed whether he recognized him or not.

So when the Mexican told him what the white Captain had said, he looked at Sull then, looked back at Sull. Sull was standing there waiting for an answer. He said, "You tell that white captain when I am dead I will surrender but not before, and not to him," and that he was going to surrender to that other captain up there, his gekova. Then he made his motion to the other one and went right on talking to his gekovah again.

Right when he made him that answer he turned loose that sapling, and had a long spear (indicating a spear head some nine inches long) with a china pole about nine feet long made fast at each end with a spear, which was sharp on each edge. The other end was made fast with a spanish knot to a buckskin lariat plaited from it, the other end around the horses neck. Just as he answered, both things were at the same time, he turned loose that sapling, and took this well arm and threw this spear at Sull that way. All Sull had to do was to be out of the way, beyond the end of the lariat.

When Nacoma saw that it didn't hit him, he just turned back to the sapling and went to talking again. Sull said to the Mexican (only the three of them were present) "That is the bravest man ever I saw. I can't shoot as brave a man as that."

The Mexican had a gun took and before he could say shoot that Mexican shot him clear loose of that sapling. He just fell loose from it. Sull run up to him then, and he was lying on his back, and he looked up at him and breathed about three times, and between breaths he gritted his teeth like a wild hog.

This Mexican, Anton, was, had been the personal slave to Nacoma, belonged to Nacoma, and he was very bitter against him. We didn't know why. He told us afterwards. He said that when he was a small boy his father was a ranchman in Mexico, not far from the Rio Grande. He said that one morning, the morning he was captured, his father and three more Mexicans were at the corral roping and catching a lot of horses, and his mother and the balance of the family was at the house. And there was a big bunch of Indians came around the corral, and it didn't take them long to kill the four Mexicans. Some of the Indians ran between them and house and circled around the corral.

Well, he said, they came to the house and his mother came out of the house and met him, Nacoma, who was leading that charge, then a young man, she met him and plead with him in Spanish, in her language, not to kill the children and not to carry them off. He said there was another Mexican woman or two there. He said they killed the women, and carried off the children, him among them, and that he saw Nacoma shoot his mother with a pistol when she was pleading with him. Nacoma kept him, he said, when they divided up the prisoners, and made a servant out of him. And that was the reason he knowed him and that woman, and knowed what they called her, Palooch.

Now by the time Ross saw the breath was out of him, Nacoma, he knew that Callahaw, another lieutenant, was out there having trouble with one Indian. Sull mounts his horse again and went to relieve Callahaw, right out of the open ground, nearly right north of where Sull and the chief were. That left the Mexican behind, and up ran two more of our men, and the Mexican told them enough that they knew it was Nacoma and that the woman was some young squaw he didn't know. He spoke a few words and ran after Ross again, but he never caught up with him till Ross got to where Callahaw and this Indian were having trouble.

The first thing he done (40ss) [Ross], was to run right up in front of them. When he run up in front of them the Indian had a buffalo robe around him, for it was a pretty cold day. She looked at him with a wild glare, and Sull hollers out to Callahaw, "Tom, this is a white woman!" Tom said, "Hell, no, that ain't no White woman," for he was mad and cussing, was an Irishman, and said, "Damn that squaw, if I have to worry with her anymore, I will shoot her!"

Sull contended she was a white woman, and he stayed in front of her himself, and finally laid hold of her horse's bridle, the Mexican runs up first, and when he is up, Sull says, "Who is she, Anton?" And he said, "IH! She is Nacoma wife."

She had a baby under that buffalo robe and held it up when Callahaw started to shoot her, and that was the reason he didn't shoot her just as soon as he run up on her. That was the first time that he knew that she wasn't a warrior. He said, "She is Nacoma's wife." And Sull said, "Well, who is she?" He said that she was a white girl they had raised and he didn't know who she was. Tom gave it up then.

Between the Mexican and Sull and Tom they got her quiet, and the Mexican talked to her in the Comanche language, telling her what she must do. They insisted on carrying her back. Just then, those two fellows that were left where Nacoma was dead run up during the time and they had scalped Nacoma, took the scalp and split it, and each one had half of it. She the woman wanted to go back there where Nacoma was killed. They carried her up there and she got down and paraded around over Nacoma a bit, and paid her respects to this other woman.

They had to force her away from there, took hold of her and just put her on her horse. The Mexican was telling her that she would make them kill her if she didn't come on. They carried her into the camp then, and they established camp. We 12 fellows hadn't come back yet, but that is the way they told it. That Mexican's name was Antonio Mortimus.

We were at Camp Cooper about three weeks afterwards when we discovered the womans identity. There were different surmises about it. There wasn't any of us that really knowed anything about it. There had been a lot of children carried off at different times in Texas. We couldn't learn from her who she was. One thing I left out, when Callahaw caught up with her, she didn't run out of the ring, for she had started off with the squaws and children but had turned back to see if they would be killed, when the circle broke she was just a little way off as if she had been in the circle. Callahaw didn't know that she was a woman. She said at the time she throwed that baby up, "Americano!" Said it over three times. Now he misunderstood what she meant. He thought she was a squaw pleading with him as an American, but he learned afterwards she meant to tell him that she was an American. (The woman was Cynthia Ann Parker)

There wasn't but 27 Indians killed that we got. They were carrying 32 Indians, when running off, wounded Indians, you might say. There were 17 dead in the circle.

Sull Ross went to meet Sam Houston, the governor, at Waco, and he took that boy (an Indian boy that was captured) with him at the time. Sull's father lived at Waco, and had several Negroes and put that Indian among them Negroes and was raised with them. He used the Indian as a cowboy as soon as he got big enough. That was the reason they caught him running with those Negroes up there. He has been right on this gallery here. That was the son of one of those warriors there.

Here is the way the boy told that to the Mexican as we came back. He said that when they went to start from the camp he had his pony ready to start, and thought he would walk a piece and shoot with his bow and arrow a little to get warmed up before he got on his horse. When this hurrah was raised and guns began popping this horse broke and run and the boy never did get to his pony. Marion Cassidy saw him dodging some horses and men. Marion took hold of his hand while the fighting was going on at the circle, which must have lasted an hour. When they were bringing Cynthia Ann in, Ross happened to see something, way out yonder, and rode out there and got him. Sull couldn't talk but just a word in a place to a Comanche, and the Indian came up to him, and he brought him in behind him. He wasn't Nacoma's boy at all. I guess he told the Mexican what Indian's son he was. We didn't care whose son he was.[20]

In another interview, Frank gave a detailed account of the identification of Cynthia Ann Parker and the first attempts to reintroduce her to civilization.

By the time we got back to the battle ground Cureton's men had come and eleven more men had come too. They had been following a trail from out of Jack and Young counties and were missing this battle several miles when they heard the noise of battle and came to investigate. A scalping party had been sent out and all the Indians found dead had been scalped except one. A squaw whom some thought a white woman had been captured, as well as a small boy seven or eight years old. The woman had a small child, a girl, whom she called Curlin. She called herself Palux. One young warrior showing to have some white blood was dead on the inside of the oblong circle that had been formed by the Indians. The woman showed more grief over the body of this warrior than she did over the bodies of the others, so this caused the scalping party not to scalp him, thinking that he might be her son. Nobody there could talk the Comanche language except the Mexican cook of Ross. He was told to ask her about this young warrior. She answered him saying "He is my boy and he is not my boy," which was no information at all.

The squaw then recognized the Mexican. He had been a slave in the family of Chief Nocona, whose squaw she was. As such, he was to be looked down upon, and from then on she answered only such questions as suited her. We learned all we could from the woman and the boy as to the possibility of other Indians being around. The woman would not talk much, but the boy told us that there was a big camp of Indians up the river, enough to kill us all, he said in a threatening way. Then it was agreed that about fifty men with the best horses would go up the river and learn about this camp the next morning. This was done, I being one of those who went. We found a large village which had been abandoned about a day before, but found no Indians.

We stayed three days near the battle ground before leaving for good. When we left we had twenty six scalps, not counting one unscalped warrior. Two of the scalped were squaws. Nocona's scalp was (s)plit open, making two parts, Jim Kelley claiming one part and Gasper Garrett the other. We had the unknown white woman and her girl baby and the Indian boy who was afterward called Pease. He was carried to Waco by Ross and turned over to his father and family. The old Captain owned some negro property, so the Indian boy was raised among the slaves until the close of the Civil War. When Sul Ross returned from the Civil War and he and Mrs. Ross started keeping house for themselves, Sul took the boy, gave him some education, treated him well, and after the Comanches came in on the Reservation he allowed him to go back to the village and stay if he wanted to. He preferred, however, to live at Waco with the Rosses and always considered that his home. During the wholesale driving of cattle from Texas to Kansas he made a few trips as trail hand, but always returned to Waco. He has been here on my farm south of Evant, Texas performing ranch service or doing other work for me several different times. He recognized me as one of the men who helped capture him, and appeared to have a special interest in all the men who had helped bring him to civilization. He told me he thought he remembered every one of the Rangers who then lived and never went near one without going to see him. Some time in the eighties he got off up the Leon river near Jonesboro and there got sick. He asked to be carried back to Captain Ross' at Waco and this request was granted. He never recovered, but died there.

Fig. 12.8 - Cynthia Ann Parker and Child. Prints & Photographs Collection, Center for American History, The University of Texas at Austin, CN Number 00087.

~The Identification and Later Life of Cynthia Ann Parker~

There was considerable speculation as to the identity of the white woman whom we had captured in the Pease river fight with the Indians. Several white children had been captured by the Indians at different times and no one knew whether she was one of them or not. She was sullen, was a hard looker, was as dirty as she could be and looked to me more like an Indian than a white woman. Some of the other men thought this too. I remember concerning this that Ross when he first saw her thought she was a white woman. He had gone up to Kalahah during the roundup after the main battle was over and saw that the latter, who was horseback,

225

was having trouble driving a squaw along. He said to Kalahah that she was a white woman and ought to be taken to camp. Kalahah, who had lung trouble and was on a fiery horse, was coughing and trying to head the dodging squaw till he had lost his temper. When Ross proposed to Kalahah that she was a white woman the latter said "White, hell, she's a damned old squaw." But the Mexican cook of Ross' who had once been a captive of the Comanches and a servant of Nocona's, ran up about that time. Ross asked him who the woman was. He said "She's Nocona's wife."

Then Ross asked "Well, who was she?"

"I don't know," he said. "She was some white girl they raised."

That settled it and the soldiers decided to keep her. She was evidently thoroughly Indian in everything else, if not in blood and some of the men begged Ross to turn her loose. But he said that there were a number of white people in Texas who had lost children through capture by the Indians and that if this woman were turned loose every one of these people would feel that this was probably his child or relative. So she was kept.

Kalahah had been the man that stopped her and Ross was the first man that had gone to him. This was just after Nocona had been killed. Ross had come direct from there. Kalahah did not kill her when she held up her baby.

By her request through the Mexican cook she was carried by Nocona's body. The Mexican was trying to talk to her all the time after he came to her, trying to tell her what she would have to do not to be killed and that she would be held a prisoner. They finally had to put her on a horse and force her to leave Nocona's body. Kelley got her baby and took it ahead, thinking that this would make her come, but she paid no attention to it.

I was not present at the Capture, for I had gone off in chase of some of the Indians that had run off during the early part of the fight, but all the details, conversation and all, were told me by the others who were there.

When they took the woman away from Nocona's body they took her back to the main battle ground, where they allowed her to look among the dead. She uttered some words of moaning for every one that was killed, but seemed to be especially grieved over the body of one young warrior. He, showing some signs of white blood, the scalping party, thinking he might be her boy, scalped all the others, but left him unscalped through respect for her.

The Mexican was told to ask if this was her boy. She replied "He's my boy and he's not my boy," which was no answer at all.

The captive, after she got over her scare and was no longer afraid for her life, would not talk to the Mexican except when it suited her—and it seldom did. She held herself above him and looked down upon him as not her equal, for she was the high chief's wife and he was only a servant or slave.

A camp was established up the creek above the battle ground and the woman and her baby were carried there. The little Indian boy of about eight years of age whom Ross had picked up was put with them and a guard was placed over them.

A cool norther blew up. The woman was made to understand that she would not be hurt or mistreated unless she tried to escape. She seemed to be in great distress. Then, through the interpretation of the Mexican, she told us how she came to be captured. When the excitement was raised from the appearance of the Rangers she had her two boys, Quanah and Grassnut, with her. They and a number of other squaws and children, according to orders, started to escape. "After I had gone some distance" she said, "I missed both my boys. I came back in search of them, coming as near to the battle as I could. In this way I was caught. I'm greatly distressed about my boys. I fear they are killed."

She then said to Antonio Martinez, the Mexican cook, according to his report of the conversation: "They may be cut off to themselves or with other children and will freeze tonight, that some of the other Indians will find them tomorrow."

In answer to the Mexican's questions she told about a larger band of Indians up the river, and said that they were on the move when the attack had been made. She told us that some of the Indians that escaped would more than likely go to the larger village and return with a large force of warriors. It was this talk and the boastings of the Indian boy that made us send out a searching party about which I have already told.

The Indian boy threatened us a great deal at first. He would talk viciously to us in his own language and the Mexican would tell us what he said. After dark it grew a good deal colder. A bed was prepared for the boy, but he wasn't satisfied to go to bed and stay there because the white men had prepared his bed. A large fire was built. He continued to give trouble to the guards. Three men, P. Cunningham, Bob Gray and Ed Tilley stood him up before the fire. All the time he was saying he wanted to freeze to death. A buffalo robe which had been captured from the Indians was wrapped around him with the wool next to him, feet and all, a small rope was taken and wrapped around this from head to foot, the boy's hands, arms, feet and legs all being securely bound. This was done while he was standing up in front of the fire. Ed Kelley shoved him over on the ground and said "Now, freeze if you can."

We heard no more of his threats about what Nocona was going to do. He did not know that Nocona was dead. The next morning he seemed to be dull. He was ready to eat, though, when food was offered him. All the men humored him and gave him friendly attention.

We left that camp on the morning of December 21, 1860. The Indian boy was allowed to keep and ride his own pony and saddle, which had been captured, and which seemed to please him very much. Nocona's wife was allowed to claim all the horses and other property that had belonged to him, that were in our possession, but she refused to take anything, saying that he had two more squaws that had the same right to the property that she had and she would take nothing unless she could have a division with them. She claimed only two horses and a saddle as her individual property, her own clothing and her baby's clothing, refusing to take the clothing of her two boys or anything that they had on the ground, saying that these belonged to the children who were not there and that they might return to get them some time. Their clothing was on the packs, all of which we captured. A lot of this extra clothing, saddles, buffalo robes and other things that we did not need we burned. She hung on to her two horses, though. One of them was as pretty a red and white paint horse as I ever saw; the other was a dark bluish roan.

The boy gave us no more trouble after we started out. The woman gave us a lot, though, trying to escape. We had no extra trouble with the horse herd. Ross' company and the twenty soldiers who had been sent to help out in the campaign had charge of the horse herd and the prisoners. On account of the scarcity of grass and water in a number of places, Captain Cureton and his men and the other eleven men traveled separately from us in returning to Fort Belknap. The only incident on the return trip that made much of an impression on my memory was when Kried Sharp accidently shot off Berry Fulcher's ear. They were riding some distance in the rear one morning when Sharp dropped a bowie knife. His gun was a shot gun. Remaining on his horse, he learned [leaned] over to pick up the knife from the ground. His horse, being wild and anxious to follow the herd, gave a jump, which caused the gun to be discharged, the load taking off a part of the top of Fulcher's ear. The wound bled profusely, but was not dangerous, of course. Dr. Neadlet dressed and trimmed the ear and soon stopped the bleeding. The boys told Berry that afterward, when he was associating with Kried, owing to the carelessness of Kried and the size of Berry's ears he had better be sure to keep them out of the way.

We were then on our return trip to Fort Belknap. When we arrived there Captain Ross got the command from Governor Houston to meet him at Waco as the Governor was billed to speak there January 12, 1861. Ross and all of us went to the headquarters camp on Elm creek. From there he left us and started to Waco. He carried the Indian boy

Donna Gholson Cook

with him, delivering him to his father, Colonel S. P. or Shapley Ross.

Ross left Lt. T. H. Kalahah in command, with instructions to take the captive woman and her baby and men enough to keep a guard and send some one after Ben Kiggins. The woman by this time had become so contrary about giving out information thru Antonio Martinez as interpreter that something had to be done. Kiggins was a man who had been a captive in this tribe of Indians. He had been bought by some Indian traders. He had not been used as a servant or a slave as Martinez had been. Word was sent ahead of the captured white woman and child that we had. Ross gave special instructions that Colonel Isaac Parker be notified. The Mexican was left with us to act as interpreter until Kiggins could be secured. According to the orders of Ross, if anyone came and identified the woman and took her off, the Mexican was to go home with them and act as interpreter till she was better reconciled or he was sent for to come back.

At this meeting at Waco the Governor proposed to give Ross another commission. He would thus disband his men and reenlist those that volunteered and fill up the company with new men. But Captain Ross declined and recommended to the Governor that Lieutenant D. A. Sublett be granted a commission as Captain for the new company. Ross returned to camp. When his commission had almost expired he made known to his men that Lieutenant Sublett had a commission to raise a new company to take the place of the old one. If any of them desired to volunteer and remain in the service on the frontier at a certain date they would be given an opportunity to do so.

The day before breaking camp on Elm Creek the opportunity was made known and part of the men volunteered to remain in the service under Captain Sublett, while the remainder, of whom I was one, went to Waco and were disbanded.

Now to get back to the woman in the story. A few early parties came before Colonel Parker did, but from what

230

information they could get from her through the Mexican interpreter they went away without laying claim to her or learning who she was.

She was still sullen and would have little to say, although she had about quit her efforts to escape. There were at the camp some women, chiefly wives of officers, who became sorry for her and decided that they would do what they could to aid her to get back to civilization. They asked Kalahah to let them have her to keep a while. He was fearful of the result, but finally consented. The women took her out of the tent in which she was staying and took her up to one of their tents. They found enough clothes to clothe her, had an old negro mammy prepare some hot water and wash her thoroughly, combed her hair and let her look at herself in a mirror. She submitted to all this willingly enough, apparently, until she got a good opportunity to get out the door of the place. When this opportunity occurred she made a dive for the door and got past the negro mammy. It was about two or three hundred yards from there to her old tent and she struck out for it. Kalahah had stationed several men near by to act as guards to prevent her from escaping, but when we saw that she was making for her tent we let her go. It was a race such as I have never seen before or since. In the lead was the squaw, jerking off clothes as she ran until she soon had on almost nothing; behind came the negro mammy frantically waving a cloth or something, two or three bewildered white women looked on and the squaw's little child, big enough to toddle around, following after, with nobody paying much attention to her. The squaw reached her tent and the next time she reappeared she had got rid of the remnants of her civilized garb and had somewhere raked up some more Comanche garments. This was the last time the women tried their hands at civilizing her.

Colonel Parker came late one afternoon. Mr. Kiggins was on hand. The Colonel looked at the woman captive, but attempted no investigation that afternoon. He had been prominent in the early days of the Republic of Texas, and was anxious to find his long lost niece and nephew, who had been carried off at the massacre at Parker's fort by the Indians when they were quite young, their father having been killed in the defense of the fort at the time, May 18, 1836.

The next morning Colonel Parker, Lieutenant Kalahah and some of the officers and soldiers that belonged to the fort Camp Cooper, I being in the group, went to the tent of the captive woman. She used a small pine box for a seat. The wind was blowing cold from the north that morning. She was sitting on her box on the south side of her tent crouched low, with elbows on her knees and the palms of her hands on her jaws. When the men assembled she paid no attention whatever to them.

Lieutenant Kalahah said "Colonel, it appears to me that the last thing she would remember of her home life would be the name that her parents and family called her."

Colonel Parker replied "I don't know if she had a double name or not, but I do know well that my brother and his wife called her Cynthia Ann."

When the woman heard this name called she stirred on her seat. Colonel Parker was asked to repeat the words. He did so and again the woman showed some commotion, stirring about uneasily, but still remaining on the box. Colonel Parker said a third time "I do know my brother and his wife called her Cynthia Ann." She rose and stood erect, fronted the man who was speaking, patted her breast and said in broken English "Me, Cincee Ann." She then repeated it and resumed her seat on the box.

This caused considerable commotion among the men. Some one said "Where is Ben Kiggins?"

"He is over yonder in one of those tents in that row of tents in a game," some one else replied.

I volunteered to go after Kiggins. "I'll go with you" said R. A. Gray, and we went.

We found Kiggins in a game of cards. I said to him "Ben, they want you up at the squaw's tent. She is about to know something."

"The hell she is," he said. He threw down his cards and asked another man to take his place. When he came out of the tent he asked us what it was she was about to know. We answered that Colonel Parker called a name in her hearing and she appeared to recognize it.

When we got near the tent Colonel Parker and Lieutenant Kalahah and a few of our boys and an officer or two at the fort met us. The Lieutenant introduced the Colonel to Mr. Kiggins. The Colonel did the talking for the group.

"Now, Mr. Kiggins," he said. "You understand better than I or any of us do how to approach her. As I called the name of the long lost niece that I am searching for she showed some commotion, leading all of us to believe that she remembered the name when she heard it."

"Give me the name, Colonel," said Kiggins. Colonel Parker repeated the name. This was not in the woman's hearing.

Kiggins then said, "Now, Colonel, don't speak a word only as I ask you."

We walked up to the tent. Kiggins commenced talking in the Comanche language in a friendly way. She arose at once and stood in front of him while he was talking to her. She would listen till he would get through talking, then answer him. He asked her what she knew about the name that we had been calling her. She made a long answer, after which Kiggins turned and translated for us what she had said.

"She says" Kiggins told us "that she much regrets it but it is a fact that once she had a pale face pa and a pale face ma and they had a name for her, and that name was Cincee Ann. She says that now, though, she has a red man pa and a red man ma and they have a name for her and this name is Palux."

Parker then said "Ask her where she was when the Indians took her into captivity." She shook her head and told him she didn't know where.

Kiggins repeated the answer to Parker, then he asked her how many people were killed when she was taken into captivity. She answered and said thirty five.

Colonel Parker then said "She may not know any better, but not that many were killed."

He then said "Ask her if there were any other captives taken away at the same time that she was."

Kiggins did so and she answered. He said "Colonel, she says that five captives were carried off at the time, she being one of the number."

"Who were they? Were they grown people or children?" were the next questions.

"Colonel," said Kiggins, "She says that there were two grown women and three children and that she was one of them and had a younger brother and his name was Juan."

Colonel Parker said that she was correct in all this, but that she was wrong in the number killed at the fort, for there were only thirty five altogether and only seventeen were killed.

Kiggins said "let me get her to describe the place where all this happened." He talked to her a good while. Then she took a stick and marked the shape of a house. She would put a large dot at one place and a small dot at another, and so on. She made a long straight mark lengthwise of the house, a little distance from it. She turned into the tent, picked up a canteen of water, filled her mouth and dropped water drop by drop in this long strait mark and trailed the water on down the length of the mark. Then she explained to Kiggins, pointing to the dots and to the mark.

Kiggins turned to us and said, "She says this is the shape of the long building they all lived in. The small dots represent windows or port holes, the larger ones represent doors, and the long line represents a running stream in front of the building."

When Kiggins made this explanation Colonel Parker turned to us and said, "Gentlemen, I actually could not make as good a picture of the old fort as she has made."

By this time we were all satisfied as to her identity but Colonel Parker kept asking questions. He asked who were the grown women and she didn't know. He asked who was the third child and she replied through Kiggins that the other child was a boy and belonged to one of the women.

Colonel Parker said, "That's right. Mrs. Plumer had a boy who was carried off with her and his name was Pratt."

Other questions were asked and answered, but enough had already been brought out to show who the squaw really was.

Preparations were made to start the next morning to the Parker home at or near Weatherford. The Colonel was asked if he wanted the Mexican to go as an interpreter until he got her home and better reconciled. He answered yes, that he would be glad to have him, so he was sent. Two of the Rangers were sent as guards and returned in a few days.

The Mexican was gone some two weeks or more. When the woman rode out of sight that morning from Camp Cooper was the last time that I ever saw her. I have been told that in less than a year her baby died. She gave so much trouble on the frontier trying to escape that she was sent to a younger brother and sister who had escaped from the Fort Parker massacre with their mother, and who at that time were living in Anderson county. I am told that she remained there with her relatives until her death, which took place about 1872. I am told, also, that she was never contented.

. . . I might add one more explanation about Cynthia Ann's strange answer as to who the young buck was that looked like a white man and about whom she said "He's my boy and he's not my boy." She told Kiggins that he was the son of another white girl who had been captured by the Comanches and had married an Indian. The girl had died a good many years before, but before doing so had made Cynthia Ann promise to look after the boy as if he were her own son.[21]

~ CARTER, WILLIS, & MORRIS ~

Frank Gholson told the stories of the death of three other settlers at the hands of Indians: Lieutenant Bob Carter in 1861; Bill Willis on Christmas Day 1866; and John Morris, killed while returning from a trail drive.

~ The Killing of Bob Carter ~

Many years ago Captain B. F. Gholson gave the following account of the killing of Lieutenant Bob Carter in a fight with Indians on October 19, 1861. "Uncle Frank" Gholson, as he was affectionately known in his later years, was one of the outstanding frontiersmen of Central Western Texas during perilous Indian times. He died at Evant, Texas, about eighteen years ago. His account of the killing of Carter follows:

In the late fifties it became necessary for the few settlers to organize one of the minute companies in Hamilton county. Bob Carter was elected lieutenant and was given command of a certain number of men, he living down near the south line of the county. He had a few men from Coryell and Lampasas counties. They divided into scouts of ten men to the scout, going out for ten days at a time. When one ten would come in another ten would go out. In this particular scout Lieutenant Carter, with nine men started out about the 10th of October. On the ninth day out, having turned in the direction of home, they nooned at the head spring of the Lampasas river. Finding they were about out of meat when they broke camp for their evening's travel, Carter directed John Witcher, an expert deer hunter to choose his side, travel separately and try to kill some game, adding: "If you don't get with us, we will camp near the round mountain at the Post Oak Spring." Late in the evening when they arrived at the spring Witcher had not shown up. Some of the men started on foot to make a little hunt, leaving their horses under guard with the other men.

F. G. Morris crossed the creek and went to the round mountain to overlook the country for Indians, game or signal smoke, or anything in their line of duty. When a short distance up the side of the mountain he stopped to view his surrounding. He was southwest of their camp on the south side of the creek, the camp being on the north side. Still further to the north and near another range of mountains he saw a big party of men, whom he took to be Indians, and they were running something, but he would not tell what it was, so he hastened to camp and told of his discoverey. By this time it was sundown. Carter ordered the men to saddle up as quickly as possible. Witcher had not yet come. They started with Grundy Morris leading, and when they got out of the timber into the open draw it was getting dark. Before they had gone a great distance their horses showed signs of excitement and they discovered that the Indians were coming in their direction. Carter ordered a charge and they met the Indians in battle array. The shooting and yelling began at once and they mixed in almost a hand-to-hand clash. When they got apart the Indians formed on the east side of the draw, which was next to the white men's camp, the rangers forming on the opposite side.

Another charge was made and the Indians met them in the draw, where another hand-to-hand conflict ensued, but was of short duration and both sides withdrew to their last positions. In the next charge they so mixed up that they changed sides of the draw. John Hurst was wounded and Simpson Loyd's horse was killed in this engagement. Calling his men together, Carter counselled with them a few moments and another charge was planned. This time the Indians resisted desperately and when both sides fell back it was found that Grundy Morris was wounded, J. R. Townsend's horse was shot and Lieutenant Carter was missing. They decided to fall back to their pack animals at the camp and take care of the wounded. The Indians withdrew to the timber on the opposite side, and when this was discovered three of the men made their way back to the battle ground to search for Carter. Failing to find him, and their wounded men growing worse, they decided to pack up and try to get the wounded over to Hurst's ranch, which was the nearest habitation. They succeeded in getting there before day the next morning, and, collecting more men, they immediately started back to the scene of battle. The body of Lieutenant Carter was found just below where the last fighting was done, and was tenderly borne by his comrades to his own home.

Still Witcher was not heard from. His brother conveyed the news to his parents at their home in what was then known as Langford's Cove, and it was generally believed that the Indians had murdered him, but late that evening Henry Carter, a ranchman, found him and brought him home on horseback. It was Witcher running from the Indians when Grundy Morris discovered them from the side of the round mountain. Witcher said they crowded him so close that he dismounted and left his horse at the edge of the brush and ran a long distance on foot. Finding that he was not pursued he stopped running and discovered he had lost his hat and shoes. Knowing the country pretty well, he was on his way to Henry Carter's when found. He was unable to travel further on foot, so Mr. Carter carried him home.

This battle took place on what has ever since been known as Lookout Mountain, on the evening of October 19, 1861, and the men of Lieutenant Carter's company were neighbors. Accounts of the fight were given by several of whom took part in it. By request of his sons Gholson sat up with the corpse of Lieutenant Carter the night after he was brought home, and assisted in the internment at Lankford's [Langford's] grave yard, now near Evant, Texas.

Following is a list of the names of the men in the scout: Bob Carter, lieutenant; John Hurst, F. G. Morris, Simpson Loyd, Joe Manning, J. M. Witcher, Jim Mitchell, Will Cotton, Adam Witcher, J. R. Townsend.[22]

~ The Killing of Bill Willis ~

One of the last deaths at the hands of Indians described by Frank was the death of Bill Willis. At the time of the killing of Bill Willis in Hamilton County on Christmas Day 1866, Frank and Adeline had been married four years.

I have been requested to write an account of the killing of Bill Willis by Indians, which occurred in Hamilton county.

On the evening of the 25th of December, 1866, there was to be a grand ball at Hamilton. The county being thinly settled people went from a great distance. Citizens of the southern part of the county and neighborhoods in the adjoining county agreed to meet at the Langford Store in Langford's care [cove?] and all who were going to go together for the protection of the women that were going. The crowd all met at the store except Bill Willis, and started to Hamilton leaving word for Bill to come on when he arrived at the store. The entire crowd went on horseback. Some three hours later I was at the store when Bill came and was told what the crowd said. He was riding a mule that was both lame and jaded and said that he had hunted ever since daylight for his other horses but failing to find them he thought he would go on on the mule. This being on the full of the moon and at the most dangerous time, I urged Bill not to go. He insisted however, and then I told him to go down by my ranch, a mile and a half off his route, and take one of my horses and turn the mule loose. My wife being present, said "Yes Bill go by and get Old Tom. We saw him and six other horses not more than a half an hour ago on the branch as we left the ranch house." He declined, saying he could make it on the mule alright. I told him it was extreme foolishness to go on that mule in its condition at that particular time. "Bill you know better, you are acting contrary to your better judgment." He patted his Spencer gun and then his six shooter and told us that he would get more of them than there was of him in case he was attacked by Indians.

Thus he rode away, mule tired and lame, to travel 18 miles to Hamilton. When he got within two miles of Hamilton he heard the war whoop raised and saw 13 Indians coming. They were a full half mile away. He spurred and whipped his mule, but the mule refused to go any faster, and the Indians ran up and began shooting arrows. He shot one Indian off his horse who had run in front of him. They then shot the mule. The mule ran a quarter of a mile. By that time they had shot it so many times that it stopped perfectly still Bill got off and took it afoot, stayed in the road and went towards town. At this time they carried the Indian away that he had shot, laid him on the prairie and left one Indian with him on his horse where he could see right down the valley to the town, while the others returned to the fight. Capt. Jim Rice lived at the outside house some distance from the town in the direction the fight was going on. The men all being in town Mrs. Rice told her girl children to run to town and tell their papa that the Indians were killing some body on the Cove Road in plain view of the house. When the children told Capt. Rice he hollered out to the men in the town that the Indians were killing somebody on the Langford Cove Road. A big crowd was in town and had their horses hitched on the square with their saddles on. The Indian on the prairie saw the movement gave a signal to the other Indians which they obeyed, leaving Willis in a few minutes time still on foot with seven wounds. When he saw the men coming, he sank down. He said, "Boys I'm badly wounded but I've got three stacked up out there." The first men ran ahead and sure enough they got to see them carrying off their three men.

It then being sun down they failed to overtake them until dark. Then they were lost. Blood hounds were put on the trail but failed to overtake them. Bill was carried to town and a man by the name of Hambright took him on his back saying "Hold around my neck Bill and I'll carry you to the doctor." Dr. Walker was called and on examination he was found to have seven wounds, five of them being arrow wounds, one six shooter wound and one large wound supposed to be a Spencer gun wound. He lingered 39 days, dying on the night of Feb. 3, 1867.

His father R. W. Willis went to him and stayed and took care of him at Hamilton until he died. He told his father, "Frank Gholson did his best to keep me from coming on on that mule. He told me if I would go, to go down by his ranch and get a horse and leave the mule. If I had done either one that he said do I would not have been in this fix."[23]

~ The Killing of John Morris ~

Frank Gholson described the killing of John Morris by Indians when Morris and his brother were returning home from a trail drive. The date of the attack is not given, but since it happened in the course of a trail drive, it was probably after the Civil War, near the end of the period of Indian attacks.

The following article was written by B. F. Gholson of Evant, Texas. The John Morris referred to was a brother of Dave Morris, Jr., who was the father of Sam and Henry Morris, who now reside in Goldthwaite.

"John Morris and his brother, W. M. Morris, sold their small stock of cattle to James Burleson, a regular driver, who employed them as trail hands to assist in driving his herd to Fort Sumner, at which place he paid them for their cattle and their wages also, giving them currency for the whole amount, except one check for $600 on some bank in Chicago. Accompanied by several of the cow hands, the Morris brothers started on their return home, coming in by way of the Concho, Jim Ned and Pecan Bayou, where their companions began to leave them and take nearest routes to their homes, and a few came as far as where Brownwood now stands.

"The Morris brothers had a wagon and three horses, and were armed with six-shooters only. When the two reached four miles northeast of the Williams ranch, Bill Morris, who was on horseback, saw several deer some distance away and went forward to kill some of the game.

"He had not gone far when he discovered a large party of Indians, some of them coming toward him, others headed for the wagon. He immediately returned to the wagon to assist his brother, John, who had climbed out of the wagon, and the fight opened.

"The Indians captured Bill's horse and shot one of the others with an arrow, causing the team to run away, leaving the boys afoot.

"The brothers knew the country well and decided to go to a certain bluff on Brown's creek, and several times they had to drive the Indians from behind trees along the way. It was a running fight and was kept so until they reached an open prairie, when John was weakening from four wounds. They finally crossed the prairie spot and reached a grove and John sank down. He told Bill he could go no further and urged him to run and try to escape.

"They had killed and wounded a number of Indians, and for the time the savages had checked up. This gave Bill an opportunity to slip away, so leaving his wounded brother, he made his way to the Williams ranch, or rather the Fowler ranch as it was then known, where he secured help and returned to assist his brother as quickly as possible. But the relief party arrived too late. The Indians were gone. John was dead and scalped and his body mutilated.

"The news of the killing reached Langford Cove that day and John Morris' father requested me to go to the Langford graveyard and prepare a grave for his son, which I did, but they decided to bury him at the Williams ranch. Thus the grave which I prepared stands open even unto this day.

"As soon as John was buried, Bill came home and then went on by the Cove. He came to my house and stayed all night. About ten nights after the killing had taken place the Indians stole thirteen horses from our place before going on.

"Bill and I followed the trail next day, and we found a horse which Bill had shot during the fight a few days before. We brought him in and learned that he belonged to Henry Ford, and had been stolen a few days before the fight.

"Twenty-six Indians engaged in this fight and seven were either killed or wounded. The wagon was plundered and the check that I mentioned and all the money carried away, except a few dollars Bill had in his pockets. The Indians were pursued but were not overtaken."

Mr. R. E. Clements talked with Edgar Burkett of Mullin regarding the John Morris killing by the Indians; he said his father, Joe Burkett, was with the party that found Morris' body and took it to Williams Ranch. The body was badly decomposed and Joe Burkett sat up with the remains all night to keep away prowling cats and dogs from the wagon.[24]

~

After his three ranger enlistments, Frank married Adeline Langford, served as a Confederate soldier, then settled down to run a stock ranch. Indian attacks were still a real fear during the early years of Frank and Adeline's marriage and continued until around 1874 with the addition of new challenges—mob rule, vigilante justice, and the Civil War.

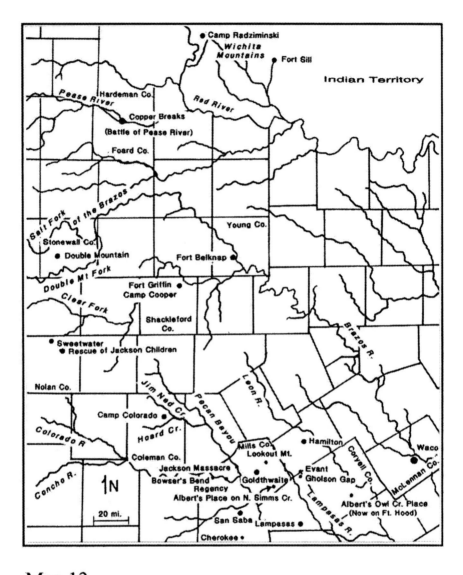

Map 13

North Central Texas counties, showing points of interest
in Chapters 12 and 13. Map compiled by author.
Copyright 2003.

Chapter 13: Vigilante Justice, Mob Rule, and Civil War Texas

Two Brothers - 1862-1865
Benjamin Franklin Gholson and
Samuel Sullivan Gholson

Texas was far removed from most of the major battlefields of the war, but the state was confronted with the fourfold problem of providing men for military service at home and in other theaters, defending the Gulf Coast against Federal attack, stamping out internal subversion, and protecting frontier residents from Indians, bushwhackers, and *renegadoes*. . . . A few Texas units, assigned to frontier defense, spent most of the war within the boundaries of the state. Others, such as Nicholas C. Gould's Twenty-Third Cavalry, patrolled the Indian Frontier of Southwest Texas until the Red River Campaign of 1864 and then, with all other available units, was shifted to Arkansas and Louisiana. Others, including the famous Frontier Regiment of the Texas Rangers, were transferred to Confederate service and fought largely east of the Mississippi. John Bell Hood's Texas Brigade—perhaps the most famous of all Texas units—fought with Robert E. Lee's Army of Northern Virginia in six of the bloodiest battles of the war, including Antietam and Gettysburg.[1]

Many books have been written about the Civil War, and the purpose here is not to rehash the war, but to establish the roles of Sam and Frank Gholson as Confederate soldiers in Texas. Although Frank's Texas Ranger experiences are recorded in great detail in several lengthy interviews, not much was written about his Civil War service. Frank's brother Sam wrote an autobiography at age eighty-two that sheds some light on the subject, particularly the series of events that led to their enlistments.

Sam and Frank narrowly escaped death at the hands of a mob in the fall of 1862. Sam had joined Sheridan's company of Confederate soldiers in the summer of 1862 but was discharged because the captain decided it was too risky for Sam to ride alone through Indian country to participate in the weekly drills. In September, he joined the company of Captain William Gallasby [Gillespie?], which would be forming at Lampasas on October 5. While he waited for the day he was scheduled to report, he took a wagonload of wheat to Lampasas to be ground so that his wife would have flour while he was away. He was waiting his turn at the mill when he received word from Doctor Steward through William Storms, the mill owner, that a mob had gone to Sam's house and arrested his wife, along with two men named Dave Purl and Aleck Williams, and were taking them all to Langford Cove (now Evant). They had also

> arrested Frank Gholson, old man Langford, old man Thomson, and took Dave Purl out to the Langford graveyard, hung him and dug a hole and rolled him in it, covered him in about 2 feet of dirt, and was hunting for Sam Gholson. They wanted to find him to hang him.[2]

If they failed to find Sam, they would put his wife in jail in San Antonio until they did. One of the mob claimed to be a provost marshal; another claimed to be a lieutenant. They were rounding up men who were rightly or wrongly accused of being deserters, and Dave Purl was at the top of their list. Dave had spent a night at the ranch of Dave Morris a couple of weeks before, and the mob "arrested the old man and took him down to Benets Creek and put a rope around his neck, then got up on a bluff and pulled him up 3 times trying to make him tell where Dave Purl was."[3] Since Purl had left Morris' ranch two weeks before, Morris had no idea where he was. After leaving Morris' ranch, Purl was riding past Sam's house and Sam invited him to get down and have dinner with him and his wife. They had never met but, as was customary, they offered hospitality to the passing stranger. Purl told Sam that he was on his way to Fort Belknap, and when he left, Sam invited him to stop in and spend the night on the way back, and when he did, that was where the mob found him.[4] It is not clear whether the mob was going to hang Sam because he harbored a deserter, because he was not in the Confederate army himself, or just on general principles.

After his flour was ground, knowing that the mob was looking for him, Sam stayed in Lampasas and sent Bill Willis (who was later killed by Indians, as described in Chapter 12) to deliver the flour to his wife. The mob was waiting for Sam on the road. They stopped Willis and asked him where Sam was, but Willis told them he did not know. The mob took Willis, the team, wagon and flour to their camp at Langford Cove. They took their prisoners, including the wives of Frank and Sam, to Lampasas and were on their way to Storms' house, when Sam was warned that they were coming and tried to escape. Sam said that he had only gone about 125 steps when they found him, and all nine of them began firing at him. He said that he "threw up his hands"[5] to surrender. Even so, the last man to reach him fired a double-barrelled shotgun at him. Sam said, "I could almost see the lead in it."[6] The man must have either been an incredibly poor shot, or just putting on a show to scare Sam, since it would have been difficult to miss such a large target at close range with a double-barrelled shotgun. They tied his hands and marched him to the public square. When Storms asked what Sam had done, they refused to answer. They were on the verge of hanging him when Captain Gallasby came up and told the leader of the mob that Sam was a member of his company, and to turn him loose. They refused to release him, took over Storms' house as their headquarters, fed his corn to their horses, and kept the prisoners under guard. The date was October 10, 1862. They brought Doctor Steward in and kept him with the prisoners until about two o'clock on the 11th, when they were all marched out to the public square. In Sam's words,

> They tied a rope around Steward's neck, then tied his hands behind him, put the rope over a big live oak limb, then tied two stake ropes to the rope around Steward's neck [and] ordered everyone to pull on the rope. Every man that refused was forced to put his hand on the rope. Two of the Greenwood brothers rode up. The mob made them get down and pull on the rope. Every man that showed up was forced to pull on the rope except 2 of the mob who standing ready to shoot me, thinking I would make a break to run when I saw them hang Steward. They had a box all ready for Steward. So they ordered everybody to say nothing about what they had seen.[7]

They used the rest of Sam's flour to pay their whiskey bill. Sam, Frank, James Scott, and Aleck Williams, all young men, and the older men, Asa Langford and John Thompson, were then taken to a camp on the Pedernales River, along with Hugh Lawhorn, who was arrested on the

247

way. There they were turned over to a man named Taylor, described by Sam as being a "very nice man"[8] who took them to San Antonio and turned over to the provost marshall (presumably a real one) where they were put in the guard house. When the charges from the man referred to by Sam as the "'Pretended' Marshall"[9] arrived and were presented to General Bee, he questioned the prisoners at length and dropped the charges. He had also received a petition signed by 500 citizens of Lampasas asking for the release of the men. General Bee told the older men to go home, including Hugh Lawhorn, and advised the four young men to enlist in Captain Bill Tobin's company and avoid going back to Lampasas until things settled down.[10] Thus, Sam and Frank found themselves in Pyron's Second Texas Cavalry, Company F.

> The 2d Regiment Texas Cavalry (also known as the 2nd Regiment Texas Mounted Rifles) was organized May 23, 1861, of companies which had previously been in the State service. (1st) Company F re-enlisted in April, 1862; was furloughed to May 31, 1862, and subsequently became Company I, Morgan's Regiment Texas Cavalry. The remainder of the regiment was re-organized in July, 1862, and (2d) Company F was organized September 27, 1862.[11]

The company was ordered to Buffalo Bayou in December 1862, then it was dismounted and sent to Galveston,[12] where Frank participated in the Battle of Galveston in January 1863.

> In 1862 he enlisted in the Second Regiment of Texas Cavalry, Colonel Pyron, of San Antonio. About the first work he was engaged in was the retaking of Galveston. He was with the forces that operated in eastern Texas and Louisiana. When Colonel Pyron was wounded the regiment disbanded. They were called together again, however, and did some good service before the surrender.[13]

The following account of the battle was given by one of the participants, W. F. Cude, who had been with the unit for some time when Frank and Sam joined it:

In June, 1862, we left the border service and went to San Antonio and joined the Second Texas Cavalry under Col. Charley Pryon [Pyron]. James Walker was lieutenant colonel. He was placed in Sibley's Brigade and Bankhead Magruder was our general. In October we were ordered to the coast near the mouth of the Brazos, where it was said Union forces were landing. Later we were ordered to Houston, and about the middle of December the Yankees captured Galveston. A call was made for volunteers to go on the steamboats to go to Galveston. As most of the volunteers were cavalrymen and as they had to fight on water they took the name of horse marines. General Magruder recaptured Galveston after a fight lasting less than an hour. This battle was fought on the first day of January, 1863. We captured one warship and two transports, sunk one warship and captured about five hundred prisoners. We had two steamboats with about two hundred men on each boat. One of our boats was sunk, but it was in shallow water and no one was drowned. Captain Pryon [Pyron] remained on the Island until June and was sent to Louisiana. General Tom Green was now our commander and our brigade soon joined the Confederate army under General Taylor. General Banks' Union army was on its way to Texas, 35,000 strong. Our army numbered about 17,000 men, and was composed of Arkansas, Texas and Louisiana troops. The two armies met about the 15th of June and fought a three days' battle in which Banks was defeated. We captured several thousand prisoners and many wagon loads of supplies.[14]

Fig. 13.1 - "Attack of Rebels upon our gun-boat flotilla at Galveston, Texas, January 1, 1863." Prints & Photographs Collection, Center for American History, The University of Texas at Austin. CN Number 06262.

Sam Gholson and James Scott were sent to Big Sandy, west of the Colorado River, to establish a horse camp, but Sam's autobiography does not state whether or not he participated in the Battle of Galveston before he went to the horse camp. Around February 10, 1863, the "'Pretended' Marshall" ran afoul of three horse hunters in Gonzales County and "was found just below a live oak limb in bad condition."[15] An order was issued by General Magruder to bring in Sam, James Scott, and Dick Newton. Aleck Williams was assigned to take Sam's place at the horse camp and take his own horse and the horses belonging to Sam and Frank to Lampasas. Sam was one step ahead of the sheriff. He asked for and got a pass to take the three horses to Lampasas County himself, so he was gone when the sheriff arrived at the camp. The sheriff sent Sergeant Shanghigh Smith and five soldiers to Lampasas County to bring Sam back, but in Sam's words,

I got word to look out, that Smith was hunting for me. I mounted my horse, went down the road toward Lampasas to watch for Smith but did not find Smith till August 1864.[16]

August 1864—a year and a half later. Sam must have been doing a little pretending himself—pretending he was looking for Smith. This may account for the notation on Sam's military service record, "Deserted March 18, 1863."[17] Sam rejoined the Confederate forces when he found Smith in Louisiana on the Tennessee Bayou. Smith told him to report to Kennedy's Company F, which he did, and stated, "Had a good time with the company."[18] He described scouting up and down the Mississippi River watching for Yankee troop movements and skirmishes where his good luck continued, with shooting all around him.[19] Since Frank was in the company until February 2, 1864, he would have been in the regiment when a British colonel named Sir Arthur James Lyon Fremantle wrote this colorful description:

> At 1.30 [Sunday, May 3, 1863] I saw Pyron's regiment embark for Niblitt's Bluff to meet Banks. This corps is now dismounted cavalry, and the procession was a droll one. First came eight or ten instruments braying discordantly, then an enormous Confederate flag, followed by about four hundred men moving by fours—dressed in every variety of costume, and armed with every variety of weapon; about sixty had Enfield rifles; the remainder carried shot-guns (fowling-pieces), carbines, or long rifles of a peculiar and antiquated manufacture. [Kentucky rifles?] None had swords or bayonets—all had six-shooters and bowie-knives. The men were a fine, determined-looking lot; and I saw among them a short stout boy of fourteen, who had served through the Arizona campaign. I saw many of the soldiers take off their hats to the French priests, who seemed much respected in Galveston. This regiment is considered down here to be a very good one, and its colonel is spoken as one of the bravest officers in the army.[20]

Sam was in Lampasas on furlough when General Lee surrendered to General Grant on April 9, 1865. He wrote, "My regiment was at Houston,

Texas, so I never got a discharge. So I am a Rebel soldier yet and expect to be one as long as I live."[21] According to Frank's pension application, which was approved, he was honorably discharged at San Antonio, Texas on May 24, 1865, although his military service record contains a notation that he deserted on February 2, 1864. He, like his brother, apparently returned to the army after some period of time.[22] During the course of the war, more than four thousand Texans deserted, some because of opposition to the Confederacy, but many for personal reasons.[23]

As a frontier state, Texas did not suffer the same degree of devastation as the other Confederate states, but by the end of 1863, a vast majority of white adult male Texans were serving in Confederate or state military forces. Many Texans never had direct contact with the enemy, but the shortages of many goods made life difficult. Items normally obtained from the northern states were no longer available and imports from Europe were kept out by the blockade of the coastline.[24] The loss of imported coffee resulted in many attempts to make substitutes from such things as rye, meal, corn, sweet potatoes and peanuts. "Salt became so scarce that some Texans dug up the floors of smokehouses and leached the dirt to recover the salt drippings."[25] Eventually, a system was developed to send cotton through Mexico, then by blockade runners to Cuba, with a final destination in Europe. Returning vessels brought war materials and other goods.[26]

The mob rule that led to the enlistment of Sam and Frank also affected other members of the family, and one incident resulted in the death of their young brother-in-law:

> Asa Langford a pioneer citizen of Center City, and ex-Texas Ranger was invited to join the mob. Mr. Langford was a property owner in both Coryelle [*sic*] and Hamilton Counties. Whatever may be said of Asa Langford, he was neither a physical nor a moral coward. Mr. Langford refused to join in killing white men. He was the father of a large family. He knew that from that time on he was in danger—and that the mob could not drive him from his home and that they would have to kill him to get rid of him. Mr. Langford while operating a general store, hauled supplies from Gatesville.
>
> One day Mr. Langford took his little son Jimmie, age 7, with him; while on the way home in a covered wagon

loaded with sewing machines, Mr. Langford, had a 44 pistol in a saddle bag on the floor in front of the high spring seat of the wagon; the little boy was driving the wagon; about half way home the mob lying in wait, hidden in the brush began firing, shooting the boy under the arm; he toppled, dropping the reins; Mr. Langford caught him pulled him up on the spring seat; the boy crawled back on a machine in the covered wagon—while Mr. Langford jumped from the spring seat to get the pistol—the firing was terrific; when Mr. Langford arose with the pistol he could see no one and the shots had set the canvas on fire. The firing continued while Mr. Langford extinguished the blaze for his little boy was hidden under the canvas. Mr. Langford was wounded in the leg. The horses were continuing down the road with no driver. Mr. Langford crawled down on the double tree of the wagon to obtain hold on the reins; a man crossed the road wearing a mask— he could not recognize him. The father found the little boy shot several times, he was dead.[27]

Another one of Langford's sons, Asa, Jr., began his short criminal career at age fourteen when he killed his first man.[28] On June 20, 1874, an arrest warrant was issued by the Clerk of the District Court of Coryell County for Asa Langford, Jr. for murder, with the following statement at the bottom: "The above defendant Asa Langford ranges about in Coleman Co. and Brown is sometimes at [Sam] Gholson's Ranch in Coleman. (Very bad man)"[29]

About four months later, Asa, Jr. was dead and a newspaper article gave the following account of his death:

Daily Democratic Statesman
Friday, Nov. 6, 1874, p 2, col 2
TEXAS ITEMS
The Chief has Hamilton locals, from which we extract the following:
. . . "Mr. Harris, of Langford Cove, Coryell county, reports that he helped bury Asa Langford, Jr., who was killed by some parties unknown, on the fifteenth instant, while on his return from Gatesville, where he had been attending court.

Some ten or twelve holes were in his body. Asa, for the last few years, has led a wild and reckless life. He was indicted for the murder of Payne and Hughes, but, for a long time, eluded all attempts to arrest, but was finally caught in San Saba, where he was about to marry the daughter of one of his victims (Hughes). He had at the time a living wife in Langford Cove, to whom he returned after his arrest and bailment."[30]

The following is an excerpt from a letter written in July 2001 by one of Frank's granddaughters who lived across the road from him and spent many days with him during the last years of his life:

The incident of the death of Asa Langford Jr. was told to me by Grandpa B. F. Gholson out on his front porch one summer day. As he, Asa Jr., was Adeline's brother Grandpa didn't talk about it in front of her and warned me to keep quiet about it. It seems that Asa Jr. was a hell raiser in general, riding through town whooping & yelling while shooting off his gun up in the air. Asa Sr. was a store keep there in the field that is adjacent to the Langford cemetery. (It was not a field then.) The citizens just got tired of Jr. acting up and told him he had to calm down & cool it for a while, but that did not set too well with him & he probably fired back at them or maybe took a shot at them. A posse was formed & Asa Jr. took to the hills in Gholson Gap and hid out for a couple of days while they hunted him on horseback. No one knows whose bullet killed him but gunfire was exchanged resulting in his death. He is buried in Langford Cemetery beside his mother. Asa Sr. gave the land for the cemetery. Don't know where Sr. is buried.[31]

Asa Langford, Jr. was around twenty-one when he died at the hands of the posse.[32] About forty miles from Evant, about a month before the warrant was issued for Langford, a more notorious criminal killed Charles Webb, deputy sheriff of Brown County. The murderer was John Wesley Hardin.[33] An excerpt from James B. Gillett's book, *Six Years with the Texas Rangers*, tells of his encounter with Hardin when Gillett was a member of Lieutenant Reynolds' Company E. The same segment also describes a portion of Asa, Jr.'s life of crime:

In the summer of 1877 Lieutenant Armstrong of Captain Hall's company, assisted by Detective Jack Duncan of Dallas, Texas, captured the notorious John Wesley Hardin. It has been said by some wag that Texas, the largest state in the Union, has never produced a real world's champion at anything. Surely this critic overlooked Hardin, the champion desperado of the world. His life is too well known in Texas for me to go into detail, but, according to his own story, which I have before me, he killed no fewer than twenty-seven men, the last being Charley Webb, deputy sheriff of Brown County, Texas. So notorious had Hardin become that the state of Texas offered $4,000 reward for his capture. Hardin had left Texas and at the time of his capture was in Florida. His captors arrested and overpowered him while he was sitting in a passenger coach.

In September, 1877, Sheriff Wilson of Comanche County, in whose jurisdiction Hardin had killed Webb, came to Austin to convey the prisoner to Comanche for trial. Wilson requested the governor for an escort of rangers. Lieutenant Reynolds' company, being in Austin at the time, was ordered to accompany Wilson and protect Hardin from mob violence. This was the first work assigned Company E under its new commander.

The day we left Austin between one and two thousand people gathered about the Travis County jail to see this notorious desperado. The rangers were drawn up just outside the jail, and Henry Thomas and myself were ordered to enter the prison and escort Hardin out. Heavily shackled and handcuffed, the prisoner walked very slowly between us. The boy who had sold fish and game on the streets of Austin was now guarding the most desperate criminal in Texas; it was glory enough for me.

At his trial Hardin was convicted, and sentenced to twenty-five years in the penitentiary. He appealed his case and was returned to Travis County for safekeeping. The verdict of the trial court was sustained, and one year later, in September, 1878, Lieutenant Reynolds' company was ordered to take Hardin back to Comanche County for sentence. There was no railroad at Comanche at that time, so a detachment of rangers, myself among them, escorted Hardin to the penitentiary. There were ten or twelve indictments still pending against him for murder in various counties, but they were never prosecuted.

Hardin served seventeen years of his sentence, and while in prison studied law. Governor Hogg pardoned him in 1894 and restored him to full citizenship.

Despite all the kind advice given him by eminent lawyers and citizens, Hardin was unequal to the task of becoming a useful man. He practiced law for a time in Gonzales, then drifted away to El Paso, where he began drinking and gambling. On August 19, 1895, he was standing at a bar shaking dice when John Selman, constable of Precinct No. 1, approached him from behind and with a pistol blew his brains out. Though posing as an officer, Selman was himself an outlaw and a murderer of the worst kind. He killed Hardin for the notoriety it would bring him and nothing more.

After delivering Hardin to the sheriff of Travis County in 1877, Lieutenant Reynolds was ordered to Kimble County for duty. Of all the counties in Texas at that time Kimble was the most popular with outlaws and criminals, for it was situated south of Menard County on the North and South Llano rivers, with cedar, pecan, and mesquite timber in which to hide, while the streams and mountains furnished fish, game, and wild cattle in abundance for subsistence.

On the South Llano lived old Jimmie Dublin. He had a large family of children, most of them grown. The eldest of his boys, Dick, or Richard, as he was known, and a friend, Ace Lankford, [Asa Langford, Jr.] killed two men at a country store in Lankford's Cove, Coryell County, Texas. The state offered $500 for the arrest of Dublin and the county of Coryell an additional $200. To escape capture Dick and his companion fled west into Kimble County.

While I was working as cowboy with Joe Franks in the fall of 1873 I became acquainted with the two murderers, for they attached themselves to our outfit. They were always armed and constantly on the watch for fear of arrest. Dublin was a large man, stout and of dark complexion, who looked more like the bully of a prize ring than the cowman he was. I often heard him say he would never surrender. While cowhunting with us he discovered that the brushy and tangled region of Kimble County offered shelter for such as he, and persuaded his father to move out into that county.[34]

There are very few recorded descriptions of the activities of the vigilante committees that administered justice in Texas during this period. Many old settlers expressed the sentiment that those times would be best forgotten. They just did not want to talk about it.

THE STATE OF TEXAS—County of Coryelle.

Any Officer of the Frontier Forces

TO ~~THE STATE SHERIFF OF CORYELLE COUNTY~~ GREETING :

You are hereby commanded that you take into your custody the body of............

Asa Langford

....if to be found in the State of Texas,

and him safely keep so that you have his body before our Honorable District Court, to be holden within

and for the County of Coryelle, at the Courthouse thereof in the town of Gatesville, on the 1st Monday

in *October* ..... A. D. 1874 ; be then and there to be and remain from day to day

and from term to term of said Court, until he be discharged by due course of law, to answer an indict-

ment, No. 458, found at the *April* Term, A. D. 1873 of the District Court of said County,

for *Murder* ....

....

Herein fail not under penalty of the law, but of this writ make due return, showing how you

have executed the same.

In witness whereof I have hereunto set my hand and the official seal of the District Court of

Coryelle County, at office, this, the 2.0. day of *June* ...... A. D. 187 4

L. M. Allen

Clerk Dist. Court Coryelle County, Texas.

The above defendant Asa Langford ranges about in Coleman Co. and Brown is sometimes at Gholsons Ranch in Coleman. (Very bad man

Fig. 13.2 - Capias No. 458, The State of Texas vs. Asa Langford, Jr., issued June 20, 1874. Texas State Archives Call No. 401-1160-311.

Chapter 14: The Stockman and the Drover

B. F. "Frank" Gholson and S. S. "Sam" Gholson
c. 1865-1875

There were worlds of cattle in Texas after the Civil War. They had multiplied and run wild while the men was away fighting for the Confederacy, especially down in the southern part, between the Nueces River and the Río Grande. By the time the war was over they was down to four dollars a head—when you could find a buyer. Here was all these cheap long-horned steers overrunning Texas; here was the rest of the country crying for beef—and no railroads to get them out. So they trailed them out, across hundreds of miles of wild country that was thick with Indians. In 1866 the first Texas herds crossed Red River. In 1867 the town of Abilene was founded at the end of the Kansas Pacific Railroad and that was when the trail really started. From that time on, big drives were made every year, and the cowboy was born. That Emerson Hough movie, *North of 36*, was supposed to show one of the early cattle drives to the railroad. It was pretty good, except that the moving picture people had Taisie Lockhard coming up the trail wearing pants. If the cowpunchers of them days had ever seen a woman wearing pants, they'd have stampeded to the brush.

Those first trail outfits in the seventies were sure tough. It was a new business and had to develop. Work oxen were used instead of horses to pull the wagon, and if one played out, they could rope a steer and yoke him up. They had very little grub and they usually run out of that and lived on straight beef; they had only three or four horses to the man, mostly with sore backs, because the old time saddle eat both ways, the horse's back and the cowboy's pistol pocket; they had no tents, no tarps, and damn few slickers. They never kicked, because those boys was raised under

259

just the same conditions as there was on the trail—corn meal and bacon for grub, dirt floors in the houses, and no luxuries. In the early days in Texas, in the sixties, when they gathered their cattle, they used to pack what they needed on a horse and go out for weeks, on a cow-hunt, they called it then. That was before the name roundup was invented, and before they had anything so civilized as mess wagons. And as I say, that is the way those first trail hands were raised. Take her as she comes and like it. They used to brag that they could go any place a cow could and stand anything a horse could. It was their life.

Most all of them were Southerners, and they were a wild, reckless bunch. For dress they wore wide-brimmed beaver hats, black or brown with a low crown, fancy shirts, high-heeled boots, and sometimes a vest. Their clothes and saddles were all homemade. Most of them had an army coat with cape which was slicker and blanket too. Lay on your saddle blanket and cover up with a coat was about the only bed used on the Texas trail at first. A few had a big buffalo robe to roll up in, but if they ever got good and wet, you never had time to dry them, so they were not popular. All had a pair of bullhide chaps, or leggins they called them then. They were good in the brush and wet weather, but in fine weather were left in the wagon.

As the business grew, great changes took place in their style of dress, but their boots and cigarettes have lasted nearly the same for more than sixty years. In place of the low-crowned hat of the seventies we had a high-crowned white Stetson hat, fancy shirts with pockets, and striped or checkered California pants made in Oregon City, the best pants ever made to ride in. Slickers came in too. In winter we had nice cloth overcoats with beaver collars and cuffs. The old twelve-inch-barrel Colt pistol was cut down to a six- and seven-and-a-half-inch barrel, with black rubber, ivory, or pearl handle. The old big roweled spurs with bells give place to hand-forged silver inlaid spurs with droop shanks and small rowels, and with that you had the cowpuncher of the eighties when he was in his glory.

In person the cowboys were mostly medium-sized men, as a heavy man was hard on horses, quick and wiry, and as a rule very good-natured; in fact it did not pay to be anything else. In character their like never was or will be again. They were intensely loyal to the outfit they were working for and would fight to the death for it. They would follow their wagon boss through hell and never complain. I have seen them ride into camp after two days and nights on herd, lay down on their saddle blankets in the rain, and sleep like dead men, then get up laughing and joking about some good time they had had in Ogallala or Dodge City. Living that kind of a life, they were bound to be wild and brave. In fact there was only two things the old-time cowpuncher was afraid of, a decent woman and being set afoot.[1]

Those were the words of E. C. "Teddy Blue" Abbott, who was born in England in 1860 and wound up in Montana.[2] He was a small child when his parents came to America, "the poorest, sickliest little kid you ever saw, all eyes, no flesh on me whatever; if I hadn't have been a cowpuncher, I never would have growed up. The doctor told my mother before we left England to 'keep him in the open air.' She kept me there, all right, or fate did. All my life."[3] Shortly after arriving from England, Teddy Blue's father bought a herd of cattle in Texas and sent him up the trail at age ten with the herd and his hired hands, with the idea that it would be good for his health.[4] His father's wagon boss was Sam Bass. According to Teddy Blue, "He wasn't an outlaw then—just a nice, quiet young fellow."[5] He also knew Calamity Jane[6] and Buffalo Bill.

Bill Cody at that time was half-owner of the C N outfit, Cody and North, with headquarters at North Platte City. He lived there for years. He was a good fellow, and while he was no such great shakes as a scout as he made the eastern people believe, still we all liked him, and we had to hand it to him because he was the only one that had brains enough to make that Wild West stuff pay money. I remember one time he came into a saloon in North Platte, and he took off his hat, and that long hair of his that he had rolled up under his hat fell down on his shoulders. It always bothered him, so he rolled it up and stuck it back under his hat again, and Brady, the saloon man, says: "Say, Bill, why the hell don't you cut the damn stuff off?"

And Cody says: If I did, I'd starve to death."[7]

Teddy Blue was a friend of the artist Charles Russell and he said, "In 1922 Charlie Russell and I were going to make a book together. I was going to tell the stories and he was going to draw the pictures, and his name would have carried it. But he died."[8] Fortunately, Teddy Blue's story did get published, leaving a precise, colorful, eyewitness description of the trail drives and the cowboys, setting the stage for this portion of the Gholson story.

Albert Gholson, the father of Frank and Sam, was in the cattle business in Texas before it became a state. At the time of his death in 1860, he was a major cattle rancher, owning thousands of acres of land in several counties. One of the first pieces of property owned by Albert was deeded to him jointly with John Chisum in 1840 by Albert's father, Samuel. Both Albert and Chisum were young men at the time. Albert was living in Harrison County and Chisum in Nacogdoches County, and the parcel of land was in Robertson County.[9] Chisum went on to become one of the most influential cattlemen in Texas.

~ Frank Gholson - Stockman ~

Frank "lived at several different places during the 15 years from 1855 to 1870 in the surrounding country,"[10] then settled on his ranch at Gholson Gap near Evant in Lampasas County and lived there for the remainder of his long life. For $400 cash, he bought 244 acres from Sam Sneed,[11] who had lived on the place since 1856, a year after Frank first saw the place. Frank moved there on October 12, 1870, with his family and around five thousand head of cattle.[12]

Many legal documents involving Frank's business are on record in Lampasas, Mills and Hamilton counties, including deeds, bills of sale, and estray reports. He was involved in an ongoing legal battle for several years, which he ultimately won. In 1871, Frank and Asa Langford posted bond for $400 for Thomas Holly, who was indicted for stealing two head of cattle. Holly failed to appear and when the court attempted to collect $400 each from Frank and Asa, a motion was filed to contest the collection of $800 on the basis that the sureties only intended to execute the bond for a total of $400, not $400 each. The matter was dismissed in State Supreme Court in 1874 on a technicality.[13]

Frank's last encounters with Indians took place around his ranch at Gholson Gap, one of them being an incident that took place at Beef Pen Spring.

Funny incident with Indians - in 1872 W. M. Thompson, W. M. Sneed, and myself made up a Kansas herd of a certain class of cattle and selected them from our own stocks. I owning the largest share in the herd made it necessary to send the most men and horses with the herd. Bill Thompson took charge and drove the herd to Wichita Kansas. I kept the lame horses, the sore backed ones, and the poor ones here at the ranch. I had five boys employed. I used them and these refuse horses to brand up the calves on the range while the best men and best horses were gone with the herd, also my ranch cook, a Mexican, went with the herd. My stock pens were a mile and a half from the ranch house. I camped the boys at the spring, known as Gholson Beef Pen Spring until now. The boys were uneasy about Indians when I would leave at night and come home. They disagreed as to who should do the cooking and frequently would fail to cook a meal. Jack Rowmines asked me that evening to let him off to go to Bud Sneed's ranch to trade horses with Bud, so I let him go. At my usual time I left the other four boys at the camp. They made their pallet on the west bank of the branch and all slept on the one pallet. At a late hour in the night Joe Straley heard some noise. He laid still and watched the direction of the noise. He wakened the other boys quietly, saying "Do you see them men younder?" Some of the boys saw them, others did not. They kept quiet, could hear nothing for several minutes, then they heard men riding directly towards them on the opposite side of the branch. A large trail came down the hill and crossed the branch right where they were sleeping. Not a word was spoken by either party. A large hole of water lay just above where the trail crossed the branch. The men rode into the water and were watering their horses when they began to talk among themselves in their own language. Up jumped the boys almost at the same minute, grabbed their six-shooters and boots and ran off in the opposite direction. The Indians, at the same moment, were as badly surprised as the boys were, whirled out of the water hole and ran back the way they had come. The boys stopped, put on their boots and clothes, put on their six-shooters, and listened until they went out of hearing. The boys made a big round on foot and came to the ranch house where I was. It was getting daylight. I was up. I saw them coming. I thought, "Those devilish boys were too contrary to cook their breakfast and are coming here for breakfast." I called out to them and said, "I wont cook." Ben Thompson spoke, saying "Worse than cooking." I asked, "What's that Ben?" "The Navajos has been after us." They told their story. I asked them if they got our horses and they answered, "We don't know. We was busy running to keep them from getting us." I had some horses at the ranch. Two of them russeled enough horses for us to ride. Breakfast was got as quick as possible. We went over there to learn that the Indians had not got any of the horses. They ran in the opposite direction from where the horses were. The cattle were in the pen all right and nothing was disturbed but the boys. When the Indians ran over the first ridge, they saw two horses grazing belonging to Sam Sneed which had not been ridden, were fat and foolish. They tried to catch them. We found that they had run a great distance after the horses. When they failed to get them, they shot two arrows into one of them. The other escaped unhurt. The Indians went down to Townshend's ranch, got a few horses, down to Bill White's, got a few more horses on down the country, and made their regular rounds, and the boys were not bothered by them any more that time. Namely, J. L. Strahley, known as Joe Strahley who died two years ago, Ben Thompson, who was killed accidently in New Mexico while driving a herd some time in the eighties to Arizona for Hunter and Evans of Fort Worth, Jim Carter I suppose living, if so near Springtown in Parker County, Jim Sparkman, Jack Rowmines missed the run by being up at Sneed's Ranch to trade horses with him.

I built an Indian proof horse lot with only one gate to it. I kept what horses were not being used under herd in daytime when I thought there was danger of Indians. I swung the gate in the nearest place of the lot to houses we lived in. It was a strong gate and was fixed so it could not be lifted off its hinges. I used a log chain and a large padlock to fasten it with at night when any horses were in the lot. One rainy night in April 1873 the Indians came to that lot. They tried to open the gate and failed. It was drizzling rain. Their moccasin tracks and pony tracks showed around the lot on the outside very plainly. The sign showed on the opposite side of the lot from the house they had put ropes on the pickets and had pulled by their horses trying to tear them down. We could see where their horses had slipped badly while pulling at the pickets. Moccasin tracks were thick at that place but they had made a failure and rode off without a horse while there were eighteen head in the lot. They did not get anything anywhere near here. They went on down the country as usual.[14]

In 1873 Frank scaled down his cattle operation, although he still owned a large farm in Lampasas County, a half interest in another stock ranch, and a half interest in the only drugstore in Evant.[15]

~ Sam Gholson - Drover ~

At the end of the Civil War, Sam owned only a few horses and no cattle. He traded the horses for a small herd of cattle, and eventually he accumulated enough of his own cattle and some belonging to other ranchers to drive them to Bosque Grande, near Fort Sumner, New Mexico, arriving February 15, 1868. "When I got to Bosque Grande, found [James] Burleson and others there with Charley Goodnight waiting for me to arrive to buy the herd."[16] Sam held the herd there until April 15, to wait for Goodnight to go to Denver to get more money, as he did not have enough to pay for the herd. Burleson and Sam returned to Texas, where Burleson collected about 3600 head, Sam collected around 2000 head and they separately started back to Fort Sumner, with Burleson in the lead. When

Burleson attempted to take his entire herd across a ninety-mile dry stretch in one group, he lost more than half of them.[17] In Sam's words,

> When we struck Castle Gap his cattle had died all the way to Horse Head Crossing. I saw cattle piled up on each other near 20 feet high. At a little mud hole in the canyon Charley Campbell of Comanche County, Texas, killed two horses and one mule trying to save the cattle. Most of Mr. Burleson's men got scared and left the cattle to find water. Some of the men pulled Campbell off of the fourth horse with his tongue sticking out and turning black.
> I got through with a loss of 16 head.[18]

Despite run-ins with Mexicans and Indians, Sam made it back to Lampasas on February 20, 1869. By May 15, he had settled up all of his cattle transactions in that area and moved to Coleman County, Texas, where he was in a partnership with G. K. Elkins from 1869 to 1871.[19] He knew how to put the fear of God into rustlers and described the reaction of one of them: "I never saw a man so bad scared as he was. He had on buckskin pants. I could hear his pants rattle and his teeth rattle as he stood and talked to us."[20] Sam was trail boss for many cattle drives and he was in several partnerships with other cattlemen, among them Crill, Miles and Taylor, and his name appears in many books and articles, among them the following:

• From "Horses Were Legal Tender":
> Another time, in 1867, Sam Gholson of Coleman County, Eugene McCrohan and Kim Ketchum of Fort Concho, and several other ranchers drove a herd to New Mexico and sold it to the government for beef. Three of the ranchers headed back home were attacked and killed by Navajos. When the rest of the party caught up to the scene, they found thousands of dollars in paper, which had been taken from the men, torn into fragments and scattered in the brush. When Indians came into possession of gold in their raids on settlers, they turned it over to smart white traders for gaudy trinkets of little value.
> If it weren't a horse, nothing held much value in the estimation of the Indian. With horses, he could buy anything from a plug of tobacco to a wife.[21]

- James Gillett was a young man of seventeen, new to frontier life and working on his first job as a cowboy in 1873 when he met Sam Gholson. Gillett was very impressed with Sam and described the meeting in his book, *Six Years With the Texas Rangers*.

> Our first work was to gather and deliver a herd of cattle to the Horrell boys, then camped on Home Creek. We worked down to the Colorado River, and when we were near old Flat Top Ranch the men with the outfit left me to drive the remuda down the road after the mess wagon while they tried to find a beef. I had gone only a mile or two when I saw a man approaching me from the rear. As he came up I thought he was the finest specimen of a frontiersman I had ever seen. He was probably six feet tall, with dark hair and beard. He was heavily armed, wearing two six-shooters and carrying a Winchester in front of him, and was riding a splendid horse with a wonderful California saddle. He rode up to me and asked whose outfit it was I was driving. I told him Cooksey and Clayton's. He then inquired my name. When I told him he said, "Oh, yes; I saw your father in Lampasas a few days ago and he told me to tell you to come home and go to school."
>
> I made no reply, but kept my horses moving. The stranger then told me his name was Sam Gholston. He said it was dangerous for one so young to be in a bad Indian country and unarmed, that the outfit should not have left me alone, and counseled me to go back to my parents. I would not talk to him, so he finally bade me good-bye and galloped off. His advice was good, but I had not the least idea of going home—I had embraced the frontier life.[22]

Sam undoubtedly saw himself in the young Gillett, and knew that it was futile to try to talk him into going home. Sam also described their chance meeting.

> He was a runaway boy like myself, a hunting more adventure, a livelier occupation than catching fish or going to school. He had the frontier fever, would not stop to listen to me, but kept moving away from my talk, so I told him my name, bade him goodby and galloped off to my own outfit. I haven't seen him since, but I read his book, "Six

Years a Ranger on the Frontier of Texas." This was in the spring of 1873.[23]

- In another excerpt from *Six Years With the Texas Rangers*, Gillett wrote:

    During the summer of 1873 John Hitsons, Sam Gholston, and Joe Franks were all delivering cattle to old John Chislom [Chisum], whose outfit was camped on the south side of the Concho River, about where the town of Paint Rock now stands. The other outfits were scattered along down the river about half a mile apart. There were probably seventy-five or a hundred men in the four camps, and at least five hundred horses. One evening just after dark the Indians ran into Gholston's outfit, captured about sixty head of horses, and got away with them. The redskins and the cowboys had a regular pitched battle for a few minutes, firing two hundred shots. This fight was in plain view of our camp, and I saw the flash of every gun and heard the Indians and the cowboys yelling. One of Mr. Gholston's men received a flesh wound in the leg and several horses were killed.[24]

Sam's autobiography further describes his wounded cowboy:

    The cowboy wounded was Richard Devlin. He was shot in the calf of his left leg and through the sweat leather and could not get off of his horse till we pulled the arrow out of his leg.[25]

- From *The West Texas Frontier*:

    Sam Gholson's Cow Hands Kill Indian.—During 1873, four or five of Sam Gholson's cow hands were out hunting cattle in Coleman County, and became separated. Two of the men struck some Indians, about five miles north of the Santa Anna Mountains, and reported to the others. The Indian trail was followed to a point about three miles east of the Santa Anna Mountains, and the savages overtaken on Lukewater. There were only a few Indians, and one of them was riding an old horse, called "old 2 D," because he wore that particular brand. The Indian riding this horse, had just stolen him from the Gholson Ranch, and Jim Jackson knowing he couldn't run very fast, singled out this particular Indian riding this horse, and ran him into the timber, where the Indian jumped to the ground and threw up his shield. But Jim Jackson killed and scalped this warrior and recovered his bow, arrows, and shield, which plainly indicated the bullet passed through this instrument before it passed into the Indian's body.

Note:—Author personally interviewed: J. B. Terrell, who with others, camped within 100 yards of the dead Indian, the following night he was killed.[26]

- From "Cattle Kings":

[Quoting Bill Hyatt] "It is possible that the last Indian depredation in this immediate section [Spur Ranch in Dickens County] was in 1883. The Comanches stole Sam Gholson's horses, and those of John and Bill Slaughter, including those named Sugar Child, Old Sorghum, and Taller Eye. The last Indian fight of any moment near here was General Mackenzie's engagement on the Tule, following which his troops killed hundreds of captured Indian horses."[27]

- From "Trailing West":

When the Indians first began to advance on us, Dutchie deserted us and I never saw him afterwards; however, he made his escape, going to S. S. Gholson's cow camp and reporting that we were all killed, and finally making his way back to the settlements at Weatherford.[28]

- In *Indian Fighting on the Texas Frontier*, Captain John M. Elkins described Sam's role in two separate incidents.

During this same year [1871] that the Indians had succeeded in carrying away the valuable herd of cattle and horses, they made a raid on Jim Ned Creek, on the bank of which my house now stands, and stole a number of horses. Sam Gholson raised a party of men for the chase.

After Sam and his band had followed the Indian trail for about one hundred miles, they saw a herd of horses being driven by the Indians. The Indians mistook the white men for another band of Indians and rode toward them. When within a short distance of the pursuers, the Indians discovered their mistake and fled for the rough country.

Sam and his men ran in between them and the cedar brakes, forcing them to retreat across the open prairie. A running fight ensued for a distance of six or seven miles. Sam, Henry Sisk, Dudley Johnson, James Manning and Ben Cooper, who were riding extra fast horses, rode on ahead of the other men and pressed the Indians until they abandoned their horses to take refuge in a branch or washout where they completely concealed themselves.

Hundreds of shots were sent from the frontiersman's guns into the woven thickets with no means of telling whether or not they were to any effect. Because of the number of stolen horses which were taken from the Indians this long chase was profitable.

A year later while I was following an Indian trail with my Minute Company, we passed near where the fight had been staged. Sam and I examined the place and found the skeletons of three Indians—likely many had been seriously injured.

During the Civil War most of the western cowmen had to go into the army or join the Frontier Rangers; this left the ranches and cattle to take care of themselves. Such was the case all along the edge of Texas settlement. The cattle were allowed to drift at will and mix from neighboring herd to neighboring herd until they roamed far from their respective ranges. At the close of the war in 1865 there were thousands of unbranded cattle which had grown up on the range from the Red River to the Rio Grande without a mark on them to identify whose they might be.

For several years after the war there was no market for cattle but the cattlemen divided the herds as best they could. They agreed among themselves that it would be a violation of no law to handle each other's cattle all along the frontier. These herds were divided according to the number of cattle each cowman could brand—the man who possessed the best horse and could rope the most cattle was the man who got into his possession the most cattle.

This "mavericking" began in December each year and when it was completed along about Christmas, all the cattlemen would come together and have a settlement. Each would have a book containing a record of the different brands he had sold and cared for; this was the only evidence necessary to establish his claim against any other of the cowmen for services rendered in caring for their estrayed cattle; and it was considered sufficient proof of the number of cattle sold that should be paid for to their owners according to the brands.

This continued eight or nine years and so far as was ever known to me, it was satisfactory to all persons concerned and gradually the herds were restored to and were brought under the direct management of their respective owners.

One of the maverick hunts which I went on was in December, 1870. Five other boys and myself rigged up a good wagon and team, with corn and grub enough to last us two weeks, and with two horses each we started out.

When we had journeyed some distance from the ranch we began branding the mavericks. We branded 100 head or more each day for several days. On the ninth day we landed in the little village of Menardville, situated on the south bank of the San Saba River. There we penned our herd of mavericks which we had gathered that day.

Not long after we had the gates all closed and our mavericks well under control in the pen, several men came to our camp where the cattle were being held. These men asked us our mission and we showed them the mavericks we were gathering, when they told us that they thought it rather early yet, that they had not begun branding the range cattle. We didn't get angry at that, we just threw the gates open and let our seventy-five or a hundred mavericks which now wore flesh brands again dash to their freedom out onto the broad range. Some of these cattle were three and four years old and ours were the first branding irons they had ever felt.

While our mavericks roamed free, back to the prairies, we went down to Menardville. I had my old fiddle with me and such a dance as we had I have never witnessed since. We danced the week out and it was certainly one enjoyable Christmas.

After our pleasant stay in the little village we began our ride across the country back to the ranch. It was a long, lonesome trip; not a house along the way and the Indians were crossing through the section of the country continuously. Every light of the moon they would do their stealing and murdering.

We crossed the Brady Mountains and there were droves of mustang ponies roaming all through them. There were hundreds of them and they were the prettiest mustangs I ever saw. They had been dropped in there by the Indians when passing through and they were gentle enough so that they could easily have been corralled and roped. Not only were those mountains covered with mustangs (though in my opinion they were the most beautiful), but deer, antelope, lobo wolves, turkey and many other kinds of wild game.

The night we arrived back at the ranch there were about fifteen boys there and we immediately planned to have what we called a stag dance. Everyone took part and we enjoyed ourselves to the fullest extent because in those days there was nothing we enjoyed more than a real stag dance.

While we were duty free and so entertaining ourselves, the Indians had to spoil it all. They sneaked up and stole every one of our saddle horses. They tore one side of the corral down and drove them out that way rather than to drive them through the gate. We slipped into our fighting clothes immediately but didn't have a horse to mount.

However, after hunting around, we mustered up enough horses to carry seven men, and work horses and mules enough to pull two wagons loaded with corn and grub enough to feed eighteen men and our stock for a period of two or three weeks. With sweet recollections of our good time which had been interrupted in such a surprising manner, we began our journey for a bloody fight.

A company of State Rangers was camped in two or three miles of us and we were joined by Captain Swisher and nine of his men. This made a total of eighteen men going on the hunt.

We followed the trail through Coleman County passing to the right of Buffalo Gap. When we had traveled about sixty miles, we found ourselves in the roughest country of Taylor County.

Knowing that we were mounted on sluggish animals and that our enemies were speeding on ahead, we were not trying to overtake the Indians but instead were riding at our leisure with the intention of killing a fat buffalo, deer or bear. We were enjoying the chase but we were not fooling ourselves—we knew that the Indians could keep well away from us if they knew we were following because our mounts could not compete against theirs.

In this leisurely manner we traveled until we were in Mulberry Canyon near two sharp peaks which sprang up near a military road which passed nearby. With four men left to guard our wagons, the remainder of our band scouted up Clear Fork to look over the situation.

It was a beautiful morning and we were enjoying the atmosphere of the country. It happened that I and two other men had started off a little ahead of the rest. Captain Swisher and his men had mounted and Sam Gholson was just riding away from them.

I saw a herd of buffalo running as if they had been disturbed. I knew in reason that we had not caused them to plunge in such a wild rush. Before calling the attention of the others or expressing my opinion, I watched the stampeded herd for a moment. Then I saw about six horses trot out into the open, then a band of Indians who were driving them following after them.

To all who had not seen the thieving band I yelled the alarm. It seemed that the Indians had suddenly ridden into the herd with a surprising dash, because buffalo, horses and Indians were so mixing and scrambling that from our view we could not determine one from the other. The Indians were about a mile from us and they had not seen us.

We quietly made our way to within 300 yards of the band, and just when we had stopped to plan an attack on them, we noticed two of the Indians skinning a buffalo within a short distance of us. Two of the boys gave chase but the Indians' fast horses soon carried them to safety.

Our men joined us and we charged the main gang. Musket balls were flying thick while we were engaged in a running fight. The first mile we sprinkled those redskins too and they were wanting to be farther from us than they were getting.

We chased them for about ten miles and they crossed two cedar brakes. They attempted to fight us from there but they could not stand our spray of lead. Our horses with the exception of one were very tired from the long run. This was a dun mare carrying Joe Franks who led the crowd from start to finish. Joe fought those Indians singlehanded when he was far in the lead of us. Several times an Indian who was riding a large bay horse dropped back in an attempt to shoot Joe from the little dun mare. He would shoot once or twice then take on more speed to get away from that Indian fighter.

The Indians disposed of all of their unnecessary luggage and continued traveling directly against the strong wind which was blowing from the northwest, thinking perhaps that their horses could push farther against the torrent of wind than ours.

Finally they halted in the cedar brakes of a canyon on the north side of a range of mountains which lay south of the Texas and Pacific Railroad in Taylor County, and south of the town of Merkel. There we fought the redskins all day.

We surrounded the cedar brakes but could not locate the spot where they were hiding. Gholson and Swisher called all of us to the top of the mountain, from where we could see their horses. We saw six Indians, riding five horses, enter there. We had shot a horse from under one of them and another had picked the rider up.

Sam Gholson, the old Indian fighter, knew what was necessary to be done. He looked over his and Swisher's men.

"Well," he said firmly, "we want six men to see after those Indians."

He looked at us again. "Now, boys, we've got them bottled up and I want to see how many cowboys will volunteer to go into those brakes after them."

Stepping out to one side, I said, "Here I am!"

My friend, Joe Franks, stepped out, followed by Wade Hampton, making half of the required number.

Our leader requested Captain Swisher to select three from among his men, which he did. Then we formulated our plans and I was placed in command of the six men because I was mighty well aware of all the tricks of those red fellows. Some of the ones who were to accompany me were never before in a battle against Indians.

We began our adventure into the thick cedar brake. I ordered the other boys to get down on their knees and begin crawling like I was doing. We entered a small ravine and followed it down, knowing that it would lead us in the direction where we had espied the Indians' horses while we were standing on the mountaintop. In double file we continued to travel the ravine; Wade Hampton was in front. I warned the boys that the first report we would have, warning us of the Indians, would be a shot from their guns.

I had no more than spoken the words until a gun banged. The bullet hit a rock between Hampton and me and the shattered rock flew in my eye. Seeing only a glimpse of one Indian, Hampton fired back. I told the boys to get out of range of the Indian's gun. We crawled out into a gully, a tributary of the ravine. There we were, right in front of two Indians who were concealed in a hole in the bank of the ravine, ten feet above its bed.

We six men sent bullets flying against the shields of those two Indians. Our repeaters were firing fast and those Indians were using those shields too. We would knock the shields down but they would have them in position over the entrance to the hold in which they were hiding by the time another bullet arrived. We had advanced toward them until we were within sixteen feet of the cliff. It was too warm for them.

One of them concluded that he could not stay so he dashed out from the hole and under our shower of bullets leaped down the cliff ten feet, falling behind a cluster of cedar where the rest of the Indian band was hiding. We had ceased firing for the moment when we noticed the other Indian making preparations to leave the hole in the cliff. I leveled my gun and waited.

He came out in plain view with his shield down. As he started his dive down to where the other Indian had descended, I fired. I hit him right between the eyes and he tumbled helplessly to the bed of the ravine. All the hollering, yelling and groaning you can imagine came off when I shot that Indian, and all of the men in the canyon came in to the fight.

The older men who were our superiors would not let us charge the band immediately after I had shot the Indian, for soon as they arrived they took charge. We could have rushed onto them and killed every one of them. Finally though, the Indians sneaked out into the cedars again.

We went to the body of the Indian I had shot. I believe that he had bled a tub full. I scalped him and my conscience didn't hurt me. Perhaps you would think it cruel but if you had known and dealt with these red rascals like I had and had seen the bodies of innocent women and children lying scalped before you, you would be like I was. I knew nothing but to fight them and seek vengeance so far as I had power to do so.

As a result of not having charged and killed those Indians while they were excited, we had to fight them all day. We saw them at least a half dozen times while they were crawling through that cedar.

My cousin, Richard Brown, and some others were curious to see the redskins and watch them fight for a while, so they climbed up onto the top of a small hill. By this time the Indians had grown more reconciled. They were using their bows and arrows. As a surprise to Richard and the others a shower of arrows flew at them. They certainly didn't lose any time in getting back to us.

While they were laughing at each other about the wild dash they had just made down the hillside, I asked Richard what he was doing with that dogwood hanging on him. He looked around and said, "Well, I hadn't felt it." Richard had got an arrow slipped in his thigh but hadn't taken time to notice it.[29]

- This story told by J. M. Franks in *Seventy Years in Texas* shows that although Sam had a well-earned reputation of being a troublemaker, he was sometimes blamed for the mischief of his younger brother:

I will tell of one little incident that happened at old Fort Gates. As I have said, there was for a long time several of the old fort houses left there, and several families were living in them. One Christmas eve there was a big candy pulling and play given by one of these families. I don't remember the name of the family, but anyway, there was a large crowd there and they were having a big time. They had their horses tied to the post oak trees that were near the house and along in the night a bunch of boys and girls who were not asked to the play, slipped up to where the horses were tied and began making mischief by first turning some of the saddles, then they proceeded to shave the manes and tails of some of the horses. I remember one old gray horse that belonged to old lady Grant, they called "Old John." He was a pacing horse. His mane and tail were shaved just as close as could be, and when he threw himself in high gear his tail would stick right straight out and I'll tell you he was a funny sight to look at. Some of the boys had ridden an old black mule that belonged to Uncle Rice Knowles and they cut off one of his ears right at his head. I was a small boy at the time [b. 1850] and it was funny to me to see those poor animals in the shape they were in, but I never could see what good those fellows got out of it, anyway.

In 1900 I was in New Mexico. Sam Golson was living up there at that time. I had not seen him since the Civil War. We were talking of old times in Coryell County and among other things this came up. I knew at that time that Sam and Frank Golson were accused of being in it, but did not know who else. Sam told me he was not there at all. He said that Frank [probably a teenager at the time] and Crockett King, Levy Rogers and Jack Smith were the ones who did the act. But in those days when anything happened in the country, if Sam Golson was there, he was the fellow who did it. Sam, in his young days, was a fine looking fellow, tall and as straight as an Indian, had black hair, always wore a Mexican hat, and was as brave as a lion. He was living a few years ago not far from Tucumcari, New Mexico.[30]

• From *The New Handbook of Texas*:

<u>Portion of entry for Curry Comb Ranch, Garza County:</u>
In 1880 the Llano Cattle Company, with capital stock of $400,000, was organized with W. C. Young as president and Ben Galbraith as manager. Sam S. Gholson, a neighboring cowman, turned in 2,500 cattle and received $50,000 in stock.[31]

<u>Portion of entry for Echo, Texas, Coleman County:</u>
Echo, on State Highway 206 four miles northeast of Coleman in central Coleman County, developed around a store established in the 1870s. In 1881 William Dibrell bought the site as part of his purchase of the Miles and Gholson ranch and renamed it Echo for the echo that resounded on a cliff at Home Creek.[32]

<u>Portion of entry for Taylor County:</u>
The earliest group of European settlers in Taylor County were buffalo hunters and bone gatherers, who arrived during the 1870s. Sam Gholson, William C. Dunn, and William E. Cureton were among the early settlers.[33]

<u>Portion of entry for Daniel Webster Wallace, born to slave parents in 1860:</u>
Tiring of his job chopping cotton near Flatonia, Fayette County, he ran away and joined a cattle drive in 1877. He drove cattle for C. C. Slaughter, Isaac I. Ellwood, Andrew B. Robertson, Sam Gholson, and C. A. "Gus" O'Keefe, and for the Bush and Tillar Cattle Company.[34]

In addition to leading many trail drives involving thousands of head of cattle, Sam was the fourth sheriff of Hamilton County from 1865 to 1866[35] and beef hide inspector of Coleman County.[36] After moving to New Mexico, Sam wrote, "I finally left the plains for New Mexico with 400 head. I have been here 25 years. I have one cow now. Don't think I will ever try cattle any more."[37]

Fig. 14.1 - "A Drove of Texas Cattle Crossing a Stream" A. R. Waud
sketch, *Harper's Weekly*, October 19, 1867. Texas State Library &
Archives Commission No. 1/103-732.

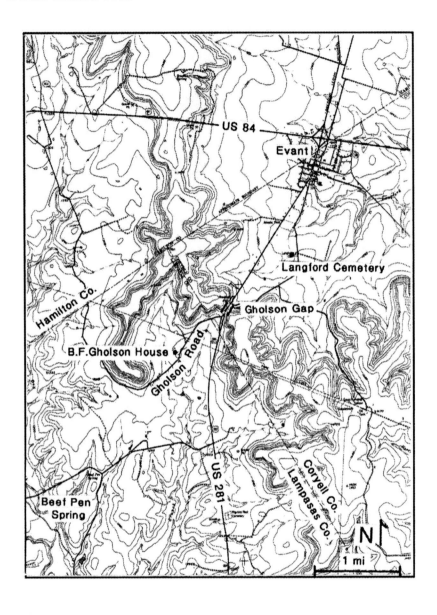

Map 14

Gholson Road area, northeast portion of topographic map from U. S. Geological Survey, 7.5 minute quadrangle, Evant, Texas, 1954, photorevised 1979.

Chapter 15: B. F. Gholson Home & Family

Fig. 15.1 - B. F. Gholson and Adeline at the 1927 reunion of Ex-Rangers. Photo courtesy of Marjory Gholson Morris.

Frank was twenty when he married fourteen-year-old Adeline, the sister of his brother's wife. Frank described their wedding in an interview many years later:

> "In riding over the country in cattle roundups and at dances, I met and fell in love with Miss Jane Adeline Langford of Langford's Cove, now Evant, in the

281

southeastern edge of Hamilton County. The wedding was
on July 18, 1862, at Adeline's home, and the preacher was
Brother Hugh M. Childers [Childress], long ago dead, for
he was an old man then. There was the customary dinner of
wild game, barbecued calves and pigs, chicken pie, cakes,
coffee for the large crowd of kinfolks and friends present.
Everybody was invited, and in the evening we all began to
dance. Those fiddlers were still sawing out the music when
the red in the east announced that it was time for everybody
to go home and get to work."[1]

For the first few years of their marriage, Frank and Adeline lived in a
log cabin. Shortly after their first child was born, Frank went out on a cow
hunt (roundup) and left his young wife at home in the cabin with the baby.
Adeline heard Indians approach and crept down into the storm cellar with
the baby. The baby remained quiet and the Indians did not find them but
they stole Adeline's saddle horse from the barn. The horse was recovered
years later, badly scarred from years of abuse by the Indians.[2]

"Adaline and I first lived in a log cabin across the hills
from here. I bought this tract of land, 244 acres, on Oct. 12,
1870, from Sam Sneed and paid him $400 cash. We paid
cash then, no installments, or land loans for us."

When asked why he had selected this particular location
with the surrounding hills, he answered readily that, "the
Indians could not sneak down over the hills and murder us
here, though they have stolen my horses and cattle from
about the place. And I built my house of rock for two
reasons: That Indians could not set fire to it nor shoot
arrows or bullets through the walls. The second reason was
that lumber had to be hauled from Waco in wagons by ox
teams and it took a long time to make the trips, especially
in rainy weather."

"We reared our family of nine children here in this
home. We are the parents of ten children, but one died in
infancy, and another, a son, Roy Gholson, died last year."

Uncle Frank then told of buying the first buggy and
harness that the people of this section of the country had
ever seen.

"Ane [*sic*] people, the folks around over this country, looked at that buggy with as much interest and almost as much amazement as we did at airplanes a few years ago," he said.

Mrs. Gholson broke in proudly with the statement:

"And Frank bought for me the first sewing machine and the first cook stove ever brought into this part of Texas. The women came for miles to do their fine sewing on my machine. He took a drove of cattle to Kansas City and sold them and brought back the machine and cook stove. I was as proud of them as any women could be of the finest radio now, or a Frigidaire. The men brought them from the city in the 'chuch [*sic*] wagons.'" . . .

The red man gone and the guns of the Civil War silenced, Uncle Frank turned to the peaceful pursuits of farming and stock raising. He put 120 acres of rich Cove land into cultivation, and still raises good crops, although he has quit the cattle, sheep, and goat industries.[3]

Fig. 15.2 - Beef Pen Spring. Photo by Donna Gholson Cook.

If its walls could talk, the two-story rock house could tell its own story. Built between 1872 and 1875[4] by Frank Gholson and a stone mason named Joe Drake,[5] the house is undergoing an extensive restoration at the time of this writing.

It is said that they built the house "between drinks", which may have affected the length of time it took. But with just two men to lay the stone, as well as quarry it, square it, and haul it by wagon from Beef Pen Spring, it probably took quite a while to finish the house.

Joseph Drake was a stonemason who had just moved to the area in 1872 with his 13-year-old son, swapping his house and lot in Bunker Hill, Illinois for 160 acres on what is now known as the Old Kingsbury Place. Most of his work was in Adamsville, and around Lampasas County. He also made tombstones, many of which can be found in the Westpoint Cemetery west of Evant near Fairview.

Door and window jambs and probably the mantels were sawn from walnut at Townsend's Mill near Adamsville, nine miles south on the Lampasas River. Floor joists, ceiling joists and rafters are of oak and were probably obtained locally. It is possible that some of the more "finished" items in the house, such as doors, window sash and shutters, were brought in from Waco.

The house has undergone a continual metamorphosis since it was first built. Originally, it was a two-story rectangular structure (24' x 32') of squared, coursed limestone, with symmetrically arranged doors and windows front and back, inside end chimneys, a hipped wood shingle roof, and 17" thick, rubble-filled walls. The two end walls have a curious juxtaposition of windows, with the upstairs window to the west, downstairs window to the east of the chimney on the south wall; and the upstairs window to the east, and downstairs window west of the chimney on the north wall. The stones are graduated in size, from very large ones at the foundation, to relatively small ones at the corbelled cornice and chimney tops. The 9-over-6 light sash windows, capped with segmental arches, all had operating shutters.

The front (east) elevation had four identical windows symmetrically spaced around four central doorways, two downstairs and two directly above. The original porch or double gallery on this elevation is still a mystery after months of research. The earliest photographs show a gabled two-story central porch, or portico. But these earliest photographs (ca. 1892) also clearly show evidence of joist holes in the stone, presumably for the purpose of attaching a full-length double gallery. The joist holes do not exist on any other elevation of the house. However, on closer examination of these photographs, it also appears that the corbelled stone cornice stops just either side of the smaller gabled porch roof, unless the shadow lines in the photograph are not strong enough under the shade of the roof to be evident. While it would appear that at one time a full-length two-story gallery was at least prepared for, and possibly built, the porch existing in these early photographs was only the width of the central bay. It had four symmetrically-placed squared columns on each level with a simple railing on both levels attached behind the columns, with central steps to the yard and a simple stair leading to the second level at the north end of the porch.

The rear (west) elevation of the house had the same number and arrangement of doors and windows on the ground floor, but no openings on the second floor.

The only woodwork that appears to be painted on the exterior of the house was the shutters and window jambs, which were green. The doors appear to have been a dark-stained wood, while the porch gable end, columns, railings and stair are unpainted. One of the later photographs of this two-story porch shows columns and railings painted white.

Inside, the house consisted of four rooms in all, with a central dividing wall on each floor and a fireplace centered on the end wall of each downstairs room. The interior walls are plastered. Originally, the plaster was scored with white lime to simulate a smooth, regular ashlar masonry wall. The floors were wood plank and ceilings were plank and bead. One of the grandsons remembers a rust color paint on the ceilings. The earliest color remaining on interior window trim and ceiling moulding is a pale blue. The fireplace mantels consisted of very simple facings to the floor, topped by a simple shelf. They were unpainted walnut, possibly stained. A simple stair with a 2" x 4" rail stood in the northeast corner of the north room.

The first kitchen for the house was probably the log structure with a large stone chimney that appears in an early photo behind the southwest corner of the house. A vent pipe appearing just northwest of the chimney might indicate that Mrs. Gholson already had her cook-stove by this time (ca. 1892). The oldest remaining grandson of the Gholsons, R. C. Gholson, remembers the log structure as a large rectangular room, later used as a smoke house.

The earliest fence around the house appears to be of split cedar rails, laid in a zig-zag pattern so that posts and post holes were unnecessary. This fence was replaced by a three-rail board fence by the late 1890's or early 1900's, in the front (east) yard, with a red picket fence across the back yard.

The earliest storm cellar was northwest of the house, with a log and earth roof. The outhouse was just outside the west yard fence. T. R. Gholson, one of the grandsons, remembers it as "Grandma's Privy", a "two-holer" with diamond-shaped cut-outs on all four sides and a shed roof sloping to the west. Besides its obvious function it was also where Adeline went to smoke her corn shucks in privacy. In later years she was allowed to smoke in the house and would send T. R. to pick up dried corn shucks in the barn which she rolled into long cigars, sitting in the rocking chair by the fire in the south room.

The original hand-dug, stone-lined well was placed in the southwest corner of the yard, with a well cap cut from a large single stone. Reportedly, the Gholson daughters disposed of all of Frank's guns, papers and other household items in this well after his death when they moved Adeline to town.

A rectangular frame dining room and kitchen addition with porches the full length of the north and south elevations was built on the north end of the west elevation of the house. This addition was probably there at least as early as 1898. The porch on the south of the addition was later screened. Mr. and Mrs. R. C. Gholson remember this porch being shaded by Madeira vines (pronounced Madeery locally). Access to the dining room was from the north room, through the west door. The small kitchen was at the west end of the addition. The grandchildren remember plain, unfinished board walls and floors, with a later addition of blue flowered wallpaper in the dining room. The cook-stove was now located in front of a window on the west wall of the kitchen. About the time of the kitchen addition, a large (8' x 12') stone or brick-lined storm cellar with a vaulted stone roof and a stone stair was constructed near the road, southeast of the house. This cellar has been tentatively located by grandchildren and old family friends of the Gholsons, but to date has not been excavated for verification.

Two log barns and corrals, as well as a vegetable garden, were across the road to the east and just south of the house. A dry-laid stone wall followed the line of the road and the south line of that pasture.

Within the earliest memory of the grandchildren (early 1900's), the hand-dug well had been replaced with a well near the southwest corner of the house with a windmill and a raised cistern with the base enclosed for use as a shower. Probably to keep the children away from the old well, the grandparents told the children that it contained a dangerous gas which had killed a man cleaning the well.

The front walk was caliche or gravel, with the yard planted primarily with native Mesquite, China Berry trees, and Mountain Juniper (locally called Cedar), with yellow and climbing roses and lilac bushes.

The most dramatic change in the house came around 1915, when Mrs. Gholson decided the house was just too large, too hard to heat and too hard to clean. She decided to have Frank, their son Sam, and grandson T. R., remove the top half of the second story. Some of the family blames this decision on the influence of the daughters, who thought a sort of bungalo-style would be more attractive. T. R.

remembers his grandfather asking Adeline where she thought he would put all the surplus stone. Her suggestion was that it be hauled off and scattered throughout the fields, which is what they did. The hipped roof form was retained, but the windows on the second floor went from 9-over-6 light to just 6 lights, with the two central doors on the east turned into windows. The new one-story front porch extended the full length of the house, its wood-shingled roof supported by turned columns. The chimneys were tapered, with a projecting course of stone at the top.

By the time the house was lowered, a Model T garage and feed granary had been added south of the house.

A wire yard fence with cedar posts and a stone front walk were added by T. R. Gholson in 1930. A bathroom had been added off the south porch of the frame addition by this time.

By 1965, the turned columns on the front porch had been replaced with square ones. The porch roof was starting to cave in, and the windows and doors were missing. The dining and kitchen addition was removed in the 1940's so that the materials could be used to build the small frame house still standing just north of the Gholson House. The log kitchen was removed and the stone storm cellar filled in after 1936.[6]

Fig. 15.3 - Earliest known photo of B. F. Gholson house, showing family members standing in front. Photo courtesy of Binnie Hoffman.

Frank and Adeline donated several acres of land for a school house to educate their own large family and other children in the surrounding area. It was "called Gholson School and nicknamed 'Rawhide,' because of the uncured lumber used in its construction."[7]

Donna Gholson Cook

Fig. 15.4 - Early photo of B. F. Gholson house, courtesy of Bonnie Gholson Gentry.

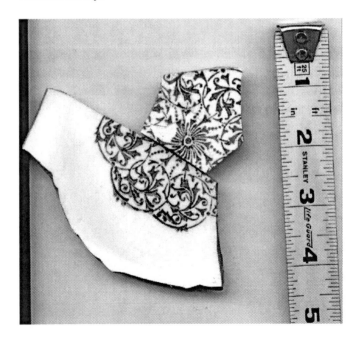

Fig. 15.5 - Dish fragment found in the rubble of the B. F. Gholson house. Photo courtesy of Binnie Hoffman.

290

One of Frank's grandsons, Conner W. Gholson, grew up nearby and spent much of his childhood with his grandfather. He recalled some additional details about the house as it appeared around 1920-30:

- There was a red picket fence around it, with pointed pickets.
- There was a windmill and tank just inside the yard at the back (about half way back, on the side) with an Aeromotor windmill.
- There was a walk from the front door to a gate held shut by a swinging weight and a chain.
- There were chinaberry trees on the north side of the house and mesquites on the south and front. The front door faced due East.
- There were two fireplaces, one in each room. The south room was used more than the north.
- An extension (about 12x20') was built along the back, which held the dining table, safe, cookstove, and dishes.
- The windows had glass panes but no screens.
- The floor was wood, but the grandson did not remember what kind of wood.[8]

Fig. 15.6 - Conner Gholson, grandson of B. F. Gholson, at the old home in 1998. Photo by Donna Gholson Cook.

291

Donna Gholson Cook

The rock house and five acres on which it was situated were purchased in 1977 by David and Binnie Hoffman who have undertaken the monumental task of restoring the rock house. The Hoffmans' credentials as restoration architects are exceeded only by their love for the Gholson place which they have made their permanent residence. What seemed to be a straightforward task has become an enormous challenge, ". . . and realizing the importance of the history of the place, several restoration alternatives have emerged, based on the three principal morphological stages of the house."[9]

The house could be restored to its configuration at the time of Mr. Gholson's death, at its present 1½-story height, with the frame kitchen, dining and bathroom addition, and one-story porch on the front (east) elevation. The interior would be finished in very smooth white plaster, with blue flowered wallpaper in the dining room, and a closet under the staircase. The yard fence would be wire, and the stone walk would remain. This would not only be a functional and relatively inexpensive approach, but from the standpoint of preservation philosophy, would be an excellent example of the morphological changes in a house over time, as the needs of the owner's family changes. The house would once again be pretty much as Frank and Adeline Gholson left it in 1932.

If the house were restored to its original two-story height with a small gabled two-story porch on the front, there would be several outbuildings that could be reconstructed, according to the needs and desires of the present owners. There would be a decision on whether or not to reconstruct the frame addition, as well as several alternatives for interior finishes. Since so much evidence for a series of small stages exists for the house in this configuration, there would be several alternatives within this framework that would be justifiable in terms of accuracy. This philosophy would also be desirable because the house would be returned to a period when Gholson was more involved in the community.

The third alternative would involve more speculation than either of the above, with a more innovative approach

292

to some of the reconstruction required. This would involve returning the house to its original two full storys and attempting to reconstruct what may have been the first front porch, a full-length double gallery, based on evidence on the house and in old photographs, using typical porches from 19th century houses in the surrounding area as models. The interior wall finish in this case would be the earliest, plaster scored with white lime. No plumbing or electricity would be installed in the house (with oil lamps used for lighting). The dining-kitchen addition would be omitted as well in a restoration to this early period. Rather than guess at the exact size and construction methods for the log kitchen, one could borrow the form and function of the kitchen and keep the large stone chimney as shown in the earliest photograph. The structure could be contemporary in the use of building materials and include modern conveniences necessary to a 20th century life-style. The best choice for the yard fence in this case, although the most expensive and possibly least utilitarian, would be the early rail fence, with gravel walks and native plantings in the yard. Since the house will most likely be used as a weekend and vacation retreat, replacing lilac and rose bushes would be impractical.

This last approach would be sensitive to the history and early function of the house, while providing a comfortable and attractive haven for 20th century occupants.

Any of the above philosophies would be a valid approach to restoration of the house. The fact that it is a relatively small, simple house makes it appealing and practical as a restoration project for a weekend home, while the richness of its history and many morphological changes make it a more interesting and rewarding project than many larger, more ornate structures.

Community interest and assistance in the project has further enhanced its value as a rewarding endeavor. Local residents and descendants of the Gholsons have lent their enthusiastic support every way possible, lending credence to long-standing assertions about southwestern hospitality and generosity.

The Gholson House is a very important structure to the community of Evant and to the state as a whole as a present-day reminder of the people who tamed and settled this area and the methods and tools with which they had to work. Both the Gholson and Langford families were highly instrumental in providing law and order for the safety of their families and those to follow, education for their children, freedom from foreign rule, and development of the cattle industry in Texas. Allowing further deterioration of their charming old home, made of local materials by methods long since lost to us, would be a disgrace. Hopefully, with continued perseverance, this will not happen.[10]

Fig. 15.7 - B. F. Gholson house in March 2001. Photo by Donna Gholson Cook.

Fig. 15.8 - The west wall of the B. F. Gholson house was the last wall standing as the stones were taken down to be reassembled. Photo courtesy of Binnie Hoffman, May 15, 2003.

~

Frank Gholson had many sides to his personality. He was attuned to nature as only a person who lives most of life outdoors can be. He was a tracker, ranger, Indian scout, cowboy, and a dreamer searching for buried treasure. He was a historian with an incredibly precise recollection of events, and much can be learned about the Old West from his numerous interviews. He was an active member of the Texas Ex-Rangers Association for as long as he was able.[11]

On September 1, 1914, Frank applied for a Confederate Pension and his application was approved the same day, to begin December 1st. The pension was discontinued in 1923 on account of his receiving an Indian War Pension from the Federal Government, then reinstated March 29, 1927.[12]

```
CAPT.B.F.GHOLSON - Standing (left)
J.MARVIN HUNTER  - Standing (right)
CAPT.DAN W. ROBERTS- Sitting
```

Fig. 15.9 - Ranger Reunion photo of B. F. Gholson, J. Marvin Hunter
(Publisher of *Frontier Times*) and Dan Roberts. Photo courtesy of
the Texas Ranger Hall of Fame and Museum, Waco, Texas.

In contrast to his tall, black-haired brother, Frank Gholson had blue eyes and was of medium height and build. He wore a white hat and smoked a briar pipe, filled from the bag of Big Bale tobacco which hung on the arm of his rocking chair.[13] He never met a stranger and he never owned a watch. According to one of his grandsons, "He just never was in enough of a hurry to need a watch."[14] Adeline cooked two eggs for Frank every morning, sunny side up, and he poured syrup on them and ate them with biscuits. He kept several cows and milked them and fed most of the milk to the cats. He had an old shepherd dog named Old Shep.[15]

Frank spent his last years retelling the stories of his ranger days to interviewers, grandchildren and any visitors who dropped in. He had a reputation for being honest to a fault and although his eyesight faded, his incredible memory never did. A recurring theme in descriptions of Frank is that he bore no animosity toward any human being.

Frank's grandsons were given nicknames in honor of the brave Indians against whom he and his father had fought—names like José Maria, Crazy Snake, Red Cloud, Tanglehair and Rain-in-the-Face. The memory of Cynthia Ann Parker was kept alive by the nicknames he gave his granddaughters—Palloch and Prairie Flower. Another granddaughter was given the nickname *Coosie Ann*, *Coosie* being the Spanish nickname for cocinero, or cook. The original Coosie was the wagon master for Charles "Chuck" Goodnight, who invented the *chuck* wagon.[16]

EPILOGUE

B. F. Gholson Tributes and Dedication of Historical Marker

Frank Gholson died at age eighty-nine on April 3, 1932,[1] just a few months before he and Adeline would have celebrated their seventieth wedding anniversary.[2] After Frank died, Adeline moved into Evant, where she died in 1940.[3] They are buried in the Langford Cemetery near Evant. The following quote is taken from Frank's obituary in the *Lampasas Record*:

> Mr. Gholson has been known as the best informed man in this section of Texas concerning its early history. He knew things that happened and could tell them, remembering them vividly, as is related by Mr. Carter below. In addition to that fact, he was a good man, a christian gentleman, having confessed his faith in Christ when only twelve years of age. He also united with the Church of Christ and followed his Lord in Baptism in 1923. One man who had known him for more than fifty years approached this writer at the cemetery and said, "I want to add just one thing to the notes you are taking and my name not be mentioned." Asked what he wanted to have said, he stated, "Uncle Frank was a peacemaker." He went on to say that he had been with him alone on many trips and in company on many occasions, and never had he heard Uncle Frank utter a disrespectful word of any human. But if differences arose between men or a group of men, "Uncle Frank would sacrifice anything except principle for peace." What a tribute to anybody! . . .
>
> Uncle Frank was a picturesque Texas character, rugged of health and strength, rugged in character; a man who stood four-square in his dealings and relationships with his fellowman; a man of undaunted courage; a man whose friendship would stand the crucial test of adversity; a man who stood a mountain of strength squarely in the path of

him who persisted in evil-doing—a man we honor and love. Truly he was a great man, not from the standpoint of statesmanship, not from the standpoint of sculpture nor art, but as a designer of human events, whose hands were instrumental in bringing to us the happy, progressive civilization that is ours to enjoy today. His long eventful life was above reproach. I have known him all my life, and have heard his name mentioned in public and private conversation more than any other man, and have never heard an unkind or disrespectful remark about him.

His wide acquaintanceship in Central Texas and his active participation in the stirring events of an earlier day, together with his vivid and phenominal [*sic*] memory of the details of the incidents of fifty, and even seventy-five years ago, made him invaluable in keeping the record of our earlier civilization authentic. . . . The book of his life is now closed, but if we had it in documentary or book form, it would be our priceless possession.[4]

Many descendants and other relatives of Frank and Adeline are also buried in the Langford Cemetery. The following description is from the *Evant News*:

Langford Cemetery

Perhaps the oldest of these cemeteries is the Langford Cemetery since the oldest known grave there is that of Eliza Lee Lankford (Langford) who died Sept. 14, 1858. She was the first wife of [Asa] Langford who established Langford Cove in the mid 1850's. Langford Cove was located about 1/2 mile south of the present town of Evant. The cemetery is about one mile south of Evant. Although Eliza Lee Langford was buried in the Langford Cemetery in 1858, Asa Langford did not deed the land for the cemetery to his heirs until 1892. The amount deeded at that time was about 1.65 acres.

In about 1967, Elmer Brooks, grandson of Evant Brooks, founder of the town of Evant, put a chain link fence around the Langford Cemetery and built a brick entrance gate. Elmer's wife and only child, a son, are buried in this Langford Cemetery. There are many descendants of Asa Langford buried in the Langford Cemetery. However, Asa Langford himself is not buried there. He is buried at Center City.[5]

The location of the cemetery was chosen by Langford's young wife, who was buried there much sooner than either of them imagined.

As the story goes, Asa Langford and his young wife, Eliza, were riding late in the afternoon on their land near their home in Langford Cove and stopped under a grove of oak trees to watch the sunset. It was a beautiful sight and Eliza told her husband she loved the spot and she hoped she could be buried there when she died. A few years later she died on September 14, 1858, when she was 32 years old. She was buried in the spot she had requested and this was the beginning of the "Langford graveyard." Through the years other family members were buried there and in 1892 Asa Langford deeded the land to his heirs to be used as a family graveyard.[6]

Fig. Ep.1 - Langford Cemetery, near Evant, Texas. Photo by Donna Gholson Cook, March 2001.

The following article from *The Four County Press* describes the Texas Historical Marker:

HISTORICAL GRAVE MARKER FOR
EARLY DAY RANGER, B. F. GHOLSON, ARRIVES

An Official Texas Historical Grave Marker for Benjamin F. Gholson—an historically significant law officer of Lampasas County—has arrived from the foundry and will soon be erected, Mrs. L. H. Baldwin, chairman of the Lampasas County Historical Survey Committee, has announced.

The marker will be placed at the Gholson gravesite in Langford Cemetery on Highway 281, one mile south of Evant.

This marker is one of a series that will record the brave deeds of Texas' most gallant lawmen from the days of the Republic to the present. The markers are sponsored through the Texas Historical Foundation by a grant given to THF by the Texas Law Enforcement Foundation. THF is the private affiliate of the Texas State Historical Survey Committee.

Inscriptions on the markers commemorate Texas Law Enforcement officers who have been killed in line of duty and or who have contributed to the development of Texas and its history, such as Texas Rangers, sheriffs and marshals.

The inscription on the Gholson marker reads:

"Benjamin F. Gholson (Nov. 17, 18[4]2 - April 3, 1932)

Born in Falls County, son of early Texas settlers Albert G. and Elidia Anderson Gholson.

After 1858-1859 service with Texas Rangers, he re-enlisted in company under Capt. J. M. Smith, and in 1860 aided in the rescue of Cynthia Ann Parker kidnaped by Comanche Indians in 1836.

Served in 2nd Regiment, Texas Cavalry in Civil War. Married Jane Adaline Langford. Prominent stockman, was active in the Texas Ex-Rangers Association.

Recorded—1967"

Frontier Texas produced a unique brand of lawmen, as it long was a border region between the U. S. and Mexico. During this time they rallied defensively against Indians and badmen; during the Republic, against invading Mexican troops. As a result, the Texas Rangers and other famous officers of the law rose to the challenge and worked heroically to keep the peace.

This marker and its location will appear in the next edition of the "Guide to Official Texas Historical Markers."[7]

State Historical Marker
For Texas Ranger B. F. Gholson Has Dedication

"I never knew a man whose word I would rather trust." This was a tribute paid to Frank Gholson, pioneer Texas Ranger and frontier Indian fighter, during the dedication of a historical marker at his grave in Langford Cemetery near Evant Sunday afternoon.

The speaker was J. P. Gerald of Hamilton who was asked to make a few impromptu remarks because he lived in the Gholson home when he was a teacher 60 years ago.

Also paying tribute to the famous pioneer Texas Ranger during Sunday afternoon's ceremonies were Lucius M. Stephens and T. K. [T. R.] Gholson of Lometa and Mrs. L. M. Baldwin and County Judge R. L. Northington, both of Lampasas.

Mrs. Baldwin is chairman of the Lampasas County Historical Survey Committee which was instrumental in obtaining the historical marker from the State.

Stephens was master of ceremonies. As a boy he was well acquainted with Frank Gholson. His father, the late John W. Stephens, worked with Gholson on a cattle ranch at Fort Concho and was a long-time friend. The Stephens family is related to Alexander H. Stephens of Georgia, Vice President of the Confederate State[s] of America.

T. R. Gholson made the response on behalf of the Gholson family at Sunday's dedication. He was one of several grandchildren of Frank Gholson who attended the unveiling. One son of the famous Ranger was present. He is Albert Gholson, 86, of Evant, the only surviving child.

About 75 people braved midsummer heat to hear legends of American folklore and history that are vital parts of the history of this country. The grandfather of Frank Gholson, Col. Sam Gholson, fought with General Andrew (Old Hickory) Jackson against the Creek Indians and against the British at New Orleans. Frank Gholson's father, Albert G. Gholson, was fighting alongside of Col. Ben Milam in the battle of San Antonio in December, 1835, when Milam was killed. Albert G. Gholson went on to fight under Gen. Sam Houston in the Battle of San Jacinto.

Frank Gholson himself first became a Texas Ranger when he was 16 years of age. Rangers were paid $12 a month and all the ammunition they needed in those days. They had to furnish their own food and clothing. His company was assigned the task of patrolling the area between the Colorado and Leon rivers to apprehend Indians out to steal horses or do other damage. The Rangers accomplished this by working in eight-man patrols through the area.

Gholson served at least three six-month hitches as a Ranger before he joined the Texas Cavalry for the Civil War. Most of his Ranger duty, part of which was while Sam Houston was Governor of Texas was spent in tracking and fighting Indians.

Gholson was a member of a patrol in 1858 which recaptured two children, Tobe and Rebecca Jackson, ages 12 and 9 respectively, from Indians near the present Sweetwater. The recapture followed two weeks of tracking the Indians from Lampasas County where they had abducted the children.

The most famous action in which Frank Gholson took part was the Battle of Pease River. In this battle, Cynthia Ann Parker, a white woman and wife of Chief Nacoma, was recaptured 24 years after she had been taken by the Comanches in a raid on Fort Parker. Gholson was in Sull Ross's Company in the Pease River Battle.

After the Civil War, Frank Gholson spent most of the rest of his life in the Evant area. He married Jane Adeline Langford, herself a member of a pioneer family of the area. The old Texas Ranger was almost 90 years of age when he passed away in 1932.

The surviving son, Albert F. Gholson, was also a Texas Ranger, from 1915 until 1918. Afterwards he spent many years in the Custom Service on the Mexican Border. He now lives in January Care Home at Evant.

The grandson of Frank Gholson who made the family's response at Sunday's dedication, T. R. Gholson of Lometa, has also spent most of his life in law enforcement work. A former Lampasas county sheriff, he also served many years as a Texas Liquor Control Board officer.

Mrs. Baldwin cut the ribbon around the new metal historical marker at Frank Gholson's grave Sunday. The marker is erected near a new concrete Civil War service marker at the foot of the grave in Langford Cemetery. At the head of the grave is a large, conventional marble monument.[8]

Fig. Ep.2 - Historical marker and Confederate States Army marker on the grave of Benjamin Franklin Gholson in Langford Cemetery, Evant, Texas. Photo by Donna Gholson Cook, March 2001.

Frank Gholson died on April 3, 1932, the one hundredth anniversary of the date his father and grandfather began their journey to Texas.

Appendix 1

Texas Land Grants

Source: Texas General Land Office
http://www.glo.state.tx.us/archives/process.html

Information for Researchers:
The Land Grant Process in Texas After 1836

The process of issuing land grants and obtaining original land titles after 1836 involved three basic steps. Records which may be found in the TGLO Archives reflect these different steps.

Step 1

Individuals received a *land certificate* for a specified amount of land if certain qualifications were met. Texas created a variety of programs with different qualifications for land.

Step 2

The *grantee* (person who was originally awarded the land certificate) or the *assignee* (person who owned the certificate) would locate available land from the public domain. Using the certificate, a grantee could have the desired land surveyed. The *field notes*, a written description of the survey, were sent to the Texas General Land Office and filed.

Step 3

After fulfilling any conditions of the grant, such as making improvements and paying any required fees, the individual could then apply for a *patent* (the original title from the government) from the Texas General Land Office.

The basic documents regarding individual land grants which may be found in the GLO Archives consist of land certificates, field notes and patents. In addition, other legal documents may be present, such as certificate transfers, duplicate certificates and powers of attorney. In certain cases, evidence had to be presented by an individual in order to prove their claim for a certificate. This evidence is often in the form of affidavits and depositions.

Several general characteristics of the land grant process are important:

- Land grant certificates were not issued for a specific tract of land. It was the responsibility of the certificate holder to find vacant public land, obtain a survey and apply for the patent.
- Land did not have to be located in the same county where the certificate was issued. For example, John Smith may have received a certificate in Harris County but actually located the survey in Travis County.
- A grantee could sell, or "assign," their land certificate to another individual. As a result, many people who received land certificates did not actually settle on the tract of land which bears their name.

Individual Name Search

If you are conducting research on an *individual* who may have been issued a land certificate, the research staff of the Archives and Records Division can conduct a search for any records that may be in the master index. This search covers the official records of Texas land grants, and will inform you of recorded land grants received by the individual, along with a summary of the documents in the files. When requesting this service, please indicate the name(s) to be searched and date(s) of immigration, if known.

Land History Search

If you are conducting research on a particular *parcel of land* and wish to know about the original grantee, please indicate the *name* of the grantee and *location* of land (county and legal description if known). The research staff will send a list of documents on file for that location from which you may then order copies. *Potential researchers should be aware that records regarding any subsequent deed transfers of land after the original patent or title are not located at the Texas General Land Office and should be sought at the county level.*

The following categories of Texas Land Grants were issued to Samuel, Albert G., and Benjamin Franklin Gholson:

Headrights (Republic of Texas, 1836-1845)
Headright grants were issued to individuals by Boards of Land Commissioners *in each county.*

First Class Headright
Issued to those who arrived before March 2, 1836. Heads of families received one league (4,428 acres) and one labor (177.1 acres), while single men received 1/3 league (1,476.1 acres).

Pre-emption Grant

Similar to the headright grants, pre-emption grants were made after statehood. From 1845 to 1854 homesteaders could claim 320 acres. From 1854 to 1856, and 1866 to 1898, up to 160 acres could be claimed. Homesteaders were required to live on the land for three years and make improvements (such as building a barn) in order to qualify for a pre-emption grant of 160 acres.

Military Land Grants

Bounty Grant:

Grants for military service during the Texas Revolution were provided by the Republic of Texas. Each three months of service provided 320 acres up to a maximum of 1,280 acres. Bounty grants for guarding the frontier (1838-1842) were issued by the Republic of Texas. Soldiers were issued certificates for 240 acres. 7,469 bounty grants were issued for 5,354,250 acres.

An individual name search was requested for Samuel Gholson, Albert G. Gholson and Benjamin Franklin Gholson. The following grants were found:

SAMUEL GHOLSON

Mexican Title for one labor of land (177.1 acres), dated February 9, 1835, to Samuel Gholston (Gholson), Robertson's Colony Land Papers, Box 37, Folder 24, Spanish Collection, Archives and Records Division, Texas General Land Office, Austin.

Translation of the title listed above (#1553).

Original Field Notes in English for the above labor of land (177.1 acres), survey for Samuel Gholson, dated February 5, 1835, Robertson's Colony Land Papers, Book B, Page 35, Spanish Collection, Archives and Records Division, Texas General Land Office, Austin.

Mexican Title for one league of land (4,428.4 acres), dated April 25, 1835, to Samuel Gholson, Robertson's Colony Land Papers, Box 35, Folder 65, Spanish Collection, Archives and Records Division, Texas General Land Office, Austin. (See end of Appendix 1 for sample and translation.)

Translation of the title listed above (#1552).

Original Field Notes in English for one league of land (4428.4 acres), Survey for Samuel Gholson, dated March 16, 1835, Robertson's Colony Land Papers, Book A, Page 55, Spanish Collection, Archives and Records Division, Texas General Land Office, Austin.

First Class Headright, Unconditional Certificate No. 181 dated September 6, 1838, for One Labor (177.1 acres) issued to Samuel Gholson by Robertson County Board of Land Commissioners, Immigration Date 1833 (Man of Family), File MIL-1-1191, Original Land Grant Collection, Archives and Records Division, Texas General Land Office, Austin.

Field Notes, survey date September 1, 1852, by virtue of certificate No. 181, acres surveyed 70.8, in current county of Bosque. Samuel Gholson's survey in Bosque County (File MIL-1-1191) was in conflict with a senior survey and was not valid.

Bounty Grant, Certificate No. 6036 dated December 29, 1838, for 1280 acres granted to George W. Morgan by the Secretary of War, for service from September 11, 1836, to July 1, 1837, File HAS-B-3, Original Land Grant Collection, Archives and Records Division, Texas General Land Office, Austin.

The following documents pertain to 1073 acres of the above bounty grant:

- Transfer of the above Certificate No. 6036 by George W. Morgan to A. G. Gholson of Robertson County on June 12, 1839 (attached to certificate).
- Transfer of Certificate No. 6036 by A. G. Gholson of Harrison County to Samuel Gholson, dated December 22, 1840 (certificate torn--signature missing).
- Field Notes of survey of 1073 acres for Samuel Gholston (Gholson) in current county of Harrison, dated February 26, 1841, by virtue of the above certificate No. 6036. Abstract No. 495.
- Affidavit dated May 14, 1841, Harrison County, wherein Sam Gholson states that 1073 acres has been surveyed for him by virtue of Certificate No. 6036, signed by Sam Gholson.
- Patent No. 253, dated December 23, 1848, issued to Samuel Gholson, for the above 1073 acres, Patent Volume 5.

The following documents pertain to the remaining 207 acres:

- Field notes of survey of 207 acres for Samuel Gholson in current county of Harrison, dated March 7, 1849, by virtue of certificate No. 6036. Abstract No. 496.
- Patent No. 600 dated August 16, 1850, issued to Samuel Gholson, for 207 acres, Patent Volume 4.

ALBERT GHOLSON

Mexican Title for a quarter-league of land (1107.1 acres), dated July 3, 1835, to Albert G. Gholson, Robertson's Colony Land Papers, Box 36, Folder 61, Spanish Collection, Archives and Records Division, Texas General Land Office, Austin.

Translation of the title listed above (#1551).

Original Field Notes in English for a quarter-league of land (1107.1 acres), survey for Albert G. Gholson, dated May 1, 1835, Robertson's Colony Land Papers, Book B, Page 101, Spanish Collection, Archives and Records Division, Texas General Land Office, Austin.

First Class Headright, Unconditional Certificate No. 47 dated February 5, 1838, for 370-1/3 acres issued to A. G. Gholson by Robertson County Board of Land Commissioners, Immigration Date March 1833 (Single Man), File BRS-1-27, Original Land Grant Collection, Archives and Records Division, Texas General Land Office, Austin.

Field Notes of survey of 369 acres for A. G. Gholson in current county of Brazos, dated May 3, 1841, by virtue of the above certificate No. 47. Abstract No. 123.

Patent No. 50 dated October 4, 1839, issued to A. G. Gholson, for two labors of land, Patent Volume 9.

Bounty Grant, Certificate No. 2115 dated January 27, 1838, for 320 acres granted to Albert G. Gholson by the Secretary of War, for service from June 13, 1836, to September 30, 1836, File MON-B-203, Original Land Grant Collection, Archives and Records Division, Texas General Land Office, Austin.

Field Notes of survey for Albert G. Gholson of 320 acres in current county of Walker, dated June 23, 1852, by virtue of the above certificate No. 2115. Abstract No. 226.

Patent No. 904, dated August 4, 1853, issued to Albert G. Gholson, for the above 320 acres, Patent Volume 5.

Pre-emption, Proof of Settlement dated March 28, 1857, made by Albert G. Gholson in Lampasas County, Affidavit No. 19, for settlement beginning before August 26, 1856, File MIL-3-1835, Original Land Grant Collection, Archives and Records Division, Texas General Land Office, Austin.

Field Notes of survey of 160 acres for A. G. Gholson in current county of Mills, dated April 5, 1857, by virtue of the above Affidavit No. 19. Abstract No. 285.

Patent No. 604 dated January 17, 1860, issued to A. G. Gholson, for 160 acres, Patent Volume 27.

BENJAMIN FRANKLIN GHOLSON

Pre-emption, Application for a survey of 160 acres made by P. W. Owens in Lampasas County, stating that he is a Citizen of Texas and 18 years of age, dated June 28, 1886, File MIL-P-5287, Original Land Grant Collection, Archives and Records Division, Texas General Land Office, Austin.

Transfer of the above pre-emption of 160 acres by A. L. Churchill and wife Hurlane to B. F. Gholson on February 17, 1890.

Field Notes of survey of 158 acres for B. F. Gholson in county of Lampasas, dated April 23, 1890. Abstract No. 1306.

Proof of Occupancy made by B. F. Gholson on August 12, 1890, in Lampasas County for 3 consecutive years of residence by P. W. Owens and A. L. Churchill on the above 160 acres.

Patent No. 521 dated January 27, 1891, issued to B. F. Gholson, for 158 acres, Patent Volume 23.

Transfer (File No. 147872) October 22, 1928, Lampasas County, S. L. Gholson and wife Ella Gholson of Lampasas County transfer the northwest part of Section 63 in Coryell and Lampasas Counties to B. F. Gholson, Original Land Grant Collection, Archives and Records Division, Texas General Land Office, Austin.

Field Notes, Description of the metes and bounds of 69 acres in Coryell and Lampasas counties, being the northwest part of Section 63, surveyed August 14, 1934, Coryell County Abstract No. 1851 and Lampasas County Abstract No. 1685.

Patent, Final Title issued to B. F. Gholson December 8, 1934, Patent 276, Volume 57-A.

Fig. Ap.1 - Sample of Mexican Title dated April 25, 1835, to one league of land (4,428.4 acres) obtained by Samuel Gholson through Sterling C. Robertson's empresario contract with the Mexican State of Coahuila and Texas. Box 35, Folder 65, Spanish Collection, Archives and Records Division, Texas General Land Office.

1552   SAMUEL GHOLSON   BOX 35
                   FOLDER 65

THIRD SEAL	[Seal of the Treasury of the Free State of Coahuila and Texas]	FOR THE BIENNIUM
TWO REALES		OF 1834 AND 1835

    Citizen Guillermo H. Steele, commissioner appointed by the Supreme Government of this State to distribute and give possession of lands and issue titles to the new colonists in the colonization enterprise of the Nashville Company;

    Whereas Samuel Gholson has been received as a colonist in the colonization enterprise contracted with the Government of the State of Coahuila and Texas by Robert Leftwick [Leftwich] on April 15, 1825, and later conceded to the Nashville Company on October 15, 1827, and the said Samuel Gholson having proved that he has a family and finding in him the requirements prescribed by the State Colonization Law of March 24, 1825; in conformity with the afore-cited law and the provisions of said contract that authorize the settlement of families within the limits of said enterprise on any part of the vacant lands for which the said company has contracted, and with the instructions governing me dated September 4, 1827, and the additional article dated April 25, 1830, and in the name of the State, I grant, confer, and put the said Samuel Gholson in real and personal possession of one league of land, which land has been surveyed by surveyor Jesse Hanna [Hannor], previously appointed for that purpose, under the following situation and boundaries:

    Beginning on the [east] bank of the [Brazos] river at a cottonwood 10 [inches] in diameter, which is the SW [sic] corner of League No. 2. Thence running up the river meandering the same N 60° W 560 varas, N 67° W 2,640 varas to a stake, from which a tree called in English a live oak 10 [inches] in diameter bears N 83° W 8 varas. Thence N 60° E, entered timber at 2,500 varas, entered prairie at 3,820 varas, crossed the Aguila River [Aguilla Creek] at 4,430 varas, bearing N 40° W, 30 varas wide, crossed a creek at 7,430 varas, at 10,817 varas set a stake for the NW [sic] corner of League No.

Fig. Ap.1a - Page one of the translation of the Mexican Title shown in Fig. Ap.1. Translation recorded in Book A, page 55, Spanish Collection, Archives and Records Division, Texas General Land Office.

Appendix 2

David Hoffman & Co.
FIRM PROFILE

The firm of **David Hoffman & Co.** represents one of the highest developments of expertise in the field of historic preservation and adaptive use in the state of Texas. Its primary professionals have demonstrated not only a thorough knowledge of preservation principles and techniques, but also they have continued to be at the forefront of the field, setting high standards that are recognized in this region.

The key professionals in the firm, **Binnie Hoffman** and **David Hoffman, FAIA**, represent a cumulative experience and proficiency in preservation planning and restoration that is unmatched. Recognized statewide for their specialization with numerous honors and awards, they have administered the restoration of hundreds of historic structures, including *National Historic Landmarks, National Register properties* and *Recorded Texas Historic Landmarks.* Their latest award, in 2001, is the Katherine Drake Hart History Preservation Award from the Austin History Center Association for their significant contributions to Austin and Travis County history.

The demands for the firm's specialization have always been statewide. While a great many restored buildings in Austin are attributed to them as architect, there are a greater number of buildings and sites around the state that have received the benefit of their expertise and guidance in matters of restoration and preservation development.

Though old buildings were once considered to be primarily interesting relics of the past, an awareness of the usefulness of historic structures has caused them to be considered invaluable resources today. The principals in the firm of **David Hoffman & Co.** have fostered this new understanding with their innovative adaptive use of older structures ... preserving the essence of the building through careful restoration of its detailing while providing for a fully functional yet compatible new use. Whether it be an adaptation of an older building for a new activity or the restoration of one to a former time, the hallmark of their practice remains: *meticulous attention to authenticity and architectural detail.*

David Hoffman, FAIA
PROFILE

In March of 1992, David Hoffman was elected to the **College of Fellows** of the American Institute of Architects. This was a national honor for his contribution to the profession of architecture through his body of work in historic preservation. This recognition for achievement in his specialized field underscores his career commitment to the principles of preservation and restoration.

While still in Architecture School at The University of Texas at Austin, Hoffman was the first recipient of the **Texas Historic Resources Fellowship**, for which he produced a historic architectural study of Roma, Texas. Historic Preservation was only beginning to be recognized as a specialization in architecture then, with a strong focus on *landmark*, high-style buildings. Hoffman began to bring into focus the importance of simpler vernacular structures as an important *genre* in his study of this small town on the Mexican border.

Hoffman set precedents again as the first Architect of the newly-formed Historic Sites and Restoration Branch of **Texas Parks and Wildlife Department** from 1971 to 1973. During that time, plans were formulated and implementation begun on an aggressive program of acquisition and development of state historic sites.

Two other architects joined Hoffman in 1973 to form the first architecture firm in Texas specializing in historic preservation. Their practice began on a statewide basis and his continues to this day as such. Many of Hoffman's projects have been recognized for excellence at local, state and national levels.

Hoffman has been an activist for historic preservation throughout his career, writing and lecturing on preservation, volunteering for many preservation groups and sharing his expertise as Adjunct Professor at **The University of Texas at Austin School of Architecture**, teaching graduate courses on Preservation Technology. He is past President of the Heritage Society of Austin and the Society of Architectural Historians, Texas Chapter.

Hoffman's primary contribution to his chosen field is the restoration under his direction of more than 100 historic buildings throughout Texas. He has many repeat and referred clients due to the integrity of his projects and the frequency with which they are concluded within Owners' parameters of time and budget. A number of buildings he has restored are of national significance (those titled *National Historic Landmark*) and almost all others are listed on the *National Register of Historic Places* and/or are *Registered Texas Historic Landmarks*. Clients include municipalities, colleges, state agencies, numerous non-profit organizations and a host of others in the private sector. He continues to serve as **Architect** for all of the firm's projects, with his involvement in all aspects of the work directly benefiting their successful results.

Donna Gholson Cook

Binnie Hoffman
PROFILE

As CEO of David Hoffman & Co., Binnie Hoffman acts as Project Manager and Project Liaison between the firm's architects, clients and state and federal agencies that are often involved in historic preservation projects in addition to researching and writing cultural and architectural histories. Her research and documentation of historic buildings and districts has been used for numerous *National Register* nominations, *Texas Historical Markers* and as information for restoration/preservation projects, historic structures reports, historic building surveys and preservation master plans.

Ms. Hoffman has administered scores of *Certified Rehabilitation* projects and consults with private and institutional/governmental clients regarding the proper application and interpretation of the *Secretary of the Interior's Standards for Rehabilitation.* She has organized and completed a number of city-wide historic building surveys according to Federal standards, including those for the cities of Waco, Gonzales and Beaumont, Texas and acted as Administrator for the Austin Historic Building Survey conducted by Hardy Heck Moore several years ago.

As an active volunteer in the field of historic preservation, she has lectured, developed curricula and conducted seminars on documentation of historic buildings and interpretation of the *Secretary of the Interior's Standards for Rehabilitation* for heritage organizations and public programs, and has been active in several heritage and professional organizations, such as the **Austin History Center Association** (President, 1989-90), the **Heritage Society of Austin** (Guild President, 1976) and the **Association for Preservation Technology** (Finance Chair, APT/Austin '86).

While still a student at **The University of Texas** from 1974 to 1978, Ms. Hoffman was a free-lance Preservation Consultant, with clients such as county historical commissions, architectural firms and the Texas Historical Commission, and she worked as a Research Assistant at **Winedale Historical Center** during the spring semester of 1975. Upon graduation, she became a member of the professional staff of the **Texas Historical Commission** as Special Projects Coordinator, developing and coordinating grants-in-aid programs for architectural surveys in cities and regions state-wide, writing and reviewing *National Register* nominations for conformity to Federal standards, administering professional workshops and conferences on preservation, and reviewing historic preservation ordinances for submission to the **U. S. Department of Interior** for certification under the 1976 Tax Reform Act.

Ms. Hoffman maintains a broad range of capabilities in the historic preservation field and continues to foster *cooperation* and *coordination* between official reviewing agencies and the firm's clients.

CHAPTER NOTES

ONE: The Immigrants
1.   Sir Winston Churchill, *The Great Republic--A History of America*, ed. Winston S. Churchill (New York: Random House, 2000), 3-19.
2.   Ibid., 23-24.
3.   Ibid., 36-41.
4.   Ibid., 42.
5.   Ibid., 43.
6.   David Freeman Hawke, *Everyday Life in Early America* (New York: Harper & Row, 1988; Perennial Library, 1989), 2.
7.   Ibid., 5.
8.   Ibid., 11.
9.   Ibid., 12.
10.   Ibid., 13.
11.   Churchill, *Great Republic,* 44-45.
12.   Angie Debo, *A History of the Indians of the United States* (Norman: The University of Oklahoma Press, 1983), 40.
13.   Virginia Baker Mitchell, *Gholson and Allied Families*, ed. Margaret Scruggs-Carruth (Dallas: n.p., 1950), Concerning Origins, 1.
14.   Lothrop Withington, *Virginia Gleanings in England, Abstracts of 17th and 18th-Century English Wills and Administrations Relating to Virginia and Virginians: A Consolidation of Articles from The Virginia Magazine of History and Biography* (Baltimore: Genealogical Publishing Co., 1980), 120-1.
15.   John Venn and J. A. Venn, comp., *Alumni Cantabrigienses: A Biographical List of All Known Students, Graduates and Holders of Office at the University of Cambridge, From the Earliest Times to 1900, Part I, From the Earliest Times to 1751, Volume II, Dabbs-Juxton* (Cambridge: At the University Press, 1922), 273.

16. Susan Myra Kingsbury, ed., *Heritage Books Archives: Records of the Virginia Company of London, Volumes 1-4*, CD (Bowie, MD: Heritage Books Archives, 1999) pdf vii, 215 ff.

17. The Rev. Silas Emmett Lucas, Jr., *Virginia Colonial Abstracts--Series 2, Vol. 3: The Virginia Company of London, 1607-1624*, abstr. and comp. Beverley Fleet, ed. The Rev. Lindsay O. Duvall (Easley, SC: Southern Historical Press, 1978), 38.

18. Hawke, *Everyday Life*, 6.

19. Ibid., 9.

20. Ibid.

21. Lucas, *Virginia Colonial Abstracts*, 38.

22. Leslie Stephen and Sidney Lee, eds., *Dictionary of National Biography, Vol. 8, Glover-Harriott,* "Goulston or Gulston, Theodore, M.D." (New York: The McMillan Company, 1908), 289.

23. Withington, *Virginia Gleanings in England*, 120.

24. Venn and Venn, *Alumni Cantabrigienses*, 274.

25. Peter Wilson Coldham, *The Complete Book of Emigrants 1661-1699: A Comprehensive Listing Compiled from English Public Records of Those Who Took Ship to the Americas for Political, Religious, and Economic Reasons; of Those Who Were Deported for Vagrancy, Roguery, or Non-Conformity; and of Those Who Were Sold to Labour in the New Colonies* (Baltimore: Genealogical Publishing Co., Inc., 1990), 238.

26. David Hackett Fischer, *Albion's Seed--Four British Folkways in America* (New York: Oxford University Press, 1989), 308.

27. Churchill, *Great Republic*, 44-45.

28. Ibid., 48-49.

29. Ibid., 50.

30. Ibid., 51.

31. Ibid., 52-55.

32. John C. Miller, ed., *The Colonial Image--Origins of American Culture* (New York: George Braziller, 1962), 15.

33. Ibid.

34. Thomas Sowell, *Conquests and Cultures--An International History* (New York: Basic Books, 1998), 80.
35. Francis Dillon, *The Pilgrims--Their Journeys & Their World* (Garden City, NJ: Doubleday & Company, Inc., 1975), 151.
36. Miller, *Colonial Image,* 86.
37. Ibid., 88.
38. Ibid.
39. Ibid., 86.
40. Ibid., 88.
41. Ibid., 86.
42. Ibid., 88-9.
43. Alden T. Vaughan, *America Before the Revolution 1725-1775* (Englewood Cliffs, New Jersey: Prentice-Hall, Inc., 1967), 5.
44. James E. Brown and Margaret Brown Altendahl, comps., *Relatives of the Browns of Mill Springs, Kentucky: Including the Fisher, Gaar, Gholson, Hutchison, Weaver and West Families* (Baltimore: Gateway Press, Inc., 1992), xxiii.
45. Mitchell, *Gholson and Allied Families*, Concerning Origins, 3.
46. New England Historic Genealogical Society, *The New-England Historical and Genealogical Register 1895, Vol. XLIX* (Boston: Published by The Society, 1895), 485.
47. John Camden Hotten, ed., *The Original Lists of Persons of Quality; Emigrants; Religious Exiles; Political Rebels; Serving Men Sold for a Term of Years; Apprentices; Children Stolen; Maidens Pressed; and Others Who Went from Great Britain to the American Plantations, 1600-1700, With Their Ages, The Localities Where They Formerly Lived in the Mother Country, The Names of the Ships in Which They Embarked, and Other Interesting Particulars, From MSS. Preserved in the State Paper Department of Her Majesty's Public Record Office, England* (Baltimore: Genealogical Publishing Co., Inc. 1968), 282, 284.
48. Nell Marion Nugent, abstr. and ind., *Cavaliers and Pioneers--Abstracts of Virginia Land Patents & Grants, 1623-1666, Vol. 1* (Baltimore: Genealogical Publishing Co., Inc., 1979), 131.
49. Miller, *Colonial Image,* 294.

50. Hawke, *Everyday Life*, 120.
51. Ibid., 123.
52. Ibid., 124.
53. Vaughan, *America Before the Revolution*, 43.
54. Churchill, *Great Republic,* 73.
55. Vaughan, *America Before the Revolution*, 6.
56. Brown & Altendahl, *Relatives of the Browns*, xxiii.
57. Ibid.
58. Churchill, *Great Republic,* 72-3.

TWO: Life in Early Virginia - 1600-1800
1.   David Freeman Hawke, *Everyday Life in Early America* (New York: Harper & Row, 1988; Perennial Library, 1989), 13-15.
2.   Ibid., 33.
3.   Ibid., 36.
4.   Ibid., 37.
5.   Ibid., 38.
6.   Ibid., 39.
7.   Ibid., 40.
8.   Ibid., 52.
9.   Ibid., 55.
10. Ibid., 56.
11. Ibid., 57.
12. Ibid., 43-4.
13. Ibid., 44-5.
14. John C. Miller, ed., *The Colonial Image--Origins of American Culture* (New York: George Braziller, 1962), 297.
15. Ibid., 298.
16. Ibid., 297-9.
17. Ibid., 301.
18. Hawke, *Everyday Life*, 84.
19. Ibid., 84-5.
20. David Hackett Fischer, *Albion's Seed--Four British Folkways in America* (New York: Oxford University Press, 1989), 311.
21. Hawke, *Everyday Life*, 81.
22. Ibid., 82.
23. Ibid., 83.
24. Ibid., 21.

25. Fischer, *Albion's Seed*, 277.
26. William Armstrong Crozier, ed., *Virginia County Records, Spotsylvania County 1721-1800: Being Transcriptions, from the Original Files at the County Court House, of Wills, Deeds, Administrators' and Guardians' Bonds, Marriage Licenses, and Lists of Revolutionary Pensioners* (1905; reprint, Baltimore: Genealogical Publishing Co., Inc., 1978), 70.
27. James E. Brown and Margaret Brown Altendahl, comps., *Relatives of the Browns of Mill Springs, Kentucky, Including the Fisher, Gaar, Gholson, Hutchison, Weaver and West Families* (Baltimore: Gateway Press, Inc., 1992), 104. From Spotsylvania County, Virginia O.B. (1724-1730), p. 324.
28. Augusta Phillips Johnson, *A Century of Wayne County, Kentucky, 1800-1900* (Louisville: The Standard Printing Company, Inc., 1939), 224.
29. F. B. Kegley, *Kegley's Virginia Frontier: The Beginning of the Southwest, The Roanoke of Colonial Days, 1740-1783, With Maps and Illustrations* (Roanoke: The Southwest Virginia Historical Society, 1938), 525-6.
30. Fischer, *Albion's Seed*, 326.
31. Ibid., 328.
32. Hawke, *Everyday Life*, 21-2.
33. Ibid., 61.
34. Ibid., 20.
35. Fischer, *Albion's Seed*, 210.
36. Paula S. Felder, *Forgotten Companions: The First Settlers of Spotsylvania County and Fredericksburgh Town (With Notes on Early Land Use)* (Fredericksburg, VA: Historic Publications of Fredericksburg, 1982), 52.
37. Fischer, *Albion's Seed*, 233-5.
38. Johnson, *Century of Wayne County*, 76. Anthony[1] also had a son named Anthony, often referred to in documents as Anthony, Jr. He was the brother of William, father of Anthony[2]. This work contains only a few references to Anthony, Jr. pertaining to Anthony[1] and his son William.
39. Fischer, *Albion's Seed*, 257. [Many older Texans still use these expressions today. When Conner Gholson, my father, was asked by one of his friends how he was doing, his answer might have been "Porely." I was often told that I "favor" my father.]

40. Ibid., 261.
41. Ibid., 258.
42. Ibid., 259.
43. Ibid., 262.
44. Ibid., 259.
45. Virginia Baker Mitchell, *Gholson and Allied Families*, ed. Margaret Scruggs-Carruth (Dallas: n.p., 1950), Concerning Origins, 3.
46. Fischer, *Albion's Seed*, 345.
47. Ibid., 347.
48. Ibid., 347-8.
49. Ibid., 347.
50. Adrienne Koch and William Peden, eds., *The Life and Selected Writings of Thomas Jefferson* (1944; reprint, New York: Modern Library, 1998), 233.
51. Fischer, *Albion's Seed*, 281.
52. Ibid., 286.
53. Ibid., 298.
54. Ibid., 300.
55. Ibid., 302.
56. Ibid., 304.
57. Ibid., 283.
58. Hawke, *Everyday Life*, 63.
59. Koch and Peden, *Life and Selected Writings of Thomas Jefferson*, 455.
60. Carl Holliday, *Woman's Life in Colonial Days* (1922; reprint, Mineola, NY: Dover Publications, Inc., 1999), 74.
61. Ibid., 105.
62. Ibid., 106.
63. Ibid., 107.
64. Ibid., 113.
65. Ibid.
66. Ibid., 114.
67. Mitchell, *Gholson and Allied Families*, 3.
68. Ibid., 11.
69. Ibid., 15.
70. Holliday, *Woman's Life in Colonial Days*, 114.
71. Hawke, *Everyday Life*, 61.

72. Stephen E. Ambrose, *Undaunted Courage: Meriwether Lewis, Thomas Jefferson, and the Opening of the American West* (New York: Touchstone, 1996), 31-2.
73. June Baldwin Bork, compiler, *Wayne County, Kentucky, Deed Book D, 1823-1828* (Apple Valley, CA: June Baldwin Bork, 1994), 42.
74. Hawke, *Everyday Life*, 78.
75. Ibid., 79.
76. Miller, *Colonial Image*, 302.
77. Ibid., 302-3.
78. Ibid., 303-4.
79. Johnson, *Century of Wayne County*, 224.
80. Joyce and Richard Wolkomir, "When Bandogs Howle & Spirits Walk," *Smithsonian Magazine* 31, no. 10 (2001): 40.
81. Ibid.
82. Ibid.
83. Ibid., 40-41.
84. Ibid., 43.
85. Ibid., 44.
86. Brown and Altendahl, *Relatives of the Browns*, 105.
87. Ambrose, *Undaunted Courage*, 30.
88. Ibid.
89. Alden T. Vaughan, *America Before the Revolution 1725-1775* (Englewood Cliffs, NJ: Prentice-Hall, Inc., 1967), 165.
90. Ibid., 164.
91. Fischer, *Albion's Seed*, 343.
92. Ambrose, *Undaunted Courage*, 32.
93. Koch & Peden, *Life & Selected Writings of Thomas Jefferson*, 262.
94. Mitchell, *Gholson and Allied Families*, 14.
95. Kegley, *Kegley's Virginia Frontier*, 513.
96. Koch and Peden, *Life and Selected Writings of Thomas Jefferson*, 564.
97. Vaughan, *America Before the Revolution*, 157.
98. Fischer, *Albion's Seed*, 313.
99. Ibid., 349-54.
100. Ibid., 314.
101. Ibid., 315.
102. Hawke, *Everyday Life*, 8.
103. Ibid., 67.
104. Ibid., 68.

105. Ibid., 118.
106. Ibid., 119.
107. Ibid., 120.
108. Ambrose, *Undaunted Courage*, 55.
109. Hawke, *Everyday Life*, 127.
110. David Brion Davis and Steven Mintz, *The Boisterous Sea of Liberty: A Documentary History of America from Discovery Through the Civil War* (Oxford: Oxford University Press, 1998), 57.
111. Hawke, *Everyday Life*, 127.
112. Miller, *Colonial Image*, 20, 31.
113. Ibid., 31.
114. Ibid., 33.

THREE: Virginia – The Planters and the Land
1. Page Smith, *John Adams, Vol. I, 1735-1784* (Garden City, NY: Doubleday & Company, Inc., 1962), 51.
2. Ibid., 259.
3. Ibid., 272.
4. Alden T. Vaughan, *America Before the Revolution 1725-1775* (Englewood Cliffs, NJ: Prentice-Hall, Inc., 1967), 23.
5. Ulysses P. Joyner, Jr., *Orange County Land Patents*, 2d ed., (Orange County Historical Society, Inc., 1999), 7.
6. Ibid., 9.
7. Nell Marion Nugent, abstr. and ind., *Cavaliers and Pioneers--Abstracts of Virginia Land Patents & Grants, 1623-1666, Vol. 1* (Baltimore: Genealogical Publishing Co., Inc., 1979), xxiv.
8. James E. Brown and Margaret Brown Altendahl, comps., *Relatives of the Browns of Mill Springs, Kentucky, Including the Fisher, Gaar, Gholson, Hutchison, Weaver and West Families* (Baltimore: Gateway Press, Inc., 1992), xi.
9. Parke Rouse, Jr., *The Great Wagon Road: from Philadelphia To the South* (New York: McGraw-Hill, 1973), 12.
10. William Armstrong Crozier, ed., *Virginia County Records, Spotsylvania County 1721-1800; Transcriptions from the Original Files at the County Court House* (Baltimore: Genealogical Publishing Co., Inc., 1978), 95.
11. Ibid., 149.
12. Joyner, *Orange County Land Patents*, 27.

13. Virginia Baker Mitchell, *Gholson and Allied Families*, ed. Margaret Scruggs-Carruth (Dallas: n.p., 1950), 1.
14. Joyner, *Orange County Land Patents*, 27.
15. Mitchell, *Gholson and Allied Families*, 1.
16. Rouse, *Great Wagon Road*, 11.
17. Philip Vickers Fithian, *Journal & Letters of Philip Vickers Fithian, 1773-1774, A Plantation Tutor of the Old Dominion,* ed. Hunter Dickinson Farish (1943; reprint, Charlottesville: The University Press of Virginia, 1996), xv.
18. Joyner, *Orange County Land Patents*, 12.
19. Adrienne Koch and William Peden, eds., *The Life and Selected Writings of Thomas Jefferson* (1944; reprint, New York: Modern Library, 1998), 248.
20. Nathaniel Mason Pawlett, *Historic Roads of Virginia, Spotsylvania County Road Orders, 1722-1734* (Virginia Highway & Transportation Research Council, n.d.), 21.
21. Ibid., 39.
22. Ibid., 44. See Explanatory Notes regarding the calendar year.
23. Ibid., 45.
24. Ibid., 81.
25. Fithian, *Journal and Letters*, xv.
26. Brown and Altendahl, *Relatives of the Browns*, 107.
27. Ibid., 105.
28. Ibid., 106.
29. Ibid., 107.
30. Mitchell, *Gholson and Allied Families*, 10. See Chapter 6 for more about Captain Joseph Collins.
31. Ibid., 11.
32. Brown and Altendahl, *Relatives of the Browns*, 145.
33. Mitchell, *Gholson and Allied Families*, 11.
34. Ibid., 10.
35. Brown and Altendahl, *Relatives of the Browns*, 198.
36. W. W. Abbot and Dorothy Twohig, eds., *The Papers of George Washington, Colonial Series, Vol. 8, June 1767-December 1771* (Charlottesville: University Press of Virginia), 568, 570. Anthony's name also appears in Vol. 9, on pages 110, 503-4, in Washington's Cash Accounts records. William's brother Anthony, Jr. apparently died in 1779, so this note must refer to William's son Anthony.

37. "Virginia Legislative Papers; From Originals in The Virginia State Archives," *Virginia Magazine of History and Biography* 13, no. 4, (1906): 412. Berkeley County, West Virginia, was formed from a part of Frederick County in 1772, and Frederick County, Virginia, was formed from a part of Orange County in 1743.
38. Ibid., 413.
39. Ibid., 411.
40. Brown and Altendahl, *Relatives of the Browns*, 200.
41. John H. Gwathmey, *Historical Register of Virginians in the Revolution: Soldiers, Sailors, Marines; 1775-1783* (Baltimore: Genealogical Publishing Co., Inc., 1979), 314.
42. Lyman Chalkley, *Chronicles of the Scotch-Irish Settlement in Virginia, Extracted from the Original Court Records of Augusta County, 1745-1800, Vol. II* (1912; reprint, Baltimore: Genealogical Publishing Co., Inc., 1974), 423.
43. Brown and Altendahl, *Relatives of the Browns*, 200.
44. Virginia Genealogical Society, *Virginia Genealogical Society Quarterly* 13, no. 2, (1975): 33.
45. Lewis Preston Summers, *Annals of Southwest Virginia, 1769-1800* (Abingdon, VA: Lewis Preston Summers, 1929), 377.
46. Brown and Altendahl, *Relatives of the Browns*, 202-3.
47. Summers, *Annals of Southwest Virginia*, 401.
48. Ibid., 405.
49. Ibid., 431.
50. Ibid., 447.
51. Mitchell, *Gholson and Allied Families*, 14.
52. F. B. Kegley, *Kegley's Virginia Frontier: The Beginning of the Southwest, The Roanoke of Colonial Days, 1740-1783, With Maps and Illustrations* (Roanoke: The Southwest Virginia Historical Society, 1938), 520.
53. David Freeman Hawke, *Everyday Life in Early America* (New York: Harper & Row, 1988; Perennial Library, 1989), 145.
54. Ibid., 146.
55. Mitchell, *Gholson and Allied Families*, 14.
56. Kegley, *Kegley's Virginia Frontier*, 500.
57. Hawke, *Everyday Life*, 146-7.

58. Fithian, *Journal and Letters*, xiv.
59. Rouse, *Great Wagon Road*, 227.
60. Brown and Altendahl, *Relatives of the Browns*, xxvii.
61. Mitchell, *Gholson and Allied Families*, 15.
62. Ibid., 14.
63. Ibid.
64. Koch & Peden, *Life & Selected Writings of Thomas Jefferson*, xxxv.

FOUR: Virginians in the American Revolution
1. David Brion Davis and Steven Mintz, *The Boisterous Sea of Liberty: A Documentary History of America from Discovery Through the Civil War* (Oxford: Oxford University Press, 1998), 3.
2. E. M. Sanchez-Saavedra, comp., *A Guide to Virginia Military Organizations in the American Revolution, 1774-1787* (Richmond: Virginia State Library, 1978), vii.
3. Sir Winston Churchill, *The Great Republic--A History of America*, Large Print version, ed. Winston S. Churchill (New York: Random House, 2000), 97-8.
4. Ibid., 98-100.
5. Ibid., 105-6.
6. Ibid., 108.
7. Ibid., 109-10.
8. Ibid., 111-12.
9. Philip Vickers Fithian, *Journal & Letters of Philip Vickers Fithian, 1773-1774, A Plantation Tutor of the Old Dominion,* ed. Hunter Dickinson Farish (1943; reprint, Charlottesville: The University Press of Virginia, 1996), 110.
10. William H. Hallahan, *The Day the American Revolution Began: 19 April 1775* (New York: William Morrow and Company, 2000), 188-9.
11. Ibid., 189.
12. Ibid., 190.
13. Benson Bobrick, *Angel in the Whirlwind: The Triumph of the American Revolution* (New York: Simon & Schuster, Inc., 1997; New York: Penguin Putnam Inc., 1998), 110.
14. Hallahan, *Day the American Revolution Began*, 190.
15. Ibid., 191.
16. Ibid.

17. Ibid., 192.
18. Churchill, *Great Republic*, 112-13.
19. Hallahan, *Day the American Revolution Began*, 177.
20. Bobrick, *Angel in the Whirlwind*, 123.
21. Ibid., 124.
22. Hallahan, *Day the American Revolution Began*, 183-4.
23. Ibid., 184.
24. Ibid., 195.
25. Ibid., 196.
26. Hallahan, *Day the American Revolution Began*, 184.
27. Ibid., 185.
28. Ibid., 197.
29. Ibid.
30. Sanchez-Saavedra, *Guide to Virginia Military Organizations*, 137.
31. Ibid.
32. Joyce Lee Malcolm, *To Keep and Bear Arms, The Origins of an Anglo-American Right* (Cambridge, MA: Harvard University Press, 1994), 138.
33. Ibid., 140.
34. Ibid.
35. Ibid., 139.
36. Adrienne Koch and William Peden, eds., *The Life and Selected Writings of Thomas Jefferson* (1944; reprint, New York: Modern Library, 1998), 205-6.
37. Malcolm, *To Keep and Bear Arms*, 143.
38. Ibid., 144.
39. Ibid., 145.
40. Hallahan, *Day the American Revolution Began*, 198.
41. Ibid., 199.
42. Ibid., 205.
43. Koch and Peden, *Life & Selected Writings of Thomas Jefferson*, xxi.
44. Davis and Mintz, *Boisterous Sea of Liberty*, 203.
45. Virginia Baker Mitchell, *Gholson and Allied Families*, ed. Margaret Scruggs-Carruth (Dallas: n.p., 1950), 14.
46. John H. Gwathmey, *Historical Register of Virginians in the Revolution: Soldiers, Sailors, Marines; 1775-1783* (Baltimore: Genealogical Publishing Co., Inc., 1979), 314.
47. James E. Brown and Margaret Brown Altendahl, comps., *Relatives of the Browns of Mill Springs, Kentucky, Including the Fisher, Gaar,*

Gholson, Hutchison, Weaver and West Families (Baltimore: Gateway Press, Inc., 1992), xvi.
48. Virginia Genealogical Society, *Virginia Genealogical Society Quarterly* 13, no. 2, (1975): 33.
49. Bobrick, *Angel in the Whirlwind*, 432.
50. *DAR Patriot Index, Centennial Edition*, Part II (Washington: National Society of the Daughters of the American Revolution, 1994), 1182.

FIVE: Over the Mountains to Kentucky
1. Frederick Jackson Turner, *The Frontier in American History* (1920; reprint, New York: Dover Publications, 1996), 37.
2. Robert L. Kincaid, *The Wilderness Road* (Indianapolis: The Bobbs-Merrill Company, 1947), 73.
3. Parke Rouse, Jr., *The Great Wagon Road: from Philadelphia To the South* (New York: McGraw-Hill, 1973), 107-8.
4. Kincaid, *Wilderness Road*, 74-5.
5. Ibid., 75-6.
6. Ibid., 78.
7. Ibid., 78-9.
8. Ibid., 80.
9. Ibid., 82-90.
10. Ibid., 98.
11. Ibid., 99.
12. Ibid., 100-101.
13. Ibid., 102-3.
14. Ibid., 103-4.
15. Ibid., 105.
16. Ibid., 106-7.
17. Ibid.
18. Ibid., 110.
19. Rouse, *Great Wagon Road*, 110.
20. Ibid., 112.
21. Ibid., 116.
22. Kincaid, *Wilderness Road*, 184.
23. Ibid., 185.
24. Ibid., 186.
25. Ibid., 187.
26. Ibid., 188.

Donna Gholson Cook

Donna Gholson Cook

27. Ibid., 189.
28. Ibid., 190.
29. Ibid., 191.
30. Virginia Baker Mitchell, *Gholson and Allied Families*, ed. Margaret Scruggs-Carruth (Dallas: n.p., 1950), 15.
31. Kincaid, *Wilderness Road*, 188.
32. Ibid., 192.
33. Augusta Phillips Johnson, *A Century of Wayne County, Kentucky, 1800-1900* (Louisville: The Standard Printing Company, Inc., 1939), 22.
34. Ibid., 24.
35. Ibid., 25.
36. Ibid., 21.
37. Ibid., 22-3, 28.
38. Ibid., 28-9.
39. James E. Brown and Margaret Brown Altendahl, comps., *Relatives of the Browns of Mill Springs, Kentucky, Including the Fisher, Gaar, Gholson, Hutchison, Weaver and West Families* (Baltimore: Gateway Press, Inc., 1992), 198.
40. Johnson, *Century of Wayne County*, 34.
41. Ibid., 35.
42. Ibid.
43. Brown and Altendahl, *Relatives of the Browns*, 204.
44. Sara Belle Upchurch, ed., "Anthony Gholson House," *Wayne County Historical Society Overview* 18, no. 1 (1997).
45. Ibid.
46. Brown and Altendahl, *Relatives of the Browns*, 206.
47. June Baldwin Bork, comp., *Wayne County, Kentucky, Deed Book B, 1811-1818* (Apple Valley, CA: June Baldwin Bork, 1993), 54.
48. Johnson, *Century of Wayne County*, 76.
49. Eric Sloane, *Diary of an Early American Boy: Noah Blake, 1805* (New York: Wilfred Funk, Inc., 1965; New York: Ballantine Books, 1974), 18.
50. Bork, *Wayne County, Kentucky, Deed Book B*, 54.
51. Anthony Gholson Biography, Gholson Family File, Wayne County Historical Society, Monticello, Kentucky.
52. Mitchell, *Gholson and Allied Families*, 15.
53. Turner, *Frontier in American History*, 19.

54. Ibid., 20.
55. Ibid., 21.

SIX: The Family of Anthony₂ Gholson of Virginia and Kentucky
1. James E. Brown and Margaret Brown Altendahl, comps., *Relatives of the Browns of Mill Springs, Kentucky, Including the Fisher, Gaar, Gholson, Hutchison, Weaver and West Families* (Baltimore: Gateway Press, Inc., 1992), 88.
2. Benson Bobrick, *Angel in the Whirlwind: The Triumph of the American Revolution* (New York: Simon & Schuster, Inc., 1997; New York: Penguin Putnam Inc., 1998), 28-9.
3. Brown and Altendahl, *Relatives of the Browns*, 90.
4. Ibid., 90-91.
5. Micah Taul Memoirs TS, No. 778, Papers of Bennett Henderson Young, 1879-1912, A\Y68, The Filson Club, Louisville, KY, 58.
6. Adjutant General of the State of Kentucky, *Soldiers of the War of 1812* (Frankfort, 1891), 154.
7. Taul Memoirs, 55.
8. Ibid., 1-3.
9. Ibid., 12.
10. Ibid.
11. Ibid., 5.
12. Ibid., 12.
13. Ibid., 13.
14. Ibid., 14-15.
15. Ibid., 15.
16. Ibid., 38.
17. Ibid., 16-17.
18. Ibid., 22.
19. Ibid., 23.
20. Ibid., 26.
21. Ibid., 27.
22. Ibid., 28.
23. Ibid., 29.
24. Ibid., 31-32. Some typographical errors corrected.
25. Ibid., 32.
26. Ibid., 33.
27. Ibid., 34.

28. Ibid., 34-5.
29. Ibid., 39.
30. Ibid.
31. Ibid.
32. Ibid., 62-5.
33. Ibid., 66.
34. Ibid., 66-7.
35. Ibid., 67.
36. Ibid.
37. Ibid., 68.
38. Ibid., 69.
39. Ibid., 70.
40. Ibid.
41. Ibid., 71.
42. Ibid., 72.
43. Ibid.
44. Ibid.
45. Ibid., 73.
46. Ibid.
47. Ibid., 74.
48. Ibid.
49. Ibid., 75.
50. Ibid., 76.
51. Ibid., 77.
52. Augusta Phillips Johnson, *A Century of Wayne County, Kentucky, 1800-1900* (Louisville: The Standard Printing Co., 1939), 38.
53. Taul Memoirs, 77.
54. Johnson, *A Century of Wayne County, Kentucky*, 224.
55. Taul Memoirs, 78.
56. Ibid., 79.
57. Ibid., 80-81.
58. Ibid., 82.
59. Ibid., 87.
60. Ibid.
61. Ibid., 88.
62. Ibid., 88-9.
63. Ibid., 89-90.
64. Ibid., 91.

65. Ibid.
66. Ibid., 92.
67. Ibid., 93.
68. Ibid., 94.
69. Ibid., 95.
70. Ibid., 99.
71. Ibid., 99-100.
72. Ibid., 100.
73. Ibid., 101.
74. Ibid., 106.
75. Ibid., addendum page 4.
76. Ibid., addendum page 27.
77. Ibid., addendum page 32.
78. Brown and Altendahl, *Relatives of the Browns*, 280.
79. Ibid., 198.
80. Ibid.
81. Taul Memoirs, 29.
82. Brown and Altendahl, *Relatives of the Browns*, 198.

SEVEN: Kentuckians in the War of 1812

1. Donald R. Hickey, *The War of 1812: A Forgotten Conflict* (Urbana, IL: University of Illinois Press, 1990), 72.
2. Ibid., 73.
3. Micah Taul Memoirs TS, No. 778, Papers of Bennett Henderson Young, 1879-1912, A\Y68, The Filson Club, Louisville, KY, 22.
4. David Brion Davis and Steven Mintz, *The Boisterous Sea of Liberty: A Documentary History of America from Discovery Through the Civil War* (Oxford: Oxford University Press, 1998), 305.
5. Hickey, *War of 1812*, 30.
6. Ibid., 46.
7. James E. Brown and Margaret Brown Altendahl, comps., *Relatives of the Browns of Mill Springs, Kentucky, Including the Fisher, Gaar, Gholson, Hutchison, Weaver and West Families* (Baltimore: Gateway Press, Inc., 1992), 198.
8. Taul Memoirs, 40.
9. Ibid., 47. This company may or may not have included Dorothy's brother Samuel. See note 29 below. The source gives an 1813 enlistment date for Samuel.
10. Hickey, *War of 1812*, 80.

11. Ibid., 82, 84.
12. Taul Memoirs, 48.
13. Ibid., 53.
14. Ibid.
15. Hickey, *War of 1812*, 85.
16. C. Edward Skeen, *Citizen Soldiers in the War of 1812* (Lexington: The University Press of Kentucky, 1999), 83.
17. Hickey, *War of 1812*, 85.
18. Taul Memoirs, 53.
19. Ibid.
20. Ibid., 54.
21. Ibid., 55.
22. Ibid., 56.
23. Ibid.
24. Hickey, *War of 1812*, 126.
25. Taul Memoirs, 57.
26. Brown and Altendahl, *Relatives of the Browns*, 198. Bartholomew Haden was married to Anthony$_2$ Gholson's daughter Catherine, the sister of Micah's wife.
27. Adjutant General of the State of Kentucky, *Soldiers of the War of 1812* (Frankfort, 1891), 154.
28. Taul Memoirs, 57.
29. Hickey, *War of 1812*, 127.
30. Ibid., 128.
31. Ibid., 131.
32. Ibid., 132.
33. Ibid., 133.
34. Ibid., 135.
35. John R. Elting, *Amateurs, To Arms! A Military History of the War of 1812* (Chapel Hill, NC: Algonquin Books, 1991; Da Capo Press, Inc., 1995), 98.
36. National Archives, Military Service Records, NWCTB Master No. 542698, SOP No. 150198.
37. Taul Memoirs, 59.
38. Ibid.
39. Ibid.
40. Hickey, *War of 1812*, 79.
41. Ibid.
42. Taul Memoirs, 59-60.

43. Ibid., 60.
44. Hickey, *War of 1812*, 137.
45. Gerard T. Altoff, *Oliver Hazard Perry and the Battle of Lake Erie* (Put-in-Bay, Ohio: The Perry Group, 1999), 59.
46. Ibid., 61.
47. Hickey, *War of 1812*, 137-9.
48. Altoff, *Perry and the Battle of Lake Erie*, 64-5.
49. Elting, *Amateurs, to Arms,* 113.
50. Hickey, *War of 1812*, 139.
51. Taul Memoirs, 61.
52. Hickey, *War of 1812*, 139.
53. Altoff, *Perry and the Battle of Lake Erie*, 65-6.
54. Taul Memoirs, 62.
55. Hickey, *War of 1812*, 182-3.
56. Ibid., 196.
57. Ibid., 198-9.
58. Ibid., 203-4.
59. Ibid., 204-5.
60. Ibid., 206.
61. Leonard V. Huber, *The Battle of New Orleans: New Orleans as it was in 1814-1815* (New Orleans: Battle of New Orleans 150th Anniversary Committee of Louisiana, 1965; reprint, New Orleans: Louisiana Landmarks Society, 1994), 3.
62. Ibid., 8-10.
63. Ibid., 38-9.
64. Hickey, *War of 1812*, 206.
65. Ibid., 207.
66. Ibid., 209.
67. Ibid., 209-10.
68. Ibid., 210.
69. Sir Winston Churchill, *The Great Republic--A History of America*, Large Print version, ed. Winston S. Churchill (New York: Random House, 2000), 208.
70. Hickey, *War of 1812*, 211-12.
71. Adjutant General, Kentucky, *Soldiers of the War of 1812*, 291-2.
72. Augusta Phillips Johnson, *A Century of Wayne County, Kentucky, 1800-1900* (Louisville: The Standard Printing Co., 1939), 60.
73. Skeen, *Citizen Soldiers in the War of 1812*, 171.
74. Ibid.

75. Hickey, *War of 1812*, 288.
76. Ibid., 212.
77. Hickey, *War of 1812*, 2.
78. Taul Memoirs, 62.
79. Hickey, *War of 1812*, 3.

EIGHT: Gone To Texas
1. Augusta Phillips Johnson, *A Century of Wayne County, Kentucky, 1800-1900* (Louisville: The Standard Printing Co., 1939), 224.
2. Virginia Baker Mitchell, *Gholson and Allied Families*, ed. Margaret Scruggs-Carruth (Dallas: n.p., 1950), 16-17.
3. John H. Gwathmey, *Historical Register of Virginians in the Revolution: Soldiers, Sailors, Marines; 1775-1783* (Baltimore: Genealogical Publishing Co., Inc., 1979), 314.
4. Johnson, *Century of Wayne County*, 33.
5. Another Researchers Publication, *Wayne County, Kentucky, Marriages, 1800-1850* (n.p., n.d.).
6. S-K Publications, *Census Images, 1810-1820-1830-1840, Livingston County, Kentucky*, CD (Wichita, KS: S-K Publications, 2001), 15-16.
7. "Recollections of B. F. Gholson, Told to J. A. Richard, August 1928," B. F. Gholson Biographical File, The Center for American History, The University of Texas at Austin.
8. Midwest Tennessee Genealogical Society, "Abstracts from Early Madison County, Tennessee, Newspapers: *Jackson Gazette*, March 21, 1829," *Family Findings*, 4, nos. 3-4 (1972); from TN GenWeb, http://www.tngenweb.org/madison/records/gazette.htm.
9. "Recollections of B. F. Gholson," Center for American History.
10. Ibid.
11. Ibid.
12. Malcolm D. McLean, comp. and ed., *Papers Concerning Robertson's Colony in Texas: Volume XI, July 26 through October 14, 1835, Nashville-on-the-Brazos* (Arlington, Texas: The UTA Press, 1984), 320.
13. "Conviction and Punishment for Passing Counterfeit Money," *Arkansas Gazette*, 28 October 1834, p. 3, col. 1, Arkansas History Commission Newspaper Collection, Little Rock.

14. "A Counterfeiter detected," *Arkansas Gazette*, 16 September 1834, p. 3, col. 1, Arkansas History Commission Newspaper Collection, Little Rock.

15. "Conviction and Punishment for Passing Counterfeit Money," *Arkansas Gazette*.

16. Ibid.

17. Ibid.

18. Ibid.

19. "Fatal Duel," *Arkansas Times and Advocate*, 29 May 1837, p. 3, col. 3, Arkansas History Commission Newspaper Collection, Little Rock.

20. Mildred Moody Nutter, contrib., "Wayne County, Kentucky Miscellaneous Court Papers from Box File," *The Kentucky Genealogist* 20, no. 2 (1978): 53-4.

21. June Baldwin Bork, comp., *Wayne County, Kentucky, Deed Book C (1819-1824),* (Apple Valley, CA: June Baldwin Bork, 1993), 16.

22. S-K Publications, *Census Images*, 15-16.

23. Bork, *Wayne County Deed Book C*, 47.

24. "A Counterfeiter detected," *Arkansas Gazette*.

25. Thomas Nuttall, *Journal of Travels into the Arkansas Territory During the Year 1819*, Savoie Lottinville, ed. (1821; reprint, Fayetteville: The University of Arkansas Press, 1999), 124.

26. Ibid.

27. Ibid., 124-5.

28. Ibid., 125.

29. Ibid., 127.

30. Ibid., 129.

31. Ibid., 127-8.

32. Ibid., 128.

33. Ibid., 243.

34. Mitchell, *Gholson and Allied Families*, 16.

35. Sherida K. Eddlemon, comp., *Genealogical Abstracts from Tennessee Newspapers, 1821-1828* (Bowie, MD: Heritage Books, Inc. 1991), 26.

36. William Ransom Hogan, *The Texas Republic, A Social and Economic History* (1946; reprint, Austin: University of Texas Press, 1969), 5.

37. Frederick Law Olmstead, *A Journey Through Texas; or, A Saddle-Trip on the Southwestern Frontier* (1857; reprint, Time-Life Books Inc., 1981), 124.
38. James Logan Morgan, comp., *Arkansas Newspaper Abstracts 1819-1845: Volume I, Obituaries and Biographical Notes from Arkansas Newspapers, 1819-1835* (Conway, AR: Arkansas Research, 1981), 72.
39. "Recollections of B. F. Gholson," Center for American History.
40. Hogan, *Texas Republic*, 6.
41. Ibid.
42. "San Felipe de Austin, Texas," ed. Charles Christopher Jackson, vol. 5, *The New Handbook of Texas,* ed. Ron Tyler (Austin: The Texas State Historical Association, 1996), 840.
43. Paula Mitchell Marks, *Turn Your Eyes Toward Texas: Pioneers Sam and Mary Maverick* (College Station: Texas A&M University Press, 1989), 25.
44. Ibid., 26.

NINE: Robertson's Colony
1. "Robertson's Colony," Malcolm D. McLean, vol. 5, *The New Handbook of Texas*, ed. Ron Tyler (Austin: The Texas State Historical Association, 1996), 623-4.
2. Ibid.
3. Malcolm D. McLean, comp. and ed., *Papers Concerning Robertson's Colony in Texas: Volume I, 1788-1822, The Texas Association* (Arlington, TX: The UTA Press, 1980), 253.
4. "Recollections of B. F. Gholson," B. F. Gholson Biographical File, The Center for American History. The University of Texas at Austin.
5. Malcolm D. McLean, comp. and ed., *Papers Concerning Robertson's Colony in Texas: Volume VII, December 6, 1831 through October, 1833, Those Eleven-League Grants* (Arlington, TX: The UTA Press, 1980), 28.
6. Ibid., 42-3.
7. Ibid., 43.
8. "Robertson's Colony," vol. 5, *New Handbook of Texas*, 623-4.
9. Mexican Title, Original Grantee Samuel Gholston, Box 37, Folder 24, Spanish Collection, Archives and Records Division, Texas General Land Office, Austin.

10. Mexican Title, Original Grantee Samuel Gholson, Box 35, Folder 65, Spanish Collection, Archives and Records Division, Texas General Land Office, Austin.
11. Mexican Title, Original Grantee Albert G. Gholson, Box 36, Folder 61, Spanish Collection, Archives and Records Division, Texas General Land Office, Austin.
12. "Surveying," vol. 6, *New Handbook of Texas*, 155-6.
13. "Robertson's Colony," vol. 5, *New Handbook of Texas*, 624.
14. Sale of Personal Property of the Estate of A. G. Gholston, October 18, 1860, Coryell County Probate Book A, page 207.
15. "Surveying," vol. 6, *New Handbook of Texas*, 155.
16. Ibid., 156.
17. "Spanish Law," Joseph W. McKnight, vol. 6, *New Handbook of Texas*, 6.
18. Ibid., 7.
19. William Ransom Hogan, *The Texas Republic, A Social and Economic History* (1946; reprint, Austin: University of Texas Press, 1969), 191.
20. Ibid., 192.
21. "Robertson's Colony," vol. 5, *New Handbook of Texas*, 624.
22. Malcolm D. McLean, comp. and ed., *Papers Concerning Robertson's Colony in Texas: Volume XIII, January 15 through March 17, 1836, The Convention at Washington-on-the-Brazos* (Arlington, Texas: The UTA Press, 1987), 733.
23. Mrs. John T. Martin and Mrs. Louis C. Hill, comps., *Falls County, Texas Records, Vol. I* (McGregor, TX: n.p., 1970), v.
24. Malcolm D. McLean, comp. and ed., *Papers Concerning Robertson's Colony in Texas: Volume IV, May through October 10, 1830, Tenoxtitlan, Dream Capital of Texas* (Arlington, TX: The UTA Press, 1977), 66.
25. Malcolm D. McLean, comp. and ed., *Papers Concerning Robertson's Colony in Texas: Volume IX, October, 1834, through March 20, 1835, Sarahville de Viesca* (Arlington, Texas: The UTA Press, 1982), 184-5.
26. Malcolm D. McLean, comp. and ed., *Papers Concerning Robertson's Colony in Texas: Volume XI, July 26 through October 14, 1835, Nashville-on-the-Brazos* (Arlington, Texas: The UTA Press, 1984), 320. Duncan's story refers to Levy Taylor, known in

history as John Taylor; however, page 319 refers to Levi Taylor's brother, John Taylor.

27. Ibid., 318-19.
28. Martin and Hill, comps., *Falls County, Texas Records, Vol I*, v.
29. Ibid., v-vi.
30. Ibid., v.
31. J. W. Baker, *A History of Robertson County, Texas* (n.p.: The Robertson County Historical Foundation), 62.
32. Ibid., 49.
33. Hogan, *Texas Republic*, 25.
34. Ibid.
35. "Architecture," Willard B. Robinson, vol. 1, *New Handbook of Texas*, 227.
36. "Dog-Run Houses," W. W. White, vol. 2, *New Handbook of Texas*, 669.
37. Baker, *History of Robertson County*, 50.
38. Malcolm D. McLean, comp. and ed., *Papers Concerning Robertson's Colony in Texas: Volume III, October, 1826, through April, 1830, The Nashville Colony* (Fort Worth: TCU Press, 1976), 190.
39. Ibid., 188.
40. "Corn Culture," Nicolas P. Hardeman, vol. 2, *New Handbook of Texas*, 326.
41. Hogan, *Texas Republic*, 32.
42. Ibid., 32.
43. Ibid., 33.
44. Ibid., 35.
45. Ibid., 34.
46. Ibid., 35.
47. Ibid., 36.
48. "Drinking and Beverages in Nineteenth-Century Texas," Ellen N. Murry, vol. 2, *New Handbook of Texas*, 701.
49. Hogan, *Texas Republic*, 38.
50. Ibid., 44.
51. "Drinking and Beverages . . . ," vol. 2, *New Handbook of Texas*, 701.
52. Hogan, *Texas Republic*, 45-6.
53. Ibid.
54. Ibid.

55. Ibid., 49.
56. Ibid., 21.
57. Ibid., 22.
58. Ibid., 24.
59. Petition by Administrator of the Estate of A. G. Gholston, Coryell County Probate Book A, p. 197.

TEN: The Republic of Texas--Early Texas Rangers
1. Mary G. Ramos, ed., *Texas Almanac, Millenium Edition, 2000-2001* (Dallas: *The Dallas Morning News*, 1999), 42.
2. Ibid.
3. Ibid.
4. Frederick Wilkins, *The Legend Begins, The Texas Rangers, 1823-1845* (Austin: State House Press, 1996), 11.
5. Noah Smithwick, *The Evolution of a State, or Recollections of Old Texas Days*, comp. Nanna Smithwick Donaldson (Austin: University of Texas Press, 1983), 71.
6. Ramos, *Texas Almanac*, 43.
7. Malcolm D. McLean, comp. and ed., *Papers Concerning Robertson's Colony in Texas: Volume IX, October, 1834, through March 20, 1835, Sarahville de Viesca* (Arlington, Texas: The UTA Press, 1982), 379.
8. Wilkins, *Legend Begins*, 12.
9. Smithwick, *Recollections*, 71.
10. Ramos, *Texas Almanac*, 43.
11. Wilkins, *Legend Begins*, 12.
12. "Bexar, Siege of," Alwyn Barr, vol. 1, *The New Handbook of Texas*, ed. Ron Tyler (Austin: Texas State Historical Association, 1996), 516.
13. Smithwick, *Recollections*, 75-6.
14. Ibid., 71-2.
15. Ibid., 75.
16. Ibid., 76.
17. McLean, *Robertson's Colony*, Vol. IX, 379.
18. Smithwick, *Recollections*, 71, 76.
19. "Bexar, Siege of," vol. 1, *New Handbook of Texas*, 516.
20. D. W. C. Baker, *A Texas Scrap-Book: Made up of the History, Biography, and Miscellany of Texas and Its People* (1875; reprint, Austin: Texas State Historical Association, 1991), 37-8.

21. "Storming of San Antonio De Bexar in 1835, From the Texas State Gazette, 1849," *Frontier Times* 9 (1932), no. 10, 515-16.
22. Malcolm D. McLean, comp. and ed., *Papers Concerning Robertson's Colony in Texas: Volume XII, October 15, 1835, through January 14, 1836, The Municipality of Milam* (Arlington, Texas: The UTA Press, 1985), 421-22, quoting *Frontier Times*, Bandera, Texas, April 1935, 303-305.
23. Falls County Historical Commission, comp. and ed., *Families of Falls County* (Austin: Eakin Press, 1987), 185.
24. "Bexar, Siege of," vol. 1, *New Handbook of Texas*, 516.
25. Ramos, *Texas Almanac*, 43.
26. "Alamo, Battle of the," vol. 1, *New Handbook of Texas*, 84.
27. Ramos, *Texas Almanac*, 43.
28. "Alamo, Battle of the," vol. 1, *New Handbook of Texas*, 84.
29. Ibid.
30. Ramos, *Texas Almanac*, 43.
31. Ibid.
32. Ramos, *Texas Almanac*, 44.
33. Malcolm D. McLean, comp. and ed., *Papers Concerning Robertson's Colony in Texas: Volume XIII, January 15 through March 17, 1836, The Convention at Washington-on-the-Brazos* (Arlington, Texas: The UTA Press, 1987), 49-50.
34. Ramos, *Texas Almanac*, 43.
35. Ibid., 44.
36. McLean, *Robertson's Colony*, Vol. XIII, 734-5.
37. Ramos, *Texas Almanac*, 44.
38. Baker, *Texas Scrap-Book*, 95-7.
39. "Barron, Thomas Hudson," Theron Palmer, vol. 1, *New Handbook of Texas*, 395.
40. Ibid.
41. McLean, *Robertson's Colony*, Vol. IX, 379-80.
42. McLean, *Robertson's Colony*, Vol. XIII, 47.
43. "Runaway Scrape," Carolyn Callaway Covington, vol. 5, *New Handbook of Texas*, 713.
44. Wilkins, *Legend Begins*, 7.
45. Ibid., 4.
46. Ibid., 5.
47. Ibid., 12.
48. Ibid., 13.

49. Ibid., 13-14.
50. Malcolm D. McLean, comp. and ed., *Papers Concerning Robertson's Colony in Texas: Volume XVII, December, 1838, through August 10, 1840, Sterling C. Robertson vs. Sam Houston, President of the Republic of Texas* (Arlington, Texas: The UTA Press, 1991), 60-61.
51. Ibid.
52. Walter Prescott Webb, *The Texas Rangers, A Century of Frontier Defense*, 2nd ed. (Austin: University of Texas Press, 1996), 30.
53. Malcolm D. McLean, comp. and ed., *Papers Concerning Robertson's Colony in Texas: Volume XIV, March 18 through July 22, 1836, The Battle of San Jacinto and the Fall of Fort Parker* (Arlington, Texas: The UTA Press, 1988), 75-78.
54. Ibid., 360-64.
55. Austin, Texas State Archives, Republic Claim AU 3128, Reel 35, p. 299.
56. "Pierson, John Goodloe Warren," Edwin G. Pierson, Jr., vol. 5, *New Handbook of Texas*, 198.
57. Austin, Texas State Archives, Republic Claim AU 3128, Reel 35, p. 300.
58. J. W. Wilbarger, *Indian Depredations in Texas* (1889; reprint, Austin, Texas: Eakin Press; Statehouse Press, 1985), 226-7.
59. Bounty Grant, Certificate No. 2115, dated January 26, 1838, for 320 acres, granted to Albert G. Gholson by the Secretary of War, for service from June 30, 1836, to September 30, 1836, File MON-B-203, Original Land Grant Collection, Archives and Records Division, Texas General Land Office, Austin.
60. Malcolm D. McLean, comp. and ed., *Papers Concerning Robertson's Colony in Texas: Volume XV, July 23, 1836, through August 9, 1837, The Gentleman from Milam* (Arlington, Texas: The UTA Press, 1989), 33.
61. Ibid., 162-3.
62. Ibid., 164-5.
63. Wilkins, *Legend Begins*, 28.
64. Ibid., 45.
65. Ibid., 59.
66. Ibid., 63.
67. Ibid., 65.
68. Ibid., 68.

69. Ibid., 69-70.
70. McLean, *Robertson's Colony*, Vol. IX, 380.
71. Malcolm D. McLean, comp. and ed., *Papers Concerning Robertson's Colony in Texas: Volume XVI, August 10, 1837, through November, 1838, The Creation of Robertson County* (Arlington: The UTA Press, 1990), 446-7.
72. Ibid., 110-11.
73. Ibid., 559.
74. Ibid., 425.
75. Ibid.
76. Malcolm D. McLean, comp. and ed., *Papers Concerning Robertson's Colony in Texas: Volume XVIII, August 11, 1840 through March 4, 1842, The End of an Era* (Arlington: The UTA Press, 1993), 171.
77. B. F. Gholson to Sam Gholson, Evant, Texas, letter, December 14, 1922.
78. J. W. Baker, *A History of Robertson County, Texas*, 5th ed. (n.p.: Sheridan Books, 1999), 88-90.
79. Falls County Historical Commission, *Families of Falls County*, 185.
80. Wilbarger, *Indian Depredations*, 361-7.
81. Austin, Texas State Archives, Army Papers, Call No. 401-5.
82. Austin, Texas State Archives, Ranger Documents, First Texas Rangers Card Catalog, Golston, Samuel, Pvt. Robertson County was established on December 14, 1837, from portions of Milam, Bexar, and Nacogdoches counties.
83. Baker, *History of Robertson County*, 63.

ELEVEN: Texas Becomes a State--Restless Years

1. Mary G. Ramos, ed., *Texas Almanac, Millenium Edition, 2000-2001* (Dallas: *The Dallas Morning News*, 1999), 45-7.
2. Deed from Sam'l Gholson to S. C. Robertson, executed October 2, 1835, in Nashville, Tennessee, recorded in McLennan County Deed Record A, 269-72.
3. J. W. Baker, *A History of Robertson County, Texas*, 5th ed. (n.p.: Sheridan Books, 1999), 36.
4. Malcolm D. McLean, comp. and ed., *Papers Concerning Robertson's Colony in Texas: Volume XVI, August 10, 1837, through November, 1838, The Creation of Robertson County* (Arlington: The UTA Press, 1990), 160.

5. Ibid., 426.
6. Deed from Sam'l Gholson of Harrison County, Republic of Texas, to Albert G. Gholson of Harrison County and John Chisum of Nacogdoches County, for one-fourth league of land located in Robertson County, executed September 21, 1840, recorded in Harrison County Deed Record A, pp. 103-106. In 1841, several documents were signed by Samuel Gholson of the Republic of Texas, County of Panola, but it is not clear how he could have been a resident of the County of Panola in 1841 since it was not created until 1846. The documents are recorded in Harrison County Deed Record B, pp. 383-4 and Harrison County Deed Record D, pp. 45-6 and 169-71.
7. Ronald Lee Gholson, comp., *Gholson and Allied Families, A Revised Golden Anniversary Edition, Reprint of "Gholson and Allied Families" by Virginia Baker Mitchell, September, 1950* (Mulberry, IN: Ron Gholson, 2002), 28.
8. Austin, Texas State Archives, Republic Claims, PD 576, Reel 163, pp. 296-305; PD 624, Reel 165, p. 707; and PD Cert. 749, Reel 189, pp. 74-90.
9. William Ransom Hogan, *The Texas Republic, A Social and Economic History* (1946; reprint, Austin: University of Texas Press, 1969), 129.
10. Malcolm D. McLean, comp. and ed., *Papers Concerning Robertson's Colony in Texas: Volume XI, July 26 through October 14, 1835, Nashville-on-the-Brazos* (Arlington, TX: The UTA Press, 1984), 320.
11. Byron Sistler and Barbara Sistler, comps. and eds., *Madison County, Tennessee, Marriages 1838-71* (Nashville: n.p., 1983), 32.
12. Mrs. John T. Martin and Mrs. Louis C. Hill, comps., *Falls County, Texas Records, Vol. I* (McGregor, TX: n.p., 1970), 33.
13. Nancy Blakeley Ruff, comp., *Harrison County, Texas, Early Marriage Records, 1839-1869*, (St. Louis, MO: Ingmire Publications, n.d.), 12.
14. Ibid.
15. Marion Day Mullins, comp., *Republic of Texas: Poll Lists for 1846* (Baltimore: Genealogical Publishing Co., Inc., 1974), 61.
16. Harrison County, Texas, 1850 Census, 1016.
17. Ibid., 1021.

18. Deed signed by the heirs of Samuel Gholson: Mary Gholson, widow of Samuel Gholson; Angelina Williams and B. F. Williams; and Albert Gholson, recorded in McLennan County Deed Record F, 229-31.

19. Malcolm D. McLean, comp. and ed., *Papers Concerning Robertson's Colony in Texas: Volume IX, October, 1834, through March 20, 1835, Sarahville de Viesca* (Arlington, Texas: The UTA Press, 1982), 379.

20. Falls County Historical Commission, comp. and ed., *Families of Falls County* (Austin: Eakin Press, 1987), 185.

21. *A Memorial and Biographical History of McLennan, Falls, Bell and Coryell Counties, Texas* (Chicago: The Lewis Publishing Company, 1893), 365.

22. Virginia Baker Mitchell, *Gholson and Allied Families*, ed. Margaret Scruggs-Carruth (Dallas: n.p., 1950), 17.

23. *McLennan, Falls, Bell and Coryell Counties*, 365.

24. Hogan, *Texas Republic*, 226.

25. Ibid., 232.

26. *Families of Falls County*, 185.

27. Harrison County Records.

28. *Families of Falls County*, 185-6.

29. Martin and Hill, *Falls County, Texas Records*, Vol. I, 46.

30. Ibid.

31. Ibid., 24.

32. "Falls County," Lisa C. Maxwell, vol. 2, *The New Handbook of Texas*, ed. Ron Tyler (Austin: The Texas State Historical Association, 1996), 943.

33. Martin and Hill, *Falls County, Texas Records*, Vol. I, 2.

34. "Justice of the Peace," Dick Smith, vol. 3, *New Handbook of Texas*, 1023.

35. Martin and Hill, *Falls County, Texas Records*, Vol. I, 2.

36. *Families of Falls County*, 185.

37. Commissioners Court Minutes & Etc., Falls County, 1852-1869, Reel 985707.

38. *Families of Falls County*, 185.

39. "Gholson, Texas," Vivian Elizabeth Smyrl, vol. 3, *New Handbook of Texas*, 148.

40. *Families of Falls County*, 185.

41. Lewis B. Porter, Sr., *Take A Journey With Me From the Washboard* (Goldthwaite, Texas: Goldthwaite Eagle Press, 1976), 86-7.
42. Ibid., 86-7.
43. Falls County Deed Records, Volume D, 6-8.
44. *Families of Falls County*, 185.
45. Coryell County Death Records 1860.
46. J. M. Franks, *Seventy Years in Texas: Memories of the Pioneer Days, Indian Depredations and the Northwest Cattle Trail* (Gatesville, Texas: 1924), 7. Another reference which may apply to Albert is found on page 64. Mr. Franks is telling a story about an event that happened in the spring of 1859-60, and said, "He went over the mountain on Henson Creek, where some men were digging a grave for some person that had died over there." Could it have been Albert? The time was about right.
47. John Warren Hunter, "B. F. Gholson's Narratives," *Hunter's Magazine* 1912: 9; B. F. Gholson file, Lampasas Historical Commission.
48. Bobbie F. Thornton, copier and typist, *Coryell County, Texas, 1860 Census & Mortality Schedule* (Plano, Texas: n.d.), Schedule 1. The ages of Albert and Mary Ann are inaccurate in the 1860 census. It is also curious that their son Samuel had the middle initial "G" in both the 1850 and 1860 censuses, perhaps having the same middle name as Albert G. In later life, however, Samuel went by "Samuel Sullivan" possibly to honor Lawrence Sullivan "Sul" Ross. He would not have been named for Ross, since they were roughly the same age, but perhaps he did change his middle name.
49. *Families of Falls County*, 331.
50. Coryell County Probate Records, Book A, County Clerk's Office, Coryell County, Texas.
51. Ibid., 197.
52. Ray Ward, abstr., "Probate Minutes, Coryell County, Texas," *Coryell Kin* 19 (2001): 80.
53. Ibid.
54. Coryell County Probate Records, Book A, County Clerk's Office, Coryell County, Texas.
55. Ibid.
56. Ibid.
57. Ibid.

TWELVE: Texas Rangers and Indians

1. "B. F. Gholson - Notes by R. J. Gerald," Bonnie Gentry Collection.
2. Ibid.
3. William Ransom Hogan, *The Texas Republic: A Social and Economic History* (1946; reprint, Austin: University of Texas Press, 1969), 66.
4. Ibid., 67.
5. "B. F. Gholson - Notes by R. J. Gerald," Bonnie Gentry Collection.
6. Ibid.
7. Untitled document 6, B. F. Gholson Biographical File, The Center for American History. The University of Texas at Austin.
8. "B. F. Gholson - Notes by R. J. Gerald," Bonnie Gentry Collection.
9. *A Memorial and Biographical History of McLennan, Falls, Bell and Coryell Counties, Texas* (Chicago: The Lewis Publishing Company, 1893), 366.
10. Sarah Harkey Hall, *Surviving on the Texas Frontier: The Journal of an Orphan Girl in San Saba County* (Austin: Eakin Press, 1996), 2.
11. "Recollections of B. F. Gholson Told to J. A. Richard, August, 1928," B. F. Gholson Biographical File, The Center for American History. The University of Texas at Austin.
12. Ibid.
13. "The Pease River Fight and the Capture of Cynthia Ann Parker," B. F. Gholson Biographical File, The Center for American History. The University of Texas at Austin.
14. "Recollections of B. F. Gholson Told to J. A. Richard, August, 1928," from the B. F. Gholson Biographical File, The Center for American History. The University of Texas at Austin.
15. Samuel Sullivan Gholson Autobiography, typescript furnished by Martha Gholson Holland and Sammy Gholson.
16. "Murder of Mr. & Mrs. Riggs and Mr. Pierce," *Frontier Times* 4, no. 12 (1927): 1-3. *(This account is nearly identical to the one found in J. M. Franks' SEVENTY YEARS IN TEXAS, but it was probably written or told by Frank Gholson, as was Franks' Chapter 27, with Gholson given credit in that instance.)*
17. "Frank Gholson as Interviewed by Felix Williams, 1931," B. F. Gholson Biographical File, The Center for American History. The University of Texas at Austin.
18. R. J. Gerald, "Benjamin Franklin Gholson, Texan," *Frontier Times* 4, no. 11 (1927): 46-51.

19. "Frank Gholson as Interviewed by Felix Williams, 1931," B. F. Gholson Biographical File, The Center for American History. The University of Texas at Austin.
20. Ibid.
21. "The Pease River Fight and the Capture of Cynthia Ann Parker," B. F. Gholson Biographical File, The Center for American History. The University of Texas at Austin.
22. J. Marvin Hunter, Sr., "The Killing of Bob Carter," *Frontier Times* 28, no. 2 (1950): 86-7.
23. John Warren Hunter, B. F. Gholson's Narratives, *Hunter's Magazine* 1912: 9; B. F. Gholson file, Lampasas Historical Commission.
24. Flora Gatlin Bowles, ed., *A No Man's Land Becomes A County* (Goldthwaite, TX: Mills County Historical Society, 1958), 54-55.

THIRTEEN: Vigilante Justice, Mob Rule, and Civil War Texas

1. B. P. Gallaway, ed., *Texas: The Dark Corner of the Confederacy, Contemporary Accounts of the Lone Star State in the Civil War*, 3rd ed. (Lincoln: University of Nebraska Press, 1999), 6.
2. Samuel Sullivan Gholson Autobiography, typescript courtesy of Martha Gholson Holland and Sammy Gholson, 4-5. "Old man Langford" was the father-in-law of both Sam and Frank.
3. Ibid., 5.
4. Ibid.
5. Ibid.
6. Ibid. Also in October 1862, mass arrests of suspected Unionists occurred in Gainesville and a mob executed forty-two of those arrested in what came to be called "the great Gainesville hanging."
7. Ibid., 5-6.
8. Ibid., 6.
9. Ibid.
10. Ibid.
11. National Archives, Military Service Records, NWCTB Master No. 542679, SOP No. 150189.
12. Samuel Sullivan Gholson Autobiography, 6. Pyron's Second Texas Cavalry "had been formed as a horse cavalry, but the inability to secure mounts had necessitated its becoming a dismounted unit." Gallaway, 156.

13. *A Memorial and Biographical History of McLennan, Falls, Bell and Coryell Counties, Texas* (Chicago: The Lewis Publishing Company, 1893), 366.
14. J. Marvin Hunter, comp. and ed., *The Trail Drivers of Texas: Interesting Sketches of Early Cowboys and Their Experiences on the Range and on the Trail during the Days That Tried Men's Souls-- True Narratives Related by Real Cowpunchers and Men Who Fathered the Cattle Industry in Texas* (Austin: University of Texas Press, 2000), 629-30.
15. Samuel Sullivan Gholson Autobiography, 6.
16. Ibid., 7.
17. National Archives, Military Service Records, NWCTB Master No. 542679, SOP No. 150189.
18. Samuel Sullivan Gholson Autobiography, 7.
19. Ibid., 7.
20. Gallaway, *Texas: The Dark Corner of the Confederacy*, 157.
21. Samuel Sullivan Gholson Autobiography, 11.
22. Soldier's Application for a Confederate Pension No. 29133, Austin, Texas State Archives.
23. Ralph A. Wooster, *Civil War Texas: A History and A Guide* (Austin: Texas State Historical Association, 1999), 43.
24. Ibid., 31.
25. Ibid., 32.
26. Ibid., 33-4.
27. Flora Gatlin Bowles, ed., *A No Man's Land Becomes A County* (Goldthwaite, TX: Mills County Historical Society, 1958), 75-6.
28. Marjory Gholson Morris, telephone conversation with author, November 3, 1999.
29. Austin, Texas State Archives, Capias No. 458, Asa Langford, Jr., State of Texas, Coryell County.
30. *Daily Democratic Statesman*, p. 2, col. 2, Article about Asa Langford, Jr., November 6, 1874, from the files of the Lampasas Historical Commission.
31. Marjory Gholson Morris, letter to author dated July 27, 2001.
32. Marjory Gholson Morris, telephone conversation with author, November 3, 1999.
33. "Hardin, John Wesley," Leon C. Metz, vol. 3, *The New Handbook of Texas*, ed. Ron Tyler (Austin: The Texas State Historical Association, 1996), 454-5.

34. James B. Gillett, *Six Years With the Texas Rangers: 1875 to 1881*, ed. M. M. Quaife (1921; reprint, Lincoln: University of Nebraska Press, 1976), 85-8.

FOURTEEN: The Stockman and the Drover
1. E. C. "Teddy Blue" Abbott and Helena Hutchinson Smith, *We Pointed Them North: Recollections of a Cowpuncher* (1939; reprint, Norman: University of Oklahoma Press, 1955), 5-8.
2. Ibid., 3.
3. Ibid., 8-9.
4. Ibid., 8.
5. Ibid., 9.
6. Ibid., 74.
7. Ibid., 51.
8. Ibid., 4.
9. Deed from Sam'l Gholson to Albert G. Gholson and John Chisum, executed September 21, 1840, recorded in Harrison County Deed Record A, 103-106.
10. "B. F. Gholson - Notes by R. J. Gerald," Bonnie Gentry Collection.
11. Binnie Depmore McCreary, "The Gholson House, Evant, Texas" (The University of Texas at Austin, School of Architecture, 1977), 31. Footnote 43 states the following: Interviews with B. F. Gholson in the 1920's and 1930's clearly state that he bought 244 acres in 1870 from Sneed. The Lampasas County Deed Records, Vol. B, p. 656, show the deed recorded Apr. 16, 1875, 160 acres for $400. Family members and a descendant of the stone mason who built the house date that event as occuring between 1873 and 1874. Perhaps the deed was recorded late, as often happened in that day and time.
12. "B. F. Gholson - Notes by R. J. Gerald," Bonnie Gentry Collection.
13. Austin, Texas State Archives, Call number M5935.
14. "B. F. Gholson - Notes by R. J. Gerald," Bonnie Gentry Collection.

15. *A Memorial and Biographical History of McLennan, Falls, Bell and Coryell Counties, Texas* (Chicago: The Lewis Publishing Company, 1893), 367.
16. Samuel Sullivan Gholson Autobiography, typescript courtesy of Martha Gholson Holland and Sammy Gholson, 16.
17. Ibid., 17.
18. Ibid., 17-18.
19. Ibid., 19-20.
20. Ibid., 31.
21. Ruel McDaniel, "Horses Were Legal Tender," *True West*, Nov.-Dec. 1963: 47.
22. James B. Gillett, *Six Years With the Texas Rangers: 1875 to 1881*, ed. M. M. Quaife (1921; reprint, Lincoln: University of Nebraska Press, 1976), 9.
23. Samuel Sullivan Gholson Autobiography, 25.
24. Gillett, *Six Years With the Texas Rangers*, 10.
25. Samuel Sullivan Gholson Autobiography, 28.
26. Joseph Carroll McConnell, *The West Texas Frontier, or a Descriptive History of Early Times in Western Texas* (n.p., n.d.), Article No. 772.
27. George A. Wallis, "Cattle Kings," *True West*, 11, no. 4 (1964): 13.
28. M. L. Johnson and E. J. Pearson, "Trailing West," *Frontier Times* 43, no. 1 (1969): 25.
29. Captain John M. Elkins, "Indian Fighting on the Texas Frontier," *Old West* 4, no. 2 (1967): 86-8.
30. J. M. Franks, *Seventy Years in Texas: Memories of the Pioneer Days, Indian Depredations and the Northwest Cattle Trail* (Gatesville, Texas: 1924), 19-20.
31. "Curry Comb Ranch," William Curry Holden, vol. 2, *The New Handbook of Texas*, ed. Ron Tyler (Austin: The Texas State Historical Association, 1996), 454.
32. "Echo, Texas (Coleman County)," William R. Hunt, vol. 2, *Handbook of Texas*, 779.
33. "Taylor, County," John Leffler, vol. 6, *Handbook of Texas*, 224.
34. "Wallace, Daniel Webster," Martha Earnest and Melvin Sance, vol. 6, *Handbook of Texas*, 804-5. Wallace learned to

read and write, saved his money to buy a ranch, and became a respected rancher, leaving an estate worth more than $1 million when he died.

35. Hamilton County Historical Commission, comp. and ed., *A History of Hamilton County, Texas* (Dallas: Taylor Publishing Company, 1979), 389.

36. Biographical Sketch of B. F. Gholson, B. F. Gholson Biographical File, Texas Ranger Museum and Library, Waco.

37. Samuel Sullivan Gholson Autobiography, 27. Sam died in Tucumcari in 1926.

FIFTEEN: B. F. Gholson Home & Family

1. Linton Otis Pendergrast, "Pioneer Tells of Indian Raids," reprinted in *Evant (Texas) News*, October 14, 1976, Bonnie Gentry Collection. Original article written October 12, 1930, probably from *Fort Worth Star-Telegram*. Adeline was born October 27, 1847, according to Confederate Widow's Application for a Pension No. 50702, Austin, Texas State Archives. Their children were born during the years 1865-1883.

2. Marjory Gholson Morris, telephone conversation with author, November 3, 1999.

3. Pendergrast, "Pioneer Tells of Indian Raids." See Chap. 14 note 11.

4. Binnie Depmore McCreary, "The Gholson House, Evant, Texas" (The University of Texas at Austin, School of Architecture, 1977), 6.

5. Ibid., 8.

6. Ibid., 8-23.

7. Ibid., 5-6.

8. Conner W. Gholson, conversation with author, Austin, Texas, June 16, 2001.

9. McCreary, "The Gholson House, Evant, Texas," 25.

10. Ibid., 25-28.

11. "Gholson, Benjamin Franklin," Carolyn Hyman, vol. 3, *The New Handbook of Texas*, ed. Ron Tyler (Austin: The Texas State Historical Association, 1996), 147.

12. Soldier's Application for a Confederate Pension, No. 29133, Austin, Texas State Archives.
13. Marjory Gholson Morris, telephone conversation with author, April 2, 2000.
14. John Banta, "Home Spared of Fate" *Waco Tribune-Herald*, July 16, 1978.
15. Conner W. Gholson, conversations with author, Austin, Texas, September 18, 2000.
16. Marjory Gholson Morris, conversations with author by telephone, April 2, 2000. Marjory was *Coosie Ann.*

EPILOGUE - B. F. Gholson Tributes and Dedication of Historical Marker
1.   Death Certificate of Benjamin F. Gholson, Lampasas County Death Records, Volume 4, page 13.
2.   "Gholson, Benjamin Franklin," Carolyn Hyman, vol. 3, *The New Handbook of Texas*, ed. Ron Tyler (Austin: The Texas State Historical Association, 1996), 147-8.
3.   Confederate Widow's Application for a Pension, No. 50702, Austin, Texas State Archives.
4.   "'Uncle' Frank Gholson Passed Away Sunday," *Lampasas Record*, April 7, 1932.
5.   J. W. Burney, Jr., "Local History Buried in Evant Cemeteries," *The Evant (Texas) News*, June 21, 19__?
6.   "Deed to the Langford cemetery at Evant, Texas," Bonnie Gentry Collection.
7.   "Historical Grave Marker for Early Day Ranger, B. F. Gholson, Arrives," *The Four County Press*, Evant, Texas, October 5, 1967, Volume 37, No. 21.
8.   "State Historical Marker for Texas Ranger B.F.Gholson has Dedication," newspaper article, source unknown.

BIBLIOGRAPHY

Legend for location of material.

ARHC = Arkansas History Commission
CAH = Center for American History, Austin
CCCL = Contra Costa County Library, Pleasant Hill, California
CorCo = Records of Coryell County, Texas
DRTL = Daughters of the Republic of Texas Library
FallsCo =Records of Falls County, Texas
FtWPL = Fort Worth Public Library
Gentry =Bonnie Gentry Collection
HarCo =Records of Harrison County, Texas
HCHM = Harrison County Historical Museum
HCGS = Hamilton County Genealogical Society
HouPL = Houston Public Library, Clayton Genealogy Library
          Branch
Int = Interviews by the author
ITC = Institute for Texan Cultures, San Antonio
LamCo =Records of Lampasas County, Texas
LCHC = Lampasas County Historical Commission
LOC =Library of Congress
McLen =Records of McLennan County, Texas
MillsCo =Records of Mills County, Texas
NARA = National Archives
NEGHS = New England Genealogical & Historical Society
OCHS =Orange County Historical Society
Own = Purchased, usually through Amazon.com
Richards =Bill Richards
SAPL = San Antonio Public Library
SMGhol =Sammy Gholson and Martha Gholson Holland,
          descendants of Samuel Sullivan Gholson
SLNC =State Library of North Carolina
TFC =The Filson Club
TorPL = Toronto Public Library
TSLAC = Texas State Library & Archives Commission
TXGLO = Texas General Land Office
TxRang =Texas Ranger Museum, Waco
VGS =Virginia Genealogy Society
WacoPL = Waco Public Library
WCHS = Wayne County Historical Society
Web =Website
WestP = Western Publications

Abbot, W. W., and Dorothy Twohig, eds. *The Papers of George Washington, Colonial Series, Vol. 8, June 1767-December 1771*. Charlottesville: University Press of Virginia. LOC.

Abbott, E. C. "Teddy Blue," and Helena Hutchinson Smith. *We Pointed Them North: Recollections of a Cowpuncher*. 1939; reprint, Norman: University of Oklahoma Press, 1955. Own.

Arkansas History Commission Newspaper Collection. Little Rock. ARHC.

Altoff, Gerard T. *Oliver Hazard Perry and the Battle of Lake Erie*. Put-in-Bay, Ohio: The Perry Group, 1999. Own.

Ambrose, Stephen E. *Undaunted Courage: Meriwether Lewis, Thomas Jefferson, and the Opening of the American West*. New York: Touchstone, 1996. Own.

Another Researchers Publication. *Wayne County, Kentucky, Marriages, 1800-1850*. N.p., n.d. HouPL.

Austin. Texas General Land Office. Archives and Records Division. TXGLO.

Austin. Texas State Library and Archives. TSLAC.

Awbrey, Betty Dooley, and Claude Dooley. *Why Stop? A Guide to Texas Historical Roadside Markers*. 4th ed. Houston: Lone Star Books, 1999. Own.

Baker, D. W. C. *A Texas Scrap-Book: Made up of the History, Biography, and Miscellany of Texas and Its People*. 1875; reprint, Austin: Texas State Historical Association, 1991. Own.

Baker, J. W. *A History of Robertson County, Texas*. N.p.: The Robertson County Historical Foundation. Own.

Banta, John. "Home Spared of Fate." *Waco Tribune-Herald*, July 16, 1978. DRTL.

"Benjamin F. Gholson, Pioneer Texas Ranger, Rests With the Fathers." *The Hamilton (Texas) Herald Record*, April 8, 1932. HCGS.

Bobrick, Benson. *Angel in the Whirlwind: The Triumph of the American Revolution*. New York: Simon & Schuster, Inc., 1997; New York: Penguin Putnam Inc., 1998. Own.

Bork, June Baldwin, comp. *Wayne County, Kentucky, Marriages and Vital Records; Deed Books A-E*. Apple Valley, CA: June Baldwin Bork, 1994. HouPL.

Bowles, Flora Gatlin, ed. *A No Man's Land Becomes A County*. Goldthwaite, TX: Mills County Historical Society, 1958. TSLAC.

Brown, James E., and Margaret Brown Altendahl, comps. *Relatives of the Browns of Mill Springs, Kentucky: Including the Fisher, Gaar, Gholson, Hutchison, Weaver and West Families*. Baltimore: Gateway Press, Inc., 1992. Own.

Burney, J. W., Jr. "Local History Buried in Evant Cemeteries." *The Evant (Texas) News*, June 21, 19__? Gentry.

Census Records of the United States.

Chalkley, Lyman. *Chronicles of the Scotch-Irish Settlement in Virginia, Extracted from the Original Court Records of Augusta County, 1745-1800, Vol. II.* 1912; reprint, Baltimore: Genealogical Publishing Co., Inc., 1974. TorPL.

Churchill, Sir Winston. *The Great Republic--A History of America*, Large Print version. Edited by Winston S. Churchill. New York: Random House, 2000. CCCL.

Coldham, Peter Wilson. *The Complete Book of Emigrants 1661-1699: A Comprehensive Listing Compiled from English Public Records of Those Who Took Ship to the Americas for Political, Religious, and Economic Reasons; of Those Who Were Deported for Vagrancy, Roguery, or Non-Conformity; and of Those Who Were Sold to Labour in the New Colonies.* Baltimore: Genealogical Publishing Co., Inc., 1990. CCCL.

Coryell County Records. CorCo.

Crozier, William Armstrong, ed. *Virginia County Records, Spotsylvania County 1721-1800: Being Transcriptions, from the Original Files at the County Court House, of Wills, Deeds, Administrators' and Guardians' Bonds, Marriage Licenses, and Lists of Revolutionary Pensioners.* 1905; reprint, Baltimore: Genealogical Publishing Co., Inc., 1978. HouPL.

DAR Patriot Index, Centennial Edition, Part II. Washington: National Society of the Daughters of the American Revolution, 1994.

Daily Democratic Statesman. Article about Asa Langford, Jr. Lampasas Historical Commission.

Davis, David Brion, and Steven Mintz. *The Boisterous Sea of Liberty: A Documentary History of America from Discovery Through the Civil War.* Oxford: Oxford University Press, 1998. Own.

Debo, Angie. *A History of the Indians of the United States.* Norman: The University of Oklahoma Press, 1983. Own.

Dillon, Francis. *The Pilgrims--Their Journeys & Their World.* Garden City, NJ: Doubleday & Company, Inc., 1975. CCCL.

Eddlemon, Sherida K., comp. *Genealogical Abstracts from Tennessee Newspapers, 1821-1828.* Bowie, MD: Heritage Books, Inc. 1991. NEGHS.

Elkins, Captain John M. "Indian Fighting on the Texas Frontier." *Old West* 4, no. 2 (1967).

Elting, John R. *Amateurs, To Arms! A Military History of the War of 1812.* Chapel Hill, NC: Algonquin Books, 1991; Da Capo Press, Inc., 1995. Own.

Falls County Historical Commission, comp. and ed. *Families of Falls County.* Austin: Eakin Press, 1987.

Falls County Records.

Felder, Paula S. *Forgotten Companions: The First Settlers of Spotsylvania County and Fredericksburgh Town (With Notes on Early Land Use).*

Fredericksburg, VA: Historic Publications of Fredericksburg, 1982. HouPL.

Fischer, David Hackett. *Albion's Seed--Four British Folkways in America.* New York: Oxford University Press, 1989. Own.

Fithian, Philip Vickers. *Journal & Letters of Philip Vickers Fithian, 1773-1774, A Plantation Tutor of the Old Dominion.* Edited by Hunter Dickinson Farish. 1943; reprint, Charlottesville: The University Press of Virginia, 1996. Own.

Franks, J. M. *Seventy Years in Texas: Memories of the Pioneer Days, Indian Depredations and the Northwest Cattle Trail.* Gatesville, Texas: 1924. Own.

Gallaway, B. P., ed. *Texas: The Dark Corner of the Confederacy, Contemporary Accounts of the Lone Star State in the Civil War.* 3rd ed. Lincoln: University of Nebraska Press, 1999. Own.

Gentry, Bonnie. Article and manuscript collection.

Gerald, R. J. "Benjamin Franklin Gholson, Texan." *Frontier Times* 4, no. 11 (1927). ITC.

Gholson, Anthony, Biography. Gholson Family File. Wayne County Historical Society, Monticello, Kentucky. WCHS.

Gholson, B. F. Biographical File. The Center for American History. The University of Texas at Austin. CAH.

Gholson, B. F. Biographical File. Texas Ranger Museum and Library, Waco. TxRang.

Gholson, B. F., to Sam Gholson, Evant, Texas, letter, December 14, 1922. SMGhol.

Gholson, Conner W. Personal communications.

Gholson, Samuel Sullivan. Autobiography. SMGhol.

Gholson, Ronald Lee, comp. *Gholson and Allied Families, A Revised Golden Anniversary Edition, Reprint of "Gholson and Allied Families" by Virginia Baker Mitchell, September, 1950.* Mulberry, IN: Ron Gholson, 2002. Own.

Gillett, James B. *Six Years With the Texas Rangers: 1875 to 1881.* Edited by M. M. Quaife. 1921; reprint, Lincoln: University of Nebraska Press, 1976. Own.

Gwathmey, John H. *Historical Register of Virginians in the Revolution: Soldiers, Sailors, Marines; 1775-1783.* Baltimore: Genealogical Publishing Co., Inc., 1979. TorPL.

Hall, Sarah Harkey. *Surviving on the Texas Frontier: The Journal of an Orphan Girl in San Saba County.* Austin: Eakin Press, 1996. Own.

Hallahan, William H. *The Day the American Revolution Began: 19 April 1775.* New York: William Morrow and Company, 2000. CCCL.

Hamilton County Historical Commission, comp. and ed. *A History of Hamilton County, Texas.* Dallas: Taylor Publishing Company, 1979. WacoPL.

Harrison County Records. HarCo.

Hawke, David Freeman. *Everyday Life in Early America.* New York: Harper & Row, 1988; Perennial Library, 1989. Own.

Hickey, Donald R. *The War of 1812: A Forgotten Conflict.* Urbana, IL: University of Illinois Press, 1990. Own.

"Historical Grave Marker for Early Day Ranger, B. F. Gholson, Arrives." *The Four County Press*, Evant, Texas, October 5, 1967, Volume 37, No. 21. Gentry.

Hogan, William Ransom. *The Texas Republic, A Social and Economic History.* 1946; reprint, Austin: University of Texas Press, 1969. Own.

Holliday, Carl. *Woman's Life in Colonial Days.* 1922; reprint, Mineola, NY: Dover Publications, Inc., 1999. Own.

Hotten, John Camden, ed. *The Original Lists of Persons of Quality; Emigrants; Religious Exiles; Political Rebels; Serving Men Sold for a Term of Years; Apprentices; Children Stolen; Maidens Pressed; and Others Who Went from Great Britain to the American Plantations, 1600-1700, With Their Ages, The Localities Where They Formerly Lived in the Mother Country, The Names of the Ships in Which They Embarked, and Other Interesting Particulars, From MSS. Preserved in the State Paper Department of Her Majesty's Public Record Office, England.* Baltimore: Genealogical Publishing Co., Inc. 1968. TorPL.

Huber, Leonard V. *The Battle of New Orleans: New Orleans as it was in 1814-1815.* New Orleans: Battle of New Orleans 150th Anniversary Committee of Louisiana, 1965; reprint, New Orleans: Louisiana Landmarks Society, 1994. Own.

Hunter, J. Marvin, comp. and ed. *The Trail Drivers of Texas: Interesting Sketches of Early Cowboys and Their Experiences on the Range and on the Trail during the Days That Tried Men's Souls--True Narratives Related by Real Cowpunchers and Men Who Fathered the Cattle Industry in Texas.* Austin: University of Texas Press, 2000. Own.

Hunter, J. Marvin, Sr. "The Killing of Bob Carter." *Frontier Times* 28, no. 2 (1950). Gentry.

Hunter, John Warren. "B. F. Gholson's Narratives." *Hunter's Magazine* 1912: 9. B. F. Gholson file, Lampasas Historical Commission. LamCo.

Johnson, Augusta Phillips. *A Century of Wayne County, Kentucky, 1800-1900.* Louisville: The Standard Printing Company, Inc., 1939. HouPL.

Johnson, M. L., and E. J. Pearson. "Trailing West." *Frontier Times* 43, no. 1 (1969). WestP.

Joyner, Ulysses P., Jr. *Orange County Land Patents.* 2nd ed. Orange County Historical Society, Inc., VA, 1999. OCHS.

Kegley, F. B. *Kegley's Virginia Frontier: The Beginning of the Southwest, The Roanoke of Colonial Days, 1740-1783, With Maps and*

Illustrations. Roanoke: The Southwest Virginia Historical Society, 1938. FtWPL.

Kentucky, Adjutant General of the State of. *Soldiers of the War of 1812*. Frankfort, 1891. HouPL.

Kincaid, Robert L. *The Wilderness Road*. Indianapolis: The Bobbs-Merrill Company, 1947. CCCL.

Kingsbury, Susan Myra, ed. *Heritage Books Archives: Records of the Virginia Company of London, Volumes 1-4*, CD. Bowie, MD: Heritage Books Archives, 1999. Own.

Koch, Adrienne, and William Peden, eds. *The Life and Selected Writings of Thomas Jefferson*. 1944; reprint, New York: Modern Library, 1998. Own.

Lampasas County Records. LamCo.

Lucas, The Rev. Silas Emmett, Jr. *Virginia Colonial Abstracts--Series 2, Vol. 3: The Virginia Company of London, 1607-1624*. Abstracted and compiled by Beverley Fleet. Edited by The Rev. Lindsay O. Duvall. Easley, SC: Southern Historical Press, 1978. CCCL.

Malcolm, Joyce Lee. *To Keep and Bear Arms, The Origins of an Anglo-American Right*. Cambridge, MA: Harvard University Press, 1994. Own.

Marks, Paula Mitchell. *Turn Your Eyes Toward Texas: Pioneers Sam and Mary Maverick*. College Station: Texas A&M University Press, 1989. Own.

Martin, Mrs. John T., and Mrs. Louis C. Hill, comps. *Falls County, Texas Records, Vol. I*. McGregor, TX: n.p., 1970. TSLAC.

McConnell, Joseph Carroll. *The West Texas Frontier, or a Descriptive History of Early Times in Western Texas*. N.p., n.d. Article No. 772. FtWPL.

McCreary, Binnie Depmore. "The Gholson House, Evant, Texas." The University of Texas at Austin, School of Architecture, 1977. Own.

McDaniel, Ruel. "Horses Were Legal Tender." *True West*, Nov.-Dec. 1963: 47. WestP.

McLean, Malcolm D., comp. and ed. *Papers Concerning Robertson's Colony in Texas*. 19 vols. Arlington, Texas: The UTA Press, 1986-1993. Own.

McLennan County Records. McLen.

Memorial and Biographical History of McLennan, Falls, Bell and Coryell Counties, Texas, A. Chicago: The Lewis Publishing Company, 1893. SAPL.

Metz, Leon C. *Roadside History of Texas*. Missoula, Montana: Mountain Press Publishing Company, 1994. Own.

Midwest Tennessee Genealogical Society. "Abstracts from Early Madison County, Tennessee, Newspapers: *Jackson Gazette*, March 21, 1829." *Family Findings*, 4, nos. 3-4 (1972); from TN GenWeb. Web. http://www.tngenweb.org/madison/records/gazette.htm.

Miller, John C., ed. *The Colonial Image--Origins of American Culture*. New York: George Braziller, 1962. CCCL.

Mitchell, Virginia Baker. *Gholson and Allied Families*. Edited by Margaret Scruggs-Carruth. Dallas: n.p., 1950. Own.

Morgan, James Logan, comp. *Arkansas Newspaper Abstracts 1819-1845: Volume I, Obituaries and Biographical Notes from Arkansas Newspapers, 1819-1835*. Conway, AR: Arkansas Research, 1981. TSLAC.

Morris, Marjory Gholson. Personal communications. Int.

Mullins, Marion Day, comp. *Republic of Texas: Poll Lists for 1846*. Baltimore: Genealogical Publishing Co., Inc., 1974. DRTL.

"Murder of Mr. & Mrs. Riggs and Mr. Pierce." *Frontier Times* 4, no. 12 (1927). TxRang.

National Archives. Military Service Records. NARA.

New England Historic Genealogical Society. *The New-England Historical and Genealogical Register 1895, Vol. XLIX*. Boston: Published by The Society, 1895. TorPL.

Nugent, Nell Marion, abstr. and ind. *Cavaliers and Pioneers--Abstracts of Virginia Land Patents & Grants, 1623-1666, Vol. 1*. Baltimore: Genealogical Publishing Co., Inc., 1979. TorPL.

Nuttall, Thomas. *Journal of Travels into the Arkansas Territory During the Year 1819*. Edited by Savoie Lottinville. 1821; reprint, Fayetteville: The University of Arkansas Press, 1999. Own.

Nutter, Mildred Moody, contrib. "Wayne County, Kentucky Miscellaneous Court Papers from Box File." *The Kentucky Genealogist* 20, no. 2 (1978). WCHS.

Olmstead, Frederick Law. *A Journey Through Texas; or, A Saddle-Trip on the Southwestern Frontier*. 1857; reprint, Time-Life Books Inc., 1981. Own.

Pawlett, Nathaniel Mason. *Historic Roads of Virginia, Spotsylvania County Road Orders, 1722-1734*. Virginia Highway & Transportation Research Council, n.d. HouPL.

Pendergrast, Linton Otis Pendergrast. "Pioneer Tells of Indian Raids." Reprinted in *Evant (Texas) News*, October 14, 1976. Gentry.

Porter, Lewis B., Sr. *Take A Journey With Me From the Washboard*. Goldthwaite, Texas: Goldthwaite Eagle Press, 1976. Richards.

Ramos, Mary G., ed. *Texas Almanac, Millenium Edition, 2000-2001*. Dallas: *The Dallas Morning News*, 1999. Own.

Rouse, Parke, Jr. *The Great Wagon Road: from Philadelphia To the South*. New York: McGraw-Hill, 1973. CCCL.

Ruff, Nancy Blakeley, comp. *Harrison County, Texas, Early Marriage Records, 1839-1869*. St. Louis, MO: Ingmire Publications, n.d. HCHM.

S-K Publications. *Census Images, 1810-1820-1830-1840, Livingston County, Kentucky*. CD. Wichita, KS: S-K Publications, 2001. Own.

Sanchez-Saavedra, E. M., comp. *A Guide to Virginia Military Organizations in the American Revolution, 1774-1787*. Richmond: Virginia State Library, 1978. TorPL.

Sistler, Byron, and Barbara Sistler, comps. and eds. *Madison County, Tennessee, Marriages 1838-71*. Nashville: n.p., 1983. NEGHS.

Skeen, C. Edward. *Citizen Soldiers in the War of 1812*. Lexington: The University Press of Kentucky, 1999. Own.

Sloane, Eric. *Diary of an Early American Boy: Noah Blake, 1805*. New York: Wilfred Funk, Inc., 1965; New York: Ballantine Books, 1974). Own.

Smith, Page. *John Adams, Vol. I, 1735-1784*. Garden City, NY: Doubleday & Company, Inc., 1962. Own.

Smithwick, Noah. *The Evolution of a State, or Recollections of Old Texas Days*. Compiled by Nanna Smithwick Donaldson. Austin: University of Texas Press, 1983. Own.

Sowell, Thomas. *Conquests and Cultures--An International History*. New York: Basic Books, 1998. Own.

Stephen, Leslie, and Sidney Lee, eds. *Dictionary of National Biography, Vol. 8, Glover-Harriott,* "Goulston or Gulston, Theodore, M.D." New York: The McMillan Company, 1908. NEGHS.

"Storming of San Antonio De Bexar in 1835, From the Texas State Gazette, 1849." *Frontier Times* 9 (1932), no. 10. WestP.

Summers, Lewis Preston. *Annals of Southwest Virginia, 1769-1800*. Abingdon, VA: Lewis Preston Summers, 1929. CCCL.

Taul, Micah, Memoirs. TS, No. 778, Papers of Bennett Henderson Young, 1879-1912, A\Y68. The Filson Club, Louisville, KY. TFC.

Thornton, Bobbie F., copier and typist. *Coryell County, Texas, 1860 Census & Mortality Schedule*. Plano, Texas: n.d. WacoPL.

Turner, Frederick Jackson. *The Frontier in American History*. 1920; reprint, New York: Dover Publications, 1996. Own.

Tyler, Ron, ed. *The New Handbook of Texas*. 6 vols. Austin: The Texas State Historical Association, 1996. Own.

"'Uncle' Frank Gholson Passed Away Sunday." *Lampasas Record*, April 7, 1932. Gentry.

Upchurch, Sara Belle, ed. "Anthony Gholson House." *Wayne County Historical Society Overview* 18, no. 1 (1997). WCHS.

Vaughan, Alden T. *America Before the Revolution 1725-1775*. Englewood Cliffs, NJ: Prentice-Hall, Inc., 1967. CCCL.

Venn, John, and J. A. Venn, comps. *Alumni Cantabrigienses: A Biographical List of All Known Students, Graduates and Holders of Office at the University of Cambridge, From the Earliest Times to 1900, Part I, From the Earliest Times to 1751, Volume II, Dabbs-Juxton*. Cambridge: At the University Press, 1922. NEGHS.

"Virginia Legislative Papers; From Originals in The Virginia State Archives." *Virginia Magazine of History and Biography* 13, no. 4 (1906). SLNC.

Wallis, George A. "Cattle Kings." *True West*, 11, no. 4 (1964). WestP.

Ward, Ray, abstr. "Probate Minutes, Coryell County, Texas," *Coryell Kin* 19 (2001). CCGS.

Webb, Walter Prescott. *The Texas Rangers, A Century of Frontier Defense*. 2nd ed. Austin: University of Texas Press, 1996. Own.

Wilbarger, J. W. *Indian Depredations in Texas*. 1889; reprint, Austin, Texas: Eakin Press; Statehouse Press, 1985. Own.

Wilkins, Frederick. *The Legend Begins, The Texas Rangers, 1823-1845*. Austin: State House Press, 1996. Own.

Withington, Lothrop. *Virginia Gleanings in England, Abstracts of 17th and 18th-Century English Wills and Administrations Relating to Virginia and Virginians: A Consolidation of Articles from The Virginia Magazine of History and Biography*. Baltimore: Genealogical Publishing Co., 1980. CCCL.

Wolkomir, Joyce, and Richard Wolkomir. "When Bandogs Howle & Spirits Walk." *Smithsonian Magazine* 31, no. 10 (2001). Own.

Wooster, Ralph A. *Civil War Texas: A History and A Guide*. Austin: Texas State Historical Association, 1999. Own.

INDEX

Duncan, Mrs. (Mahala), 127
Duncan, Newton C., 104, 105, 126, 127
Duncan, Thomas, 160
Dunmore, Lord, xxvii, 41, 43, 47, 48
Dunn, William C., 278
Durram, Hannah, xxvi, 14
Dwight, G. E., 138
Dyer, Capt. Jno. N., 145
Eades, Thomas, 56
Eagle Pass, Texas, 179
Earl, Miss Ellen, 202
East India Company, 40
Eastland County, Texas, 102
Eaton, Alfred, 160
Echo, Texas, 278, 354
Edmiston, Zebulon, xxx, 93
education, early Virginia, 16
Edwards County, 200
El Paso, Texas, 256
Elizabeth I, Queen of England, xxv, 3
Elizabeth, ship, 9
Elk River, 68
Elkins, Capt. John M., 269, 354
Elkins, G. K., xxxiv, 266
Elliott, Lt., 76
Ellwood, Isaac I., 278
Elm creek, 229
Elms, Dave, 198, 200
Elms, Mr., 198
emancipation of slaves, 48
Embry, Dr., 174
England, xxi, xxv, xxvi, 3, 4, 5, 6, 7, 8,
    9, 12, 13, 15, 16, 18, 25, 28, 38, 39,
    41, 46, 48, 261, 319, 320, 321, 361,
    363, 365
English common law, 46
Erath County, Texas, 102, 174
Erie, Lake, ix, xxix, 75, 76, 77, 78, 337,
    358
Evans, Hunter and, 264
Evans, Peter, sons, 14
Evant, Texas, xi, xix, 178, 182, 197,
    224, 236, 238, 241, 246, 254, 262,
    265, 281, 284, 300, 304, 346, 356,
    360, 361
Everett, John E., 174, 175

Exelet, Illinois, 88
Fairview, Texas, 284
Falls County, Texas, 102, 106, 146,
    166, 167, 169, 171, 178, 182, 341,
    342, 347, 348, 357, 362
Falls of the Brazos, 104, 107, 155, 168
False Washita River, 141
Fannin, James, 117, 126
Farmer, John, 172, 174
Faulkner County, Arkansas, 91
Fauntleroy, F. W., 175
Fayette County, Kentucky, 34, 62
Fayette County, Texas, xxvii, 34, 278
Federalists, 72
Fields, C. T., 165
Fields, J., 165
Fields, W. C., 165
Finley, John, 50
fires, range, 203
First Continental Congress, 41, 42
Fitzhugh, Capt., 211
flag, "Come and Take It," 114
Flat Top Ranch, 267
Flatonia, Texas, 278
Flores and Cordova fights, 154
Florida, 72, 255
*Flowers and Fruits From the
    Wilderness*, 106
food, early Texas, 109
food, early Virginia, 11, 22
Ford, Henry, 242
Fort Belknap, ix, xxxiii, 201, 203, 205,
    208, 209, 211, 229, 246
Fort Boone, xxvii, 54
Fort Cobb, 203, 205, 211
Fort Concho, 266, 302
Fort Defiance, 74
Fort Detroit, xxix, 73
Fort Gates, 277
Fort Jennings, 74
Fort McHenry, xxix, 81
Fort Parker, ix, xxx, 94, 105, 107, 137,
    143, 144, 207, 235, 303, 345
Fort Radsminskie (Camp Radziminski),
    204
Fort Sumner, xxxiv, 241, 265

guides, Battle of San Antonio, xxx, 118, 122
Guilford Court House, Battle of, xxviii, 49
Gulf Coast, 81, 245
Gulf of Mexico, 38, 142
Gulston, Dr. Theodore, xxv, 3, 5, 6, 8
Gulston, Jane, 6
Gulston, John, 6
Gulston, Nathaniel, 6
Gulston, William (John's son), 6, 8
Gulston, William (Nathaniel's son), 6
Gulstonian lecture series, 6
gun rights, application of, 46
guns, xx, 11, 23, 25, 46, 47, 52, 83, 103, 126, 146, 151, 197, 216, 222, 251, 268, 270, 275, 283, 286
Gunston, Antho., 9
Haden, see Hayden
Hadley, Joshua, 105, 106
Haigwood, Henry, 160
hair and beard styles, early Texas, 110, 267
Hall's Company, Capt., 255
Hambright, Mr., 240
Hamilton County, Texas, 102, 174, 197, 209, 238, 252, 262, 278, 282
Hamilton, Texas, 238, 302
Hammond, John, 56
Hampton, Wade, 275
Hancock, John, 44, 48
Hand, John, 153
Hanner valley, 185
Hardin, John Wesley, 254, 255
Harris, Mr., 253
Harrison County, Texas, 164, 262, 347, 357, 363
Harrison, William Henry, 73, 75, 85
Hayden (Haden), 2nd Lt. Bartholomew, 56, 71, 75, 336
Hayden, Kitty, 14
Haynes, J. A., 175
headrights, early Virginia, 27
Heard, Jim, 153
Henderson, Bennett, 65, 333, 335, 364

Henderson, Capt. William F., 151, 152, 153
Henderson, Col. Richard, 53, 54
Henry, Anne, 32
Henry, Gen. C., 78
Henry, Hugh A., 160
Henry, John R., 160
Henry, Maj. Robert P., 78
Henry, Patrick, ix, xxvii, 32, 39, 40, 41, 42, 43, 45, 46, 48
Henry, Susannah (sister of Patrick), 33
Henry, William, 73, 75, 85, 160
Henson Creek, 172, 349
Hill County, Texas, 102
Hill, George Washington, 153
Hinchey, 156
historical marker, B. F. Gholson, x, xv, 301, 302, 304
History of the Battle of New Orleans, Smith's, 85
Hitsons, John, 268
Hoard creek, 185
Hoffman, Binnie Depmore McCreary, 187, 193, 194, 292, 316, 318, 353, 355
Hoffman, David, 292, 316, 317, 318
Hogan, William Ransom, xvii, 176, 339, 341, 347, 350
Hogg, Governor, 256
Holly, Thomas, xxxiv, 262
Holtzclaw, B. W., 105
Home Creek, 267, 278
Hood County, Texas, 102
Hopkinsville, Kentucky, 108
Horrell boys, 267
horse racing, early Virginia, 21
horse stealing, 90
Horsehead Crossing, 184, 266
Hough, Emerson, 259
House of Burgesses, Virginia, 45, 48
houses, early Virginia, 17
Houston *Chronicle*, 178
Houston, Andy, 153
Houston, Sam, ix, xxxi, 116, 117, 122, 125, 132, 137, 145, 149, 163, 178,

La Bahía, 126
La Bahía Road, xxx, 144
La Grange, Texas, 166
Lafitte, Jean, 82
Lamar, Mirabeau B., 137, 162, 163
Lambert, Gen. John (British), 84
Lampasas County Historical Survey
  Committee, 301, 302
Lampasas County, Texas, 102, 179,
  190, 236, 250, 262, 265, 284, 302
Lampasas Historical Commission, 186,
  349, 351, 352, 359, 361
Lampasas River, 180, 236, 284
Lampasas, Texas, xiii, 170, 196, 198,
  246, 247, 248, 250, 251, 266, 267
land grant, Kentucky, 48
land grants, early Virginia, 28
land grants, Texas, xv, 104, 305
Landreth, Al, 57
Lane, Walter, 153, 153
Langford (Lankford) Cemetery, x,
  xxxiii, 238, 242, 254, 298, 299, 300,
  301, 302, 304
Langford (Lankford) Cove (Evant),
  182, 238, 239, 240, 242, 246, 247,
  253, 254, 256, 281, 299, 300
Langford family, 179
Langford gang, fictitious, 178, 179
Langford Store, 239
Langford, Asa, Jr., xxxiv, 253, 254,
  256, 258, 352, 359
Langford, Asa, Sr., xxxiv, 179, 182,
  246, 247, 252, 262, 300
Langford, Eliza Lee (Mrs. Asa), 299,
  300
Langford, Jimmie, 252
Lawhorn, Hugh, 247
Lawrence, Commodore Perry's ship, 76
Lee County, Texas, 102
Lee, Ambrose, 199
Lee, Capt. John D., 182
Lee, Gen. Robert E., 245, 251
Leftwich, Robert, 102
Leftwich's Grant, 102
legal system, early Texas, 104
Lemmon, William F., 173

Leon, Juan, 209
Leon River, 181, 188, 224, 303
Lewis and Clark expedition, 70
Lewis, Susannah, 59
Lewis, Zachary, xxvi, 26, 28, 59
Lexington, Battle of, xxvii, 43, 44
Lexington, Kentucky, 69, 74, 76
Limestone County, Texas, 102, 163,
  164, 165
Lincoln, Thomas, 54
literacy rates, early Virginia, 16
Little River, 128, 150, 160
Little Wichita River, 207
Livingston County, Kentucky, xxix, 88,
  91, 338, 363
Llano Cattle Company, xxxiv, 278
Llano River, 102
Llano River, North, 256
Llano River, South, 256
Lockhard, Taisie, 259
log cabin, description of, 107
Logan, Col. John, 54
Lometa, Texas, 302
London Company (Virginia Company
  of London), xxv, 4, 5, 6, 7, 13, 15,
  27, 320, 362
London, xxvi, 5, 7
Long Island (Kingsport, Tennessee), 53,
  54
longhorns, Texas, 259
Lookout Mountain, ix, 188, 238
Lost San Saba mine, 103
Louisiana, 179, 245, 248, 249, 251, 337,
  361
Louisiana militia, 83
Louisiana Purchase, xxix, 34, 64, 85
Louisiana State Museum, 82
Louisiana Territory, 34, 82
Louyers, D. W., 175
Love, William, 151, 152, 153, 162
Loyd, Simpson, 237, 238
Loyola mission, 178
Lubbock, Francis R., 109
Lukewater, 268
Luther, Martin, 3
Mackenzie, Gen., 269

Ward, 159, 160, 349, 365
Ward, Capt. Thomas William, 121
Washington County, Texas, 144
Washington, D. C., 62, 81, 131, 206
Washington, George, ix, xxvii, 23, 31,
    39, 41, 42, 44, 45, 54, 327, 358
Washington, Samuel, xxvii, 31
Washington-on-the-Brazos, ix, xxx,
    125, 126, 132, 341, 344
Washita River, 203, 205
Wayne County, Kentucky, xxviii, xxix,
    34, 55, 56, 58, 61, 63, 64, 67, 70, 72,
    74, 91, 325, 332, 338, 339, 358, 363
weapons requirement, Virginia, 46, 47
Weatherford, Texas, 235
Webb, A. J., 160
Webb, Charles, Deputy Sheriff, 254
Webb, Walter Prescott, 137, 345
Welch, Tom, 176
Welsh, John, 160
West Texas Frontier, 268, 354, 362
West Virginia, 31, 34, 56
West, Isaac, xxx, 56, 63, 92
West, Isaac, Jr., xxx, 92
Westport Cemetery, 284
Wheeler, Joseph, 56
White House, burned, 81
White, Bill, 264
White, Capt. Carey, 114, 133
Wichita mountains, 201, 203
Wicker, 179, 182
Wier, R. N., 167
Wilderness Road, xxviii, 54, 55, 331,
    332, 362
Williams' ranch, 187, 241
Williams, Aleck, 246, 247, 250
Williams, Capt. John, 185, 187, 190,
    197
Williams, Col. John, 65
Williams, Jackson, 168, 169
Williams, Jenkin, 88
Williams, Mrs. John, 195, 196
Williamsburg, Virginia, 28, 46, 48
Williamson County, Texas, 102
Willis, Bill, xxxiv, 235, 238, 239, 246
Willis, R. W., 240

Wilson, President, 206
Wilson, Samuel, 65
Wilson, Sheriff, 255
Winchester rifle, 267
Winchester, 59
Winchester, Kentucky, 65, 68
Winchester, Tennessee, 68, 69
Witcher, Adam, 238
Witcher, J. M., 236, 237, 238
women, duties, early Virginia, 17, 18
women, education of, early Virginia, 18
Wood County, Texas, 164, 166
Woods, A. M., 199
Worthington's Marsh, 31
Yellow prong of Brazos River, 209
Young County, Texas, 208, 223
Young, W. C., 278
Zacatecas, 113

ABOUT THE AUTHOR

Donna Gholson Cook was born in San Angelo, Texas, with Texas roots six generations deep. Her love of the history of the Old West was fueled by family stories about her great-grandfather, one of the first Texas Rangers. Spare time in her teenage years was spent reading western books and riding horses. Her spare time in recent years has been used to research her Gholson ancestors, who were not only among the first Texas colonists, but the first American colonists as well, crossing paths with many famous Americans in their journey. GHOLSON ROAD will give the reader a glimpse into the lives of some of the Americans who fought to create this great nation and to maintain our freedom.

CPSIA information can be obtained at www.ICGtesting.com
Printed in the USA
BVOW05s1525191014

371328BV00001B/58/P